The Art and Craft of Judgment Writing

A Primer for Common Law Judges
Max Barrett

Author
Max Barrett

Managing director
Sian O'Neill

The Art and Craft of Judgment Writing: A Primer for Common Law Judges
is published by

Globe Law and Business Ltd
3 Mylor Close
Horsell
Woking
Surrey GU21 4DD
United Kingdom
Tel: +44 20 3745 4770
www.globelawandbusiness.com

Printed and bound by CPI Group (UK) Ltd, Croydon CR0 4YY, United Kingdom

The Art and Craft of Judgment Writing: A Primer for Common Law Judges

ISBN 9781787428577
EPUB ISBN 9781787428584
Adobe PDF ISBN 9781787428591

© 2022 Globe Law and Business Ltd except where otherwise indicated.

The right of Max Barrett to be identified as the author of this work has been asserted by him in accordance with sections 77 and 78 of the Copyright, Designs and Patents Act 1988.

All rights reserved. No part of this publication may be reproduced in any material form (including photocopying, storing in any medium by electronic means or transmitting) without the written permission of the copyright owner, except in accordance with the provisions of the Copyright, Designs and Patents Act 1988 or under terms of a licence issued by the Copyright Licensing Agency Ltd, 5th Floor, Shackleton House, 4 Battle Bridge Lane, London, England, SE1 2HX, United Kingdom (www.cla.co.uk, email: licence@cla.co.uk). Applications for the copyright owner's written permission to reproduce any part of this publication should be addressed to the publisher.

DISCLAIMER
This publication is intended as a general guide only. The information and opinions which it contains are not intended to be a comprehensive study, or to provide legal or financial advice, and should not be treated as a substitute for legal advice concerning particular situations. Legal advice should always be sought before taking any action based on the information provided. The publishers bear no responsibility for any errors or omissions contained herein.

Table of contents

Preface ———— 5
Sir Robin Jacob
University College London

Foreword ———— 7
Mr Justice Max Barrett

Part I: The theory of ———— 13
the art and craft of
judgment writing
   1. On judgments ———— 15
   2. Judgments: ———— 29
      purpose and audience
   3. Judgment length ———— 39
   4. Judgment style ———— 47
   5. Judgment structure ———— 79
   6. Dissenting and ———— 103
      concurring judgments
   7. Children, families ———— 119
      and immigrants
   8. Authors and judges ———— 135

Part II: The practice ———— 151
of the art and craft of
judgment writing
   9. Three great and ———— 153
      pioneering women
      judges:
      Justices O'Connor,
      Ginsburg and Wilson

  10. Three great ———— 187
      American judges:
      Justices Holmes, Jackson
      and Scalia
  11. Three great ———— 219
      British judges:
      Lords Atkin, Denning
      and Bingham
  12. Some great judges ———— 253
      from the wider
      common law world

Part III: *Ex tempore* ———— 285
judgments
  13. The art and craft ———— 287
      of *ex tempore*
      judgments

Appendix: The ———— 303
judgment as the art
of truth

Table of cases ———— 309

Select bibliography ———— 315

Index ———— 353

About the author ———— 371

About Globe Law ———— 373
and Business

As always, I have tried to make my meaning clear. That is necessary if you are to influence others. As St Paul said: 'For if the trumpet give an uncertain sound, who shall prepare himself to the battle? So likewise ye, except ye utter by the tongue words easy to be understood, how shall it be known what is spoken? For ye shall speak into the air.'
Denning[1]

Write an opinion, and read it a few years later when it is dissected in the briefs of counsel. You will learn for the first time the limitations of the power of speech, or, if not those of speech in general, at all events your own. All sorts of gaps and obstacles and impediments will obtrude themselves before your gaze, as pitilessly manifest as the hazards on a golf course. Sometimes you will know that the fault is truly yours ... Sometimes you will feel that the fault is with counsel who have ... misread the obvious ... Sometimes, though rarely, you will believe that the misreading is ... malicious, in which event you will be wise to keep your feelings to yourself.
Cardozo[2]

---

1 Denning (1983), vi–vii.
2 Cardozo (1939), 123.

Preface

Sir Robin Jacob
University College London

A book review once ran something like this: "Every book reviewer should say at least one nice thing about it. Well, it is printed on very nice paper." This book is miles from such a book. It is entertaining, hugely researched, and above all makes you think. It is a joy to read. You can do that straight through or by dipping into it from time to time. Or, better, both. Having read it through I shall henceforth be a regular dipper!

The subject is very serious. Independent, strong judges are vital to the rule of law in any democratic system – "Be you never so high, the law is above you" was written by the 18th-century cleric Thomas Fuller and made famous by Lord Denning in 1977.[1] Though true, it is not enough. Fully independent judges could provide austere, un- or barely reasoned, "the court hereby rules" kind of judgments, but these would not convey any sense of legitimacy. People need more, a sense of humanity and fairness, from judges' decisions. That needs well-expressed reasons, not just the answer. The common law system provides the greatest freedom for judges to do that.

In some countries the system suppresses judicial individualism. Courts (even first instance) are a panel who have to produce a single judgment.[2] A few years ago my Serbian PhD student said he was amazed to read a judge using "I" rather than the impersonal "the court" when he first started seeing common law judgments. A common law judgment is expressed to be the work of the judge who gives it.[3] Judgments are individually crafted. There is no prescribed

---

[1] See *Gouriet v U.P.W.* [1977] QB 729 (CA), 762.
[2] A Dutch friend once said to me: "There is a judgment out there with my name on it and I don't agree with a word of it!"
[3] Sometimes a judicial assistant ('law clerk' in the US) may do some of the work, though not much in the UK or Ireland. Lazy judges sometimes leave most of it to them.

formula. The potential for variation of style, language, amount of detail and so much more, is huge. With that flexibility comes responsibility. A thinking judge must work out what is best for her or him and for the case in hand. Who is the audience for this judgment? The parties obviously – especially the loser.[4] But who else? The press? Lawyers in general? Academics? There may be other considerations too – those I personally would eschew. For the judge, to show how clever he/she is and how many authorities he/she can cite? Should the judge try to lay down the law in a series of numbered propositions as if they were the Tablets of Stone of Moses or the laws of the Medes and Persians. There are other considerations too – for instance, do different types of case call for different sorts of judgment? For example, many sensitive family cases, where there is seldom a good or clear answer, really involve choosing which possible answer is the least unsatisfactory. On the other hand, a commercial case calls for a tight clear, well-reasoned and certain answer.

One thing I was looking for in the book I could not find. A solution to the problem of increasingly long judgments, sometimes further bloated by long citations of passages from authorities or documents, so easily put in by cut and paste. Sometimes I think we should have a rule about judgment length (I think one or two US state courts have one). Or perhaps a rule that judgments must be handwritten by the judge and another that they can only be written on a particular, very expensive paper for which the judge must pay himself.

Max has addressed and debated all these questions and more. Any common lawyer worth his or her salt will enjoy this book – nothing like it has even been attempted before (as far as I know). What civil lawyers will make of it remains to be seen.

I end by saying Max Barrett has honoured me twice. First, he kindly cites a couple of my judgments. Second, by asking me to write this preface. It was not difficult to say yes. Or to write it. May this book's readers enjoy, treasure, think, and learn from it.

---

[4] Who, as one US judge had on a permanent note on his desk saying "is the most important guy in court"!

Foreword

Mr Justice Max Barrett

> *Those with a taste for fairy tales seem to have thought that in some Aladdin's Cave there is hidden the Common Law in all its splendour and that on a judge's appointment there descends on him knowledge of the magic words 'Open Sesame'. Bad decisions are given when the judge has muddled the password and the wrong door opens. But we do not believe in fairy tales anymore.*
> Lord Reid[1]

This book considers the art and craft of judgment writing. It examines how legal judgments are written and might better be written. It does this in two ways: first, by considering theories of good judgment writing, as posited by academics and judges from around the common law world; and second, by considering the judgments of great judgment writers from the United States, the United Kingdom and the wider common law world – in particular, the nations of Australia, Canada, India, Ireland, Israel and New Zealand. Though slightly outside the scope of a work on judgment writing, the book also touches on the art, craft and delivery of *ex tempore* (ostensibly impromptu) judgments – a judgment form still extensively relied upon in common law jurisdictions.

I am a serving judge of the High Court of Ireland and have written many hundreds of reserved judgments to this time. However, this book is humbly tendered to readers with the intention of showing what I have learned of judgment writing from *others*, not from a presumptive sense of what I can teach from experience. My hope is that a consideration of the extensive academic and professional commentary on judgment writing by

---

1 Reid, 22.

someone who works as a judge will be of interest to novice superior court judges, their more seasoned colleagues and all who have an interest in judgment writing and legal writing more generally (including legal practitioners, law teachers and students of law). Lower-court judges called upon to write judgments will also, I hope, find this book of value. And judges at all levels will, I hope, find Part III (on *ex tempore* judgments) to be useful.

No one reader will agree with all the precepts and propositions identified hereinafter. Likely all judges will have deviated from those propositions. I know that I have. This is because no form of writing can be confined by unyielding principles or rules. However, this is not to say that the quest to identify such principles and rules is pointless. The opposite is true: perfection in the art and craft of judgment writing is unattainable; self-improvement is always possible.

A brief synopsis of this book follows.

Chapter 1 ("On judgments") considers what is meant by the term 'judgment'. It looks at why reasons should be given, types of reasoning, the inherent inadequacy of reasoning and some aspects of *ex tempore*, oral and written judgments.

Chapter 2 ("Judgments: purpose and audience") looks at judgment purpose. It considers the precedential functions of judgments, potential audiences for judgments and how perceived audience/s can impact on judgment form.

Chapter 3 ("Judgment length") considers the important question of judgment length. It looks at the position that pertained historically; considers possible reasons for the greater length of contemporary judgments; addresses the attractions of brevity, clarity and simplicity in judgment writing; and examines the barriers to same. It also considers the potential of short-form judgments in addressing 'judgment overload' within common law systems.

Chapter 4 ("Judgment style") focuses on issues of style. It looks at stylistic types, and considers the use of literary allusion, academic references, footnotes, metaphors, aphorisms and epigrams. It also looks at common pitfalls in judgment writing.

Chapter 5 ("Judgment structure") considers different approaches to judgment writing offered by various experts/practitioners. It also considers how to approach the task of judgment writing.

Chapter 6 ("Dissenting and concurring judgments") examines the potential, role, merits and drawbacks of dissenting and concurring judgments; the motivations of dissenting/concurring judges; and the writing of dissenting/concurring judgments.

Chapter 7 ("Children, families and immigrants") looks at the particular need for simplicity in judgments concerning child/family/asylum/immigration law. In it I contend that appending a simplified 'plain language' note to such judgments is a useful innovation.

Chapter 8 ("Authors and judges") considers writing tips offered by some prominent novelists and poets and brings them to bear in the context of judgment writing.

Chapter 9 ("Three great and pioneering women judges") considers the lessons in judgment writing to be gleaned from the careers of three prominent judges from the pioneering generation of women appointed in recent decades to the apex courts of their home jurisdictions. The three are Justices O'Connor and Ginsburg of the US Supreme Court, and Justice Wilson of the Supreme Court of Canada.

Chapter 10 ("Three great American judges") considers what lessons might be gleaned from the judgment-writing styles of three prominent US Supreme Court justices: Justices Holmes, Jackson and Scalia.

Chapter 11 ("Three great British judges") considers what lessons might be gleaned from the judgment-writing styles of three prominent British 'law lords': Lords Atkin, Denning and Bingham.

Chapter 12 ("Some great judges from the wider common law world") considers what lessons in good judgment writing might be gleaned from the judgments of leading judges of the wider common law world: Sir Owen Dixon (Australia); Bora Laskin (Canada); Hans Raj Khanna (India); Brian Walsh (Ireland); Shimon Agranat (Israel); and Sir John Salmond (New Zealand). (One clear lesson arising from this chapter is that there is significant potential for a future book looking at the lessons in judgment writing to be gleaned from the judgments of more great judges from the wider common law world, including but not limited to the common law jurisdictions of Africa and the Caribbean.)

I should emphasise in passing that Chapters 9 to 12 do not seek in any way to criticise the judges considered in those chapters – all of whom were outstanding practitioners of the art and craft of judgment writing, as well as being people who attained high judicial office in their respective jurisdictions. Instead, those chapters are written in a spirit of appreciation of the world-class talents of the judges considered and seek merely to identify such lessons in judgment writing as emerge in the all-too-brief consideration of their remarkable careers that can be undertaken in a general text such as this.

Chapter 13 is entitled "The art and craft of *ex tempore* judgments". Many *ex tempore* (essentially 'on-the-spot') judgments continue to be delivered in all common law systems, especially at lower-court level. So although this book concerns itself with judgment *writing*, it would seem remiss not to include a chapter on the art and craft of *ex tempore* judgments, which may in any event involve some written preparation and/or be reduced to written form following delivery.

In the appendix, I consider some aspects of what the philosophy of aesthetics and art/literary theory have to teach us about judgments and judges. I have deliberately consigned this text to the appendix because the issues it touches upon, though interesting, are not this book's primary focus.

Throughout this book, I have used the feminine form in referring to the notional judge. I do not mean to cause any offence in this regard to male or non-binary judges. There are all kinds of fine judges whose diversity of background, being and experience enriches and adorns the global bench. (I use the phrase 'global bench' advisedly. The international nature of the judicial profession is a striking feature of judicial life. Judges across the world are engaged in much the same task in their daily labours, yielding a commonality of experience which makes cross-border comparisons, such as those undertaken herein, possible, sensible, informative and helpful.)

References in this book to a 'judgment' are, unless the text/context otherwise indicates, to a written reserved legal judgment rendered by a government-appointed judge in a court of law. When writing of the American context, I often use the word 'opinion' – essentially an Americanism for what is typically called a 'judgment' in many other common law jurisdictions. I am mindful too that members of the Appellate Committee of the House of Lords (the forerunner of the UK Supreme Court) technically delivered speeches, not judgments. However, for ease of reference, I generally refer to these speeches as 'judgments' (which in substance is what they were).

In terms of footnote references, this book adopts a modified version of the Chicago referencing style. When referring to a particular book/article, instead of inserting, eg, '(Sivakumar, 274)' in the main text and thus potentially interrupting the flow of reading, the reference 'Sivakumar, 274' appears as a footnote. Hence, a reader who wishes to read this book without bothering much with footnotes is given a smooth reading experience, while a reader who wishes to consult a work referred to in a footnote, will find the full source details in the bibliography. (In the example given it is "Sivakumar, S, "Judgment or Judicial Opinion: How to Read and Analyse" (2016) 58(3) *Journal of Indian Law Institute* 273" (at p274)). Case references appear in full in the footnotes.

I am deeply grateful to Sir Robin Jacob for his comments on an earlier draft of this text and for kindly agreeing to write the preface. My brother, Professor Gavin Barrett of University College Dublin's Sutherland School of Law, offered his customary unhesitating support and welcome insights, for which I am most grateful. I must also thank Professor Laura Cahillane of the University of Limerick Law School and Professor Keith O'Sullivan of the School of English at Dublin City University for their comments on an earlier version of this text. I am grateful also to the anonymous reviewer of a previous version of this text who suggested a number of useful amendments. Mum, Dad and Conor, as always, were forthcoming with kindness and reassurance. I must also thank Ms Katie Winder for undertaking a valuable proofread of the late-draft text and suggesting useful amendments.

This book does not make or seek to make, nor should it be construed as making, any comment on the careers or judgments of any serving judges or any judges who have departed from judicial service but whose working life continues (whether as a judge or otherwise).

This book is written in a personal capacity. All opinions expressed by me (and any errors) in this book are mine alone.

As this book goes to print a terrible war is being visited on Ukraine. All after-tax royalties earned by the author from sales of this book will be donated to the Ukrainian relief efforts of the International Red Cross and Red Crescent Movement.

This book is dedicated with love to Agapi, Athena, Petros and Mikhalis.

Part I: The theory of the art and craft of judgment writing

1. On judgments

This chapter considers what is meant by the term 'judgment'. It looks at why reasons should be given; types of reasoning; the inherent inadequacy of reasoning; and some aspects of ex tempore, *oral and written judgments.*

Law is a dynamic medley of concepts, evolving over time, differing across cultures. Melded by lawmakers and moulded by judges, these concepts form and inform the 'rule of law' – the critical infrastructure on which liberal democracy is constructed. As with all infrastructure, the rule of law requires "maintenance, upkeep and renovation".[1] Judgments play an important part in this process. This is because laws "are a dead letter without courts to expound and define their true meaning".[2] What, however, is a 'judgment'?

1. Definition

The current *Oxford Dictionary of Law* defines a 'judgment' as a "decision made by a court in respect of the matter before it"[3] and the "process of reasoning by which the court's decision was arrived at".[4] This definition is, arguably, not great. If a judgment is a "decision made by a court", then only the decision is the judgment, not the reasoning for the decision. However, in colloquial parlance, a 'judgment' comprises both the reasoning and the decision. Additionally, when one considers matters more deeply, one quickly realises that the concept embraces more than the decision/reasoning processes. It extends to the imaginative process of

---

1 French.
2 Hamilton.
3 Law, 378.
4 *Ibid*, 379.

arriving at a decision; the creative process of judgment writing; the performative element of judgment delivery; and any enduring text that remains. Central to all this is the judge. She is the author of her imagination, judgement and performance. Lord Macmillan, a onetime 'law lord', touches on the creative aspect of judging when he describes it as "a literary composition ... subject to certain conventions".[5]

Bearing the foregoing in mind, can one iterate a more refined definition of what constitutes a 'judgment'? In practical terms, a 'judgment' is a decision given by one or more judges in respect of a particular dispute. In colloquial terms, a 'judgment' comprises the reasons for a decision. But in truth, a judgment is so much more. It is a performative act: "not just an explanation for a legal outcome, it brings that outcome into existence."[6] It is a violent act: a judge "articulates her understanding of a text, and as a result, somebody loses his freedom, his property, [etc]".[7] And it is an attempt at persuasion, seeking "to persuade the relevant audience that the outcome is justified".[8]

2. Persuasiveness

The general view is that the more persuasive a judgment is, the more authoritative it is.[9] There is an alternative view that judgments are not written to persuade but simply to communicate and/or establish precedent.[10] However, the better view is that a judgment needs to be persuasive. It needs to persuade the litigants, the media and wider society that the judgment is correct. If appealed, it will need to persuade a majority of appellate judges that it is correct by their lights. There is also self-persuasion at play – that is, a judge seeks also to persuade herself that her decision is correct. All these persuasive acts require communication via judgment.

A question arises as to whether, in the Information Age, the task of marshalling persuasive arguments in favour of a particular conclusion will remain the exclusive provenance of human judges,

---

5   Macmillan (1948), 491.
6   Murynka, 630.
7   Cover (1986), 1601.
8   McCormick (1995), 454.
9   Bianchi, 43.
10 Cappalli, 286.

1. On judgments

given the abundance of information which now typically confronts judges in each case. It has been suggested that artificial intelligence (AI) "may not be aware of the reasons for a particular conclusion ... but that does not mean that AI ... could not ... marshal arguments in favour of such a conclusion".[11] There is a sub-set of legal literature on the task of judging in the Information Age – a discrete subject beyond this book's scope. However, one early commentator largely captured the key possible advantages and drawbacks presenting in this regard.[12] The advantages are likely savings in time/money, a greater sense of impartiality and a decline in unpredictability. But the drawbacks are significant: a freezing of precedent, a dehumanisation of the justice process and a propensity for strange results if rationality is brought to bear without emotion being prayed in aid. Ultimately computer-*aided* justice rather than computer-*administered* justice seems the more likely future.

We live in an age when the continuing vitality of the common law system is challenged by 'information overload'. By this I mean not just that the length and number of judgments are increasing. Rather, I mean to refer also to the amount of case law and commentary now available online. This super-abundance of information – a superfluity of which is often provided to deciding judges – has led to judges facing a "crisis of volume".[13] In this context, it seems necessary to explore whether there are alternatives to existing standard methods of adjudication. Kirby, a retired Australian judge, offers two possible alternative approaches: "[1] [T]he court ... could prepare a draft opinion based on the papers. The advocates ... could then attack, or support, this document. [2] Alternatively ... parties could be required to draft an opinion for adoption (with adaptations) by the court."[14]

Kirby's proposal is the type of radical solution required if the common law system is not to drown in the tidal wave of precedent and commentary available online. Even so, his proposal seems unlikely to enjoy much purchase in the legal world. As Kirby observes: "The law is resistant to ... original thinking ... especially

---

11 Abdullah, 8.
12 See D'Amato.
13 Martineau, 119.
14 Kirby (2001), 15–16.

... when it affects the methodology of its operations."[15] Lawmakers need not show the same innate conservatism. Even so, perhaps a surer first step – one more likely to command general support – would be for judges to adhere in judgments to the 'gold standard' of brevity, clarity and simplicity canvassed for by prominent English judge Lord Bingham and considered hereinafter.

3. **Reasons**

There are at least five reasons for giving reasons. The first is to explain how and why a decision is made.[16] Second, in giving reasons, a judge is required to work rationally through applicable law and facts to arrive at a decision. (While some judges are capable of extensive *ex tempore* reasoning, there is something about judgment writing that allows reason to settle and logic to flow.) Third, reasons enable a higher court to understand the thinking of a lower court. However, appellate courts need to be sensible as to what is required in this regard if the triple standard of brevity, clarity and simplicity is to be attainable at trial court level. A fourth 'reason for reasons' presents in the specific context of judicial review cases – that is, cases in which an applicant challenges a decision made by central government or a public body. In such cases, the provision of reasons should assist decision makers in improving their processes and future decisions. Fifth, in providing written reasons, a judge seeks to inspire faith in the neutral decision-making capacity of the courts and to deflect criticism.[17]

Personal motivations can inform a judge's decision to give extensive written reasons:

> *Transplants from academia may feel irresistibly driven to communicate their intellectual processes and products ... Refugees from the world of politics and public affairs write to persuade ... colleagues and the public that they are moving law in the right direction. Some judges write for the personal gratification that comes from being quoted,*

---

15 *Ibid*, 16. A late-2021 burst of online commentary (admittedly in the quiet end-of-year period) on the decision of the UK Supreme Court to issue its judgments in Calibri typeface, rather than the more traditional Times New Roman (possibly in a bid for greater accessibility/readability through use of a modern font style) is testament to how even slight changes in the legal system can excite comment. (See generally Hussain.)
16 Downes, 3.
17 Ferguson, 207.

With Compliments

The Hon. Mr. Justice Donal O'Donnell
CHIEF JUSTICE

Thanks peter

Supreme Court of Ireland | Four Courts, Inns Quay, Dublin 7, Ireland

cited, and republished ... with the side benefits of invitations to lecture, [and] write in law reviews ... Ambitious judges may write in hopes of promotion.[18]

Some judges, it might be added, may just like to write. If the 'transplants' would curb their enthusiasm, the 'refugees' would contain their desire to persuade, the self-indulgent would refrain from seeking self-gratification, the ambitious would place litigants' interests ahead of their own and devotees of writing would consider occasionally directing their talents into other writing forms, one suspects that lengthy written judgments would be fewer in number – and that litigants and the legal system would be the better for it.

Despite the merits intrinsic to written judgments, there is no acknowledgement in early common law cases that a judge was under an obligation to give written reasons. In the courts of England and Wales, for example, it is not until the late 16th century that one finds references to other cases in judicial reasoning. And it is only in the late 17th century that one finds Chief Justice Vaughan opining that a judicial decision is the best source of law.[19] (One might quibble with this: a judicial decision is *a* source of law; however, only the better-written judgments, it is submitted, are the *best* source of law.) Notwithstanding Vaughan's observations, the prevalence of jury trials to the mid-19th century meant that all fact finding and much related reasoning was done secretly by jurors. Even as the superior courts of England and Wales began to give written reasons, they appeared satisfied for lower courts not to do so. North of Hadrian's Wall, there was the same reluctance as there was 'down south' at producing written judgments or even written records of oral judgments. Lord Reid, a onetime Scottish 'law lord', recounts that: "when about 1800 Lord Justice Clerk Eskgrove [a Scottish judge] saw a man taking notes he said indignantly – 'the man's takin doun ma verry words'. But things were then changing ... And very likely English influence had its effect."[20]

Today, the prevailing view in the common law world is that identified by the Supreme Court of Canada in *R v Sheppard*:[21]

---

18 Wald, 1995(1), 1372.
19 *Bole v Horton* (1673) 124 ER 1113, 1124 (CtCP).
20 Reid, 24.
21 [2002] 1 SCR 869 (SC).

"[J]ustice must not only be done but must be seen to be done, [and] ... it is difficult to see how justice can be seen to be done if judges fail to articulate ... reasons for their actions."[22] Things have come a long way from the days when 18th-century British judge Lord Mansfield is said to have observed – perhaps in jest – that a judge should never volunteer reasons for a judgment, "for your judgment will probably be right, but your reasons will certainly be wrong".[23] It is unlikely that any modern judge would heed such advice (and it is not clear that it was ever intended as serious guidance). But the fact that, historically, lengthy reasoning was not always considered necessary, yet society continued to function should give pause to judges who consider that without their always providing lengthy written reasons, the justice system will inevitably be tarnished and society necessarily the poorer.

Paradoxically, the giving of reasons is unlikely to ensure that a completely reasoned judgment is given in a case.[24] This is because the reasoning underpinning a judgment is "more nuanced than [a] ... judgment can ... convey".[25] In other words, reasoned judgments will never perfectly attain what they seek to achieve because judgments, as human creations, are necessarily imperfect. "[P]ublished reasons can only be an outline of the main factors which have led to the judge's conclusion."[26] It follows that the litigant or appellate court that seeks complete reasons in any one judgment is to some extent seeking what can never be given.

There is a (now-dated) piece of research which suggests that English judges subscribe to five different reasoning types:[27]

- deduction from clearly worded statute;
- inductive reasoning;
- reasoning by ruling out alternative solutions (*reductio ad absurdum*);
- reasoning by analogy; and
- application of precedent.

---

22 *Ibid*, para 15.
23 Campbell (1849), 588.
24 Murray, 546.
25 Murynka, 637.
26 Kirby (2003), 45.
27 Goutal, 46–49.

Although one would expect that judges in the United States – a fellow common law jurisdiction – would utilise precisely the same deductive techniques as judges in the United Kingdom, in fact there are differences. Thus, the same research points to a uniquely American form of reasoning: the statistical syllogism, whereby if a set of cases has received a certain treatment, the next such case could well deserve similar treatment.[28] And it finds that deduction from statutory wording, reasoning by example, *reductio ad absurdum* and reasoning by analogy do not enjoy the same popularity among American judges.[29] (There is also, in the United States, a merged form of precedential deduction, whereby a governing rule is stated in a telegram-style sentence, a conclusion is stated and one or more authorities are cited.)[30] A number of additional reasoning types can also be deployed in judgments – for example:

- reasoning that proceeds on some sense of shared rationality;
- reasoning that proceeds on an 'It goes without saying … ' basis;
- reasoning that has recourse to legal presumptions; and
- reasoning that deploys a rule/exception paradigm.[31]

If nothing else, the foregoing points to the variety of legitimate reasoning techniques open to a common law judge tasked with judgment writing. However, it seems unlikely that many judges, when they commence writing a judgment, resolve to deploy a particular reasoning type. Rather – and this goes back to the issue of persuasiveness – an individual judge seems more likely to settle on whatever one or more reasoning types seem to her to be desirable or necessary to make her judgment more persuasive.

4. Clarity

The institutional role of judges is "discharged most directly in the writing of judgments".[32] Those judgments form a part of the law and operate as a guide to future judges. So there is a need for maximum clarity and certainty in judgment writing. This is because

---

28 *Ibid*, 52.
29 *Ibid*.
30 *Ibid*, 53.
31 Bianchi, 38–39.
32 Keane, P, 13.

it is unreasonable to expect lawyers and non-lawyers "to wade through multiple judgments, pondering the subtle nuances which emerge and how they impact on the *ratio decidendi*, if there is one".[33] The US Federal Judicial Center has posited, as an (uncontroversial) ideal in this regard, that an opinion "should fairly, clearly, and accurately state the significant facts and relevant rules of law".[34]

Lord Neuberger, a former UK Supreme Court president, has made a number of useful observations concerning clarity in judgment writing. These include the following.

First, clarity does not demand length. "Judgment-writers should be braver and appeal courts … more robust."[35] (To use a colloquialism, 'it takes two to tango' – that is, trial judges are unlikely to be braver if appellate courts are unwilling to be more robust.)

Second, judges should avoid the twin sins of engaging in an "anxious parade of knowledge" and being "too clever" – that is, yielding to smarminess.[36] Perhaps a useful practice note for judges in this regard is the advice offered by the headmaster of Charterhouse to the poet Robert Graves as the latter quit his *alma mater*: "Well, good-bye, Graves, [he said,] and remember that your best friend is the waste-paper basket."[37] The author of a notable pen-picture of Vice-Chancellor Bacon, a prominent 19th-century English judge, also strikes a cautionary note for all judges in the observation that "[h]is fault, like … other men of confident judgment, was … cocksureness".[38]

Third, not every judgment will be understood by everyone, but the aim should be to make every judgment as accessible as possible – not least to the public.[39] As Lord Bingham has observed, it is a requirement of the rule of law that the law "be accessible and so far as possible, intelligible, clear and predictable".[40] The issuance of judgments that are as brief, clear and simple as possible honours the rule of law. A good judgment, it is submitted, should be sufficiently

---

33 Heerey, 463.
34 Federal Judicial Center (2013), 1.
35 Neuberger (January 2012), para 31.
36 Ibid.
37 Graves, 51.
38 Anon (1901), 381.
39 Neuberger (November 2012), para 30. A question arises as to whether enough is yet done to ensure accessibility of judgments to people with disabilities.
40 Bingham, T (2011), 37.

well written to enable interested and reasonably intelligent non-lawyers to understand who the parties were, what the case was about, what decision the judge reached and why.[41] Achieving the foregoing can be a challenging task for judges, to whom the complex can seem readily comprehensible.[42] Nonetheless, some level of greater clarity and simplicity is typically desirable and attainable through the condensed brevity that rigorous editing brings.

Fourth, a short summary at judgment start is desirable.[43] In my own judgments, I now place a three or four-sentence summary as a form of headnote ahead of the main body of the judgment. In an age when more judgments are written (and hence a lower proportion formally reported), the provision of this summary is a service to litigants and future readers.

Fifth, judges should consider giving in-judgment guidance to the structure and contents of long(er) judgments.[44] A table of contents goes a long way towards achieving this. Ideally, tables of contents are presented in a smaller font size, the aim being that they should occupy only a page or two of text. (Otherwise, they quickly become more obstacle than aid to comprehensibility. Tables of contents also serve a useful function in judgment editing. When one prepares a table of contents, it swiftly becomes apparent where there has been any duplication/overlap of observations in the main text.)

Sixth, judges should be rigorous in cutting judgment length.[45] (And when a judgment re-treads existing legal ground, it is not clear that previous case law requires to be considered at any length.)

Seventh, there could *perhaps* be fewer dissenting judgments. Certainly, they should tend to be shorter than majority judgments.[46] The subject of dissenting judgments is given fuller consideration in Chapter 6.

Eighth, a concurring judgment should perhaps be given only when a topic would benefit from "judicial dialogue".[47] (Concurring judgments are also considered in Chapter 6.) As will be seen, a

---

41 Neuberger (November 2012).
42 *Ibid*.
43 *Ibid*, para 16.
44 *Ibid*, para 17.
45 *Ibid*, para 20.
46 *Ibid*, para 28.
47 *Ibid*, para 29.

question mark has been raised as regards the desirability of concurring judgments. My own sense is that they are beneficial. A great strength of liberal democracy is its commitment to free speech. Concurring judgments are a form of free speech.

The flipside of wariness about concurring/dissenting judgments is a perception that composite judgments (single judgments which set out the common view of multiple judges) help to achieve the following sensible ideal identified by the European Court of Human Rights (ECtHR) in *Sunday Times v United Kingdom*:[48]

[T]he law must be adequately accessible: the citizen must be able to have an indication that is adequate in the circumstances of the legal rules applicable to a given case ... [A] norm cannot be regarded as a 'law' unless it is formulated with sufficient precision to enable the citizen to regulate his conduct ... if need be with appropriate advice.[49]

5. Composite judgments

Though the ECtHR was treating with the law generally, its observations have resonance in the specific context of composite judgments. This is because instinct suggests that a single judgment will bring that certainty and clarity which the ECtHR considers desirable. However, my own view in this regard respectfully aligns with that of Lord Reid, who once observed:

We are often told that there should only be one judgment instead of ... five speeches in the House of Lords. At first sight that seems good sense: the law will then be clear ... The trouble is ... it won't work and experience has shown that ... [i]f you compare the quality of Privy Council judgments [a composite judgment being common in the Privy Council] with speeches in the House of Lords ... Privy Council judgments have been ... inferior ... Yet the same Law Lords have sat and ... taken just as much trouble ... The truth is ... it is often not possible to reach a final solution of a difficult problem all at once. It is better to put up with some uncertainty ... for a time than to reach a final solution prematurely. The problem often looks rather different the second time ... Second thoughts are not always best but they generally are.[50]

Other problems present. The issuance of a single composite

---

48   [1979] ECHR 6538/74.
49   *Ibid*, para 49.
50   Reid, 29.

opinion by a multi-judge panel deprives the world of that richness of views which concurring/dissenting judgments provide. Moreover, a single composite opinion is so authoritative it may 'chill' the future evolution of the law. By contrast, a smorgasbord of judgments (lead/concurring/dissenting) yields a hint as to how the law may or should evolve in the future and holds out the promise of such evolution to each succeeding generation.

6. ***Ex tempore* judgments**

It is an old adage that justice delayed is justice denied. When a case hearing ends, a judge must decide whether to give an *ex tempore* judgment or a written reserved judgment. An *ex tempore* judgment is, ostensibly, an impromptu judgment that is delivered orally, either immediately or very soon after the hearing of a case ends, with an approved transcript or a written-form judgment often following thereafter. By contrast, a reserved judgment is one that is postponed to a future time, so as to allow the deciding judge to think over matters further and write a well-crafted judgment. In truth, it is typically possible to write a relatively lengthy reserved judgment within a few days and a reserved judgment – even one written at an accelerated pace – is, it is submitted, more desirable in terms of offering clarity and certainty to litigants. If work pressures mean that a reserved judgment cannot be written quickly, Sir Frank Kitto, a onetime member of the High Court of Australia, has offered a solution: half-write it. "It is much easier," he observes, "to come back to a half-written judgement than to a clean slate."[51] Fundamentally, it would seem much more desirable that a judgment be reserved than delivered *ex tempore*. This is because, whatever the other advantages of *ex tempore* judgments may be, they are rarely models of lucidity:[52]

> *[F]ew judges are gifted with the skills necessary to produce an* ex tempore *oral judgment of the same quality as a written reserved judgment. To do so entails the judge being exceptionally articulate ... able to marshal his thoughts logically and rationally and ... able to express himself orally with the same economy and facility of language*

---

51   Kitto (2003), 71.
52   Mous, 638.

as he can on paper ... [W]here the case entails legal issues, an ex tempore judgment demands that the judge ... be completely au fait with the relevant principles of law and in a position to state them accurately and apply them appropriately.[53]

There are some judicial *wünderkinder* who possess all of these talents. Back in the 19th century, Sir George Jessel – the first Jewish master of the rolls – was renowned for his skill in oral judgment, as in "the great *St Leonards Will Case* in which he delivered a luminous judgment, entirely oral, extending over seventeen pages of the Law Reports, affirming the proposition that the contents of a lost will ... may be proved by secondary evidence".[54] (We also have a sense of how Jessel spoke. London-born, he apparently had the habit – like Eliza Doolittle – of dropping his aitches. Thus, the possibly apocryphal tale is told that when he was once advised that a whale had been stranded in Oban, Jessel's reply was "Impossible! A whale in 'Olborn! It must be a 'oax".)[55]

Judges with the memory and skills of Jessel tend to be rare. Yet *ex tempore* judgments continue to have their aficionados. So, for example, it has been suggested that it is in the public interest that, "if ... appropriate", judgments should be given on an *ex tempore* basis.[56] A considered view as to the merits or otherwise of *ex tempore* judgments was offered in *Hadid v Redpath*.[57] That was a case in which the New South Wales Court of Appeal decided that the inadequacy of reasons given by a trial judge in a personal injuries lawsuit had yielded a substantial miscarriage of justice. In the course of his judgment in the appeal, Justice Heydon said of *ex tempore* judgments:

> *Vigorous and combative methods, lack of regard for tender feelings, and impatience need not necessarily accompany the practice of giving unreserved judgments, but they commonly do ... The faults of expression typical of unreserved judgments are often said on appeal to manifest errors of thought.*[58]

---

53 Corbett, 119.
54 Manson, 231.
55 St George Stubbs, 155.
56 Mahoney, 103.
57 [2001] NSWCA 416.
58 *Ibid*, para 50.

This seems a polite way of saying that unreserved judgments can be too punchy, show insufficient empathy/sympathy and come across as impatient. Heydon acknowledged that *ex tempore* judgments do offer a means of avoiding the dangers of delay in judgment.[59] Even so, if counsel and/or litigants push for judgment to be given *ex tempore*, it may be prudent for the judge so prevailed upon to heed Polonius' advice to Laertes: "Take each man's censure but reserve thy judgment."[60]

Why is a written reserved judgment so often desirable? At a fundamental level, "[r]eading maketh a full man; conference a ready man and writing an exact man".[61] However, there are more workaday advantages. Thus, a written reserved judgment:

- maximises the probability that a judge will give the best possible judgment[62] (because it is only in writing and revising that one can arrive at "the requisite intensity of penetrating thought");[63]
- counters any tendency towards arbitrariness;
- is beneficial to the legal process, illustrating to all that the judge has taken time to assess a claim and perhaps giving solace to a losing party that her case has been heard and understood[64] (that said, "disappointed litigants will rarely [if ever] feel ... that a judgment not in their favour was ... right");[65]
- entails the potential for "exacting ... reasoning" by a judge;[66]
- offers a firm basis on which to construct an appeal;
- is of greater use as precedent (most *ex tempore* judgments suffer from the impression of having been delivered in haste. Judgments that are never reduced to writing are "legal untouchables");[67]
- offers valuable guidance in a relatively permanent form on how the law may be evolving and may also identify a need for

---

59 *Ibid*, para 45.
60 *Hamlet*, I.iii.
61 Bacon, "Of Studies".
62 Gageler, 203.
63 *Ibid*, 190.
64 Gorman, 302-03.
65 Murynka, 630.
66 Gorman, 305.
67 *Ibid*, 307.

lawmakers to intervene where "judicial decision making ... is ... systematically unfair or out of touch";[68]
- exposes a judge to proper public scrutiny[69] (such scrutiny can be a bruising experience, but society is the better that it occurs, provided that any criticism is fair);[70] and
- allows for "a freedom of expression and thought which an oral judgment can never match"[71] – that is, the written form offers a potential for comprehensiveness and eloquence which the spoken word does not typically entail.

Perhaps the last word on the merits of written judgments ought to go to the eminent American judge, Richard Posner, who has observed as follows:

Reasoning that seemed sound when 'in the head' may seem half-baked when written down, especially since the written form of an argument encourages some degree of critical detachment in the writer... Many writers have the experience of not knowing except in a general sense what they are going to write until they start writing. A link is somehow forged between the unconscious and the pen. The link is lost to the judge who does not write.[72]

In this chapter, I have considered in a general sense what is meant by the term 'judgment'; the reasons for giving reasons; some aspects of judicial reasoning; and the merits of written reserved judgments. In Chapter 2, I focus in more detail on judgment purpose; the precedential function of a judgment; and the matter of audience (for whom a judgment is written) and how the intended audience/s for whom a judge writes may impact on judgment form.

---

68   Murynka, 630.
69   Gorman, 302.
70   Arguably, the best recent example of unfair criticism is the attack launched by the *Daily Mail* against three senior English judges as "Enemies of the People" after they gave judgment, on 3 November 2016, that parliamentary consent to the United Kingdom's formal notification of 'Brexit' to the European Union was required. The headline appeared in the *Daily Mail* on 4 November 2016. The irony of this criticism was that the three judges in their judgment affirmed the sovereignty and primacy of Parliament within Britain's parliamentary democracy and so were championing 'people power', not opposing it.
71   Gorman, 304.
72   Posner (1995), 1447–48.

2. Judgments: purpose and audience

This chapter looks at the purpose of a judgment. It considers the precedential functions of judgments and the potential audiences of a judgment. It also looks at how perceived audiences may, can and do impact on judgment form.

1. Purpose

Reasoned judgments serve multiple purposes. They decide the issues in dispute.[1] They seek to impart justice to affected parties.[2] They seek to persuade multiple audiences that the court has arrived at a proper answer.[3] They constrain judicial arbitrariness.[4] They legitimate judicial creativity.[5] They seek to guarantee consistency, predictability and stability in the legal system. They advertise the integrity of the legal system.[6] They serve the democratic process by offering a medium whereby "judges speak to ... citizens".[7] They facilitate inter-generational discussion about the nature of our society.[8] They invite judges in the future to think and speak as the court has done.[9] They remind members of the least democratic branch of government "that they must operate by more than ... judicial fiat".[10] (In this last regard, one finds echoes of Bentham's long-ago assertion that "Publicity is the ... soul of justice".)[11] They enable a judge to go through the law and facts and come to a

---

1 Sivakumar, 274.
2 *Ibid.*
3 *Ibid.*
4 *Ibid.*
5 *Ibid.*
6 Horwitz, 101.
7 *Ibid*, 109.
8 *Ibid*, 110 *et seq.*
9 White (1995), 1366.
10 Horwitz, 109.
11 Bentham, 316.

considered judgment. (Integrity is required in this process if the facts that a judge chooses to relate are not to be "inherently selective";[12] judges are not immune from the "human temptation to ignore or ... minimize inconvenient facts".)[13]

Reasoned judgments also enhance the 'soft power' of a nation. English judgments are an example *par excellence* of this. The decisions of the English superior courts have long informed the jurisprudence of those nations that were once within the British Empire. And for so long as the United Kingdom was in the European Union, the judgments of its superior courts on EU law were a valuable resource for judges from other EU member states. However, as the days of Britain's empire recede into more-distant history and as the United Kingdom has quit the European Union, neither avenue of influence seems likely to continue as before.

Immediately after the Second World War, the US Supreme Court was a standard bearer for the proper articulation of rights and freedoms in liberal democracies. Certainly, it was looked to as such by the Irish courts in the 1960s and 1970s. However, this influence appears to have diminished of late, for various reasons. These include "an American judicial trend towards intentional isolation from the influence of legal developments in the courts and legal systems of other nations".[14]

There are, it is submitted, four purposes to a written judgment:
- clarification of thought;
- explanation of a decision;
- public communication of reasons; and
- provision of reasons for an appellate court to consider.[15]

When it comes to clarification of thought, one reality of which judges are keenly aware is the extent to which there are no easy answers to the legal questions posed in court proceedings. As US Chief Justice John Roberts, while a Supreme Court nominee, observed of his time as a federal appellate judge: "I've found that I have to spend far more time than I thought I would just getting to

---

12   Juliano and Schwab, 558–59.
13   Fletcher, 297.
14   Van Detta, 53.
15   See generally Atkinson.

2. Judgments: purpose and audience

... what the right answer should be."[16] (This observation, as it happens, raises issues of its own. For what Chief Justice Roberts means to refer to is the right answer *by his own reckoning*. There is oftentimes no 'right' answer as such. To borrow from Lord Reid, there is not some 'Open Sesame' formula that rolls back the stone to the common law cave and reveals the truth within.[17] For all that many people believe that when a higher court says 'nay' after a lower court said 'yea', or *vice versa*, the lower court got matters wrong (and sometimes it will have done), as often as not the appellate court may – as is its right – simply have taken a different view on one or more close-run issues).

As to the role of written judgments in explaining a decision, litigants and lawyers obviously need to know how and why a decision has been reached. It has been suggested that it is "particularly important that the losing party knows why ... she ... lost".[18] This perception of a judgment as a 'letter to a loser' is not new or radical.[19] It is, however, a concept consistent with the modern notion of therapeutic jurisprudence. This is a notion which arose initially in the mental health context and conceptualises the ideal legal resolution process to be one which "allow[s] a party ... [to] move on from a legal encounter in a positive way".[20] It is, therefore, a departure from the perception of the common law as adverse to "empathic reasoning".[21] And empathy is wanted in judges – albeit that it is sometimes wanting in judges and invisible in judgments, "banished from the better legal neighborhoods and from explicit recognition in legal discourse".[22] This divorce of legal reason from emotion and the related notion that a judge must avoid displays of empathy "reflects an impoverished view of reason and understanding ... that focuses on cognition in its most reductionist sense".[23]

In explaining a decision, a judge is neither required nor expected to embark upon an academic excursus. Judgments are not intended

---

16 See Reynolds, M.
17 Reid, 22.
18 Atkinson, 3.
19 Murray, 549.
20 *Ibid*, 551. See also Hunter *et al*, 344–46, 352.
21 Murray, 556.
22 Henderson (1987), 1575.
23 *Ibid*.

Part I: The theory of the art and craft of judgment writing

to be quasi-PhD theses.[24] Legal judgments are not the place to answer "big questions".[25] It may sometimes be appropriate for an appellate court to "articulate law beyond the immediate facts"[26] so as to bring necessary clarity to a particular area; though when it comes to such clarifications, there is the alternative view iterated by Lord Macmillan in *Read v J Lyons and Co Ltd*[27] that the task of a court "is to decide particular cases between litigants ... not to rationalise the law".[28] That said, the contemporary abundance of composite judgments issued by the superior courts of the United Kingdom suggests a departure from Macmillan's worldview towards a process of engagement with "law's supposed intellectual disorderliness".[29]

As to the role of written judgments in the public communication of reasons, judges communicate to the public uniquely through their judgments. In order to communicate effectively, a judgment must be "clear, precise, and say everything that needs to be said ... and no more",[30] though sometimes a judge may feel compelled to say a little more in the interests of justice.

Judgments in common law jurisdictions interpret the current position at law and also simultaneously create precedents which assist in future case determination.[31] They achieve the latter task by providing later judges with a "beaten track" to follow.[32] A consequence of all this is that judges do not view themselves as giving judgment in "unconnected instances".[33] Rather, they recognise themselves to be "sustaining a continuum, a total heritage which has potential for further development".[34] This consciousness of writing not just for the present time but potentially for all time has an impact on how judgments are written. When a judge writes a judgment, she is writing not just for the parties in front of her, but with an awareness of the precedential/normative significance of her

---

24 Jacob.
25 Mortimer, 285.
26 Bagaric and McConvill, 42.
27 [1947] AC 156 (HL).
28 *Ibid*, 175.
29 Munday (2002b), 349.
30 Atkinson, 3.
31 Sivakumar, 273.
32 Elias, 483.
33 Macrossan, 201.
34 *Ibid*.
35 Barak-Erez, 273.

words.[35] Judges are well aware that in a system constructed on precedent, "[t]oday is not only yesterday's tomorrow; it is also tomorrow's yesterday".[36]

2. Audiences

A 1960 survey of higher US appellate court judges indicated that judges saw themselves to be writing for the following ensemble:
- posterity;
- the bar;
- future judges;
- lawmakers;
- law students;
- the informed public;
- the writing judge;
- the loser (and the other lawyers and parties in the case); and
- (on a multi-judge panel) fellow judges whose vote one wishes to sway.[37]

Another audience – at least for apex courts – is the lower courts, to which such courts provide guidance.[38] One way of conceiving of these various audiences is to imagine them as being like planets around the sun. In the inner orbit are those most closely concerned with a case. In the middle orbit (when it comes to appellate judgments) is the court whose judgment has been appealed. In the outer orbit are the media, the legal profession, legal academics, law students and the public. With so many satellites orbiting around, which ought to be the subject of most focus? Justice Alito of the US Supreme Court has described the key target audience for judgments in the following terms:

I think I am first writing for myself ... Then ... if I am attempting to write a majority opinion – I am writing for the other ... judges whom I hope will be part of the majority ... Then I am ... writing for ... those who will have to apply the opinion in future cases: trial judges and lawyers ... [W]e are [also] writing for an audience that includes some people who will not try to understand what we really mean, but will

---

36 Schauer, 573.
37 Leflar (1961), 813–14.
38 Waye, 296.

try to use our words to support whatever position they, in a professional way, feel they need to take on behalf of their clients.[39]

With the growth of administrative government in liberal democracies since the Second World War, it is unsurprising that "the general public now pays ... more attention to judicial opinions".[40] Indeed, the breadth of the contemporary audience for judgments is such that the identity of the precise audience for any one judgment has become, it is submitted, rather indistinct.[41] This blurring into indistinction offers a possible reason why modern judgments are so often prolix. Judges may be seeking to satisfy multiple audiences, even though different audiences are looking for different things – sometimes contrary things (eg, comprehensiveness/simplicity) – in the same judgment. As long ago as 1971, US Chief Justice Warren Burger called on American judges "to write briefly if reasons must be given [and] ... to make extensive treatment the exception rather than the rule".[42] At least in the common law jurisdictions on the European side of the Atlantic, the opposite of Burger's ideal seems often to present.

Lord Bingham has suggested that the parties to a case may be the sole audience for the unreserved judgment of a lower court. However, when it comes to appellate courts, he considers their judgments to have a wider reach:

[Their] wider audience will probably include ... members of the legal profession who may be asked to advise on the point at issue ... courts who have to apply the law ... law teachers who have responsibility to summarise and discuss the law ... [even] non-legal professionals ... [and in] a case which has attracted ... [media] interest ... the general public.[43]

In summary, the following potential audiences, in no particular order, are identified by Leflar, Wanderer and Bingham:
- the writing judge;
- on a multi-judge panel, fellow judges whose vote one wishes to sway;

39	Alito (2009), 40.	
40	Mikva, 1366.	
41	Murray, 546.	
42	Laskin (1972), 346.	
43	Bingham, T (2009), 607.	

- the parties to a case, perhaps especially the losing party;
- for an appellate court, the court whose judgment has been appealed;
- the legal profession;
- lawmakers;
- judges generally;
- public officials;
- law teachers/students;
- non-legal professionals;
- the media;
- the public; and
- posterity.

The precise configuration of a court's audience in any one case will depend on the court's institutional role. In a court with a primary dispute resolution function, the parties (Bingham indicates) will be the primary audience, though "there are other audience categories … [G]overnments, and their agencies, are likely to be interested".[44] In a law-revealing court, the wider audience base will include:
- the parties;
- courts tasked with applying the revealed law;
- the legal or allied professions;
- the academy; and
- the public.

(A question arises as to whether academics and the legal professions rightly comprise part of a judgment's intended audience. After all, academics are paid to consider and write about the law, "and have no need of judges to do their work for them";[45] and the legal professions will remain interested in judgments without judges writing their judgments as though the professions were a target.)[46] The nature of the audience written for will impact on judgment form, with judgments being "adjusted to the particular exigencies of the audience".[47]

---

44 Mortimer, 284.
45 Jacob.
46 *Ibid.*
47 Bianchi, 38.

When it comes to posterity as an audience, it is probably wise for judges to heed the observation of former US Supreme Court Justice Felix Frankfurter as to "the evanescent fate of decisions of even the greatest ... judges".[48] With some judges, their descent into the ranks of the relative unknown is not for want of trying. It is said of the 19th-century lord chief justice, Lord Cockburn, that he "liked a page of *The Times* daily devoted to him ... and ... picked out of the general list cases which would afford him that gratification".[49] Doubtless, such behaviour is unknown today (and it is notable that, despite these efforts at self-aggrandisement, Cockburn has disappeared into relative obscurity). There are, of course, exceptional judges – such as Oliver Wendell Holmes, Jr (in the United States) and Lord Denning (in the United Kingdom) – whose judgments/names will likely always enjoy some level of renown. Even so, it is notable that the judgments and names of long-ago judicial greats (eg, Lord Mansfield) have eventually receded into some level of obscurity.

The primary audience of a judgment comprises the parties to the proceedings. However, the losing party, as previously mentioned, is often viewed as a particular focus of attention. This is not a new idea. Sometime around 2,000 BCE, Ptah-Hotep, an ancient Egyptian observer, observed that: "[A] good hearing soothes the heart."[50] A judgment written for the loser will suggest that such a hearing is precisely what has been afforded, hopefully with like effect. A distinction falls to be made between the 'primary audience' – that is, the court itself (which may be an audience of one in the case of a trial judge) – and a 'secondary audience', which includes litigants, the legal profession, other courts and the general public.[51] Of the primary audience, when a judge writes the lead/sole judgment, she must obtain the agreement of a sufficient number of other judges to command a majority. When a judge sits alone, she must be satisfied with the finished product that she crafts. Writing a judgment with which one's colleagues are satisfied runs the risk that one will excise desirable material to win majority backing. Writing a judgment

---

48   Frankfurter (1951), 503.
49   Manson, 162.
50   Murray, 545.
51   Bosielo, 12–13.

2. Judgments: purpose and audience

with which the individual judge is satisfied raises the possibility that she will continuously write in a manner that satisfies her natural biases.

Some commentators have suggested that a judge should write to the entirety of the intended audiences for a judgment. "Writing in a way that can engage all likely members of the [intended] audience is ... a desirable aim."[52] However, such views are not without difficulty. After all, a judgment written for strangers to a dispute will take a very different form from one that is written for the litigants involved. (Not least, the factual context provided in a judgment will likely need to be longer for non-litigants.) If brevity in judgments is to rescue the common law system from a superfluity of precedent, a necessary first step is for national judiciaries to take a firm stance on who they are writing their judgments for. In truth, judges may be caught in a "terrible irony"[53] in this regard. This is because they must seek to be transparent and accountable to an informed but limited audience. Yet they are sometimes called upon (though perhaps not as often as individual judges might imagine) to write detailed and potentially lengthy judgments that do not speak to the wider community. However, this 'terrible irony' may not be so terrible as first appears. Serious media outlets are perfectly capable of taking a detailed and/or lengthy judgment and reducing it to a form that is comprehensible by the general public, while still accurate. And there is nothing to stop a court from appending a brief 'plain language' addendum to a judgment which explains the substance and outcome of the judgment in simple, non-condescending terms.

In this chapter, I have looked at the issues of the purpose and precedential function of, as well as the potential audiences for, a judgment; and some related consequences for judgment form. In Chapter 3, I move on to consider the critical issue of judgment length.

---

52   Mortimer, 284.
53   Waye, 296.

3. Judgment length

This chapter considers the question of judgment length. It looks at the position that pertained historically. It considers possible reasons for the greater prolixity of judgments in modern times. It identifies the attractions of brevity, clarity and simplicity in judgments. It examines what barriers present to better/briefer judgment writing. And it considers the potential of short-form judgments.

1. Historical background

Writing in the 17th century, Francis Bacon observed that: "An over-speaking judge is no well-tuned cymbal."[1] Four centuries later, some judges appear not yet to have absorbed fully the lesson that Bacon taught, with one learned commentator not entirely facetiously observing: "Life is too short to read modern judgments."[2] In the 19th century, judgments of the English courts were typically short, yet society functioned. Some of the more significant judgments were notably short, "bad decisions seem[ing] to coincide all too often with ... excessive length".[3] So, for example, the judgment of US Chief Justice Marshall in *Marbury v Madison*[4] occupies fewer than 28 pages of text. Closer in time, Lord Atkin's landmark judgment in *Donoghue v Stevenson*,[5] which grounds and rationalises the modern law of negligence, runs to a mere 20 pages or so.

Changes in perception as to the need for public accountability suggest that brief 19th-century style judgments may not sit well with 21st-century audiences. However, modern judges seem as a

---

1 Bacon, "Of Judicature".
2 Jacob.
3 Forrester, 175, 177.
4 5 US 137 (1803).
5 [1932] AC 562 (HL).

whole to be moving to a very different position as regards the desirable length of judgments from that adopted by their 19th-century forbears. Today, dissertation-length judgments rich in detail and quotations abound, for example, in the English law reports. But why have judgments become so long? Why do they depart so often from the "felicitous terseness"[6] that one finds in the judgments of some of the great judges of the past? A number of possible reasons present.

First, certain judicial behaviours have perhaps contributed to the problem:

- There is a tendency for judges to engage in "minute analysis of earlier decisions, with copious citation of earlier judicial formulations".[7]
- There can be a tendency to address unnecessary points and to seek to persuade multiple audiences – all at a time when "[g]iven the explosion of judicial opinions ... we can no longer afford judicial encyclopaedists".[8]
- There has been a change in judgment-writing culture, such that "[e]veryone has almost come to expect long judgments".[9]
- There is a possible lack of time on the part of busy judges to finesse their judgments into shorter texts. As Vice Chancellor Megarry noted in *Cayne v Global Natural Resources plc*: "Brevity takes time."[10] (An alternative presents, succinctly identified by the character of Lincoln in Steven Spielberg's eponymous 'bio-pic' of the great American president: "As the preacher said, I could write shorter sermons but once I start I get too lazy to stop.")
- There may also be ambition involved, with some judges not wanting to acquire a reputation for "'cutting corners' in the[ir] analysis".[11]
- There may be an abiding sense among some judges that "for later generations, the reputation of a judge rests on the quality of his judgment";[12] when the truth is that most judges will quickly be forgotten.

---

6   Manson, 319.
7   Andrews, 29.41.
8   Mikva, 1366.
9   Jacob.
10 [1982] Lexis Citation 569 (Ch D).
11 Andrews, para 29.43.
12 Mason (2008), 39.

Second, attorney/litigant behaviour has likely played a part. In an age when counsel can (and do) place abundant references to case law and academic works before the courts, the "increased length of judgments ... may ... indicate that [judges] ... are [simply] responding to the changing nature of material placed before them".[13]

Third, technology-related behaviour is a factor. Modern technology has yielded a situation in which it has become the work of seconds to replicate swathes of text "hoovered up"[14] from legal databases. This represents a sea change from a past when only the best judgments were published in law reports of limited size and hence only a limited number of judgments were able to shape the law. Today, the challenge confronting judges/lawyers is "how best to use ... increasing accessibility of precedent ... without being swamped".[15] Separately, in an age when written judgments are typically published online by courts and "achieve immortality on the court's webpage", there may be pressure on judges to ensure that every judgment is "a paragon of judgment writing".[16] Fundamentally, the exponential increase in available data has made judiciaries "a micro example of the general phenomen[on] ... of information overload ... which pervade[s] modern life".[17]

Fourth, there is what might be styled 'pace of change' behaviour. Thus, the post-Second World War growth of the administrative state, and, in the European Union, the voluntary establishment by member states of an additional supranational lawmaker have seen a "relentless expansion of the volume of the law".[18] As Lord Macmillan once memorably put matters: "The itch to legislate is an unhappy disease of democracy."[19] As democracies grow older and as mutually advantageous cooperation between most European democracies deepens, there is a lot for judges to analyse and adjudge upon.

Fifth, in a modern liberal democracy, the public (and litigants)

---

13 Groves and Smyth, 264.
14 Munday (2006), 866.
15 Gibson, J, 5–6.
16 McColl, 55.
17 Waye, 297.
18 Groves and Smyth, 264.
19 Macmillan (1927), 48.

would likely consider it unreasonable if judges were simply to "drop new rules like oracles"[20] without providing adequate reasoning.

Sixth, in times of change, the law changes. For example, in the United Kingdom, a gradual lengthening of judgments occurred around the time of the Industrial Revolution as judges sought to accommodate new *modes de vie*.[21] In a similar vein, during the 20th century, English appellate cases concerned with contract law tended to become longer as judges grappled with the need to adapt earlier precedents to meet changed societal conditions. As the world proceeds through the Information Age, similar developments can be expected. As I write this chapter, I am myself confronted with a case which deals with certain consequences of the online issuance of insurance contracts.

2. Brevity, clarity and simplicity

Whereas brevity, clarity and simplicity are much touted as virtues in judgment writing – that is, "giving good reasons, not just more reasons"[22] – they can be missing virtues in contemporary judgments. Lord Bingham, in 2009, had the following remarks to make about each of these virtues:[23]

> [On brevity] *Brevity is ... an underrated virtue in judgments, which have in most common law jurisdictions ... become much longer than they were ... [P]erhaps the main reason why judgments have become ... more prolix is to be found in a judicial desire ... to be seen to be doing a good professional job ... This is ... laudable ... but there comes a point at which assiduity becomes a vice.*
>
> [On clarity] *This is ... a feature of all good writing, but ... a particularly important feature of legal writing since ... a loose or ambiguous expression can be a potent source of mischief. [Cardozo has suggested that "[T]he sovereign virtue for the judge is clearness*[24]*".] ... [T]he challenge is ... to write good, accurate English, perhaps slightly formal ... avoiding ... a style that is stilted, pompous, portentous or archaic and ... one that attempts to be racy or resorts to slang or is populist in tone.*

---

20   Goutal, 63.
21   *Ibid*, 62.
22   Murynka, 642.
23   Bingham, T (2009), 609–610.
24   Cardozo (1939), 121.

[On simplicity] *There are some subject matters which cannot, without distortion or caricature, be made ... simple. But simplicity should ... be a constant aim ... [T]he most distinguished and influential judgments tend to leave the law simpler than it was ...*

There is nothing new in the identification of simplicity as a goal. Lord Reid, writing in the early 1970s, put matters well when he observed of common law judges:

We are here to serve ... the common ordinary reasonable man. He has no great faith in theories ... What he wants ... is an explanation in simple terms which he can understand. Technicalities and jargon are all very well ... but ... if you cannot explain your result in simple English there is probably something wrong with it.[25]

Half a century on, some judges seem to continue to view complexity almost as though it were a professional value. Yet simplification, it is submitted, is a "necessary concession to our limited knowledge" and simpler theories "possess greater methodological, epistemological, and aesthetic ... value".[26]

There is a certain oddity to the fact that as ever more judgments accumulate in each common law jurisdiction,[27] there has (arguably) been a collective failure among judges to recognise that where once-fluid laws have crystallised, greater brevity of judgment writing is possible without any related compromise as to the quality or effectiveness of individual justice systems. The authors of an editorial published in 2014 under the auspices of India's National University of Juridical Sciences observe as follows in this regard:

[T]he Indian Supreme Court has ... given ... judgments that run into millions of pages, since 1950. With so many judgments rendered, judges are realizing that a lot of the law has already been crystallized and [that] many cases can be disposed by succinct, clear and well-structured judgments. Writing brief judgments, without compromising on reasons, will ... speed up the process of justice delivery. Though the focus has been on length of judgments, considerations such as struc-

---

25 Reid, 25.
26 Schuck, 1–2.
27 In Ireland, for example, more than four times as many written judgments issued from the High Court in 2019 – the last proper year of court services before the arrival of the COVID-19 pandemic – than in 2000. Thus, in 2000, 227 written judgments were delivered (Courts Service (2000), 38); in 2019, 947 written judgments were delivered (Courts Service (2019), 82).

turing of judgments, gender neutral language, schedule[s] of cases, footnotes etc. will go a long way in bringing clarity to the law.[28]

The same is doubtless true of many common law jurisdictions. A sometimes-proffered example of the ideal approach to be adopted in this regard is the decision of the House of Lords in *Rylands v Fletcher*,[29] which has been described as a "telling example of [the] ... simple, clear and short".[30] (However, this may not be the best of examples. After all, it is the "famous judgment"[31] of the future Lord Blackburn in the Court of Exchequer Chamber – from which the appeal to the House of Lords was brought – that is the most renowned of the judgments delivered in the case. The embellishments of the House of Lords in *Rylands* are viewed by some as less than superlative.)[32]

3. Barriers to better judgment writing

There are a number of barriers to writing brief, clear, simple (and hence more accessible) judgments. So, for example, some judges are inclined to "write out"[33] – that is, to write extensively as they reason through facts and law. Length is also a consequence of in-judgment quotations from case law and commentary. (The use of a plethora of such quotations is attributable to technology and also perhaps to "a lack of intellectual confidence – or even of ... intellectual indolence".)[34] A further barrier to the key principles is a changed appreciation of the need for public accountability,[35] some judges clearly thinking that this means that they must invariably give an account that is as comprehensive as possible. Thanks also to the "tremendous proliferation of judgments"[36] available for consultation and citation, whereas once a single case might have sufficed to be quoted in support of a proposition, several may now (seem to) need to be cited. This tendency to multiplicity of citations can perhaps best be overcome if judgments are taken as an opportunity to

---

28 Anon (2014), iv.
29 [1868] UKHL 1 (HL).
30 Anon (2014), iv.
31 Murphy, J, 644.
32 See, eg, Newark, 562.
33 Mortimer, 287.
34 Munday (2006), 866.
35 Bingham, T (2009), 609.
36 Mortimer, 288.

(re)state applicable principle in simpler terms, rather than to quote extensively from precedent.

Among trial judges, there is a possible embedded systemic disincentivisation of brevity. Thus, it has been suggested:

[I]f trial judges were permitted to address matters summarily or were not expected to recite every single argument made by parties to demonstrate it had been considered; were not expected to go into great detail about all the evidence before them and instead concentrate on the evidence used to make their findings ... we would see quite a change to the length of trial judgments. In turn, those judgments would be more digestible, and more accessible to ... parties ... the general community [and] ... appellate courts.[37]

The manner in which courts conduct trials can aid in generating judgments of great length. Agreed statements of fact, agreed document bundles and the rigorous imposition of page/word limits can all yield less documentation, focus attention on key issues in dispute and lead ultimately to shorter written judgments.

Finally, there may also be a perceived need among trial judges to close out the potential for appeal on the ground that an argument was not considered. Appellate courts have a role to play in this regard:

If a judge says she ... has considered the arguments made, then in the absence of a factor in the reasons which obviously contradicts that statement, I do not see why an appeal court would not accept the statement at face value.[38]

4. Short-form judgments

At appellate level, there is a case for shorter-form judgments, where there is no issue of law/precedent or other matter of general significance presenting, and where the relevant facts and documentary material are set out in the judgment under appeal and are not in dispute. Perhaps the ideal to be aimed for in this regard is a situation where reasons "can be given ... briefly and ... not ... preceded by a lengthy narrative of the facts ... and ... arguments".[39] However,

---

37   *Ibid*, 289.
38   *Ibid*, 291.
39   Gault, 645.

two problems would perhaps need to be overcome before such an innovation could be widely introduced. The first is the need to preserve the "[i]ndividual judicial voice, so essential to the impression that a judge has given a case serious thought".[40] The second is to identify criteria by which the absence of need for a longer judgment could be gauged. Among the "obvious indicators"[41] pointing to a need for a long/short or no written judgment are "complex expert evidence, an unusual or novel point of law or a multiplicity of issues of fact".[42]

To this point, I have considered various functional dimensions of judgment writing, such as:
- what a judgment is;
- for whom it is written;
- the purposes which it serves (including its precedential function);
- the audiences for a judgment; and
- (in this chapter) the issue of judgment length.

In the next chapter, I depart from this functional consideration of judgments and look at the question of judgment style.

---

40 Murynka, 634.
41 Barrow, 437.
42 *Ibid.*

4. Judgment style

This chapter addresses the importance of style. It looks at stylistic types and considers the use of literary allusion, academic references, footnotes, metaphors, aphorisms and epigrams. It also looks at common pitfalls in judgment writing.

1. **Aspects of style**

    Style matters. It is "not an evil in the Sahara of a judicial opinion".[1] It separates the wheat from the chaff, making the difference between a judgment that is forgettable and one that is memorable. "It is almost a truism to acknowledge the importance of style in judicial reasoning."[2] This is because, as touched upon in Chapter 1, judgments seek to persuade and persuasiveness is linked in part to style.[3] When it comes to style, Lord Macmillan, in his characteristically eloquent prose, has observed that a judgment as an intellectual creation stands in a class of its own:

    The judge speaks with authority and what he says should therefore be spoken with befitting dignity. He should not affect grandiloquence but he should be impressive. The strength of a judgment lies in its reasoning and it should therefore be convincing. Clarity of exposition is always essential. Dignity, convincingness and clarity are exacting requirements but they are subservient to ... the main object of a judgment ... to do justice.[4]

    Style is not a mere matter of dressing or ornamentation. In truth, style and substance are inseparable. As former US Supreme Court Justice Benjamin Cardozo has observed: "Form is not ... added to

---

1 Cardozo (1939), 121.
2 Bianchi, 30.
3 Macdonald, 144; Bianchi, 30.
4 Macmillan (1948), 491.

substance as a ... protuberant adornment. The two are fused into a unity."[5] This does not mean that a judge has to descend to purple prose, writing "judgments beginning with élan and proceeding with breathless zest, holding the reader entranced to the ... satisfying and dramatic dénouement".[6] It means merely that style is an essential component of any successful judgment, "if for no other reason than we cannot think or act without it".[7] In "Judges' Writing Styles (And Do They Matter?)", Richard Posner, an American judge, defines 'style' in the following terms:

> We can think of it most broadly as the specific written form in which a writer encodes an idea, a 'message,' that he wants to put across. His tools of communication are, of course, linguistic. But they include not only vocabulary and grammar but also the often tacit principles governing the length and complexity of sentences, the organization of sentences into larger units such as paragraphs, and the level of formality at which to pitch the writing. These tools are used not just to communicate an idea but also to establish a mood and perhaps a sense of the writer's personality.[8]

Posner then moves on to consider a number of aspects of style – namely:

- style as what is left out by paraphrase ("Some judicial opinions ... lose something ... maybe a lot, in being paraphrased");[9]
- style as "good writing";[10]
- discretionary style ("undetermined by content, by meaning");[11]
- literary style ("detachable from the specific setting");[12] and
- style as signature/voice[13] (Lord Denning's short, staccato style is perhaps the classic example of style of this form).

Drawing on Penn Warren's concepts of pure and impure poetry,

---

5 Cardozo (1931), 5.
6 Kitto (2003), 69.
7 Horwitz, 113.
8 Posner (1995), 1422.
9 Ibid.
10 Ibid, 1423.
11 Ibid, 1424.
12 Ibid.
13 Ibid, 1425.

Posner writes of judgments as being 'pure' or 'impure' in form. Judgments pure in form have a lofty tone and speak with certitude.[14] They "tend to be long ... solemn ... polished and artifactual".[15] Impure judgments "tend to be more direct, forthright, colloquial, informal, frank, even racy, even demotic", and mercifully brief.[16]

2. Stylistic types

Lord Macmillan once observed that "[t]he style of any composition is necessarily dominated by its purpose".[17] The process of adjudication is informed by a seriousness of purpose and a desire for clarity. So it is perhaps surprising that despite this constancy of purpose, judgments present in a variety of styles. Between them, Wigmore and Heydon identify 10 styles of judicial reasoning:

- the brisk and muscular style, which distils facts and law to the most basic discussion possible;
- the business-like style, which is business-like in thrust but less pared down than the muscular type;
- the cautious approach, which seeks to resolve a case on fine points;
- the circular style, which dances around the point almost until the end;
- the factual style, which focuses on the facts and contains no useful statement of law;
- the loaded style, which involves a judge identifying facts and applying law without any mention of case law until the end;
- the non-routine style – the only point of commonality between this and other styles is that it is non-routine;
- the rambling style, which drifts on without offering much real guidance;
- the 'reasoning by reference' style, which involves lots of citations and not a lot of discussion; and
- the 'slow boiler' style, which involves the slow development of complex, inter-related themes.

---

14   *Ibid*, 1426.
15   *Ibid*, 1429.
16   *Ibid*, 1426.
17   Macmillan (1948), 491.

If nothing else, this list of reasoning styles points to the rich breadth of styles open to a common law judge to deploy when writing a judgment. It also suggests that any reluctance to evolve current standard judgment form into something shorter is fundamentally misfounded, as there is no ideal style (and hence current judgment form cannot be seen as somehow ideal). One thing, however, seems clear. Given the super-abundance of available precedent in the Information Age, there needs to be a return to brisk/business-like forms of adjudication if judge-centred, precedent-focused common law systems are not to lose their "capacity for growth and ... ability to slough off outmoded precedents".[18]

One early commentator on judgment-writing styles merits special mention. In a mid-1920s article, the then future US Supreme Court Justice Benjamin Cardozo identifies six overlapping styles of judgment:
- the magisterial/imperative style;
- the laconic/sententious style;
- the conversational/homely style;
- the refined/artificial style;
- the demonstrative/persuasive style; and
- the tonsorial/agglutinative ('cut and paste') style.

Each style type merits some consideration.

In a judgment that adopts the magisterial/imperative style, Cardozo writes, "We hear the voice of the law speaking by its consecrated ministers."[19] This style is typically (though not unfailingly) associated with an age when judges – ordinary people vested with extraordinary power – misconstrued their fortune in life as somehow divinely ordained. In a secular and un-deferential age, such pretension, it is submitted, is no substitute for persuasive judgments. As examples of the magisterial style, Cardozo offers Chief Justice Marshall's judgment in *Marbury v Madison*[20] and Lord Mansfield's judgment in *Somerset*.[21]

Marbury is a seminal decision of the US Supreme Court, albeit now

---

18 Schaefer, 6.
19 Cardozo (1931), 10.
20 5 US 137 (1803) (SC).
21 *Somerset v Stewart* (1772) 98 ER 499 (KB).

recognised "by many serious students of ... constitutional law [as having] rested on debatable constitutional grounds".[22] It arose from US President John Adams' decision, in the last weeks of his one-term presidency, to fill various government positions, "including some for friends and needy relatives".[23] Somewhat unfairly, these many court appointments became known as 'midnight appointments' – a term which suggests that they were made in a frenzied last-minute rush, when in truth they were more considered.[24] Mr Marbury was one of a number of people appointed by Adams to be a federal justice of the peace (a type of lay magistrate). Two decades after *Marbury v Madison* was decided, Thomas Jefferson – the man who succeeded Adams as president – recounted the details of the case in a private letter which suggested that as yet he did not accept the validity of the Supreme Court's decision in the case. Thus, Jefferson observed that the "practice of Judge Marshall, of travelling out of his case to prescribe what the law would be in a case not before the court, is ... very censurable".[25] He then proceeded to the following account of *Marbury*:

> *[A]mong the midnight appointments of Mr Adams were commissions to some federal justices of the peace for Alexandria. These were signed and sealed by him, but not delivered. I found them on the table of the department of State, on my entry into office, and I forbade their delivery. Marbury, named in one of them, applied to the Supreme Court for [an order compelling] ... the Secretary of State (Mr Madison) to deliver the commission intended for him.*[26]

In his ensuing judgment for the Supreme Court, Marshall held that Marbury had a right to have the physical document that was the commission delivered to him. However, he also held that the statutory provision which would have allowed the court to order delivery of the commission was itself unconstitutional. So the order sought by Marbury could not be made.

---

22 Nielson, 389.
23 McCullough, 563.
24 *Ibid*.
25 Letter of 12 June 1823 to William Johnson (a US Supreme Court justice). Johnson was the Supreme Court's original 'great dissenter' before that mantle was assumed in the 20th century by Justice Holmes (whose judgments are considered in more detail in Chapter 10), though Johnson's style lacks the "metaphoric finality" of Holmes' (Levin, 529). To borrow from Cardozo's terminology, Johnson's prose is laconic (ie, eloquently succinct) rather than magisterial. But whatever his talents as a lawyer, Johnson's standing as a slave-owning anti-abolitionist makes him a notably unattractive (frankly immoral) character.
26 *Ibid*.

Marshall's judgment in *Marbury*, albeit perhaps of questionable correctness from a constitutional perspective, has long been seen as possessed of real genius. It sidestepped the showdown that would have ensued between the executive and the judiciary if the Supreme Court had ordered delivery of the commission (because the Supreme Court had no means of compelling performance of its order). But it also established judicial review – the notion that the courts could examine the constitutionality of the actions of the other branches of government – as a foundational concept of American law. Marshall's magisterial style is evident throughout his judgment – for example, where he describes the exclusive role of the courts as arbiters of law:

> *It is emphatically the province and duty of the judicial department to say what the law is. Those who apply the rule to particular cases, must of necessity expound and interpret that rule. If two laws conflict with each other, the courts must decide on the operation of each. So if a law be in opposition to the constitution; if both the law and the constitution apply to a particular case, so that the court must either decide that case conformably to the law, disregarding the constitution; or conformably to the constitution, disregarding the law; the court must determine which of these conflicting rules governs the case. This is of the very essence of judicial duty.*[27]

As for *Somerset*, it was among the most prominent court cases of its day. Its facts make for harrowing reading. James Somerset was a young African slave bought in the United States by Charles Stewart, a Scotsman. (Stewart appears to have been working in North America as a customs officer.) On his return to England in 1769, Stewart brought Somerset with him. In England, Somerset came into contact with freed slaves and abolitionists. At some point, he was baptised and acquired some abolitionist godparents. In 1771, Somerset ran away from Stewart. Unfortunately for him, he was eventually recaptured and stowed in a ship on the Thames pending an intended forced return westwards across the Atlantic, likely to end his days on a cotton or sugar plantation. Then some Londoners, who appear to have been Somerset's godparents, stepped into the fray and made a *habeas corpus* application. This required that

---

27   5 US 137, 177–78 (1803) (SC).

4. Judgment style

Somerset be produced in Lord Mansfield's court so that the legality of Somerset's detention might be tested.

Somerset was perhaps fortunate that his case ended up before Mansfield, who was foster-father to Dido Elizabeth Belle, a woman of colour who had been born in the British West Indies to one of Mansfield's nephews and a woman by the name of Maria Belle (a possible sometime slave).[28] This foster arrangement may have given Mansfield a particular insight into the plight of slaves that many of his colleagues on the bench did not possess. In any event, following one of the great show trials of the day, Mansfield held that Somerset was not lawfully detained and required that he be set free. He also, in effect, held slavery to be illegal in England and Wales, his judgment culminating with the following paragraph:

The state of slavery is of such a nature, that it is incapable of being introduced on any reasons, moral or political; but only positive law, which preserves its force long after the reasons, occasion, and time itself from whence it was created, is erased from memory: it's so odious, that nothing can be suffered to support it, but positive law. Whatever inconveniences, therefore, may follow from a decision, I cannot say this case is allowed or approved by the law of England; and therefore the black must be discharged.[29]

One physically cringes at the diminishing, racist reference to Somerset as 'the black', as though Somerset was an object defined by his being a person of colour. Were a judge to express herself so today, she would rightly face calls for her resignation. A further problem with the just-quoted text is that it offers a 'get-out' clause for those who supported slavery through its assertion that slavery could validly be established by way of positive law, such as statute. Thus, "[w]here positive law sanctioned slavery [as in Britain's North American colonies], Mansfield explicitly conceded the supremacy of such positive law".[30]

Why did Mansfield proceed as he did? One view is that, having failed to get the parties to settle matters between themselves (and so obviate the need for judgment), Mansfield undertook what he

---

28 Jeffries.
29 (1772) 98 ER 499, 510 (KB).
30 Cover, 17.

53

perceived to be "an exercise in damage limitation",[31] issuing a judgment that would be as inoffensive as possible to pro-slavers. In consequence, the decision did not end slavery in the British Empire. Nor did it end the slave trade in England. All it achieved (though this was an achievement) was to prevent slaves who came to England from being repatriated into slavery. Thus, the judgment took a small step towards righting the evil of slavery, albeit that a bigger step might have been taken. As one learned commentator has observed: "To suggest that Somerset foreshadowed the end of slavery is ... too simplistic ... Mansfield's decision in *Somerset* was carefully phrased to ensure ... it did not introduce a major change in the status of slaves."[32]

Cardozo writes of Mansfield that he shows "sure and calm conviction"[33] in his judgments; that he writes as a man conscious of his power[34] and as someone who perceives himself to be the very "mouthpiece of divinity".[35] But there is surely a danger in a judge casting herself in sacral guise, writing as the mouthpiece of God (if there is a God), and showing the sure and calm conviction of one who considers herself assuredly correct. Majestic prose is no substitute for moral substance. In preparing to countenance that slavery was acceptable if sanctioned by positive law, Mansfield surely descended from the magisterial to the morally offensive.

The next two forms of judgment identified by Cardozo are laconic/sententious judgments and conversational/homely judgments. Cardozo treats these two judgment types together, observing: "There has been no stage of our legal history in which these methods have been neglected."[36] When it comes to the laconic/sententious style, Justice Holmes of the US Supreme Court (whose judgments are considered at some length in Chapter 10) has been described by Cardozo as one "who can vie with the best".[37] As to the conversational/homely style, it brings "the author down nearer to the human level of the litigants",[38] yielding a more human

---

31 Paley, 662.
32 *Ibid*, 663–64.
33 Cardozo (1931), 13.
34 *Ibid*, 14.
35 *Ibid*.
36 *Ibid*, 17.
37 *Ibid*, 21.
38 Wald (1995), 1418.

judicial process. Lord Denning (whose judgments are considered in more detail in Chapter 11) is an iconic example of a judge who wrote in the conversational/homely style. The difficulty with this style is that it risks seeming less authoritative – not when deployed by a judge as accomplished as Denning, but certainly when it comes to lesser judges. My own sense of how to combine the need for authority with the attractiveness of the conversational is to append to the end of a traditional-form judgment a brief plain-language note to the parties as to what the substantive judgment states. This enables the writing of a judgment that is technically satisfactory, while also facilitating the production of an associated text that is accessible to litigants and later readers in a meaningful way.

Turning to the remaining categories of judgment identified by Cardozo, when it comes to refined/artificial judgments, he refers to this type of judgment as "smelling a little of the lamp"[39] – by which he seems to mean that it has been worked and reworked so that "it verges ... upon preciosity and euphuism".[40] The opinions of Cardozo himself are perhaps the best example of this type of writing. Thus it has been observed, for example, that "There is often a feeling of strain when one reads Cardozo";[41] that "Cardozo's prose is all too patently worked over";[42] and even that "Cardozo attained eminence ... not because but in spite of his style".[43] A good example of Cardozo's writing in this regard is his judgment in *Reed v Allen*,[44] where he writes of the need for the law of restitution to bend towards practical justice:

A system of procedure is perverted from its proper function when it multiplies impediments to justice without the warrant of clear necessity. By the judgment about to be rendered, the respondent, caught in a mesh of procedural complexities, is told that there was only one way out of them, and this a way he failed to follow. Because of that omission he is to be left ensnared in the web, the processes of the law, so it is said, being impotent to set him free. I think the paths to justice are not so few and narrow.[45]

---

39 Cardozo (1931), 23.
40 *Ibid*.
41 Mous, 636.
42 *Ibid*, 637.
43 *Ibid*.
44 286 US 191 (1931) (SC).
45 *Ibid*, 209–10.

It is not just Cardozo's judgments in which an inclination to excessive refinement (preciosity) and elaborate writing (euphuism) present. In his book, *The Growth of the Law*, one finds a like inclination/sentiment to those featuring in the last-quoted text – for example, where Cardozo observes:

> Judges march at times to pitiless conclusions under the prod of a remorseless logic which is supposed to leave them no alternative. They deplore the sacrificial rite. They perform it none the less, with averted gaze, convinced as they plunge the knife that they obey the bidding of their office. The victim is offered up to the gods of jurisprudence on the altar of regularity.[46]

Though the refined/artificial approach has its charms, Cardozo (ironically perhaps) found it left him occasionally "yearning for ... more robust and virile [language]".[47]

As to demonstrative/persuasive judgments, Cardozo means in this regard to refer to a style that is not far removed from the magisterial/imperative style. It differs in being "suggestive of the scientific seeker for the truth and less reminiscent of the priestess on the tripod".[48] The need for judgments to be persuasive has already been considered; so one can skip over what Cardozo describes as the demonstrative/persuasive style of judgment to the tonsorial/agglutinative style. What Cardozo anticipated in this regard was the modern problem of cutting and pasting passages from precedent into judgments. Writing of this judgment form, Cardozo observes: "I will not expatiate upon its horrors ... The dreary succession of quotations closes with a brief paragraph expressing a firm conviction that judgment for plaintiff or for defendant ... follows as an inevitable conclusion."[49]

Almost a century later, this has become a commonly encountered form of judgment, facilitated by modern technology but still possessed of the deficiencies that Cardozo identifies.

In recent years, Australia and India have been to the fore among common law countries in seeking to improve judgment writing in their respective jurisdictions. In Australia, there has been a deliberate reassessment of how judgment writing is approached. One

---

46   Cardozo (1963), 66.
47   Cardozo (1931), 25.
48   *Ibid*, 25–26.
49   *Ibid*, 31–32.

commentator, writing in 2007, observed: "Until ... recently, decisions of courts ... in Australia were written quite differently to the way they are now coming to be written."[50] India has moved to a point where, for example, there has even been a proposal that aspirant judges might be tested on their précis writing skills (this already happens in some Indian states), their capacity for judgment writing using computer technology and their judgment writing as a skill.[51] One recent article published in the journal of India's National University of Juridical Sciences points to a number of useful stylistic innovations in which Australian judges have engaged:

> *[J]udgments use 'opening words' that provide a sentence or two on the issue at hand ... Use of sub-headings is another significant tool that helps structure the judgment ... Another significant change ... is the gradual abandonment of Latin terms and phrases ... More remarkable developments ... include ... gender-neutral language, inclusion of footnotes and provision of a schedule of cases.*[52]

3. Issues of style

There are a number of stylistic issues to which any judge determined to improve her writing style might have regard. These are considered below.

First, general issues of style. These include the following:

- One cannot communicate ideas in writing except by writing well. A judge has failed if her words do not convey her thoughts to her readers. Reasoning should be vivid and concrete. A strong and honest opinion is preferable to one that appeals only to the legal profession.
- The central purpose of a judicial opinion is to explain – candidly and precisely – the reasons for a decision.
- Judges should try to write reasoning in a way that makes it accessible to intelligent lay persons. That aids in "keeping the law in tune with human and social needs ... and avoiding the legal professional's natural tendency to ... obscurity and preciosity".[53]

---

50 Downes, 3.
51 See Kaushik and Singh.
52 Anon (2014), iv.
53 Friedman *et al* (1993), 47.

- 'Interesting' is not the same as 'entertaining'. "Flamboyant rhetoric and evangelical fervour have no place."[54]
- Language should not be rhetorical or reflect contrived effort by a judge.
- Greater concision is desirable. Superfluous facts/words/phrases should be avoided. "A narrative of facts, some relevant and some not, is likely to distract and confuse."[55]
- When a draft judgment seems done, it should be laid aside, then returned to with a view to editing/improvement. "All writing requires editing. All editing takes time."[56]
- It is preferable to use gender-neutral terms and not to use language that excludes/offends.
- A judge should avoid seeking in every judgment to lay down the law for all future generations; not all judgments (not even all judgments of an apex court) possess the same significance.
- A judge should always have a style guide to hand. A good work in this regard is Williams and Bizup's *Style: Lessons in Clarity and Grace*, a volume renowned in the United States and deserving of a wider international audience.
- A judgment must decide a case as the judge determines best but ought not to read like a partisan brief or deride the loser or her arguments.

Second, the relationship between audience and style. In this regard, the following points might be made:
- A judge should think about her audience and pitch her reasoning appropriately. "The tragedy of much modern official legal writing ... is its [refusal] ... to expand the community of readers."[57]
- A judge should help readers understand:
  - what the issue presenting is;
  - why it is important;
  - what the law says;
  - what sources/constraints apply;

---

54 Richardson (1981), 10.
55 Dessau and Wodak, 120.
56 McLachlin (2001), 701.
57 Macdonald, 142.

4. Judgment style

- what the judge makes of the arguments;
- why she has favoured one side; and
- that she has been fair.
* It is a good idea to read text aloud to an imaginary audience so as to ensure that, as written, it has a pleasing rhythm.
* Editing should be done from the vantage of the reader.

Third, the relationship between style and judgment openings. Again, a number of points might be made:
* Beginnings should be "concise and uncluttered by unnecessary detail".[58]
* The scene should be set simply and clearly "as a prelude to any further or complex description or analysis".[59]
* The issues for determination should be succinctly identified and the judgment should disclose "where it is heading and any relevant background".[60]
* It is useful to state the key question in the first sentence.
* A well-written first paragraph gives a reader "enough preliminary information to enable him to read ... with understanding" and "simplifies ... drafting ... the rest of the [judgment]".[61]
* The first page of a judgment is "prime real estate"[62] of inestimable value in terms of scene setting and reader engagement.
* A point of outstanding importance should usually be discussed first, though alternative sequencing can be appropriate.

Fourth, the style of reasoning. In this regard, the following points might be made:
* Shorter, clearer reasoning is desirable.
* There is no such thing as 'too simple'. Judges should use the fewest words to convey meaning and the simplest words to convey each thought/concept. (This is not the same as 'dumbing down'.)

---

58 Dessau and Wodak, 119.
59 *Ibid*.
60 *Ibid*.
61 Smith, G (1973), 1207.
62 *Ibid*.

- The basic analysis should be expressed in no more than three propositions.
- It can be useful to proceed as if having a conversation.
- Brevity in judgments is not best achieved by discarding text but by not committing it to writing to begin with. "[O]nce the written word gets itself on paper, it is as tenacious of life as a cat with its nine lives."[63]
- Extensive discussion of facts may lend colour but is often unnecessary. The reader need only be told what she needs to know to understand the legal ruling.
- Each step in an exposition should be like a pyramid, with the point at the beginning and the support underneath.
- Excessively formal text, legalisms, abstract text and fashionable words should be avoided.

Fifth, style is of relevance even when it comes to a court's treatment of the law. In this regard the following points might be made:
- It is essential to identify/detail the legal principles applied. "The best judgments ... clearly state the legal principle on which they are based."[64]
- Expressions of law should be lean, follow from existing precedent and be comprehensible to an intelligent non-lawyer.
- Superfluous, decorative, quasi-scholarly discussions of the law should be avoided.
- The practical/equitable rules for a particular rule of law should be considered. Not infrequently, this will give a judgment "that touch of wisdom that demonstrates ... the rightness and justice of the decision".[65]
- If applicable law has been thoroughly discussed, its origins/interpretation need not be elaborated upon. If a rule is less well developed or requires elaboration, then precedent, the new direction of the law and the effect of the decision should be considered.

---

63   *Ibid*, 1205.
64   Macmillan (1948), 498.
65   Smith, G (1973), 1207.

- A well-reasoned decision needs to demonstrate that it is reasonable/logical.
- One learned commentator (Benson) has listed numerous unhelpful legal writing forms that should not be over-relied upon – for example:
  - long words;
  - rare words;
  - Latin phrases;
  - common words with uncommon meanings;
  - Norman-French terms;
  - terms of art;
  - professional argot;
  - formalistic formulas;
  - vague expressions;
  - doublets;
  - unusual prepositional phrases;
  - use of 'said' and 'such' as articles;
  - long, complex sentences with embedded clauses;
  - the passive form;
  - negatives;
  - misplaced phrases;
  - illogical ordering;
  - absent pronouns;
  - too many ideas in each sentence;
  - extreme precision (which can often yield confusion);
  - impersonality;
  - declarative sentences;
  - conditional sentences;
  - pomposity/dullness;
  - poetic devices; and
  - odd presentation (eg, solid prose blocks with little punctuation).

Sixth, style and the writing of a conclusion. A conclusion should resolve the issues identified at the start. There is no reason why the conclusion and/or a summary of same cannot also appear at the start of the judgment. Indeed, it can be helpful in terms of rendering what follows more comprehensible to begin with the end

– albeit that the ending may need to be restated, even if only by reference, at the end.

Seventh, the inter-relationship between style and grammar. A detailed consideration of the rules of grammar is beyond the scope of this book. Even so, a few general points can usefully be made about the need for good grammar and certain related matters:

- Judicial reasoning should feature good grammar and sentence structure.
- Latin terms should, so far as possible, be avoided. Nowadays, few people have the benefit of a classical education and use of Latin tends therefore to make a judgment less clear, even if the Latin is a legal term of art such as *'inter alia'* or *'mutatis mutandis'*. (My own practice as regards these particular phrases is to state instead, 'among other matters' and 'subject to any necessary changes'.)
- Each page should be broken into a small number of paragraphs, with one-sentence paragraphs best avoided.
- A judge is not writing a novel; there is no need for 'elegant variation' (ie, the same phrase/word can be repeated).
- Defined terms generally make it easier to read a judgment, provided that they are not overused.
- Care should be taken to know the meaning of words and to use the most fitting words.
- Citations/quotations/*dicta* should be kept to a minimum; they can encourage a descent into confusing prolixity. (Footnotes are considered in more detail later below.)
- Humour, puns and witticisms, it is submitted, are generally inappropriate. Litigants do not like to be laughed at. The law is not sport. Judgments are not a vehicle for showing how clever a judge is. "[W]riting opinions is a 'damnable serious business'."[66] And there is always a risk that humour may misfire. One of the 19th-century law lords, Lord Blackburn, once tried a personal injury case in which the plaintiff's counsel dwelt at length on how the loss of an eye had blighted his

---

66   Wald, 1995, 1416.
67   Manson, 261.
68   Adalberto, 726.
69   Cardozo (1939), 131.

4. Judgment style

client's career. "I have lost the sight of an eye, Mr X," Blackburn observed lightly, "and it has not blighted my career." The jury was apparently impressed by this remark and awarded trifling damages. Though it was not a judgment that caused the jury to act so, the story points to the perils of judicial levity at any point in proceedings.[67] All that said, judicial humour is not without its aficionados. So, for example, it has been observed that: "Judicial ... humor need not be dreadful. When used appropriately, figurative language can add levity, help make a point, or simply make an opinion fun to read."[68] However, the position adopted by Cardozo seems, with respect, more convincing:

> *Flashes of humor are not unknown, yet the form of opinion which aims at humor from beginning to end is a perilous adventure, which can be justified only by success, and even then is likely to find its critics almost as many as its eulogists. The story is told by Bernard Shaw of a man who wished to consult the writings of the great naturalist Buffon, and who startled the clerks in the bookstore by the pompous and solemn query, 'Have you the books of the celebrated Buffoon?' One of the difficulties about the humorous opinion is exposure to the risk of passing from the class of Buffons where we all like to dwell and entering the class of the celebrated Buffoons. The transition at times is distressingly swift, and when once one has entered the new class, it is difficult, if not indeed impossible, to climb over the fences and back into the old.*[69]

- It is submitted that sarcasm ought also to be avoided. One cannot but recall in this regard the judgment of Lord Justice Knight Bruce in *Thomas v Roberts*,[70] a judgment written "in a fine vein of sustained sarcasm".[71] In that case, Mr Thomas, a religious sect member who had no property of his own, married another sect member, who had a fortune of about £5,000, under circumstances which suggested that the marriage was brought about by the sect leader. Subsequently, Thomas deserted this wife to head off with the sect leader and the other sect members, while his wife returned to her family

---

70   *Thomas v Roberts* (1850) 64 ER 693 (VC Ct).
71   Manson, 33.

Part I: The theory of the art and craft of judgment writing

home, where she gave birth to a baby boy. The boy was cared for by his mother and maternal grandmother, and it was held that this was a proper case for restraining the father from taking custody of the boy. In his judgment, Lord Justice Knight Bruce observes, for example, that "It must not be inferred ... that Mr Thomas left his wife and child to starve ... [H]e has from time to time transmitted or permitted to be paid to her the income or part of the income of the property that he acquired in her right"[72] – that is, Thomas kindly allowed his deserted wife the use of money that morally was her own even though it fell to Thomas by law. There is no doubt that Thomas was no gentleman and no suggestion that the case should have been decided otherwise than it was. Yet a strange feature of Lord Justice Knight Bruce's sustained sarcasm is that it seems to diminish both him and the literary quality of his judgment.[73]

3.1 Allusion

A particular stylistic device not uncommonly encountered in common law judgments is that of literary allusion. Lord Macmillan considers that: "[A]n occasional happy literary quotation [is] ... both legitimate and desirable."[74] Certainly, literary allusion can serve a number of useful ends. It can enliven a judgment, commanding the attention of a reader. It can adorn a judgment, rendering it beautiful. Drawing on the literary canon to explain or illustrate a point can "drive home the universal validity of a particular point".[75] It "helps to ensure that the law in its written form remains in touch with literary sources outside the narrowly confined and inbred world of legal precedent and terminology".[76] And it may be appropriate in set-piece legal cases where judges wish to mark the momentous nature of proceedings.[77]

---

72 *Supra*, at 697.
73 Lord Justice Knight Bruce also succumbs to offensive anti-Roma sentiment, observing of the possibility that he would allow the boy to live with his father and other sect members: "God forbid ... I should be accessory to condemning any child to such a state of probable debasement; as lief would I have on my conscience the consigning of this boy to a camp of gypsies" (*supra* at 773). This is an observation for which a judge would doubtless (and rightly) be called upon to resign were she to make such a comment today.
74 Macmillan (1948), 493.
75 Corbett, 127.
76 Elms (2008), 57.
77 *Ibid*.

4. Judgment style

In the last decade, to take one jurisdiction, there have been various allusions by the courts of England and Wales to the works or words of such literary stalwarts as Burns, Byron, Johnson, Milton, Pope, Shakespeare and Tennyson. (For some reason, the works and words of female authors appear not to have been relied upon.) In *Re C (Interim Care Order)*,[78] some of Robert Burns' words – "O, wad some Power the giftie gie us/To see oursels as ithers see us!" – were used by Lord Justice Ward regarding a mother who showed an inability to see her actions as her daughter saw them.[79] In *SS v NS (Spousal Maintenance)*,[80] Mr Justice Mostyn, when asked to assess a husband's future income, managed to refer to Lord Byron, Niels Bohr and Mark Twain in a single paragraph.[81] In *R (Forge Care Homes Ltd) v Cardiff and Vale University Health Board*,[82] Lord Justice Laws, when describing an arrangement whereby suitably qualified nurses had to be present in a care home even when the nursing skills which only the registered nurse could provide were not being called upon, quoted Milton's renowned line: "[T]hey also serve who only stand and wait."[83] In *H v H*,[84] where an abusive husband threatened to (but did not) make an application for custody, Mr Justice Mostyn echoed Pope at his most eloquent when describing the husband as "willing to wound and yet afraid to strike".[85] In *Lau v Chu*,[86] Lord Briggs observed that: "The contest between law and equity ... has been fought over many years and is graphically illustrated by the contest between Shylock and Portia in Shakespeare's *The Merchant of Venice.*"[87] And in *Distinctive Properties (Ascot) Ltd and Secretary of State for Communities and Local Government*,[88] Mr Justice Keene commenced his judgment with the words: "'The woods decay, the woods decay and fall', wrote Lord Tennyson, but this appeal is

---

78 [2011] EWCA Civ. 918.
79 See para 18.
80 [2014] EWHC 4183 (Fam.).
81 See para 55.
82 [2016] EWCA Civ. 26.
83 See para 55. Milton has latterly enjoyed something of a burst of popularity worldwide, being referred to, for example, in the Supreme Court of India judgment of Chief Justice of India Dipak Misra in *Shine v Union of India* (2018) 46 BHRC 637, para 32 (admittedly in a cross-reference to a previous judgment); and in the judgment of Judge Pinto de Albuquerque of the ECtHR in *Hutchinson v United Kingdom* [2017] ECHR 57592/08, para 39.
84 [2020] EWHC 9 (HC).
85 *Ibid*.
86 [2020] UKPC 24 (PC).
87 *Ibid*, para 92.

concerned with the consequences of human intervention in the life of woodlands."

What is interesting even from this limited selection of literary allusions is that they seem often to serve a real purpose. So, for example, Lord Justice Ward's observation concerning the mother seems less wounding when couched in Burns' words. In *H v H*, Mr Justice Mostyn paints a brilliant pen picture of the husband through his use of Pope's words, in a way that he might not otherwise have achieved. In *Lau*, Briggs – though he refers to *The Merchant of Venice* – does not draw on Shakespeare's language, but rather makes the point that: "The contest between law and equity has been going on for so long it even features as a plot in a Shakespearean play." What judges (at least English judges) seem *not* to do is to make meaningless references to literature. Rather they deploy a literary reference to meet a specific end. One commentator has drawn a distinction in this regard between allusions that enhance "the texture of judicial prose and [sustain] ... a learned and authoritative judicial tone" and "allusions [that] do not ... add ... useful information ... or ... rhetorical weight".[89] He also suggests that literary sources tend to be used for one of five reasons:

- for lexicographical purposes;
- as an apt phrase;
- as a repository of wisdom;
- as a means of reinforcing simple truths; and
- as a means of strengthening/attenuating a sense of connection with the past.

Ultimately, use of literary allusion is perhaps attributable to the fact that judges are well-educated people. Well-educated people often use literary allusions, even in ordinary conversation. So it is hardly surprising that such allusions should creep into their work product. Even so, deployment of literary allusion within a judgment can be controversial. For example, in *Standard Fire Insurance Co v Reese*,[90] a decision of the Supreme Court of Texas, Judge Steakley was moved to remark in his dissenting judgment that while the

---

88 [2015] EWHC 729.
89 Meehan, 431.
90 (1979) 584 SW 2d 835 (Texas SC).

majority had sought to rely on a variety of quotations from the great authors, "our own writings are more in point".[91] (His criticism of the majority may not have been entirely merited. The majority sought to make the point that while it had been sought to criticise some hyperbole in the oral argument of counsel for an insurer, "[s]uch [hyperbolic] arguments are a part of our legal heritage and language".[92] The majority then proceeded to give various examples of such arguments from non-legal literature.)

As to the use of poetic quotes, it has been suggested that there are three reasons for their deployment in written judgments:
- to make comment;
- as a diversion from legal analysis; and
- as an introduction.[93]

There is also a fourth reason, which is to clarify some aspect of the case before a court. Perhaps the best-known example of this last-mentioned reason occurs in *Plaut v Spendthrift Farm Incorporated*,[94] a decision of the US Supreme Court. There, a particular statutory provision was held by each tier of the US federal courts to involve an unconstitutional contravention of the separation of powers. In his judgment for the majority, Justice Scalia observed:

Separation of powers, a distinctively American political doctrine [sic – Montesquieu was French and a form of tripartite government is a hallmark of all modern constitutional democracies], profits from the advice authored by a distinctively American poet [Robert Frost in "Mending Wall"]: Good fences make good neighbors.[95]

Justice Breyer, though he concurred with the majority, brought his own perspective to bear, observing:

As the majority invokes the advice of an American poet, one might consider as well that poet's caution, for he not only notes that 'Something there is that doesn't love a wall,' but also writes, 'Before I built a wall I'd ask to know/What I was walling in or walling out'.[96]

Neither Scalia nor Breyer was interested so much in Frost's

---

91   *Ibid*, 842.
92   *Ibid*, 838.
93   Petersson, 105.
94   514 US 211 (1995).
95   *Ibid*, 240.
96   *Ibid*, 245.

"Mending Wall" as they were in using Frost's imagery and language to buttress a point that fell to be made in any event. Even so, their reliance on Frost's poetry is of note, being "a rare acknowledgement of the formative power of cultural context upon the law".[97]

Perhaps the most unusual deployment of poetry in a common law judgment came in *Fisher v Lowe*,[98] a decision of the Michigan Court of Appeals, in which the court elected to give its decision by way of a poem authored by the court. The appeal arose from an action in tort concerning damage done to an oak tree by an automobile. Affirming the lower court, the appeals court held:

We thought that we would never see
A suit to compensate a tree
A suit whose claim in tort is prest
Upon a mangled tree's behest;
A tree whose battered trunk was prest
Against a Chevy's crumpled crest;
A tree that faces each new day
With bark and limb in disarray;
A tree that may forever bear
A lasting need for tender care.
Flora lovers though we three,
We must uphold the court's decree.

One has to wonder whether the plaintiff/appellant was amused by the court's sudden venture into writing poetry. One suspects that he was not.

Returning to literary allusion (as opposed to 'literary' creation), the use of such allusion has not always met with universal approval. Thus, a number of potential downsides to this practice have been suggested. First, numerous citation studies indicate that such allusions "are generally slight and inconsequential".[99] Second, there is a concern among some commentators as to whether literary allusions are "too frivolous [for] ... the serious task of judgment".[100] Third, if literary allusion is used too often, it can descend into

---

97 Dolin, 204.
98 333 NW 2d 67 (Mich Ct App 1983) (Michigan CA).
99 Keith, 108.
100 *Ibid.*
101 Elms (2008), 58.

cliché.[101] Fourth, it is important to have regard to one's audience if allusion is not to pass unappreciated.[102] Fifth, if one wishes to cultivate the image of a legal system that is accessible, classical language and other 'highbrow' quotes seem best avoided. Sixth, the anonymous authors of a review published in 2014 under the auspices of India's National University of Juridical Sciences urge caution when it comes to literary allusion in judgments, observing that: "In doing so ... there is a danger of judgments going completely off track which manifests in unnecessary lengthy and complicated legal scholarship."[103] Seventh, if the relevance of a literary allusion is tangential, it will seem boastful.[104] One learned commentator has written in this regard of "giving the impression of striving for effect or of literary and intellectual ostentation".[105] Arguably, Lord Denning succumbed to this last weakness in *George Mitchell (Chesterhall) Ltd v Finney Lock Seeds*,[106] a case arising from the fact that the plaintiffs had requested one form of cabbage seed and been provided with another, in which Denning opens his judgment as follows:

> Many of you know Lewis Carroll's "Through the Looking Glass." In it there are these words (Ch. IV):
> "'The time has come,' the Walrus said,
> 'to talk of many things:
> Of shoes – and ships – and sealing-wax –
> Of cabbages – and kings – '"
> Today it is not "of cabbages and kings" – but of cabbages and whatnots.[107]

3.2 Academic references

Closely related to literary allusion is the inclusion of academic references. Jacob observes that: "[I]f you think of a judgment as a quasi-Ph.D. thesis it will need to be long." Perhaps as good a sign as any of a judge who is taking a 'PhD approach' to her judgment

---

102 *Ibid.*
103 Anon (2014), iii.
104 *Ibid.*
105 Corbett, 127.
106 [1982] 3 WLR 1036 (CA).
107 *Ibid*, 1040.

writing is a judge who writes a judgment that is rich in academic references. In one way, the inclusion of academic references is perhaps even more surprising than the inclusion of literary allusion. After all, judges have to resolve substantive legal disputes; academics address the 'big questions' but are not required to bring resolution to their considerations.[108] So the two professions are engaged in different tasks, even if treating with the same law. This is not to criticise academic endeavour which "offers a valuable service to the law",[109] as repeatedly recognised by prominent judges. So, for example, former Chief Justice Brennan of Australia observes that: "The press of litigation and the tyranny of judgment writing are not conducive to reflective doctrinal research. Such research is the Academy's invaluable contribution to the judicial process."[110] Sharlow – a Canadian judge – has struck a similarly supportive note, once observing to a conference of legal scholars that: "[E]ach one of you can teach judges something that will eventually become part of the fabric of our law ... And there is no limit to what you can teach us."[111] In the recent *TuneIn* case,[112] the current master of the rolls even opines that: "Summaries of legal principles are ... generally better undertaken by academic commentators rather than by judges deciding live cases."[113] This is the first example I am aware of in which a superior court judge has canvassed the proposition that the synoptic exposition of legal principle is best left to academic commentators – an approach to judging that arguably sits uneasily with the onetime observation of Lord Macmillan that: "The more we are swamped with precedents the more do we need the lifebelt of principles."[114]

At least on the European side of the Atlantic, the judicial embrace of the academy is a relatively recent development. Historically, the refusal to look beyond statute and case law was a product of an anti-intellectual stance that prevailed in many common law jurisdictions well into the 20th century.[115] However,

---

108   Barak-Erez, 273.
109   French, 21.
110   Brennan, G, 8.
111   Sharlow, 20.
112   *TuneIn Inc v Warner Music UK Ltd* [2021] EWCA Civ 441 (CA).
113   *Ibid*, para 193.
114   Macmillan (1927), 48.
115   Sharpe and Proulx, 552.

by the end of the 20th century, change was well in the air. So, for example, in *White v Jones*,[116] the then Lord Justice Steyn – a future lord of appeal – complained that the judges of the Court of Appeal in that case "were not referred to a single piece of academic writing".[117] Matters have proceeded with such speed that, in Canada, case law and academic treatises now enjoy "more or less equal footing".[118]

The principal attractions of academic writings are perhaps threefold:

- They facilitate the resolution of unresolved law;[119]
- They offer the potential for a "symbiotic and dialogic" relationship between the courts and the academy;[120] and
- They provide social context to legal issues.[121]

However belatedly it has come, the 'intrusion' of a reasonable level of academic commentary into judgment writing seems a welcome development, provided that it is not merely deployed as "a form of decoration"[122] or to clothe the untenable with the lustre of learning. Nonetheless, there are some possible drawbacks to reliance on such commentary. First, such reliance may signify a forsaking of the common law for "an openly instrumentalist form of judicial decision-making".[123] Second, it may involve judges abandoning their role as guardians of liberty and see them become partners in expanded government. Third, it is an approach that can involve judges undertaking general socio-economic and political analysis, which is simply not for courts to do. Fourth, on a related note, it may involve the interjection of unelected judges into the democratic process. Fifth, it may enable elected lawmakers to offload their due responsibility by improperly leaving resolution of controversial policy issues to the judiciary. Sixth, it may threaten public perception of the judiciary as impartial. Seventh, it may

---

116 [1995] 2 AC 207 (CA).
117 *Ibid*, 235.
118 Sharpe and Proulx, 551.
119 *Ibid*, 563.
120 *Ibid*, 567.
121 *Ibid*, 569.
122 Mason (2003a), 5.
123 Gava (2002), 575.

"reduce the authority of the judge and present him as a research student recording by citation his research material".[124]

Two issues of style have not yet been treated with: first, the extent to which a judge relies on precedent; and second, the use of harsh language.

3.3 Precedent

As to the extent to which a judge relies on precedent, even common law judges, it is submitted, need to be careful not to quote excessively from previous judgments. "While there is nothing inherently wrong in mentioning ... previous decisions ... a reference [may] ... serve the purpose."[125] That, at least, is the ideal. If parties submit various cases to a court for consideration, they expect that many or all of them will be included in any ensuing judgment. Counsel too can have an unwelcome tendency to supply the governing precedent (from an apex or appellate court) and then to provide judgments which merely apply the higher precedent. Three points might be made in this regard:

- A judge referred to various authorities can always elect to deal with the critical authorities in detail and dispose of the others briefly (even by reference only).
- Unless lower court precedents add something to a higher court precedent, they do not need to be furnished or treated with.
- As to referring to merely persuasive authority when a point has already been addressed in binding authority, this seems unnecessary.

3.4 Harsh language

As to the use of harsh language, judges typically enjoy immunity from suit in respect of their judgments. If that immunity is not to be abused, judges must show moderation in their language. Of interest in this regard is the decision of the Supreme Court of India in *State of Gujarat v Justice RA Mehta (Retd)*.[126] There, a trial judge had been notably critical of the chief minister of Gujarat. Addressing the

---

124 Fausten *et al*, 743.
125 Sivakumar, 304.
126 [2013] 1 SCR 1 (SCI).

4. Judgment style

issue of the use of harsh language, Justice Chauhan of the Supreme Court observed as follows:

> *Judges must act independently and boldly while deciding a case, but should not make atrocious remarks against the party, or a witness, or ... the subordinate court. Judges must not use strong and carping language, rather they must act with sobriety, moderation and restraint ... [C]ourts should not make any undeserving or derogatory remarks against any person, unless the same are necessary for the purpose of deciding the issue involved in a given case. Even where criticism is justified, the court must not use intemperate language and must maintain judicial decorum at all times keeping in view always ... that the person making such comments is also fallible. Maintaining judicial restraint and discipline are necessary for the orderly administration of justice and courts must not use their authority to 'make intemperate comments, indulge in undignified banter or scathing criticism' ... [W]hile formation and expression of honest opinion and acting thereon, is a necessity to decide a case the courts must always act within the four corners of the law. Maintenance of judicial independence is characterised by maintaining a cool, calm and poised mannerism, as regards every action and expression of the members of the judiciary and not by using inappropriate, unwarranted and contumacious language. The court is required 'to maintain sobriety, calmness, dispassionate reasoning and poised restraint'.*[127]

Sometimes even great judges descend into impoliteness. Lord Blackburn, one of the more prominent 19th-century law lords, once suggested that if a particular county court judge had given the direction to a jury that he did, then he should be reported to the lord chancellor. This was perceived to be an unnecessarily tart remark – so much so that the county court judge "was much comforted ... not long afterwards, by an address of confidence from ... legal practitioners".[128] The lesson from this episode seems to be this: had Blackburn used polite understatement to make much the same point, he could likely have made his criticism without exciting the local practitioners into their embarrassing counteraction.

The duty of politeness, it is submitted, extends to dissenting

---

[127] *Ibid*, para 73.
[128] Manson, 261.

judges. Undoubtedly, "the imperative of judicial civility toward other judges" sits in tension with "the duty ... to account candidly for their differences".[129] However, as former US Chief Justice Charles Evans Hughes once observed: "A judge may be a strong judge without being an impossible person."[130] A judgment is not meant to be an exercise in self-justification – that is, it is not expected to explain why the judge is right and others wrong. "[R]ather, it should appear as a logical conclusion of facts and legal principles."[131]

One last point when it comes to politeness is that judges seem best advised to refrain from condemning witnesses in a judgment unless strictly necessary. "The judge is there to decide the case rather than to denounce human evil or folly."[132] When it comes to making comment on individuals in a judgment, Kitto offers the sage advice that: "Commendation or condemnation of individuals has a place in a judgment if, but only if, it advances the argument by which the Judge reaches his conclusion."[133]

4. Footnotes

Turning next to the use of footnotes in a judgment, I once attended a conference at which there was incidental discussion of this practice. One of the judges present suggested that the topic might usefully be the subject of a full day's analysis at some future date. I am not sure that the use of footnotes merits such thorough consideration. Nonetheless, some consideration is merited. There are, it is submitted, a number of advantages to (at the least) consigning citations to footnotes:

- The main text becomes an easier read.
- Judges are thereby enabled to vary and shorten sentence length.
- With greater variety in sentence length comes the potential for more coherent/forceful paragraphs.
- When a text is crowded with citations, ideas can get crowded out.

---

129   McGlynn Gaffney, 583.
130   Hughes, 68.
131   Sivakumar, 305.
132   Gibbs, 497.
133   Kitto (2003), 71.

- Extensive citations mid-text can be "camouflage for poor writing and poor thinking".[134] Citations are perhaps best viewed as "numerical hiccups".[135] Just as hiccups interrupt speech, citations disrupt narrative free flow.

Although footnotes can serve a legitimate purpose, there does seem to be a general aversion to their usage. Oliver Wendell Holmes, Jr is known to have remarked in private correspondence that an opinion (judgment) should not be like "an essay with footnotes".[136] Closer in time, one American commentator has suggested that judges should "quit using footnotes – cold turkey",[137] thereby eliminating the potential for footnotes to become a wasteland of needless *dicta*. On the European side of the Atlantic, there has been a creeping abundance of footnotes in English judgments, judges seemingly proceeding on the assumption that to include footnotes "is non-contentious ... reflects a welcome modernity ... and is not ... an issue requiring debate prior to implementation".[138] One learned commentator has suggested that:

- this increase in footnote use might be related to increasing judgment length;[139]
- it marks a significant change in legal method and "deserves to be considered with care";[140] and
- there is a possible want of clarity as to the precedential standing of footnotes.[141]

As to the precedential point, a question perhaps arises as to whether this is a problem in practice. After all, footnoted text contains either the *ratio decidendi* or some element of the same (and offhand, it seems unlikely that the *ratio* would be consigned to a footnote). If text does not comprise the *ratio decidendi*, then it is *obiter* and the usual rules apply. Ultimately, in terms of whether/when to consign text other than a citation to a footnote,

---

134 Garner (2001), 9.
135 *Ibid*, 12.
136 Holmes (1953), 675.
137 Mikva, 1367.
138 Munday (2006), 864.
139 *Ibid*, 866.
140 *Ibid*, 867.
141 *Ibid*, 869.

judges can perhaps usefully observe the general rule that: "If the substance of the footnote is relevant and worth a dip of the head, it should be woven into the text."[142]

5. Metaphors, aphorisms and epigrams

I turn next to consider the use of metaphors, aphorisms and epigrams in judgment writing. One might imagine that there would be little use for metaphor in law. However, as Lord Macmillan has observed: "[W]ell-chosen metaphors ... are both legitimate and desirable."[143] Certainly, a dry area such as competition law is enhanced and clarified by the use of metaphors such as 'bottleneck' or 'price squeeze' – language that gets to the heart of what is at play in a judgment far more succinctly than more prosaic language would achieve. But the danger with metaphors is that they can "tend to run away from us. Then we find that our thinking is directed not by the force of argument at hand, but ... the interest of the image in our mind".[144]

Aphorisms and epigrams are a not uncommon feature of judgments. In the 19th century, English judge Lord Justice Knight Bruce enjoyed renown as an epigrammatist, his judgments including such pithy observations as: "'The light of justice is waning in August' [when the courts have risen for the long vacation] [and] ... 'There are callings in which to be convicted of literature is dangerous'"[145] – perhaps thinking of the judicial profession in this regard. He was also skilled in the use of aphorisms – observing, for example, in *Pearse v Pearse*,[146] that: "Truth, like all other good things, may be loved unwisely – may be pursued too keenly – may cost too much."[147] Coming closer in time, Justices Holmes and Jackson of the US Supreme Court (whose judgments are considered in more detail in Chapter 10) were master epigrammatists. The problem, however, with aphorisms and epigrams is that while they are enjoyable to read, they can involve substituting wit for analysis ("containing more wit than reason"),[148] and they can be

---

142 Forrester, 186.
143 Macmillan (1948), 493.
144 Bosmajan, 38.
145 Manson, 31.
146 (1846) 63 ER 950 (Ct Ch).
147 *Ibid*, 957.
148 Horwitz, 119.

unclear. Once constructed, they may also engender a reluctance to amend one's judgment for fear of having to drop an aphorism/epigram that one considers particularly fine. As will be seen, Justice Holmes' fondness for epigrams did not always enhance the clarity of his judgments; though, by contrast, Justice Jackson enriched his judgments with epigrams that were typically (albeit not invariably) easy to understand.

Having looked at judgment style in this chapter and at judgment function in previous chapters, I turn next to the question of how a judgment might (best) be structured.

5. Judgment structure

This chapter is primarily concerned with eight different approaches to judgment writing offered by various judges/experts. It also considers how to approach the task of judgment writing and different forms of judgment. The chapter ends with a consideration of editing.

1. **Introduction**

    Part of the judgment-writing task involves a judge recognising what type of judge she is and swinging away from the excesses to which that type of judge can incline. In essence, there are three judge types:
    - those who emphasise the philosophy/literature of the law;
    - those who feel compelled to write exhaustive judgments; and
    - those who decide the particular case and no more.[1]

    So many modern judges seem to come within the second category that it is perhaps worth quoting what one learned commentator, writing as long ago as 1948, had to say in this regard:

    > *[Such judges] think that in every opinion all the law touching all the legal points raised or those that could be raised should be pursued to the minutest detail, and every case that may be found in the digest and the reports having any bearing should be analyzed, with quotations from many ... Cases involving many points and fine distinctions are much to their liking. They are sometimes more interested in busying themselves in the technical aspects of the case than they are in a correct decision of the case on its merits.[2]*

    Such judges are perhaps at risk of forgetting that litigants come

---

1   See Gregory, 363.
2   *Ibid*, 363–64.

to court for a resolution of the issues presenting, not for a ride on the whirligig of legal theory.

Some judgments all but write themselves. "They are purely mechanical and can be dealt with quickly."[3] Other judgments concern complex facts and require deeper thought.[4] Some cases involve facts and/or legal issues which are so sophisticated as to yield judgments that read like statute law, "with introductions, formally divided chapters, [and] normative precision".[5] Before a judge begins to write a judgment, she ought usefully to decide in her mind, it is submitted, "what purpose the opinion [judgment] will serve and how to write it to suit that purpose".[6] Three inter-related factors of relevance present in this regard:

- the complexity of the facts and the nature of the issues;
- the intended audience; and
- whether it is intended that a judgment will be published.

Each factor is worth considering in more detail.

1.1 Complexity of the facts and the nature of the issues

As to the complexity of the facts and the nature of the issues, situations will present in which the law is well or less well developed. In the former situation, judges might usefully consider whether another comprehensive judgment would assist in the development/explanation of the law or simply intrude itself into a well-settled area of the law. If a judgment will tread legal ground that has been well trodden in previous case law, it need not elaborate in detail on the law. This applies particularly where there are one or more decisions of an apex court that crystallise the law. Unless that court has left some omission that requires to be addressed, no narrative comment on that binding precedent is required. Where there is such an omission or a case otherwise steps into a new area of the law, the US Federal Judicial Center has suggested that a judge should "discuss and analyze [i] the precedents in the area, [ii] the new direction the law is taking, and [iii]

---

[3] Atkinson, 1.
[4] *Ibid.*
[5] Macdonald (2001b), 30.
[6] Federal Judicial Center (2013), 3.

the effect of the decision on existing law".[7] The recitation of facts is of notable importance in judgments that tread new legal ground, as the facts essentially stake out the area to which the judgment applies. Thus:

> *[iv] the opinion should present sufficient facts to define for other readers the precedent it creates and to delineate its boundaries ... [and] [v] [t]he relevant body of precedent – and the relevant policies – should be analyzed in sufficient detail to establish the rationale for the holding.*[8]

Whether [ii] and [iii] are necessary is perhaps a moot point; these seem matters best left to academic commentary. My own general preference is to take the law as I identify it and apply it to the case/facts at hand, leaving any commentary on how the law is evolving to academic commentators. Items [iv] and [v], though important, have the potential to considerably lengthen a judgment, and care is required in this regard to go as far as is necessary in stating facts and analysing precedent, but no further.

As well as judgments that tread old ground and those that tread new ground, occasionally the wealth of case law in an area is such that a judge may consider it necessary to synopsise existing law. I have always found it useful when judges do this. However, the practice has recently been the subject of negative comment by Master of the Rolls Sir Geoffrey Vos in the *TuneIn* case,[9] where he observes:

> *I am not convinced that it is helpful to try to summarise wide-ranging areas of law in numbered principles. That is not really how the common law operates. The common law is at its best when cases are decided by the finding of facts in the particular case and by the application of the law applicable at the relevant time to those facts.*[10]

That traditional approach, it is submitted, has yielded the contemporary 'information overload' that presents in the common law system. As a consequence, it would seem (certainly, it is arguable) that the principles-based approach adopted by Lord Justice Arnold in the same case is to be preferred. Occasional

---

7   *Ibid*, 4–5.
8   *Ibid*.
9   *TuneIn Inc v Warner Music UK Ltd* [2021] EWCA Civ 441 (CA).
10 *Ibid*, para 192.

synopses surely assist in shortening the length of judgments that follow thereafter and thus facilitate the attainment of that brevity, clarity and simplicity in judgment writing which has been posited as an ideal by, for example, Lord Bingham.[11] My own practice when writing such synopses is to consider each previous case in some detail and identify the particular principles for which it stands. At the end, I then restate all the principles and put the name of the relevant case/s in brackets after each stated principle. This gives the reader the assurance that I have considered the relevant case/s in detail while also providing a bullet-point statement of principles that can be applied in future cases. What can be unhelpful are judgments where a judge simply states that: "I have read X Case, Y Case and Z Case, and the following principles present." While the stated principles may be correct, the reader does not have the comfort of knowing this unless she sees the writing judge go through the detail.

1.2 Audiences

Different judgments will be written for different target audiences. The issue of intended audience has already been touched upon in Chapter 2. The US Federal Judicial Center has in the past distinguished in this regard between five forms of judgment, as follows:

- judgments that are written primarily for the litigants and their lawyers ("The parties will be familiar with the facts and will generally not be interested in an extensive exploration of the law");[12]
- judgments that may say something to someone other than the parties ("Judges may assume a certain level of sophistication ... on the part of lawyers. But if the case involves an arcane area ... more discussion of the factual and legal background will be needed");[13]
- judgments that remand a case to a lower court (the judgment tells the lower court what is expected on remand);
- judgments that identify guidelines for trial courts. These, the Federal Judicial Center recommends, should state the factual/

---

11   Bingham, T (2009), 609–10.
12   Federal Judicial Center (2013), 5.
13   *Ibid.*

legal/policy basis for the guidelines with sufficient clarity to enable trial judges to apply them correctly;[14] and
- judgments that address an issue of general public interest or are likely to attract media attention ("[Such a judgment] should be written in a manner that will ensure it cannot be misunderstood").[15]

Care should also be taken when writing a judgment not to leave 'hostages to fortune' – that is, observations (or a want of elaboration on observations) such as to yield confusion.

The option of whether to publish a judgment is ultimately a matter for the writing judge, at least when she sits alone. However, in the Information Age, there is pressure for judgments to be published online at the earliest opportunity and there can be criticism if they are not. The factors that might prompt a judge to authorise judgment publication include whether the judgment:
- is being given in the first case to raise the issue/s touched upon;
- alters/modifies/clarifies a rule of law;
- considers an aspect of the law that has previously received little attention;
- questions the law (though an issue presents as to whether it is the task of judges to question the law or simply to apply it);
- resolves an apparent conflict in earlier decisions;
- reverses a lower court decision or affirms it on different grounds; or
- warrants publication in light of other factors making it a case of public interest.[16]

1.3 Publication

Sometimes after a judgment is published, counsel may indicate that there is some form of typographical error in the text. My own practice is to correct such typographical errors only if they do not change my intended meaning and never to amend a judgment substantially. A useful practice whenever amendment to a judgment

---

14 *Ibid.*
15 *Ibid*, 6.
16 *Ibid.*

is required post-publication is to proceed as reputable online newspapers proceed and to indicate, for example, that: "This judgment was amended on [stated date] because Ms X was wrongly referred to in paragraphs (a) and (b) when the reference should have been to Ms Y." In jurisdictions which allow circulation of judgments to counsel before they are pronounced in court or otherwise formally issued, such errors will hopefully be identified and excised pre-publication. However, those jurisdictions then face the problem of how to deal with challenges to a proposed judgment.

1.4 Further observations

Judgment form is more a matter of convention than law. In trial court judgments, a judge often (though not always in this sequence) recites the subject matter, identifies key issues presenting, highlights particular factual concerns and applies the relevant laws to the facts – a process which culminates in the judge's ultimate conclusions. By contrast, appellate court judgments often (though not always in this sequence) summarise the lower court decision as to the facts and then consider points of law in detail. Many commentators over the years have decried the perception of judgment writing as "exhaustive essay writing",[17] and still the problem presents.

Because litigants only ever see the end product of judgment writing, they and the legal world do not see how "well-written, fluent, cogent judgments conceal the thoughts ... feelings, the backwards and forwards motions involved in their making ... [and the] erratic ... even contradictory, pathways towards decisions".[18] Moreover, because judgments are typically declaratory in style, litigants and the wider world may not appreciate just how close a decision can be and that the law, as confidently stated by a judge, often does not in fact clearly favour one side over another.

A number of commentators/judges have broken down judgments into various components and offered guidance on what is at play in the various limbs. Some of this guidance is short, some long; all of it is useful when it comes to judgment writing. Eight

---

17 Cowen, 252.
18 Herz, M, 126.

5. Judgment structure

approaches are considered hereafter – those of Atkinson, Bingham, Bosielo, Corbett, Mahoney, Strong, the US Federal Judicial Center and Wanderer. Between them, they consider the various segments of a judgment to comprise the elements outlined in Table 1.

Table 1. Alternative judgment formats

Atkinson	Bingham	Bosielo	Corbett
Facts	Central point	Introduction	Introduction
Law	Salient facts	Facts	Facts
Application	Litigation history	Issues	Law and issues
Consideration	Parties' contentions	Law	Application
	Lower court reasons	Application	Relief
	Ratio	Remedy	Order
		Order	

Mahoney	Strong	Federal Judicial Center	Wanderer
Issues	Opening	Introduction	Nature of action
Law	Issues summary	Issues	Facts
Facts	Material facts	Facts	Questions
Conclusions	Legal analysis	Legal principles	Determination
Order	Conclusion	Conclusion	Disposition/ mandate

2. Atkinson

Atkinson, a onetime Australian judge, canvasses the 'Facts, Law, Application, Conclusion' (FLAC) structure as a useful skeleton on which to construct a judgment. As to 'F' (the facts), in a civil case the facts in issue are determined by the pleadings. It is important for the decision maker to resolve the facts in issue. A central challenge for judgment writers when it comes to the facts is to outline them in sufficient detail that it will not be necessary to amplify upon them at a later stage in judgment, yet also to keep the outline of the facts sufficiently curtailed that it does not detract from the judgment as a whole.[19] Excessive iteration of facts is distracting. A perceived need to focus greatly on facts may in part explain why modern judgments have become so long. For all judges, deciding what detail to leave out of a judgment can be a challenging task; however, it is worth bearing in mind that: "All stories are ... equivocal and contingent ... Only part of any story is recounted by a text."[20] As to procedural history, this should, it is submitted, be referenced only if it is relevant to the findings.[21]

When it comes to 'L', the 'law', Atkinson observes that:

It is important to the resolution of any legal dispute that we set out the relevant statute and case law ... [I]n clarifying for ourselves the right decision to come to we have to know what the law is and to ... state it clearly and persuasively ... Sometimes you will set out the law before the facts.[22]

There are fewer judgments in which the law needs to be set out before the facts; though as Atkinson observes, this can sometimes be necessary. (If counsel finds it necessary in court to outline the law before, for example, hearing from any witnesses, this is a sign that a similar approach might usefully be adopted in the ensuing judgment.)

As to 'A' ('application') and 'C' ('conclusion'), parties will accept a judgment more willingly if they see objective application of the law to the facts before them, with the conclusion being the result of the application of the law to the facts.

---

19 Sivakumar, 288.
20 Macdonald (2001a), 677.
21 Sivakumar, 288.
22 Atkinson, 6.

One 'A' that is arguably absent from the 'FLAC' acronym is 'Argument'. Many judges consider it appropriate to outline the legal arguments posited by counsel for each side – perhaps so that each side gets a sense that what it came to court to assert has at least been heard; though it is difficult not to recall in this regard the cautionary observation of the US Federal Judicial Center that: "Lengthy statements of ... parties' contentions ... are not a substitute for analysis and reasoning, and ... should be avoided."[23]

Outlines of the legal arguments for both sides are often followed by a 'Discussion' section, in which the judge will seek to resolve the legal points arising before moving onto 'A' ('Application'). So it may be that the 'FLAC' acronym ought rightly to be 'FLAAC' – that is, Facts, Law, Arguments, Application, Conclusion. When it comes to 'Argument', one question presenting is whether a trial judge should ever copy (adopt as her own) the submissions received from the winning side and present the copied text to the parties as her judgment. The reasons why a trial judge might do so are not always to do with laziness; she may feel that the arguments are so well expressed that they cannot be bettered, and/or that the case is so overwhelmingly in favour of one party that there is nothing to be said for the loser. The Supreme Court of Canada has given judgment on this point and, it is submitted, arrived at a sensible and balanced approach, holding that:

> *Only if the incorporation is such that a reasonable person would conclude that the judge did not put her mind to the issues and decide them independently and impartially as she was sworn to do, can the judgment be set aside.*[24]

3. Bingham

Lord Bingham, a onetime English judge, has suggested the following to be essential ingredients of an appellate court judgment:
- a succinct identification of the central point of the case at the outset of the judgment;
- a summary of the salient facts;
- some account of the litigation history;

---

23   Federal Judicial Center (2013), 15.
24   *Cojocaru v British Columbia Women's Hospital & Health Center* [2013] 2 SCR 357 (SC).

- a summary of the parties' contentions;
- some attention to the reasoning of the judge against which appeal has been brought; and
- identification of the reasons for affirming/dismissing the appeal.[25]

4. Bosielo

Bosielo, a onetime South African judge, has offered a more refined version of the 'FLAC' approach, deploying the acronym 'IFILARO': 'Introduction, Facts, Issues, Law, Application, Remedy, Order'. Bosielo suggests that a judgment should indicate by way of introduction what the case is about, how it came before the court and what the court is required to decide. He considers it important that the nature of the proceedings also be described – for example, whether it is an appeal or an interlocutory application. This section, he writes, "must be simple, crisp and succinct but sufficiently inform the reader/listener what the case is ... about".[26]

Bosielo identifies the facts as the most important part of the judgment. In terms of resolving disputed facts, he indicates that a judge "can determine them whilst discussing the facts"[27] – presumably expressly or simply by stating particular facts to apply. Alternatively, Bosielo suggests that resolution of conflicts of fact can be left to a later stage in the judgment when dealing with the issues presenting. The next section of a judgment, Bosielo suggests, should deal with issues of credibility, reliability and probabilities or improbabilities, all in the context of evidence evaluation. Such issues may relate to:
- the facts only;
- the law only;
- the facts and law; or
- the application of the law to the facts.

"Ordinarily such issues are determined when findings on the facts are made."[28]

---

25 Bingham, T (2009), 608–09.
26 Bosielo, 18.
27 *Ibid*, 19.
28 *Ibid*, 25.

Any judgment must identify the law and legal principles applicable. However, Bosielo cautions against what might be called 'over-egging the custard' in this regard. Thus, he observes that: "Only those cases which are relevant and ... support your decision need to be ... analysed."[29] This is a useful note for judges concerned that a case might be appealed successfully because a case mentioned was not considered; this could only happen where the case in question was critical to the decision that fell to be reached or its absence otherwise pointed to some fatal flaw in the deciding judge's reasoning. Bosielo urges judges to read applicable case law, understand it, and (in their judgments) demonstrate how a particular case supports a particular conclusion, suggesting that: "In many cases, once the facts and the applicable law have been decided, the answer becomes self-evident."[30]

The relief to be granted, Bosielo observes, is largely determined by the findings of law and fact. The order, he observes, simply "records the end result".[31] One of the more surprising features of life as a judge – at least in Ireland – is that while the judge delivers judgment, she does not formulate the order that ensues. That is done by a senior civil servant who liaises with the parties and only contacts the judge if the precise form of the order to issue is unclear from the judgment.

5. Corbett

Corbett, a former South African chief justice, recommends a six-stage structure to a "logical, flowing judgment":[32]
- an introductory section;
- a setting out of facts;
- identification of the law/issues presenting;
- application of the law to the facts presenting;
- a determination of the relief to be ordered; and
- the order of the court.

The introductory section, per Corbett, should:
- "set the stage";[33]

---

29 *Ibid*, 26.
30 *Ibid*.
31 *Ibid*, 27.
32 Corbett, 126.

- identify how the matter came before the court;
- state who the parties are;
- briefly describe them and their activities; and
- give a broad sense of what the case is about.

This section often gets written last.

A difference between judgments of common law courts and their civil law counterparts is, in the common law world, "a growing obsession with setting out the facts".[34] This preoccupation with facts may be attributable to an absence in the common law scheme of an overarching or underpinning conceptual system. Additionally, by identifying the facts, a judge ensures that she does not go beyond deciding the case put before her; judges are not "roving ambassadors for the rule of law".[35] Facts may be gleaned from the pleadings (to the extent they are agreed) and any disputed facts resolved on the evidence. Although Corbett rightly considers the indication of applicable facts to be "a most important part of the judgment",[36] he also emphasises the need for selectivity and concision in this regard:

You will find that ... a vast amount of material has been placed before the court, much of which was either irrelevant from the start or became irrelevant as the case developed ... Ignore this material in your judgment ... There is nothing worse than a judgment which consists of a surfeit of quotations from pleadings, affidavits, evidence and documents, and a minimum of reasoning.[37]

There is a degree of subjective judgment in the selectivity/concision urged by Corbett. But any notion that a fully objective statement of universal truths can ever be distilled by a judge from all that is before her seems false. Everything that appears in one judge's judgment is a product of her mind and perceptions. It has been suggested that really what judges are doing in this regard is making 'truth claims' – that is, asserting truths "which, although presented as truths are ... but claims as to the truth".[38] A related

---

33 *Ibid*, 122.
34 Munday (2006), 866.
35 Richardson (2004), 118.
36 *Ibid*, 122.
37 *Ibid*, 123. As Cardozo observes: "There is an accuracy that defeats itself by the over-emphasis of details" (1931, 7).
38 Burns, 226.

difficulty which also presents is that: "Individual perceptions of ... material facts can differ subtly but critically ... More fundamentally ... attempts to state ideas in particular sets of words can alter the ideas as the words change."[39]

The identification of the issue/s at play before the court is a critical aspect of any judgment. In this regard, it has been suggested that:

The real creativity in a judicial decision lies in the question that judges decide to accept as the basis of their deliberations ... Every court makes a fundamental decision about the question before it, and the wording in that first decision controls all others.[40]

The structure of the law/issues segment of the judgment will depend on what is in play in a particular set of proceedings. Corbett identifies a number of different scenarios that may commonly present in this regard – namely, a dispute:
- solely as to law;
- solely as to facts;
- where both facts and law are in issue; and
- where there is no dispute about facts or law but there is a dispute about the result to be arrived at.

This segment of the judgment will determine how the case is to be decided, with one commentator referring to the "rhetoric of inevitability" deployed by judges whereby they "compulsively ... associate their own views with a correct course in history".[41] (Another possibility as to why judges proceed so is not from compulsion but from necessity. The necessity is this: in a system of law based on precedent, a judge must try to slot her view of matters into the schema of existing precedent, even when departing from it.)

6. Mahoney

Mahoney, a onetime Australian judge, suggests sequencing a judgment in the following way:
- issues to be determined;
- applicable law;

---

39   Heydon (2013), 205.
40   Ferguson, 208.
41   *Ibid*, 214.

- facts;
- conclusions; and
- an identification of any orders to be made.

He suggests that in all cases it is useful to have the parties agree on the particular questions to be decided. Presuming that such agreement proves possible (and it may not), this eliminates as a ground of appeal the claim that the judge did not answer all issues presenting. Mahoney also cautions that the question/s to be resolved should be elicited from counsel, rather than imposing the judge's formulation of the determinative question/s. When it comes to the law, Mahoney recommends that a judgment should state:

- how the deciding court has jurisdiction;
- how the case comes before the judge;
- the law with which the dispute is concerned (this may be covered by the statement as to jurisdiction); and
- the particular legal principles/provisions by reference to which the dispute falls to be resolved.

Often there will be no issue between the parties as to the basic facts presenting. In such instances, a summary chronology of facts will suffice. But in other instances, there will be a dispute as to the facts, yielding an immediate dilemma for a trial judge as to what facts require to be stated. Lord Macmillan offers the traditional view that:

> *The first judgment [ie, the trial court judgment] rightly covers the whole ground. In the court of appeal much is usually shed, but the first judge cannot foretell what points may commend themselves on appeal and he ought to provide all the material which may conceivably be regarded as relevant on a reconsideration of the case.*[42]

As the trial judge is not a soothsayer, such an approach leads to the almost inevitable approach on the part of a trial judge that 'more is better'. Mahoney identifies the dilemma that arises:

> Prima facie *it might be thought that a statement of the facts will be sufficient if it [i] indicates the context of the dispute, so that the principle chosen for decision can be understood, and [ii] ... communi-*

---

42   Macmillan (1948), 499.

> *cates to the parties involved that the judge appreciated the nature of their dispute. However ... it may be prudent for the judgment to record [iii] not merely the substance of the factual context but the details of the evidence which has been placed before the court ... because an appellate court may otherwise infer that that which has not been recorded has been overlooked or not taken into account.*[43]

Until this dilemma is resolved, trial judges will doubtless continue to err on the side of caution and state facts in fulsome detail. The problem could likely quickly be resolved if appellate courts were to take the sensible view that all that is required of a trial judge is that her statement of the facts include solely the facts which are part of the essential reasoning process of the trial judge's judgment. By maintaining such a stance and departing from it only in cases of egregious error, appellate courts could go a long way in terms of reducing the systemic difficulty that treating with facts presents for trial judges. Clearly, to the extent that facts are in dispute: "It is necessary for a judge ... to record how he decided between the competing versions of them."[44]

The conclusion of a judgment is what the parties to a case are most interested in and, to them at least, is the most important part of the judgment. (For non-parties, other aspects of the judgment, such as discussion of any legal issue presenting, may be of more interest.) When it comes to conclusions of fact, various reasoning processes may be relied upon, including syllogisms, inference and intuition. In or following the judgment, one or more orders will be made.

7. Strong

Strong, an American commentator, mentions as the "most often-used and well-regarded structural framework"[45] one derived from the principles of classical rhetoric: "an opening paragraph ... (*exordium*) ... a summary of the issues to be discussed (*divisio*) ... a recitation of material adjudicative facts (*narratio*) ... an analysis of ... legal issues (*confirmatio a. confutatio*) ... and ... a conclusion (*peroratio*)."

---

43 Mahoney, [8].
44 *Ibid*.
45 Strong, 117.

The opening paragraph (*exordium*) should give the reader a roadmap of where she will be brought by the author. It should also contain enough information to let a reader know whether it is worthwhile continuing with the read. It can usefully answer five questions:
- Who?
- What?
- When?
- Where?
- How?

The summary of the issues to be discussed (*divisio*) outlines the law which will be brought to bear on the material facts. The recitation of material facts (*narratio*) follows. The analysis of legal issues (*confirmatio a confutatio*) analyses the legal issues in detail and identifies the rationale for reaching the outcome reached. The law, Strong indicates, should not be applied "mechanistically".[46] Rather, the case for and against different conclusions should be argued. The conclusion (*peroratio*) is typically a sentence to a paragraph in length and indicates the form of the order to be made.

8. **US Federal Judicial Center**
The US Federal Judicial Center offers perhaps the most thoroughgoing consideration of how judgments should be written. It has suggested that every "full-dress" judgment[47] – that is, every judgment that requires structured discussion of facts, legal principle and governing authorities – should contain five elements:

> *(1) an introductory statement of the nature, procedural posture, and result of the case; (2) a statement of the issues to be decided; (3) a statement of the ... material facts; (4) a discussion of ... governing legal principles and resolution of the issues; and (5) the disposition and necessary instructions.*[48]

The purpose of an introduction should be "to orient the reader".[49] It can usefully state:

---

46 *Ibid*, 126.
47 Federal Judicial Center (2013), 3.
48 *Ibid*, 13.
49 *Ibid*.

5. Judgment structure

- who the parties are;
- the basis for the court's jurisdiction;
- any relevant prior proceedings and how the case got to the court;
- what the case is about;
- the legal subject matter; and
- the result.

The statement of issues is the "cornerstone" of a judge's reasoning.[50] It determines which facts are material and what are the governing legal principles. The Center cautions against confusing identifying issues with reciting contentions.

The Center posits the uncontroversial propositions that only the facts necessary to explain a decision should be included and that excessive factual detail can be distracting.

The Center considers the consideration of legal principle to be at the heart of a judgment. This consideration must, the Center suggests, "demonstrate that the Court's conclusion is based on reason and logic ... [and] persuade the reader of the correctness of the decision".[51] However, not every case/contention raised by the parties requires to be addressed. What is required is that the discussion "be sufficient to demonstrate to the losing party that the court has fully considered the essentials of its position".[52]

The Center also offers guidance on case citations, secondary sources and quotations. When it comes to case citations, it considers that most legal points are adequately supported by citing the latest decision, and that it is only if "an opinion breaks new ground ... [that] the court should marshal existing authority and analyze the evolution of the law sufficiently to support the new rule".[53] When it comes to secondary sources (law review articles, treatises, texts and non-legal sources), the Center opines that "they should be cited sparingly and only to serve a purpose".[54] When it comes to quotations, the Center offers the view that while quotes

---

50 *Ibid*, 14.
51 *Ibid*, 16.
52 *Ibid*.
53 *Ibid*, 18.
54 *Ibid*.

from another case can be more informative than simply citing the case, "[t]he impact of a quote ... is inversely proportional to its length".[55]

9. **Wanderer**

Wanderer, an American commentator, suggests that there are five essential elements to any judgment: "[Identifying] the nature of the action, the statement of the facts, [identifying] the questions to be decided, the determination of the issues, and the disposition and mandate."[56] The opening paragraph, he maintains, should lay out the 'who' and 'what' of the case. This is critically important "because it tends to forecast the quality of the entire product".[57] A good beginning gives reason to believe that the author has something to say and will say it well. In addition, Wanderer observes, a judgment should state all facts that are legally significant or necessary to establish context. Diagrams and maps should be included if they will aid understanding. Facts should be stated as a narrative, in the past tense and usually in chronological order. Dates should be inserted only where they will help readers understand the flow of events or where they serve another purpose – for example, identifying applicable law. Although the issues may be introduced in the opening paragraph, Wanderer suggests that the legal questions to be decided should appear in the paragraph following the statement of facts, and before the determination of the issues.

As to the determination/disposition section, this portion of a judgment, per Wanderer (and, it is respectfully submitted, he is right in this), is the heart of the judgment. In it, competing law and policy are analysed and a reasoned decision is reached by reference to the facts at hand. Wanderer suggests that when discussing a legal issue, it is helpful to proceed as follows:

- Identify the discrete issue;
- Identify the legal rule that applies and show how it has been applied in like cases; and

---

[55] *Ibid.*
[56] Wanderer, 55.
[57] Re, 12.

5. Judgment structure

- Apply that rule to the facts at hand by presenting both parties' arguments and reach a conclusion as to which is the more persuasive.

The last paragraph of a judgment, Wanderer suggests, should provide a clear, precise resolution of the case, stating the decision that has been reached and the relief that is to be granted.

Turning from the forms of judgment to the substance of a judgment, and specifically to the issue of editing, it remains the case that common law judges have tremendous – almost absolute – freedom as to what they say and how they say it. Thus, save insofar as a court has stylistic rules or an in-house editing department, no one can typically force an edit on a judge – not even fellow judges on a collegiate court. It is unsurprising, therefore, that some judges "succumb to the prolixity of our age"[58] and "become self-satisfied with their opinion-writing … [because no one] ever tells them that there is something wrong with it".[59] This problem, however, is not confined to appellate court judges. Editing is therefore a matter to be addressed by all judges. It has been suggested that a good editing process should include the following:

[i] using a checklist of topics or issues to ensure that … all issues are resolved … [ii] checking names, dates, figures and other data for accuracy … [iii] eliminating repetition … [iv] excluding irrelevant findings of fact … [v] pruning lengthy quotations … [vi] removing and replacing Latin expressions, jargon or outmoded expressions … [vii] eliminating explanations of the obvious … [viii] using the active voice … wherever possible … [ix] simplifying … complex sentences and adopting short sentences, where appropriate … [x] checking the use of punctuation to avoid ambiguity and facilitate comprehension … [and] [xi] scrutinising the length and content of paragraphs.[60]

The US Federal Judicial Center has in the past urged judges, when it comes to editing, to focus on whether there is any:

- wordiness (eg, verbosity, trying to convey too much, covering too many issues or simply writing too much);

---

58 Mikva, 1366.
59 Leflar, 816.
60 Dessau and Wodak, 11.

- lack of precision and clarity (vagueness being a common concealer for ignorance);
- poor organisation;
- cryptic analysis;
- pomposity; or
- humour, which it observes "works better in after-dinner speeches than in judicial opinions".[61]

But perhaps the most comprehensive editing checklist is offered by Wanderer,[62] who suggests that in the course of an editing process, the following questions can helpfully be addressed:

Does the court have jurisdiction? Are all ... factual statements ... supported by ... the [pleadings] ... ? Are the questions to be decided laid out clearly? Are all ... legally significant facts included in the statement of the facts? Are all direct quotations ... perfectly accurate? Have the facts supporting the losing party been stated? Have all issues been addressed? Have the arguments of the losing party been stated and ... addressed? Do the cases cited stand for the propositions ... asserted? Are the conclusions ... supported by clear reasoning and legal authorities? Is the court's ruling stated clearly and succinctly? Have all omissions from quotations been indicated by ellipses? Are all dates, numbers, and citations accurate? Is the opinion readable, grammatical, and correctly punctuated? Is any use of figurative language or humor ... likely to help the reader ... ? Have all the parties been treated with respect?

The various suggested 'checks' arising from the assorted commentary considered above can perhaps be reduced to the following:
- Does the court have jurisdiction?
- Does the judgment embrace all it should and resolve all issues?
- Are the questions to be decided identified clearly?
- Have names, dates, quotes and so on been checked for accuracy?
- Has unnecessary repetition been eliminated?

---

61   Federal Judicial Center (2013), 22.
62   Wanderer, 70.

- Are all legally significant facts included?
- Are the facts supporting the losing party stated?
- Have irrelevant findings of fact been excluded?
- Are all factual statements supported by the evidence?
- Are conclusions supported by reasoning and authorities?
- Do all cases cited stand for the propositions asserted?
- Have all quotations been pruned as much as possible?
- Are all omissions from quotations indicated by ellipses?
- Have all Latin, jargon and outmoded expressions been excised?
- Have explanations of the obvious been eliminated?
- Does the judgment use the active voice where possible?
- Have lengthy/complex sentences been simplified and short sentences adopted?
- Has punctuation been checked?
- Has the length/content of paragraphs been scrutinised?
- Have cryptic analysis, pomposity and humour been eschewed?
- Is any use of figurative language or humour likely to aid readers?
- Is the ruling stated clearly and succinctly?
- Have all parties been treated with respect?

10. Conclusion

Before closing this chapter, it is worth pausing to consider a striking analogy that has been drawn in the academic literature between the roles of judges and architects. Thus, Devlin points to five challenges which confront architects and which are also useful in helping judges to appreciate their role: "integrating function, structure and beauty; balancing the technical and practical with the visionary and conceptual; calibrating continuity and change; resolving the tensions between the individual and the community; and seeking the infinite within the finite".[63] Devlin also draws a distinction between monumental architecture (which he suggests may be more the provenance of appellate judges) and vernacular architects (whom he compares to trial judges). In truth, his analogy between

---

63   Devlin, R, 291.

judges and architects seems to work for judges at all levels, without the need for this further monumental/vernacular distinction.

When it comes to integrating function, structure and beauty, Devlin points to the need for judges not to become overwhelmed by the amount of law before them and to remember the primary function that the/a law serves. Structure comes into play in best deciding how to give effect to that primary function. As to balancing the technical and practical with the visionary and conceptual,[64] one cannot better Devlin's eloquence in his observation that:

> The good architect [judge] needs to be able to integrate ... science and art, the pedantic and the creative, the intellectual and the emotional ... the intuitive and the deliberative. In pursuing this synthesis, the architect must address the relationships between efficiency and aesthetic solid and void, light, texture and colour, simplicity and ornamentation ... the minimal and the sensual.[65]

As regards calibrating continuity and change, just as a good architect must be alive to the *'genius loci'*, so too judges, when it comes to writing a judgment, need to be aware of (and sensitive to) the legal geography, topography, landscape, climate and environment. Even if taking Frost's path less travelled, a judge needs to set her judgment in context and explain by reference to existing law why taking that path represents the best route forward in the dispute presenting.

When it comes to resolving tensions between the individual and the community, just as an architect has a dual task *vis-à-vis* the commissioning client and the community into which a particular architectural endeavour will be integrated, a judge must be alive to the individual and community aspects of her judgment. Finally, when it comes to seeking the infinite within the finite, Devlin refers to what is perhaps the most satisfying part of being a judge: glimpsing the universal within the incidental.[66]

I turn now from the question of how judgments in general might (best) be structured, and from the consideration in previous

---

64 Ibid.
65 Ibid, 295–96.
66 Pérez-Gómez, 206

chapters of certain functional and stylistic aspects of all judgments, to a more focused consideration of two major types of appellate court judgment: dissenting and concurring judgments.

6. Dissenting and concurring judgments

This chapter examines the potential, role, merits and drawbacks of dissenting judgments; the motivation of dissenting judges; the writing of concurring judgments; and the need for good manners in judgment writing.

1. **Dissenting judgments**
    There are, broadly speaking, three approaches to how appellate courts issue their judgments. These have been succinctly described by the late US Supreme Court Justice Ginsburg in the following terms:

    In the civil-law tradition ... courts ... issue a collective judgment ... in stylized, impersonal language. The author of the judgment is neither named nor ... identifiable. Disagreement, if it exists ... is not disclosed. The British common law tradition lies at the opposite pole. In appeals in that tradition, there was conventionally no 'opinion for the court'... Instead, the judges hearing the case composed their own individual opinions which, taken together, revealed the court's disposition. Changes in British practice and in some European tribunals have brought these divergent systems closer together ... Our [American] system occupies a middle ground ... Opinions that speak for the Court remain the custom ... But unlike courts in civil-law systems ... each member of the Court has the prerogative to write separately ... In civil-law systems, the nameless, stylized judgment ... are thought to foster the public's perception of the law as ... stable and secure. The common law tradition ... prizes the independence of the individual judge ... and the transparency of the judicial process.[1]

    Perhaps the biggest difference between an appellate court and a

---

1   Ginsburg (2010a), 2–3.

trial court is that appellate courts typically operate (and/or are perceived by their members to operate) on a collegiate basis, which requires members to proceed on the basis of consultation, discussion and compromise, with each member expected to bear her share of the court's workload. In a collegiate court, a judge is as responsible for the judgment on which she 'signs off' as she is for a judgment that she has authored (which is the reason why a 'signing off' judge gets to make comment on a judgment that another judge is writing).[2] It has been contended that even when a judge in a collegiate court is not 'signing off' on a judgment, she "has a collegial responsibility to ensure that the judgment remains as good as it can be as a product of the Court".[3]

A common difference between trial and appellate courts – save where the former sit as multi-judge divisional courts – is that appellate courts typically sit in multi-judge panels, yielding the potential for dissent. (By contrast, trial judges typically sit alone.) Views on the merits of dissenting judgments vary. Some commentators view them positively, taking the view that "[t]he right to dissent is the essence of democracy ... an effective safeguard against judicial lethargy ... [and its] effect ... the essence of progress";[4] and that "[t]he only sincere questions in judicial opinions [judgments] ... appear in dissents".[5] Other commentators view dissenting judgments as "the *enfant terrible* of appellate practice".[6] The onetime US Supreme Court Justice Potter Stewart once described them, perhaps not wholly humorously, as "subversive literature".[7] Even Justice Holmes, the so-called 'Great Dissenter' – though in fact, he dissented less often than most of his colleagues[8] – observed in *Northern Securities Co v United States*,[9] in which he wrote his first Supreme Court dissent, that the practice of dissent is "useless and undesirable, as a rule";[10] and still he persisted in dissenting.

When it comes to the differing views of the dissenting judge,

---

2 O'Regan, 4.
3 *Ibid*.
4 Carter, 118.
5 Ferguson, 210.
6 Traynor, 211.
7 Flanders, 403.
8 Ginsburg (1990), 142.
9 193 US 197 (1904).
10 *Ibid*, 400.

these range from viewing her "as noble juridical warrior ... [and/or] curmudgeonly recalcitrant ... [and/or] activist ideologue".[11] But regardless of the view one takes of a dissenting judge (and of the stance taken by a dissenting judge in any one case), there is wisdom in the observation of Lord Neuberger that: "The undoubted right of each appellate judge to write his or her own judgment, like all rights, carries with it responsibilities, one of which is to provide clear, practical guidance."[12]

Though doubtless perceived by some as "an undisciplined act of judicial egotism",[13] dissenting judgments have traditionally served three functions:
- reinforcing democracy;
- inspiring clearer majority judgment writing; and
- facilitating change.

Each of these is now considered in turn. First, dissenting judgments demonstrate that a societal norm of democracy (freedom of speech) exists within the judiciary, thereby affirming that norm.[14] As William Douglas, a former US Supreme Court Justice has observed: "Judges, like other leaders of thought, must be free to choose – and, being free, must have the daring to let their inner conscience cast their votes."[15] In issuing dissenting judgments, judges show that freedom to present. Second, dissenting judgments tend to stimulate clearer judgment writing by majority judges and undoubtedly throw the majority view into sharper relief[16] – the all-time prize for throwing the majority view into sharp relief surely going to Justice Mussmano of the Supreme Court of Pennsylvania. His dissent in *Commonwealth v Robin*,[17] a case concerned with the distribution of an allegedly obscene book entitled *Tropic of Cancer*, opens with the following powerful lines:

The decision of the Majority of the Court in this case has dealt a staggering blow to the forces of morality, decency and human dignity

---

11   McIntyre, 431.
12   Neuberger (January 2012), para 24.
13   Lipez, 346.
14   Carter, 123.
15   Douglas (1948), 107.
16   Flanders, 407.
17   421 Pa 70 (Pa 1966).

> *in the Commonwealth of Pennsylvania. If, by this decision, a thousand rattlesnakes had been let loose, they could not do as much damage to the well-being of the people of this state as the unleashing of all the scorpions and vermin of immorality swarming out of that volume of degeneracy called the 'Tropic of Cancer.' Policemen, hunters, constables and foresters could easily and quickly kill a thousand rattlesnakes but the lice, lizards, maggots and gangrenous roaches scurrying out from beneath the covers of the 'Tropic of Cancer' will enter into the playground, the study desks, the cloistered confines of children and immature minds to eat away moral resistance and wreak damage and harm which may blight countless lives for years and decades to come. From time immemorial civilization has condemned obscenity because the wise men of the ages have seen its eroding effects on the moral fiber of a people; history is replete with the decadence and final collapse of mighty nations because of their descent into licentiousness and sloth.*[18]

The majority were likewise uneasy about the text of the book but considered themselves compelled by binding federal precedent to conclude that the book enjoyed free speech protection. (The book, a novel by American author Henry Miller, was first published in 1934 and heralded the candid discussions of sex/uality that are now commonplace in literature. Though explicit, Miller's book arguably manages to capture "the immediacy, energy, seediness and glorious beauty of life".)[19]

Stemming from the notion of any one judgment as being but "the temporary crystallisation"[20] of the law, a third attraction of dissenting judgments is that they facilitate the evolutionary process of change.[21] As former US Chief Justice Charles Evans Hughes once put matters: "A dissent ... is an appeal to the brooding spirit of the law, to the intelligence of a future day."[22] (Lord Bingham has spoken in more prosaic terms of how "the dissent of today may become the orthodoxy of tomorrow".)[23] By sowing the seeds of doubt, a dissenting judge may harbour the hope that a majority decision will

---

18	*Ibid*, 73–74.
19	Sweeney Byrne.
20	Murphy and Rawlings, 59.
21	Lynch (2003), 726.
22	Hughes, 68.
23	Bingham, T (2009), 607.

not stand the test of time, even if "the majority of a court ... is more likely to be right on the average than the minority".[24] That said, those hoping to be immortalised as 'the one who stood for truth' would perhaps do well to heed the observation of Justice Scalia of the US Supreme Court that dissents "need not be read after the date of their issuance".[25]

There are other perceived merits to a dissenting judgment:

- A dissenting judgment "unmasks the false appearance of unanimity [where] ... unanimity does not exist".[26] If judges conceal disagreements by over-reliance on convergent judgments, this "denies ... people ... the right to evaluate and criticise ... judicial choices".[27]
- Dissenting judgments remind the public that:
  - the law is not always clear;
  - unanimity is not always attainable; and
  - there are areas of the law which are uncertain or which are capable of development and which require the dialogue which a dissenting judgment invites.[28]
- Former US Chief Justice Hughes has even cautioned against the undue pursuit of unanimity, observing that: "[U]nanimity which is merely formal, which is recorded at the expense of strong, conflicting views, is not desirable in a court of last resort, whatever may be the effect upon public opinion at the time."[29]
- Dissenting judgments serve a valuable purpose because of the benefits which flow from a "contest of ideas".[30] "Judicial history shows that the dissenting opinion has exercised a corrective and reforming influence upon the law."[31]
- Dissenting judgments help preserve a "vital inheritance" of the common law heritage whereby "each judge in a multimember panel will reach a reasoned decision on the correct legal conclusion".[32]

---

24 Gregory, 366.
25 Scalia, 42.
26 Flanders, 406.
27 Kirby (2005), 5.
28 Steel, 145.
29 Hughes, 68.
30 Steel, 144.
31 Carter, 118.
32 Hogg and Amarnath, 129.

- As former US Chief Justice Harlan Stone has noted, a dissenting judgment, with its appeal to scholarship, history and reason, "sounds a warning note [to a majority/court] that legal doctrine must not be pressed too far".[33]
- Paradoxically, a dissenting judgment also restores "power and influence to the truly unanimous judicial opinion".[34]
- Issuance of a dissenting judgment is a hallmark of a process that has integrity as its focus, providing reassurance to the public that judges are trying to do right by the law.[35]
- A "dissent ... expose[s] the deliberative character of ... decision-making"[36] and affirms public faith that what unfolds behind court doors is a careful consideration of the issues at stake.
- A dissenting judgment keeps an appellate court in the vanguard of the law's intellectual development,[37] placing it "center stage for significant legal debate".[38]
- Even if a dissenting judgment eventually goes unpublished, it "serve[s] the internal corrective functions of checking the court's preliminary thinking".[39]
- A dissenting judgment indicates to a losing party that her arguments were heard.[40]
- A dissenting judgment can aid in a more complete resolution of a case.[41]
- As a literary accomplishment, a dissenting judgment often "exude[s] an infused passion, an expressive potency, and even a tell-tale hint or two of not-so-latent literary leanings – together with other dynamic and imaginative qualities that are typically lacking in more homogenized majority opinions".[42]
- A dissenting judgment can provide solace to a trial judge who

---

33 Stone (1942), 78.
34 Flanders, 406.
35 Lipez, 347.
36 Stack, 2236.
37 Flanders, 407.
38 Scalia, 39.
39 Flanders, 409.
40 See Steel, 145.
41 McIntyre, 457.
42 Flanders, 410.

is being reversed,[43] though this is a minor concern and rather assumes that a trial judge may perceive herself to be in need of solace.
- The process of dissent can contribute to the personal satisfaction experienced by appellate court judges (admittedly another minor point). Writing in this regard, William Douglas, a onetime US Supreme Court Justice, has even suggested that: "[T]he right to dissent is the only thing that makes life tolerable for a judge of an appellate court."[44]

Despite being generally supportive of dissenting judgments, Lord Bingham considers that there are some instances in which a single judgment of an appellate court better serves the rule of law:
- judgments on issues of professional conduct/responsibility;
- judgments concerned with criminal law and practice; and
- judgments issued in instances where the law has become unduly complex and requires "a single lapidary and authoritative statement setting out the law shorn of ... superfluous excrescences".[45]

When it comes to criminal law and practice, Bingham's view – though now perhaps the prevailing view – is not uncontroversial. Half a century ago, Lord Reid took a contrary stance, observing:

For a time it was customary in the House of Lords to have only one speech in criminal appeals. But after the disaster of Smith v DPP we changed that. I don't believe that decision would have been so bad if there had been more than one speech. Differences would have been expressed which would have taken the edge off it.[46]

There is much to recommend this view. There is also a danger with composite judgments that the law to some extent may be 'set in aspic'. Perhaps the ideal compromise between 'Bingham-ites' and 'Reid-ites' lies in the pragmatic approach canvassed for by Lord Neuberger:

---

43 Steel, 145.
44 Douglas (1960), 4.
45 Bingham, T (2009), 610–12.
46 Reid, 29. *DPP v Smith* [1961] AC 290 (HL) had indicated that 'grievous bodily harm' (as an element of intent for murder) meant 'really serious harm'. This conclusion was "highly controversial" (Keane (2002), 3). Reid was a law lord when Smith was decided; however, he was not on the panel that decided it, which may explain why he was so candid in the above-quoted observations.

> *Where the law is being developed in a significant area on a case-by-case basis there will be much to be said for a multi-judgment decision so that ... judges, lawyers and academics can feel their way in a discursive manner. Where a practical rule is being propounded for application in the County Courts, it is ... better to have a single authoritative judgment.*[47]

Paradoxically, it is possible to dissent without writing a dissenting judgment. Thus, it has been suggested that while "it is of the first importance that every judge [on a multi-judge panel] should decide each case conscientiously ... that does not mean that one must publish a separate judgment".[48] However, the US Federal Judicial Center has in the past observed that: "Rarely should a judge dissent without opinion; doing so communicates no information."[49] To utilise a renowned, if perhaps apocryphal, observation of the Duke of Wellington: if a judge dissents, she should likely "publish and be damned!"[50]

The motives that may prompt a dissenting judge to dissent – some of which have been touched upon already as advantages of the dissenting judgment – include the following:

- a perceived need to protest "because you cannot abide the result";[51]
- because there may be scope for dissent in the "glorious generalities" of the law;[52]
- to offer a consolation prize to the loser – that is, "you feel so strongly about the wrongness of an outcome that you want the losing party to know it";[53]
- because in the judgment writing stage a judgment has become a minority judgment and ought not to go wasted;[54] or
- because one considers that there is a want of sensitivity in the trial judge's approach.[55]

---

47 (November 2009), para 24.
48 Keane, P, 18.
49 Federal Judicial Center (2013), 29.
50 See Longford, 110.
51 Lipez, 328.
52 *Ibid*, 330.
53 *Ibid*.
54 *Ibid*, 331.
55 *Ibid*, 333.

6. Dissenting and concurring judgments

Perhaps the most innovative recent analysis done on why/when judges dissent is the law and economics analysis undertaken by Epstein, Landes and Posner. They offer a theory of dissent grounded on self-interest, done by reference to judges with life tenure:

> *[Such] judges have leisure preference or ... effort aversion, which they trade off against their desire to have a good reputation and to express their legal and policy beliefs and preferences ... We use this model to explore the phenomenon of judicial dissents, and in particular what we call 'dissent aversion,' which sometimes causes a judge not to dissent even when he disagrees with the majority.*[56]

A consideration of this line of analysis is outside the scope of this work, though one has to wonder whether "dissent aversion" is but a 'law and economics' recognition of what might euphemistically be described as judicial inertia.

Notwithstanding the advantages touched upon above, there are also perceived drawbacks to the issuance of dissenting judgments. A first perceived drawback of dissenting judgments is that they can yield "harm ... to the institution [of a court] ... especially ... in the case of ... persistent dissent over a particular issue".[57] So, for example, when it comes to the US Supreme Court, there is a sense among some commentators that "individualistic judging"[58] (of which dissenting judgments are, arguably, a symptom) is harming that court; and that "[a] return to institutional judging will restore the power of dissent and foster stability, predictability, and respect for constitutional law".[59] Remarkably, given the scale of dissent that presents within the modern US Supreme Court, from 1923 to 1972 the American Bar Association (ABA) Code of Judicial Ethics contained the following anti-dissent observation (inserted at the behest of onetime US Chief Justice Taft):

> *A judge should not yield to pride of opinion or value more highly his individual reputation than that of the court to which he should be loyal. Except in case of conscientious difference of opinion on fundamental principle dissenting opinions should be discouraged in courts of last resort.*[60]

---

56 Epstein *et al*, 102.
57 Lynch (2003), 768.
58 Bennett, 255.
59 *Ibid*.
60 See Alder, 244.

In truth, the just-quoted segment of the old ABA Code seems disparaging of judges, suggesting that a dissenting judge – who has taken a judicial oath of office – might elect to contravene that oath and take the view that a majority judgment is wrong not because she believes that to be so, but rather because of "pride of opinion" or some sense of "individual reputation". The ABA provision perhaps derived from a perception that there is an "institutional connection"[61] between a court and the rule of law, with dissenting judgments challenging the perception of a court's decisions as legally determinate.[62] However, there is a contrary view that the institutional approach "reflects the misguided notion that the authority of the law depends on the myth of the one right answer".[63] Fuld, a onetime American judge, perhaps puts matters best in this regard:

Dissents ... destroy the illusion of absolute certainty and ... judicial infallibility, but ... the reputation and prestige of a court ... depend on something stronger and more substantial than ... illusion. Certainty ... and flawless adjudication may be highly desirable ideals. We are not, however, discussing whether we shall ever attain them, but only whether we should seek to maintain the appearance of an impeccability which does not ... exist. We should not deplore the destruction of this illusion. Honest and reasonable disagreement exists in every field.[64]

Additionally, in a system which allows a majority view to prevail in the face of a dissenting view, the majority view enjoys all the legitimacy it requires.[65]

A second perceived drawback of dissenting judgments springs from the sense that an unmitigated quest for convergence in judgment writing could, by stifling clarification of legal principle, "be counter-productive and ... serve to undermine the clarity, ascertainability and predictability of the law".[66] A third perceived drawback is the imprecision of language to which a dissenting judge may succumb because her words do not have legal effect.[67] A fourth

---

61   Stack, 2239.
62   *Ibid*, 2244.
63   Lipez, 313.
64   Fuld, 928.
65   Scalia, 35.
66   Bagaric and MacConvill, 42.
67   Cardozo (1939), 35–36.

perceived drawback is that sharp divergences between judges may suggest their true division to be on political grounds.[68] A fifth perceived drawback is that if dissenting judgments occur too frequently, they may disrupt the smooth running of an appellate court.[69] At the very least, dissenting judgments create more work for fellow appellate court members if they consider it necessary to respond to what is said in a dissenting judgment.[70] However, any added workload issues that a dissenting judgment presents can be attenuated by internal mechanisms within a court's working practices – for example, by "minimizing the number of circulations of draft judgments, [so as] to avoid an 'endless loop' of drafts being circulated among a panel".[71]

How should one approach writing a dissenting judgment? Steel makes a number of useful observations in this regard.[72] These include the following:

- It is not necessary to repeat the facts and history set out in the majority judgment unless one is disagreeing with those facts and that disagreement is crucial to the difference of opinion.
- It is not necessary for a dissenting judgment to adopt the structure of its reasons from the judgment of the majority.
- It is useful to keep dissenting judgments "short and sweet and focus[ed] on the essential point of disagreement".[73]
- It is not necessary for judges to "ride on the merry go round"[74] whereby the majority replies to a dissenting judgment and the dissenting judgment then replies to the reply, and so on.
- Personalised language is unnecessary; all judges are engaged in a search for justice.[75] The US Federal Judicial Center has suggested that: "When commenting on an opinion

---

68 Hogg and Amarnath, 136.
69 *Ibid*, 131.
70 Steel, 144.
71 Hogg and Amarnath, 137.
72 Steel, 146–47.
73 *Ibid*.
74 *Ibid*.
75 One cannot but recall in this regard the possibly apocryphal story told of Lord Coleridge, a noted 19th century English judge, that when travelling to court one morning, his carriage was involved in an accident in Grosvenor Square. Worried that he would be late for work, he decided to let his driver deal with the accident and hailed a cab, telling the cab driver to bring him to the Courts of Justice. "'And where be they,' the cab-driver said. 'What!', said Coleridge. 'A London cabby, and don't know where the Law Courts are at old Temple Bar?' 'Oh! the Law Courts, is it? But you said Courts of Justice'" (Manson, 361).

[judgment] written by another judge, it is always appropriate to comment on the substance of an opinion, but inappropriate to comment on matters of style."[76]
- It is important that the language used in a dissenting judgment acknowledges the difficulty of the case and disagrees in a reasonable, temperate manner.
- Dissenting judgments generally benefit from strong opening/closing sentences and paragraphs. "[B]eginnings and endings ... are particularly important in framing the debate with the majority. The beginning should explain why you are dissenting; the ending should be a forceful last word."[77]

2. Concurring judgments

Whether concurring judgments are possessed of as many virtues/drawbacks as dissenting judgments is a question which has received surprisingly little attention. What is a concurring judgment? It has been described as:

a weaker form of judicial self-expression than the dissent. The judge ... has reached an identical conclusion by a different route, [and] feels the duty or desire to set matters out in his own words, perhaps wishes to add a personal gloss ... or to address a point passed over in his colleagues' judgments. Yet ... for these self-same reasons, the concurring judgment is also a more intense form of judicial self-expression. Despite the fact that he does not differ in the result and his utterances in likelihood will have no palpable effect on the result ... the judge nevertheless feels prompted to make a contribution to its final resolution.[78]

In short, concurring judgments are (to borrow a phrase from children's author JK Rowling) somewhat 'fantastic beasts' with less clear-cut reasons for their existence than dissenting judgments:

[Though] not as threatening as dissents ... [they] raise more collegial eyebrows, for in writing separately on a matter where the judge thinks the majority got the result right, she may be thought to be self-indulgent, single-minded, even childish in her insistence that everything be done her way.[79]

---

76 Federal Judicial Center (2013), 28.
77 Lipez, 339.
78 Munday (2002a), 639.
79 Wald (1995), 1413.

Kitto persuasively suggests, however, that the good reason which exists for the writing of judgments generally "tends in favour of the conclusion that a Judge ... set out his own reasons".[80] When it comes to the form of a concurring judgment, the US Federal Judicial Center has in the past contended that "Judges should include in their concurring opinions a statement of reasons why they are concurring specially"; and that "The arguments should be principled and the tone should be instructive but not pedantic".[81]

McCormick identifies eight different types of concurring judgment that have featured in the Supreme Court of Canada, although his observations have a more general resonance:

- Bridging judgments: These agree with some of what the majority and minority have to say, but align with the majority;[82]
- 'Let me add' judgments: These agree with the majority, but volunteer some additional reasoning;[83]
- Narrower grounds judgments: These are essentially the converse of the 'let me add' opinion;[84]
- 'Except for' judgments: These agree with the majority, but except elements of same from the general agreement (they are to some extent comparable with a dissenting judgment);[85]
- Different route judgments: These agree with the outcome but disagree with the method of arriving at that outcome;[86]
- 'Ditto' judgments: These are a very brief form of concurrence which essentially state, 'As in X case, so in this case';[87]
- Seriatim judgments: These involve a succession of judges issuing their own judgment, each of which, to a greater or lesser extent, converge/diverge;[88] and
- Other judgment forms.

A number of advantages can be attributed to a concurring judgment:

---

[80] Kitto (2003), 78.
[81] Federal Judicial Center (2013), 30.
[82] McCormick (2008), 149.
[83] Ibid,149–51.
[84] Ibid,152–55.
[85] Ibid,155–56.
[86] Ibid,156–57.
[87] Ibid,157–59.
[88] Ibid,159–62.

- It shows that "it matters how a solution is arrived at";[89]
- It may encompass tomorrow's orthodoxy and/or a refinement of prevailing opinion;
- The prospective issuance of a concurring judgment may incentivise the majority judgment author/s to craft a better judgment;
- It assures litigants that the matters in issue "have been accorded fitting attention by all members of the tribunal";[90]
- It "resist[s] a simple winner-loser dichotomy and suggest[s] a variety of directions in which the prevailing point of view could be nudged in future";[91] and
- It may "enhance rather than detract from the power of the lead judgment".[92]

Writing in this last regard, Lady Hale has suggested that a concurring judgment can:
- give an executive summary to a decision;
- lend a certain 'dramatic touch';
- involve a dissociation from certain passages of the lead judgment (though this could also be seen as a form of dissent); and
- add a distinct perspective.

Ultimately, she favours "short, separate concurrences in appropriate cases":

This is not to justify grandstanding or self-indulgence. Most of this could perhaps be achieved by a more collegiate approach to judgment writing, which is common elsewhere in world where plurality judgments are the norm – for example in the US and Canadian Supreme Courts or the European Court of Human Rights. But they too allow short additional concurrences, without which something distinctive would be lost. And I doubt whether some different perspectives could always or even often be accommodated in the plurality view.[93]

---

89   Munday (2002a), 640.
90   *Ibid*, 641.
91   McCormick (2008), 166.
92   Hale.
93   *Ibid*.

6. Dissenting and concurring judgments

By way of disadvantage, Steel considers that concurring judgments can "[i] cause more harm to the coherence of the law ... than dissents ... [ii] dilute the thrust of the case and [iii] make it difficult to determine the ratio".[94] Her practice is to confine the writing of concurring judgments to instances where "[a] the majority has decided the case on a different rationale than I would have and ... [b] ... I believe that the development of the law in the area is sufficiently important for me to give my opinion".[95]

When it comes to concurring and dissenting judgments, it is submitted that it behoves appellate court judges to demonstrate good manners towards lower court judges. As the US Federal Judicial Center has observed: "Appellate opinions ... need not attack a trial court's wisdom or judgment, or even its attitude ... [and] should avoid unnecessary criticism."[96] One commentator has observed that "appellate judges are not at war with anyone"[97] – though the occasionally combative opinions of US Supreme Court Justice Scalia (some of which are considered in Chapter 10) can give the impression of a judge who is sparring with his colleagues. Côté offers the following useful tips on diplomacy and politeness in one's dealings as an appellate judge, though some of them have a wider resonance for judges at all levels:

[1] Once in a while, it really is necessary to write something firm and stern in a judgment ... On these occasions ... [u]se old-fashioned language, not modern turns of phrase ... [and] [a]void extreme language ... [2] More frequently, it may be necessary to write a judgment disagreeing with a proposition being adopted by a colleague. In this situation, do not mention the colleague at all ... Instead (where possible) disagree with the view of the party whose submission the colleague accepts ... And if no party so argued, simply begin with 'One might wonder whether [here state the proposition being adopted by one's colleague], but no party so argued on this appeal' ... [3] Remember that we all err occasionally, and that it is usually more tactful to criticize a piece of work, rather than its author ... [4] Do not say that the judge under appeal overlooked or left out vital points. Do

---

94   Steel, 146.
95   *Ibid.*
96   Federal Judicial Center (2013), 19.
97   Côté (2015), 32.

not say even that he or she erred ... Instead, say that the reasons for decision (or jury instructions) of the trial court did so ... [5] Sign no reasons for judgment beyond the routine, until someone who was not on the panel has read and commented on the draft. Such comments should touch on readability, ease of understanding, tone, and phrasing, which is likely also to detect unfortunate terms that might produce misinterpretations, misunderstandings, or offence ... [6] And remember that there is one comment which is never safe to ignore: that a draft judgment is hard to understand, ambiguous, or could be read as suggesting something unintended.[98]

One further impossible-to-ignore comment is that one's draft judgment is marred by error.

In this chapter I have moved from a general consideration of judgments and focused on two major types of appellate court judgments: dissenting and concurring judgments. In the next chapter, I bring this closer focus to bear on the particular need for briefer, clearer forms of judgment in child, family, asylum and immigration cases. I also consider how appending a 'plain language' addendum to judgments may enhance their accessibility and comprehensibility.

---

98   *Ibid*, 35.

7. Children, families and immigrants

This chapter looks at the particular need for simplicity in judgments concerned with child, family, asylum and immigration law. The chapter contends that the appending of a simplified 'plain English' note to such judgments would be (and is) a useful innovation to adopt. It also suggests that such a step might usefully be taken in respect of all judgments.

1. **'Plain English' notes**
One of the pleasures of being a High Court judge in Ireland is that one does not spend an entire career hearing a single category of cases. Instead, one is rotated between different classes of case. In recent years, I have moved from the Commercial Court and tended to hear asylum and immigration cases and, latterly, child and family cases. Three things quickly became apparent to me when I started hearing asylum/immigration and child/family cases. First, many people who come to court find the language of traditional-form judgments difficult to understand – even incomprehensible. Second, in a whole swathe of cases, the parties presenting in court just do not understand what is going on in court, to the point of throwing occasionally desperate looks to the judge as if to ask her to advise what on earth is happening. (I always respond to such looks by pausing to explain in plain language what is being said/done.) Third, in child law proceedings, traditional-form judgments are "usually impenetrable to the children directly affected by them".[1]

With all the above in mind, when doing child/family/asylum/immigration cases, I now generally append to my judgments a note in which I try to set out clearly what a particular judgment means

---

1   Stalford and Hollingsworth, 1035.

for the child, the family member/s, the asylum seeker, the immigrant or other parties involved. After all, "the law does not belong to lawyers, judges or law professors – it belongs to the people who come before the courts to have their disputes resolved".[2] As new generations of people come before the courts, it is necessary for the court system to re-legitimate itself as an arbiter of disputes that is fit for purpose when it comes to society's evolving needs. Kane touches on this point when he writes of the International Criminal Court that to ensure its continuing legitimacy, it must "create and deliver a product that is needed and wanted by its consumer base".[3] That is an observation which, it is submitted, has a much wider resonance.

The idea of appending a 'plain English' note to a judgment is different from the approach adopted by the English judge, Mr Justice Jackson, in *Re A: A Letter to a Young Person*,[4] where he wrote the entirety of his judgment in the form of a note to the affected child. Instead, I write the judgment in a traditional form and attach a simple explanation of the judgment in the form of a note to the affected child/immigrant, etc. That way, the lawyers get the legal judgment that they have come looking for and the child/immigrant, etc gets a distilled version of the judgment. Other approaches have been tried. Thus, Mr Justice Jackson also wrote a plain English judgment in *Lancashire County Council v M*,[5] though in a more conventional form than in *Re A*. Sheriff Anwar, a Scottish judge, also took a 'child-friendly' approach to the form of the judgment that she wrote and delivered in *Mr Patrick v Mrs Patrick*, a parental contact dispute.[6] That seems to have been a one-off case in which the sheriff was advised that it was necessary that the children hear the decision as to contact from a neutral third person. As with Mr Justice Jackson, the sheriff's letter is a model of clarity and a useful resource in terms of identifying the type of text that can be used in such correspondence.

In part, these differing efforts can be seen as part of a global evolution of judgment writing. Writing at the turn of the century,

---

2 Sharpe (2002), 611.
3 Kane, 8.
4 [2017] EWFC 48 (HC).
5 [2016] EWFC 9 (HC).
6 [2017] Lexis Citation 282.

Chief Justice McLachlin of Canada observed of the Canadian judiciary – though a similar trend is discernible in judgments from courts of other jurisdictions – that judges are becoming increasingly aware that getting the right answer to a tricky legal question is not enough; and that "we can maintain and enhance public confidence in the legal system not only by providing quality service, but also by doing so in a compassionate, respectful way".[7]

My approach of appending to a judgment a 'plain language' note summarising the effect of a judgment, offers, it is submitted, a practical answer to the question posed by Mr Justice Munby, then the president of the Family Division of the High Court of England and Wales, when in a public lecture on the involvement of children and vulnerable persons in the justice system, he asked:

> *Should the judge be writing a letter for the child to read today, written in the kind of language appropriate for the child having regard to their present age or understanding? Or should the judge be writing a letter for the child to be read by the child at some – and if so what – point in the future?*[8]

Providing a technical judgment that is, to borrow from the United States' Plain Writing Act 2010, "clear, concise, well-organized and [which] follows other best practices appropriate to the subject or field and intended audience",[9] followed by a 'plain language' note, one achieves, it seems to me, the two objectives identified by Mr Justice Munby. Thus, one provides texts that can be understood now and in the future by the child (including when she becomes an adult) and also the relevant legal audience. Notably, Mr Justice Munby also highlights the risks of issuing the final judgment in child law cases in unwritten *ex tempore* form. Doing so means that there will be children who will have no idea in the future as to why a judge made a particular decision, and "Knowledge of who one is, who one's family is (or was) ... is fundamental to ... human beings ... [and] an aspect of ... private life which ... the European Convention on Human Rights requires the State to respect".[10]

---

7 McLachlin (2002), 280.
8 Munby, 6.
9 124 Stat 2862, s 3(3).
10 Munby, 6.

Writing a simplified addendum to a judgment also neatly advances the therapeutic potential of judgments, both in the child law context and more generally, with one Canadian commentator observing as follows:

Applying a similar approach to the child protection context has the potential to yield therapeutic benefits. A negative judgment in a child protection matter can, for example, acknowledge parents' strengths and positive motivations. Inclusion of this information has the potential of providing the parent with the comfort that their efforts, and usually their love for the child, were recognized, even though the frailties of their position have led to them ultimately being found unable to continue caring for their child.[11]

In 2021, a photograph of one of my end-of-judgment notes was posted on Twitter along with a kind remark. Within a couple of days, almost 20,000 people indicated that they liked the note and hundreds of people made constructive comments. A few days later, my judicial assistant drew my attention to what had happened. I read the online comments and found them interesting for a number of reasons. First, they were overwhelmingly positive. So I knew that I was, to use a colloquialism, 'on to something' in terms of a helpful evolution of my judgment-writing style. Second, some of the observations gave a helpful sense of how I might improve further on what I had done, even pointing to some useful literature in this regard. Third, a number of commentators suggested that end-of-judgment notes need not be confined to children's cases. (They did not know that I was doing something similar in asylum/immigration cases also; however, I agree with their suggestion that this approach could be more widely deployed.) Fourth, with so much brainpower brought to bear by so many well-intentioned people, I was given something of a 'roadmap' by which to navigate how I might improve what I was doing.

The various tweets suggested the following:
- There is an appetite for an explanatory note at the end of judgments.
- When writing such a note, a useful exercise is not to write as the judge, but to write it through the mind-set of the recipient/s.

---

11 Kierstead, 39.

- Kindness and a want of condescension are necessary traits of any such note.
- If the addressee is being addressed in anonymous terms, it is useful to explain why this is being done.
- While some level of standardisation will inevitably creep in, it is important that each note be personalised.
- Each note should be down to earth, hopeful, respectful, empathetic and informative.
- Short sentences and the simplest vocabulary should be used (it cannot be too simple).
- Multi-syllable words are best avoided.
- It is useful to include a line in judgments aimed at children requesting that a lawyer or guardian *ad litem* should take the time to read the note with/to the addressee and make sure that the child understands it.
- There is no reason why similar explanatory notes cannot be appended to all judgments. As CS Lewis once wrote in an essay on writing for children (which I consider hereinafter), "the neat sorting-out of books into age-groups, so dear to publishers, has only a very sketchy relation with the habits of any real readers".[12] Likewise, to suggest that simplified text belongs only in children's judgments is to diminish child-litigants and other litigants alike.

What might children think of child-friendly judgments? Research done under the auspices of the Council of Europe suggests that they would welcome it: "[C]hildren ... [are] critical of many officials ... for not respecting them, for not appreciating their special needs as children and for not showing them empathy ... [C]hildren want to be heard, they want to receive information in a form that they can understand."[13]

Herz, a one-time German judge, writing in a related vein, recalls "sitting on the bench and seeing a young defendant's eyes searching mine, desperate to make a personal emotional contact".[14] In civil cases, my experience is that children want kindness and respect

---

12 Lewis, CS, 3.
13 Kilkelly, 39.
14 Herz, R, 132.

because they think kindness and respect are owing to them as people – and they are right to think so.

Consistent with the sense that, consequent upon the UN Convention on the Rights of the Child (1989), judges have a *duty* to enhance the access and availability of child citizens to justice, the Council of Europe in 2010 adopted a series of 'Child Friendly Justice Guidelines'. (These guidelines find echo in the 'Guidelines on Children in Contact with the Justice System' adopted in 2017 by the International Association of Youth and Family Judges and Magistrates.) A number of the guidelines point to the need for a transformation of traditional judgment styles when it comes to children:

> 49. *Judgments and court rulings affecting children should be duly reasoned and explained to them in language that children can understand, particularly those decisions in which the child's view and opinions have not been followed ...*
>
> 75. *The child's lawyer, guardian ad litem or legal representative should communicate and explain the given decision or judgment to the child in a language adapted to the child's level of understanding and should give the necessary information on possible measures that could be taken, such as appeal of independent complaint mechanisms ...*
>
> 124. *... [C]hild-friendly justice ... implies that children understand the nature and scope of the decision taken, and its effects. While the judgment and the motivation thereof cannot always be recorded and explained in child-friendly wording, due to legal requirements, children should have those decisions explained to them, either by their lawyer or another appropriate person (parent, social worker, etc.).*

My own experience suggests that Guideline 124 is not entirely correct. Sometimes the substantive issues in child proceedings are complex and the law needs to be reasoned through in detail. However, while reality can sometimes seem "resistant to explanation by simplification",[15] I have yet to encounter an issue/response that cannot be distilled into a child-friendly note that can be

---

15   *Ibid.*

appended to a judgment. And ultimately, who better to explain to a child what she has decided than the deciding judge herself?

Stalford and Hollingsworth, in an engaging article, have pointed to a number of objections that might be and/or have been raised by judges about conveying the outcome of their decisions directly to parties, in particular children. These are considered below.

First, there may be concern about exposing children to sensitive information that might impact on familial relationships.[16] (I share such concerns. However, in terms of the notes that I append to judgments, I have not found this to be a real concern. This is because such notes largely reflect the conclusions reached and explain them in child-friendly language. Regardless of the form of judgment that issues, a child will obviously learn of the judge's conclusions. It cannot but help a child for an explanation of those conclusions to be furnished by the judge in language that is clear but not condescending.)

Second, judges are often required to deal with complex factual and legal issues that may be too technical or nuanced to capture in a judgment addressed directly to a child.[17] (I am respectfully unconvinced that this is so. To the extent that it is true, this does not, it is submitted, offer good reason why a comprehensive technical judgment cannot be followed by a child-friendly explanation.)

Third, demands for efficiency in the justice system may run contrary to the additional work involved in "seemingly superfluous and time-consuming innovations in the form of child-friendly judgments".[18] (I am not myself sure that this is a convincing proposition when it comes to appending a child-friendly explanation to a technically complex judgment. Immediately after writing a complex judgment, when its every nuance is still fresh in my mind, I find it takes little time to reduce the substance and thrust of a judgment to a 'plain language' note.)

Fourth, the independence of the judiciary means that judges may legitimately resist incursions on their freedom to decide the form and tone of their judgments.[19] (I respectfully do not agree with

---

16 Stalford and Hollingsworth, 1039.
17 *Ibid*, 1040.
18 *Ibid*.
19 *Ibid*.

this line of possible resistance. The concept of judicial independence has never extended to writing judgments that are incomprehensible to their recipients and the traditional judgment form is beyond comprehensible for many.)

Fifth, judges may consider that their neutrality and impartiality would be compromised by a "more 'involved', emotive" form of judgment.[20] (However, detached language does not make one any less 'involved'. It is difficult, in particular, to see how a detached document followed by an explanatory note of that detached language renders a judge more 'involved' than she already is.)

Sixth, there may be a concern that simplified text is less precise. Questions arise, it might be suggested, "as to whether a judge can alter the words and style of a judgment ... whilst still retaining the [precision] ... required for an 'appeal-proof' decision ... [T]hrough simplification ... the persuasive power of [a] ... judgment may be lost too".[21] (A number of observations might be made regarding this concern. There is, it is submitted, no such thing as an 'appeal-proof' decision. If an appellate court would have done things differently, it will decide matters so. The judgments of Lord Denning are proof that simplification enhances comprehensibility and persuasiveness.)

In truth, there seems to be no ethical or legal reason why a judgment cannot be written in a manner that meets Lord Bingham's gold standard of brevity, clarity and simplicity. And there is legal basis – not least in the UN Convention on the Rights of the Child and (for Europeans) the fair trial provisions of the European Convention on Human Rights (Article 6) – for the issuance of intelligible judgments. "The uniquely universal vulnerability of children ... demands that this obligation ... extends to them with force."[22] But there is another reason for brevity, clarity and simplicity that is evident from the tweets that I have referred to above: judges are perceived by many people as the physical embodiment of the legal system – that is, the human link between law/justice and litigants. It therefore behoves all judges, it is submitted, to show that the legal/justice system has feeling and is caring. These relational attrib-

---

20 *Ibid*, 1041.
21 *Ibid*.
22 *Ibid*, 1043.

utes of their role seem better achieved through judgments which take the time to explain their substance in age and litigant-appropriate language. Why age and litigant appropriate? Because although the six comments drawn from Stalford and Hollingsworth are concerned with judgments that issue to children, they have a resonance in the area of family law more generally in areas such as asylum and immigration, where one is treating with people who may not have perfect English, and in cases when one is treating with persons with intellectual disabilities. (Indeed, not unlike the UN Convention on the Rights of the Child, the UN Convention on the Rights of Persons with Disabilities (2007) requires that justice be accessible to persons with disabilities.) In truth, the case for simplification applies generally to all forms of judgment – not least, though not only because, when it comes to the wider public, complex judgments require deconstruction and "when law is [so] transmitted ... distortions are bound to occur".[23]

2. Practical steps for producing child-friendly judgments

In terms of practical steps that can be taken as regards producing child-friendly judgments (and judgments that are more 'friendly' to litigants generally), the following useful measures have been identified:

First, children and young people's views and lived experiences should be the starting point for developing the resource ... Second, the resource should be easy to follow ... Third, the resource should focus on facilitating understanding, rather than just conveying information. Fourth [and in terms of judgment writing, this seems to be a key point], a child friendly resource has to be appealing, requiring presentation in a format or range of formats that children will want to use. They should not be too lengthy or complicated and the amount of text used should be kept to a minimum ... Key points or words should be emphasised through repetition.[24]

Are there any wider rules when it comes to writing judgments for children? There is an abundance of texts on writing for children generally. However, perhaps the best advice in this regard has been given by CS Lewis, author of *The Chronicles of Narnia* and so one of

---

23 Wolff, 1041.
24 Marshall *et al*, 213–14.

the all-time 'greats' of children's literature, as well as a leading intellectual of the 20th century. In his essay, "On Three Ways of Writing for Children", Lewis makes various observations that can be brought to bear in the context of judgment writing.

First, Lewis is opposed to the notion of children as a special public, to whom one gives what they want, however unpleasant it may seem to the author. He considers that it is not possible – in truth, it is disrespectful – "to regale the child with things calculated to please but regarded by yourself with indifference or contempt".[25] In the judgment-writing context, what Lewis effectively points to in this regard is the need to show empathy and avoid condescension.

Second, Lewis observes how "[i]n any personal relation the two participants modify each other". The process of hearing and adjudging upon a case is intensely personal. For example, a trial judge spends hours with people in a courtroom. She then goes home and spends hours in their imagined company as she constructs her judgment. She then issues to the parties a judgment written by her for the parties. So, for all that the language of a judgment may be detached, it is actually a very personal (and interpersonal) task, with the judge affected by what the parties have said and the parties affected by how the judge responds. In writing, as in life, Lewis observes: "You would become slightly different because you were talking to a child and the child would become slightly different because it was being talked to by an adult."[26] In judgment writing, a judge when writing for a child (and for other vulnerable categories of person) must become slightly different and be conscious that what she has to write will impact at several levels. Thus, care and consideration are called for.

Third, Lewis subscribes to the theory that one should only write a children's story when that "is the best art-form for something you have to say".[27] Bringing this to bear in the judgment-writing context, what Lewis essentially points to is that one should write with children in mind when writing a child law judgment. However, this does not mean that simplicity is to be avoided when writing judgments for other audience categories.

---

25   Lewis, CS, 1.
26   *Ibid*.
27   *Ibid*.

Fourth, Lewis observes that: "*Sentimentality* is apt to creep in if we write at length about children as seen by their elders ... For we all remember that our childhood, as lived, was immeasurably different from what our elders saw."[28] What Lewis is getting at in this regard is the need, when writing for children, to 'get into their shoes': to see the world as they see it and to write accordingly. This goes back to the point, made above, that when writing for children and other vulnerable persons, a judge should 'get into their shoes' and view the world through their mind-set.

Fifth, Lewis posits that "a children's story ... enjoyed only by children is a bad children's story".[29] By this he means that when a children's story is the right form in which to recount a story, it will be appreciated and read (and re-read) by children of all ages. This offers good reason for taking time to draft and add a 'plain English' addendum to a judgment. Unlike the judgment proper, it is likely to be read and re-read by the addressee and others, so it is important to pitch it right in terms of substance and tone. (And just as adults can enjoy the nostalgia of a children's book, an adult who was once the child to whom a judgment was addressed may in later years enjoy and appreciate the kindness shown by the judge to the child that was.)

Sixth, to judges who might shrink from writing child-friendly text, Lewis offers a useful word of caution when he observes that: "To be concerned about being grown up ... to blush at the suspicion of being childish; these things are the marks of childhood and adolescence."[30] In a sense, what he suggests is that grown-ups should not be afraid to 'descend' to childish words if that is necessary to achieve empathy. While no one wants a judge who emotes from the bench, there is nothing wrong with a judge who writes in language that is empathetic.

Seventh, Lewis suggests that writing for children "imposes certain very fruitful necessities about length".[31] In this, Lewis means that stories for children are typically shorter than other forms of story; though his use of the word 'fruitful' also carries the

---

28   *Ibid*.
29   *Ibid*, 2.
30   *Ibid*.
31   *Ibid*, 3.

suggestion that such shortness is enriching. Two points arise from this. First, when writing a judgment for a child or other vulnerable person, the need for brevity which presents in all judgments should be to the fore. Second, brevity aids clarity and enriches a judgment.

Eighth, Lewis accepts that: "A ... serious attack on the fairy tale as children's literature comes from those who do not wish children to be frightened."[32] As touched upon above, a like concern presents when it comes to writing judgments that will be read by children: one does not want, as a judge, to make an oftentimes bad situation worse by writing something that may adversely affect a child. My own sense is that this is a very real concern. Certainly, it is one reason why I prefer writing a technical judgment in the traditional style that deals with the detail of a case (and which may be read by the child when older), while focusing in the child-friendly addendum on what the immediate implications of a judgment are for the child, addressing the substance of the case at a more 'headline' level. This is more conservative (though, it is submitted, correctly so) than the stance taken by Lewis when it comes to writing potentially frightening fairy tales:

> *Those who say that children must not be frightened may mean two things. They may mean (1) that we must not do anything likely to give the child those haunting, disabling, pathological fears against which ordinary courage is helpless ... His mind must, if possible, be kept clear of things he can't bear to think of. Or they may mean (2) that we must try to keep out of his mind the knowledge that he is born into a world of death, violence, wounds, adventure, heroism and cowardice, good and evil. If they mean the first I agree with them: but not if they mean the second. The second would indeed be to give children a false impression and feed them on escapism in the bad sense.*[33]

Whatever about fairy tales, when it comes to judgment writing, children ought never to be frightened by the substance of a judgment, by court processes more generally and, least of all, by the presiding judge/s.

Ninth, Lewis cautions against moralising – and the same point might be made of judgments. Moralising, Lewis suggests, is likely to

---

32 *Ibid*, 4.
33 *Ibid*, 5.

lead a writer into platitudes and falsehoods. But he also considers it disrespectful, for "in the moral sphere [children (and litigants)] ... are probably at least as wise as we".[34]

Tenth, Lewis cautions against patronising children, but also against idealising them. In terms of judgment writing, this again points to the need for empathetic text that is understanding, while at the same time bringing an adult understanding to the facts presenting. "We must of course try to do them no harm: we may ... sometimes dare to hope that we may do them good. But only such good as involves treating them with respect."[35]

3. General conclusions

Much of the commentary in the last few pages has pertained specifically to judgments concerning children and child law. However, that commentary can also be applied to asylum and immigration law judgments, as well perhaps as to judgments more generally. When it comes to this more general context, the following points might usefully be made:

- Judges are often perceived as the human link between law/justice/litigants. It therefore behoves judges to show that the legal/justice system has feeling and is caring.
- Getting the right answer to a tricky legal question is not enough; it is important to proceed compassionately/respectfully.
- Many people who bring cases to court can find the language of traditional-form judgments difficult to understand. A useful innovation is to append, to a technical standard-form judgment, a 'plain language' note that sets out clearly but without condescension what a judgment means for the parties. A number of points might be made regarding such notes:
  - When writing such a note, a useful exercise is not to write as the judge, but to write it as though one were the person being written to.
  - Kindness and want of condescension are necessary traits in any such note.

---

34 Ibid, 6.
35 Ibid.

- If an addressee is addressed in anonymised terms, it is useful to explain why.
- Some level of standardisation will inevitably creep in; however, each note should be personalised.
- Each note should be down to earth, hopeful, respectful, empathetic and informative.
- Short sentences and the simplest vocabulary should be used.
- Multi-syllable words are best avoided.
• Writing a simplified addendum to a judgment advances the judgment's therapeutic potential.
• For a court system to enjoy legitimacy, it must create and deliver a product that is needed and wanted by its 'consumer base'.
• The notion that demands for efficiency in the justice system may run contrary to the additional work involved in preparing 'time-consuming' litigant-friendly judgments is unconvincing. Immediately after writing a complex judgment, the time/work needed to reduce it to 'plain language' is not great.
• As regards wider rules to writing for litigants in a manner that better meets their needs, the following might be posited:
  - A judge must be conscious that what she writes will impact at several levels, so care and consideration are called for.
  - While no one wants a judge who emotes from the bench, there is nothing wrong with a judge who writes empathetically.
  - When writing a judgment for a person of limited language abilities, the need for brevity which presents in all judgments is very much to the fore; brevity typically aids clarity, thus enriching a judgment.
  - A judge should avoid moralising; it will likely lead her into platitudes/falsehoods and assumes a moral wisdom that may not present.

- One should neither patronise nor idealise litigants. While a judge should lean towards empathy, she must bring critical understanding to a case.

In this chapter, I have considered the particular need for briefer, clearer, simpler forms of judgment. Continuing with this issue of accessibility and comprehensibility, in the next chapter, I consider how some of the writing tips of a few of the great English-language authors can be brought to bear by a judge minded to improve her judgment writing.

8. Authors and judges

In this chapter, I consider what various leading English-language authors have had to say about the art and craft of writing generally. I then seek to transpose their observations into the judgment-writing context. In doing so I proceed on the notion that: "The problem of composing good judicial writing cannot ... be so very different from the problem of composing any ... good writing."[1] For reasons of space, I confine myself to observations made by five famous and accomplished authors: Somerset Maugham, George Orwell, Edgar Allen Poe, Mark Twain and Edith Wharton.

1. **Somerset Maugham**

    Somerset Maugham is remembered today as the author of numerous works marked by elegance, restraint and a sharp eye for observation. These are all talents that a judge tasked with judgment writing can, it is submitted, usefully seek to bring to bear in her labours. In *The Summing Up*, Maugham makes various comments on writing style that repay careful consideration.

    First, he writes, one should not seek to write perfect prose, for "perfection has one grave defect: it is apt to be dull".[2] Likewise, unless a judge writes judgments that are engaging, reader attention is likely to wander.

    Second, good writing does not require literary genius. Maugham considered that he had only "an acute power of observation ... a logical sense, and [an ability to write with] lucidity, simplicity and euphony".[3] These are abilities which most good judges likely possess and can bring to bear in their judgment writing.

---

1   Gibson, W, 134.
2   Maugham, 18.
3   *Ibid*, 20.

Third, there are three causes of obscurity in writing:
- negligence;
- wilfulness; and
- uncertainty as to what one means to say.[4]

These are attributes that, it is submitted, the good judgment writer should seek to avoid.

Fourth, lucidity is a more obvious merit than simplicity.[5] It seems almost a trite observation that judges should seek invariably to be lucid, though simplicity of expression is also desirable.

Fifth, Maugham writes, simplicity "by no means comes by nature ... [I]t needs rigid discipline".[6] This is also true of judgment writing.

Sixth, good prose is essentially rococo in nature – that is, "the natural expression of persons who [value] ... a civilized life".[7] It is an approach to writing that requires taste, decorum and vigour. Judgment writing, it is submitted, is the same.

Seventh, Maugham lauds euphony – that is, the quality of writing that is pleasing to the ear.[8] When it comes to judgments, euphony seems a quality that retains its importance whether or not the entirety of a judgment is read out in court (not least as judgments continue to be written as though they were to be read out in court). Overall, however, Maugham prefers simplicity to euphony.[9]

Eighth, Maugham is un-rigorous when it comes to grammar.[10] He acknowledges that English grammar is difficult and that few writers avoid making mistakes in it. However, he cautions that "grammar is common speech formulated ... I would prefer a phrase that was easy and unaffected to a phrase that was grammatical".[11] That may be good advice when it comes to fiction writing. But when it comes to judgment writing, a disregard for grammar "can only tarnish the dignity of the court".[12]

---

4   *Ibid*, 21.
5   *Ibid*, 22.
6   *Ibid*, 23.
7   *Ibid*, 26.
8   *Ibid*, Chapter 13.
9   *Ibid*.
10 *Ibid*.
11 Maugham, 27.
12 Komar, 30.

Ninth, Maugham cautions that good writing takes time.[13] Good writing needs to be written and rewritten. In this, the judges of today have perhaps an easier time than the writers of Maugham's day. In the Information Age, the task of rewriting has become less time consuming, with what is ostensibly the 'first' draft of a judgment often being the result of hundreds of backspace deletions and retyped text.

Tenth, Maugham maintains that one should write in the manner of one's period.[14] Language is alive and constantly changing. So, for a judge to try to write like an earlier generation of judges can only yield artificiality of style and remoteness of tone. Maugham even suggests that one should not hesitate to use common phrases if they give vividness and actuality.[15] However, in the judgment-writing context, care is required if the dignity of the court is not to be diminished by colloquialisms. When I use a colloquialism, I tend to use the formula '… to use a colloquialism, [colloquialism stated]'. That enables the use of a colloquialism while also acknowledging that one is descending from the more heightened level of prose being deployed generally throughout the judgment.

Eleventh, although he encourages writing in the manner of one's period, Maugham suggests that: "An acquaintance with the great works of the past serves as a very good standard of comparison."[16] When it comes to judgment writing, it is also beneficial to read some of the past masters of judgment writing. In Part II of this book, I consider some prominent judges and judgments of the United States, the United Kingdom and the wider common law world, and seek to identify some writing tips that can be gleaned from their judgments.

Twelfth, Maugham accepts that to digress is human.[17] However, he suggests that digression must be avoided even more than saints avoid sin: "[S]in may be venial, digression is mortal."[18] When it comes to writing judgments, if a paragraph commences 'In passing …', it is probably best excised.

---

13 Maugham, 29.
14 *Ibid*, 30.
15 *Ibid*.
16 *Ibid*, 64.
17 *Ibid*, 84.
18 *Ibid*.

Thirteenth, Maugham suggests that one should "stick to the point and whenever [one] ... can, cut".[19] This seems equally good advice when it comes to judgment writing.

Fourteenth, Maugham maintains that good judgment writing is a career-long exercise. The judge, like Maugham's paradigm author:

learns by ... trial and error. His early works are tentative; he tries his hand at various subjects and various methods ... By a simultaneous process he discovers himself ... what he has to give and learns how to display this ... to the best advantage. Then, in full possession of his faculties, he produces the best of which he is capable.[20]

2. George Orwell

George Orwell – best known today as the author of *Animal Farm* and *1984* – is renowned for the sterling quality of his prose. In his essay on "Politics and the English Language", Orwell identifies a number of means whereby English can better be deployed "as an instrument for expressing and not for concealing or preventing thought".[21] His observations are readily transferable to the judgment-writing context.

First, Orwell observes that poor deployment of language, while it may spring from another cause, can "become a cause, reinforcing the original cause and producing the same effect in an intensified form".[22] One can see this in judgment writing when, for example, a tendency to write long and convoluted judgments becomes a habit, even though it is not necessary as a matter of form. The particular difficulty which this presents in judgments is that "slovenliness of ... language makes it easier to have foolish thoughts".[23]

Second, Orwell observes that bad writing is curable: bad habits, which spread by imitation (in the legal context, by judges following the poor example of compeers who write bad judgments), can be avoided "if one is willing to take the necessary trouble. If one gets rid of those habits one can think more clearly"[24] – and clarity of thought is surely a desirable end goal for any judge desirous to do right by litigants.

19	*Ibid.*
20	*Ibid,* 123.
21	Orwell, 8.
22	*Ibid,* 3.
23	*Ibid.*
24	*Ibid.*

8. Authors and judges

Third, Orwell points to what he considers are two particular excrescences of English-language writing: staleness of imagery and lack of precision. Imagery may seem something that a judge need not be concerned with; but what is a judge doing when writing judgment facts other than creating an image in the reader's mind of the salient facts? A past master at such image setting is Lord Denning, whose best judgments offer imagery as good as any novel, employing prose that is "colourful and personal ... an exuberant celebration of a self-confident bench, unafraid of allowing the impassive judicial mask to slip".[25] Some of the more prominent judgments of Denning, who "few would dispute ... was the greatest English judge of the twentieth century",[26] are considered in Chapter 11.

Moving on, Orwell points to a number of deficiencies in the use of written English that can usefully be avoided, it is submitted, by those tasked with judgment writing. First, what Orwell describes as "operators"[27] or "verbal false limbs" should be avoided.[28] This is such a common deficiency of modern judgment writing that it is perhaps worth quoting Orwell's observations and confining oneself to the observation that they apply with equal rigour to judgment writing:

Operators, or verbal false limbs ... pad each sentence with extra syllables ... The keynote is the elimination of simple verbs ... In addition, the passive voice is wherever possible used ... and noun constructions ... used instead of gerunds ... The range of verbs is further cut down by means of the –ize and de– formations, and banal statements ... given an appearance of profundity by means of the not un– formation. Simple conjunctions and prepositions are replaced by ... phrases ... and the ends of sentences are saved from anti-climax by such resounding commonplaces as greatly to be desired, cannot be left out of account ... and so on and so forth.[29]

There can be few judges who have not succumbed to some such literary ploys and it takes the sharp journalistic eye of Orwell to see this approach to writing for what it is: an excrescence. Other

---

25 Munday (2002a), 629.
26 Goff (b).
27 Orwell, 4.
28 *Ibid.*
29 *Ibid.*

deficiencies identified by Orwell include "[p]retentious diction"[30] and "[m]eaningless words".[31] As regards the former, Orwell suggests that pretentious diction is used "to dress up simple statements and give an air of scientific impartiality to biased judgments".[32] As regards the latter, Orwell observes that in certain kinds of writing, "it is normal to come across long passages which are almost completely lacking in meaning".[33]

Orwell's overarching criticism of modern English (and the same criticism can arguably be made of modern judgment writing) is that, at its worst, "[i]t consists of gumming together long strips of words ... and making the results presentable by sheer humbug".[34] Though one would hesitate to describe any judicial observation as 'humbug', it is difficult not to see, in the modern tendency of quoting extensive chunks of earlier precedents and stringing them together with a line or two of one's own text, a form of the linguistic abuse of which Orwell makes mention. What is the solution to such abuse? Orwell suggests the following:

A scrupulous writer, in every sentence ... he writes, will ask himself at least four questions ... : What am I trying to say? What words will express it? What image or idiom will make it clearer? Is this image fresh enough to have an effect? And he will probably ask himself two more: Could I put it more shortly? Have I said anything that is avoidably ugly?[35]

Orwell cautions against use of hackneyed phraseology that transforms writing into "a lifeless imitative style",[36] observing that the person who succumbs to such phraseology becomes a form of machine, "almost unconscious of what he is saying".[37] No doubt every lawyer has encountered a judgment where a judge with unbecoming dreariness recites the facts, the law, the issues at play, the arguments of one side and the conclusion, all in a manner that is as indigestible as it is immemorable.

Notably, Orwell does not seek to canvass in favour of some form of standard English. Rather, he canvasses for "using the fewest and

---

30   *Ibid.*
31   Orwell, 5.
32   *Ibid*, 4.
33   *Ibid*, 5.
34   *Ibid*, 6.
35   *Ibid.*
36   *Ibid.*
37   Orwell, 7.

8. Authors and judges

shortest words that will cover one's meaning ... [and] to let the meaning choose the word ... not the other way around".[38] To this end, he suggests the following rules, which, it is submitted, can be borne in mind by a judge tasked with judgment writing:[39]

(i) *Never use a metaphor, simile or other figure of speech which you are used to seeing in print.*
(ii) *Never use a long word where a short one will do.*
(iii) *If it is possible to cut a word out ... cut it out.*
(iv) *Never use the passive where you can use the active.* [One commentator has observed in this regard that "Lawyers love the passive voice. They think it gives objectivity to their statements. But taking the action out of writing does not add to its power. Quite the reverse."][40]
(v) *Never use a foreign phrase, a scientific word or a jargon word if you can think of an everyday English equivalent.*

3. Edgar Allen Poe

Poe's posthumously published critical essay on the art of poetry writing, "The Poetic Principle", contains several observations that can be brought to bear in the judgment-writing context. Various of his propositions are stated below and their relevance to judgment writing then considered.

1. *[A] long poem does not exist ... [T]he phrase, 'a long poem,' is simply a flat contradiction in terms ... That degree of excitement which would entitle a poem to be so called at all, cannot be sustained throughout a composition of any great length ... [R]evulsion ensues – and then the poem is ... no longer such.*[41]

Long judgments happen, and oftentimes litigants and counsel have no one but themselves to blame that this is so. If they come to court and raise a great number of arguments and cite a great number of previous cases, then they can expect that the judgment they receive in return will, in dealing comprehensively with the many

---

38 *Ibid*, 8.
39 *Ibid*.
40 McLachlin (2001), 698.
41 Poe, 1431.

141

arguments and cases raised, run to many pages. What Poe points to is a need for caution in this regard. A judgment needs to be as long as it needs to be, but no more.

2. *"On the other hand, it is clear that a poem may be improperly brief. Undue brevity degenerates into mere epigrammatism ... There must be the steady pressing down of the stamp upon the wax"* (to make an impression).[42]

Though a thorough consideration of a dispute is always warranted, brevity in judgment writing is generally desirable, especially when there is nothing about a decision that is likely to render it of precedential value. When it comes to judgment writing, there are means of shortening judgments without resorting to epigrams. The facts need not always be stated in exhaustive detail. A summary chronology of relevant facts may suffice. Venerable precedents can be referenced without the need for extensive quotes. And the arguments of each side need not be extensively referenced before proceeding to a consideration of the key arguments presenting.

3. Poe is opposed to what he calls *"the heresy of the Didactic"*,[43] whereby *"[e]very poem ... should inculcate a moral; and by this moral is the poetical merit of the work to be adjudged"*.[44]

There can be a tendency on the part of some judges to seek to write each judgment as a classical exposition of whatever proposition is canvassed for. But few judgments become classics, and even those judgments are subject to amplification and interpretation. To seek to find an enduring proposition (moral) in every case is a fool's errand. Judges, to borrow from Jacob, should "[e]schew trying to lay down the law on the subject in hand for all future generations".

4. *"[T]he tone, in composition, should always be that which the mass of mankind would adopt – and must perpetually vary ... with the occasion."*[45]

42	*Ibid*, 1433.
43	*Ibid*, 1435.
44	*Ibid*.
45	*Ibid*, 1440–41.

What Poe posits – and it can equally be contended of judgment writing – is that one's writing should be comprehensible. However, what is more interesting is the sense that tone should vary with the occasion. So, for example, when writing a judgment in a home repossession case, it may be necessary to write the judgment in a more elemental form than if one were writing a judgment in a commercial case.

4. Mark Twain

In an acerbic essay on "Fenimore Cooper's Literary Offences", Twain assails the writing style of the by then long-dead author of such classics as *The Last of the Mohicans*. His essay – despite the occasional descent into objectionably racist language (excised from the quotes that follow) – identifies a number of rules on romantic fiction writing, several of which can, (perhaps surprisingly) also usefully be borne when it comes to judgment writing:

> [1] *That a tale shall accomplish something and arrive somewhere.*
>
> [2] *... [T]hat the episodes of a tale shall be necessary parts of the tale and shall help to develop it ...*
>
> [3] *[T]hat the personages in a tale ... shall exhibit a sufficient excuse for being there ...*
>
> [4] *... [T]hat ... the talk shall sound like human talk and be talk such as human beings would be likely to talk in the given circumstances, and have a discoverable meaning, also a discoverable purpose, and a show of relevancy, and remain in the neighbourhood of the subject in hand, and be interesting to the reader, and help out the tale, and stop when the people cannot think of anything more to say ...*
>
> [5] *... [T]hat when the author describes the character of a personage in his tale, the conduct and conversation of that personage shall justify said description ...*
>
> [6] *... [T]hat when a personage talks like an illustrated, gilt-edged, tree-calf, hand-tooled, seven-dollar Friendship's Offering in the beginning of a paragraph, he shall not talk like a ... minstrel in the end of it ...*
>
> [7] *... [T]hat crass stupidities shall not be played upon the reader ...*
>
> [8] *... [T]hat the personages of a tale shall confine themselves to possibilities and let miracles alone ...*

In addition to these large rules are some little ones. These require that the author shall:
[9] ... Say what he is proposing to say, not merely come near it ...
[10] Use the right word, not its second cousin ...
[11] Eschew surplusage ...
[12] Not omit necessary details ...
[13] Avoid slovenliness of form ...
[14] Use good grammar ...
[15] Employ a simple and straightforward style.

Is it possible to distil Twain's observations into a set of rules with more direct applicability to the task of judgment writing? The following rules might be stated:

- A judge, in every judgment and every part of a judgment, should seek to arrive at a particular end.
- Every element of a judgment should be necessary to that judgment and any unnecessary element excised.
- Any person or event included in a judgment should be included for a reason.
- The language employed by a judge in her judgment should, to the greatest extent possible, be ordinary language and have a discernible meaning/purpose/relevance.
- What is stated in a judgment should be relevant to the facts at hand.
- A judge should stop writing any judgment or point in a judgment when there is nothing more to be said.
- Descriptions of the conduct or personage of anyone who features in a judgment should be polite and contained to the necessary.
- The language/tone of a judgment should be consistent.
- A judge/judgment must reason through the law, not around it, arriving at an end the reasons for which are clear, cogent and convincing.
- A judgment should confine itself to the facts pleaded and not posit hypotheticals based on alternative facts.
- A judgment should state what the writing judge means it to state.
- The writing judge should use the right word for what she wants to state, "not its second cousin".

- A judgment should not contain surplus language or evince slovenliness of form.
- A judgment should omit unnecessary detail (the converse is also true) and feature good grammar.

5. **Edith Wharton**

Edith Wharton was not 'just' the eloquent author of such works as *The Age of Innocence*; she was also an accomplished garden and interior designer, and hence had a practised eye for the aesthetic. In her work, *The Writing of Fiction*, Wharton makes a number of observations on telling a short story and the construction of a novel that are also of interest when it comes to authoring a judgment.

When it comes to the art and craft of telling a short story, Wharton makes perhaps a dozen points of interest from the perspective of a judge interested in improving her judgment-writing style:

- The opening page should contain the germ of the whole: its "trajectory is so short that flash and sound nearly coincide".[46] (One is reminded in this regard of the observation that the first page of a judgment is "prime real estate".)[47]
- Every phrase should be a signpost and never a misleading one.[48] (In terms of judgment writing, perhaps the lesson to be derived from this and the next-considered of Wharton's observations is that digression is best avoided.)
- The least touch of irrelevance or chill of inattention will undo the author's spell.[49]
- Some of the greatest short stories owe their vitality to the dramatic rendering of a situation.[50] (Lord Denning is perhaps the most renowned judge in the English-speaking world in terms of injecting drama into his judgments.)
- The author (judge) must know not only from what angle to present her tale, but also why that angle is the right one.[51] (Likewise, when it comes to judgment writing – and this would also seem the lesson of the next-considered of

---

46 Wharton, 51.
47 Dessau and Wodak, 3.
48 Wharton, 37.
49 *Ibid*, 38.
50 *Ibid*, 47.
51 *Ibid*, 49.

Part I: The theory of the art and craft of judgment writing

- Wharton's observations – it pays to think through what one means to write before one writes it.)
- The author (judge) must turn her subject over and over and walk around it before it can be volunteered to the reader as "a natural unembellished fragment of experience".[52]
- It takes genius to make an end, to give a sense of inevitability to any work of art.[53] (Genius is not necessary for good judgment writing. Likely all that is required of a good judgment is that "it should appear as a logical conclusion of facts and legal principles".)[54]
- The seemingly simplest sauces are the most cunningly combined and completely blended.[55] (In the context of judgment writing, brevity, clarity and simplicity are the product of effort and planning.)
- Deep familiarity with her subject will protect the short-story writer from the danger of contenting herself with a sketch of the selected episode.[56] (When it comes to judgment writing, deep familiarity with the subject matter facilitates the selection of the most relevant facts, thus engendering a desirable brevity, clarity and simplicity to one's judgment.)
- Wharton suggests that one should not replace resentment of "the dense and the prolix"[57] with an overestimation of "the tenuous and the tight".[58] (For the judgment writer, perhaps the lesson to be learned is that brevity should not descend to summariness.)
- Most beginners crowd into their writing twice as much material as needed.[59] (Prolixity in judgment is perhaps suggestive of a similar deficiency of approach.)
- When it comes to writing, "[e]conomy and expenditure must each bear a part ... but they should never degenerate into parsimony or waste".[60] (When it comes to judgment writing,

---

52   *Ibid*, 49.
53   *Ibid*, 50.
54   Sivakumar, 305.
55   Wharton, 53.
56   *Ibid*, 54.
57   *Ibid*.
58   *Ibid*.
59   *Ibid*, 56.
60   *Ibid*, 57.

there is something of a 'Three Bears' dimension to this aspect of Wharton's advice – that is, a judgment should neither be too long nor too short, but just right.)

In relation to the art and craft of constructing a novel, Wharton makes another dozen points of interest from the perspective of a judge who is keen to improve her judgment-writing style:

- The mode of presentation to the reader must always be determined by the nature of the subject.[61] In judgment writing, the nature of the dispute and whether the applicable facts and/or law are complex will contribute to the mode of presentation, though a sense of the audience for which one is writing will also be necessary. "The argumentative tools used ... must be adjusted to the particular exigencies of the audience."[62]
- Convention is the first necessity of all art.[63] (This is also true of judgment writing, though there may be a need for a fundamental reassessment of the conventional form of common law judgments if the common law system is not to collapse under the weight of precedent that has become available to judges and lawyers in the Information Age.)
- Narrative should furnish substance.[64] (In the judgment-writing context, excessive/digressive text requires to be excised in the editing phase so that all that is stated always advances the judgment and never unduly lengthens it.)
- A critical question presenting for the author is where to begin.[65]
- Length needs to be determined by subject. (For the writing judge, she should always be able to say "'It might have been longer,' never: 'It need not have been so long'".)[66]
- A mediocre book is always too long and a great one usually seems too short.[67] There is undoubtedly a lesson in this for judgment writers.

---

61 *Ibid*, 72.
62 Bianchi, 38.
63 Wharton, 72.
64 *Ibid*.
65 *Ibid*, 100.
66 *Ibid*, 102.
67 *Ibid*, 102–03.

- "The great writers of fiction ... all had a sense for the proportion of their subjects and knew that great argument requires space."[68] (Great judgments, like great arguments, require the space necessary for consideration and exposition of the points addressed.)
- Even the weakest novels of the greatest writers seek "to complete what in life seems incoherent and fragmentary".[69] (In judgment writing, this observation points to the role of the judge as the actor responsible for weaving all the threads of fact and argument before her into a complete whole.)
- No conclusion can be right unless it is latent in the first page.[70] (One is again reminded in this regard of the observation that the first page of a judgment is "prime real estate".)[71]
- There must be a sense of inevitability about the ending.[72] (Likewise, the end of a good judgment, it is submitted, "should appear as a logical conclusion of facts and legal principles".)[73]
- An author who does not know when her story is finished but keeps on adding additional episodes weakens the ending and robs what went before of significance.[74] (Again, the lesson seems to be that a judge should state what needs to be said and end her judgment there.)
- "At the conclusion of a novel the illuminating incident need not only send its ray backward; but it should send a long enough shaft of light to meet the light cast forward from the first page."[75] (A good judgment, it is submitted, should do likewise.)

In this chapter, I have considered how some of the writing tips of a few of the greatest English-language authors can be brought to bear by a judge minded to improve her judgment writing. In the

---

68   *Ibid*, 105.
69   *Ibid*, 107.
70   *Ibid*, 108.
71   See Dessau and Wodak, 3.
72   Wharton, 108.
73   Sivakumar, 305.
74   Wharton, 108.
75   *Ibid*, 110.

next three chapters, I consider the lessons for better judgment writing to be gleaned from the judgments of some of the greatest judges. In doing so, I turn from a consideration of the theory of the art and craft of judgment writing to a consideration of its practice.

Part II: The practice of the art and craft of judgment writing

9. Three great and pioneering women judges: Justices O'Connor, Ginsburg and Wilson

After graduating near the top of my class at Stanford Law School in 1952, I was unable to obtain employment in a private law firm. I did receive one contingent offer of employment – as a legal secretary. O'Connor[1]

People ask me about the US Supreme Court, 'When will there be enough [women justices]?' My reply: 'When there are nine!' Ginsburg[2]

When I was appointed to the Supreme Court ... many women ... telephoned, cabled, or wrote to me rejoicing in my appointment. 'Now,' they said, 'we are represented on Canada's highest court. This is the beginning of a new era for women.' So why was I not rejoicing? ... I knew ... that the law does not work that way. Change in the law comes slowly ... It responds to changes in society; it seldom initiates them. Wilson[3]

1. Introduction

Since the 1970s, women have been appointed to the highest judicial office in many jurisdictions. One immediately thinks of distinguished judges such as:

- Rose Bird (the ill-fated first female chief justice of California whose dislike of the death penalty led eventually to her "humiliating ouster from the bench");[4]

---

1   O'Connor (2004).
2   Ginsburg (2012–13), 299.
3   Wilson (1990), 507.
4   Uelmen, 150. Professor Uelmen moves on to describe how, a decade after Bird's eviction from office, she:
        remained at the fringe of the legal community and, some say, of society. She was found working as a volunteer running the copy machine at the Stanford Law School poverty law clinic. She had become ... reclusive [and] ... was then not even licensed to practice law in California.
    After a years-long battle with cancer, Bird died in 1999 at the relatively young age of 63.

- Susan Denham (lately chief justice of Ireland);
- Lady Hale (lately president of the UK Supreme Court);
- Susan Kiefel (the chief justice of Australia);
- Beverley McLachlin (lately chief justice of Canada);
- Dame Helen Winkelmann (the chief justice of New Zealand); and
- Winkelmann's predecessor in office, Dame Sian Elias.[5]

Even so, there continues to be an "under-representation of women in judicial office in many countries".[6] Given this under-representation, it is appropriate to devote a specific chapter of this book to the art and craft of judgment writing as practised by three pioneering women judges. In truth, I was rather spoiled for choice in this regard. In the end, I decided to focus on the art and craft of judgment writing as practised by three great North American judges. The first is Sandra Day O'Connor, the first woman appointed to the US Supreme Court. The second is Ruth Bader Ginsburg, the first Jewish woman appointed to the US Supreme Court and a judge whose celebrity status latterly made her something of a 'pop icon' among Americans, akin to Lord Denning's status with the British public of his day.[7] The third is Bertha Wilson, whose remarkable life story saw her emigrate to Canada from her native Scotland in her mid-twenties, become a practising lawyer in her mid-thirties and win appointment to the Supreme Court of Canada in her early fifties. All three women were great judges. All three were pioneers in the sense of being in the first generation of women to make it to the highest courts in their home jurisdictions. All three have much to teach about the art and craft of judgment writing.

2. Sandra Day O'Connor

A "great jurist"[8] and "prolific opinion writer",[9] Sandra Day

---

[5] New Zealand appears to be the only independent common law nation where its first female chief justice has been followed by a second female chief justice, thereby creating a second 'first' (and a new norm) after generations of men succeeding men in the highest judicial office.

[6] Feenan, 491.

[7] Ginsburg's pop icon status was cemented with the release of two films in 2018 on aspects of her life: *On the Basis of Sex* (a 'bio-pic') and *RBG* (a documentary film). These were followed by a further documentary film in 2019: *Ruth Bader Ginsburg: In Her Own Words*.

[8] Hall, K, 205.

[9] Brown *et al*, 1229.

9. Three great and pioneering women judges: Justices O'Connor, Ginsburg and Wilson

O'Connor (1930–) was the first woman appointed to the US Supreme Court – an appointment with which, it has been said, "the axis of the legal world for women shifted, never to return to its old position".[10] Nominated by President Reagan, O'Connor had previously served as a Republican member of the Arizona Senate and was a serving member of the Arizona Court of Appeals – itself a notable achievement given an apparent want in diversity on US state courts.[11] O'Connor was later to laud Reagan for his history-making nomination of her, praising him for building "a bridge to equality" and observing that: "Reagan knew ... his decision wasn't about Sandra Day O'Connor; it was about women everywhere."[12]

Testament to the small number of law schools from which contemporary Supreme Court justices tend to be drawn, O'Connor graduated from Stanford Law School in the same year as William Rehnquist (who was a fellow associate justice when O'Connor joined the Supreme Court and served as chief justice during her later tenure).[13] Rehnquist's advancement to the Supreme Court was, of course, unimpeded by his gender (though also facilitated by his genius). Thus, "[w]hile ... Rehnquist headed off to a clerkship with Justice Robert Jackson, his future colleague on the Court scrambled for legal work despite her top grades".[14] In his autobiography, Reagan indicates that what he was looking for in his nominee was "the antithesis of an ideological judge".[15] In O'Connor, he got what he was seeking. For though O'Connor was "quite conservative"[16] and "a law and order Justice",[17] her "open-mindedness"[18] defied "any ideological label".[19] She preferred "to work to consensus"[20] – a trait that yielded opinions in which she combined "centrist and independent viewpoints",[21] "deciding each case ... on its own merits"[22] rather than through some ideological prism.

---

10 McGregor, R, 1245.
11 Goelzhauser, 761.
12 O'Connor (2004).
13 Anon, "Stanford Stories".
14 Ginsburg *et al* (2006), 1251.
15 Reagan, 280.
16 Choper and Sullivan, 56.
17 Moore, 147.
18 Ginsburg *et al* (2006), 1242.
19 *Ibid*.
20 Hall, K, 204.
21 *Ibid*, 205.
22 Bales, 1710.

O'Connor's pragmatic approach to judging did not escape criticism. One of her colleagues (Justice Brennan) criticised her majority opinion in *Engle v Isaac*[23] as too "result-oriented".[24] However, O'Connor's style of decision making had attractive characteristics, such as:

- a preference for concreteness over abstraction;[25]
- an emphasis on responsibilities over rights;[26] and
- a recasting of issues to create "new options in resolving the dispute".[27]

Her approach was later to be praised by the ideologically different Justice Ginsburg, who observed that O'Connor's opinions "presented ... disagreement plainly and professionally. She wasted no words castigating colleagues' opinions as [for example] ... 'a jurisprudential disaster'"[28] (these particular words of castigation are drawn from the opinion of Justice Scalia in *Lee v Weisman*).[29]

Ultimately, O'Connor's willingness to seek consensus and "her refusal to cast herself into a single political or ideological mold"[30] led her to occupy a centre-field position among the court's members, offering a crucial fifth vote to 'tight' five-to-four majority decisions time and again. Her deciding vote became so critical that it was at one point even suggested that the Supreme Court should be seen as "the O'Connor Court ... not a very principled [ideologically pure] institution, but ... also not extreme".[31] In *Rosenberger v Rector*[32] – a case concerned with the university funding of religious/secular student publications – O'Connor offered a principled reason for favouring "narrow, context-specific solutions to legal problems"[33]

---

23 456 US 107 (1982) (SC).
24 *Ibid*, 144.
25 Behuniak-Long, 427.
26 *Ibid*.
27 *Ibid*.
28 Ginsburg *et al* (2006), 1241.
29 505 US 577 (1992), 644. In *Lee v Weisman*, the Supreme Court held that having clergy offer prayers as part of an official public school graduation ceremony violated the Establishment Clause of the First Amendment (whereby the US government cannot establish an official religion or unduly favour one religion over another). In his dissenting opinion, Justice Scalia also described the majority view as "psychology ... by amateurs" (636), "nothing short of ludicrous" (637) and involving "distortions of the record" (640).
30 France, 39.
31 Rappaport, 370.
32 515 US 819 (1995) (SC).
33 Appleton, 6.

and "concurrences that limit[ed] the reach of majority decisions", pointing to "the flaws and dangers of a Grand Unified Theory that may turn out to be neither grand nor unified".[34]

In a onetime article on music and law, O'Connor made a number of points about the judicial role that are of relevance to a book on judgment writing, as follows:

- As Bacon once observed, "an over-speaking judge is no well-tuned cymbal"[35] (which suggests that O'Connor preferred brevity to wordiness in judgment).
- There is a parallel between the public performative roles of judges and musicians. "However good our private reasoning or practicing skills, we are judged by the quality of what we do publicly."[36] (So it is necessary to be attentive to the art and craft of judgment writing because a judgment is the only tangible product that issues publicly post-hearing, aside from whatever order is made.)
- A key element of the judicial role is the persuasive role whereby judges have "to convince the public that [their] ... take on the law ... is ... correct".[37]
- The musicians we remember and admire – and O'Connor seems also to have judges in mind when she makes this point – "are not those who were the most original; they are those whose originality makes a deep connection to the audience".[38] (It is difficult to read this and not to recall Lord Denning and his connection with the British public of his day, due to "the appeal his pronouncements made to popular common sense ... and the simple and comprehensible prose in which he made them".)[39]
- Lawyers, like musicians, "write not just for the audience of their own time, but ... for audiences of the future",[40] noting the need for judicial courage to go against conventional wisdom and that: "In law, like music, the best [works] are

---

34 *Supra*, at 882.
35 Bacon, "Of Judicature". See O'Connor (2005), 41.
36 O'Connor (2005), 44.
37 *Ibid*.
38 *Ibid*.
39 Sedley (1999).
40 O'Connor (2005), 45.

sometimes ahead of their own time."[41] (The concept of judicial courage features repeatedly in O'Connor's writing. She has observed separately that: "[T]he Rule of Law requires judges to act with great courage ... against ... public opinion and the power of the legislative and executive branches.")[42]

- The job of law involves doing work in concert.[43] (This may be true of multi-judge appellate panels, but is less true of life as a trial judge.)
- "At their best ... law and music are a fusion of reason and passion; learning and living; erudition and inspiration."[44] One need only read an opinion of Oliver Wendell Holmes, Jr – whose dissenting opinions have been described as "written with 'cold Puritan passion'" – to see the truth of this.[45]

One of O'Connor's clerks has offered additional insights into O'Connor's approach to the art and craft of judgment writing. She did not like footnotes, observing: "If you have something to say ... say it. Don't weasel around down in the brush."[46] She always did her best to write her best opinion in any one case and did not revisit it thereafter.[47] She was very much a traditional-form common law judge, "rarely ... deciding more than she [had] ... to" in any one case, and evincing "resistance to any new theory until its implications were teased out through ... a series of cases".[48] And when preparing her opinions, she attended to the facts of each case "in excruciating detail".[49]

2.1 Some key opinions

In terms of analysing O'Connor's judgment writing, it has been a challenge to settle upon just a few opinions of interest from the many that might have been discussed. O'Connor "long criticized the election of state and local judges".[50] So her opinion in *Republican*

---

41 Ibid.
42 O'Connor (2009), 1171.
43 O'Connor (2005), 45–46.
44 Ibid, 46.
45 Frankfurter (1938), 26.
46 Syverud, 1731.
47 Ibid.
48 Ibid, 1731–32.
49 Ibid.
50 Greco and Wermiel, 25.

Party of Minnesota v White[51] is of interest because it treats with a subject on which she is known to have had strong views, thus offering a lesson on how to hold a view yet proceed judicially. O'Connor's opinions also typically evince a deep-held belief in equality, as can be seen in, for example, *Mississippi University for Women v Hogan*[52] and *Grutter v Bollinger*.[53] One of O'Connor's most significant 'swing votes' was in *Planned Parenthood of Southeastern Pennsylvania v Casey*,[54] a case which upheld key elements of *Roe v Wade*,[55] the seminal (if now perhaps imperilled)[56] American case concerning a woman's freedom of choice, while also exposing *Roe* to limitation at the state level, leaving one commentator to observe of freedom of choice post-*Casey* that it was an example of "now you see it, now you don't".[57] Finally, there is O'Connor's part in *Bush v Gore*[58] – easily the most politically charged case in which she participated while on the Supreme Court.

At issue in *White*[59] was the constitutionality of a Minnesota canon of judicial conduct which prohibited candidates for elected judicial office from offering views on controversial legal/political issues. O'Connor joined the majority judgment in its conclusion that the canon violated the First Amendment (which protects free speech). However, she wrote a separate concurring opinion to express concern about judicial elections generally.[60] Her key points were that:

- "if judges are subject to regular elections they are likely to feel that they have ... some personal stake in the outcome of every publicized case";[61] and

---

51 536 US 765 (2002) (SC).
52 458 US 718 (1982) (SC).
53 539 US 306 (2003) (SC).
54 505 US 833 (1992) (SC).
55 410 US 113 (1973) (SC).
56 The possibility that *Roe v Wade* may yet be reversed has come about because of *Dobbs v Jackson Women's Health Organization*. That is a case concerned with the constitutionality of a Mississippi law which seeks to ban almost all abortions after 15 weeks of pregnancy. Argument in the case was heard by the Supreme Court in early December 2021 and judgment is expected in July 2022. The tenor of the questioning by some of the justices at the hearing and the fact that the US Supreme Court is a more conservative institution than it was when *Roe* and *Planned Parenthood* were decided have led some to believe that the court may depart from those cases (see generally Glenza).
57 Linton, 7.
58 531 US 98 (2003) (SC).
59 536 US 765 (2002) (SC).
60 *Ibid*, 788.
61 *Ibid*.

- "Elected judges cannot help being aware that if the public is not satisfied with the outcome of a ... case, it could hurt ... re-election prospects."[62]

(Conversely, it could be contended that – at least in theory – unelected judges might refrain from issuing decisions that go against a government with which the power of advancement rests. So there is likely no perfect system of selecting judges.) O'Connor's opinion in *White*, as it happens, was criticised for having "ignored reality – the difficulty of ending judicial elections";[63] American voters, it seems, rather like state judge elections.[64]

In form, O'Connor's concurring opinion in *White* is, to borrow from McCormick,[65] best seen as a 'let me add' judgment (albeit that what is added is not so much additional reasoning as a diversion into the drawbacks of judicial elections), or an 'other form' opinion (offering a view on an issue about which O'Connor felt strongly). In substance, her concurring opinion meets the US Federal Judicial Center standard of including a statement as to why the concurrence has issued. In addition, the arguments are principled and instructive;[66] and – consistent with the observations of Lady Hale on concurring judgments[67] – it adds a distinct perspective and is relatively brief. It offers, in short, a good example of when and how to write a concurring judgment.

In *Mississippi University for Women v Hogan*,[68] a case which ushered in the "twilight"[69] of single-gender schools in the United States, the Supreme Court held the single-sex admissions policy of the Mississippi University for Women's School of Nursing to be unconstitutional. (Mr Hogan, a male nurse who sought to obtain a formal nursing qualification, was refused admission on his desired basis when a female candidate similarly positioned would have been admitted.) O'Connor delivered the majority opinion in *Hogan* and her preference for narrow opinions is obvious from the start:

---

62 *Ibid*, 789.
63 Schotland, 8.
64 *Ibid*.
65 See Chapter 6.
66 (1991), 30.
67 See Chapter 6.
68 458 US 718 (1982) (SC).
69 Steigelfest, 375.

her very first sentence reads: "This case presents the narrow issue of whether a state statute that excludes males from enrolling in a state-supported professional nursing school violates the Equal Protection Clause of the Fourteenth Amendment."[70] Having stated the critical issue arising, O'Connor then outlines the facts and the procedural history of the case, commences her legal analysis with a statement of principles (and a consideration of related case law) and then turns to the arguments advanced by Mississippi for maintaining the single-sex admissions policy, eventually concluding that the nursing school's policy violated the Equal Protection Clause of the Fourteenth Amendment (which prohibits states from denying to any person in their jurisdiction the equal protection of the law). Thus, O'Connor takes an Issue–Facts (including procedural history)–Law–Application–Conclusion approach in her reasoning. This approach, in essence, conforms to that espoused by the US Federal Judicial Center,[71] though it is also akin to the approaches espoused by Atkinson and Mahoney.[72]

The form of discrimination in *Hogan* was unusual in that it involved discrimination against males (not usually the primary target of discrimination); whereas, as O'Connor noted: "History provides numerous examples of legislative attempts to exclude women from particular areas."[73] The opinion is something of a joy to read, being written in simple but eloquent English that simultaneously belies and enhances the significance of what was being decided by the court. It is also unceasingly logical in tone and thrust; albeit that O'Connor is, arguably, a little harsh in her criticism of the minority opinions of Justices Powell and Blackmun.[74] Justice Ginsburg was later to offer two notable insights regarding *Hogan*. The first was that: "Sandra appreciated that there's nothing better you can do for a field that historically has been dominantly female than to get men to do the job as well. When men get into the field in numbers, pay tends to go up."[75] The second was that the decision 'cut both ways' in gender terms. Thus, in *United States v*

---

70 458 US 718 (1982) (SC), 719.
71 See Chapter 5.
72 *Ibid*.
73 458 US 718, 725 (1982) (SC).
74 *Ibid*,724.
75 Ginsburg (2013), 928.

Virginia,[76] a case in which the all-male admission policy of Virginia Military Institute was deemed unconstitutional, *Hogan* was the principal authority favouring women who wanted to attend the Institute.

In *Grutter v Bollinger*,[77] the Supreme Court held that a non-quota affirmative admissions policy that was designed to enhance student body diversity but involved "individualized inquiry into the possible diversity contributions of all applicants"[78] did not violate the Equal Protection Clause. O'Connor delivered the majority opinion. In form, the opinion commences with a brief identification of the critical issue presenting: "This case requires us to decide whether the use of race as a factor in student admissions by the University of Michigan Law School ... is unlawful."[79] It then moves on to a lengthy consideration of the facts coupled with an account of the procedural history and certain of the evidence. Thereafter, it proceeds with an analysis of applicable law (including leading case law) and applies the law to the facts presenting, before concluding that: "[T]he Equal Protection Clause does not prohibit the Law School's narrowly tailored use of race in admissions decisions to further a compelling interest in obtaining the educational benefits that flow from a diverse student body."[80] So again, the judgment takes an Issue–Facts–Law–Application–Conclusion approach to its reasoning that conforms most closely to the judgment-writing approach espoused by the US Federal Judicial Center.

O'Connor's opinion in *Grutter* is, arguably, a more challenging read than her opinion in *Hogan*; but overall, it achieves a redemptive clarity, as well as being inspirational in its commitment to an inclusive, heterogenous America – at points rising to the rousing, such as where she states that:

> [T]o cultivate a set of leaders with legitimacy in the eyes of the citizenry, it is necessary that the path to leadership be visibly open to talented and qualified individuals of every race and ethnicity. All members of our heterogeneous society must have confidence in the

---

76   518 US 515 (1996) (SC).
77   539 US 306 (2003) (SC).
78   *Ibid*, 341.
79   *Ibid*, 311.
80   *Ibid*, 343.

> *openness and integrity of the educational institutions that provide this training ... Access ... must be inclusive of talented and qualified individuals of every race and ethnicity, so that all members of our heterogeneous society may participate in the educational institutions that provide the training and education necessary to succeed in America.*[81]

Despite clearly arriving at a helpful end result in terms of promoting diversity (an undoubted good), *Grutter* has attracted some criticism – for example, for a perceived want of penetrating analysis of the law school's admission practices, with one commentator observing that: "I had hoped that [such an] ... analysis would force all of us to undertake a serious re-examination of our admissions practices ... I fear that [it] ... will encourage many ... to conduct 'business as usual.'"[82] *Grutter* has also been criticised for having prohibited the use of racial quotas in affirmative action programmes.[83] Whatever one makes of these criticisms, it is perhaps fair to state that the decision in *Grutter*, though liberal in thrust, also has a conservative hue.

In *Planned Parenthood of Southeastern Pennsylvania v Casey*,[84] at issue were Pennsylvanian legislative provisions that sought to discourage women from having an abortion by making their freedom of choice more cumbersome to exercise. O'Connor joined Justices Kennedy and Souter in issuing a plurality opinion, with other members of the court concurring in part. (A plurality opinion is the lead minority opinion in a case without a majority opinion; however, the various parts of the plurality opinion in *Casey* attracted sufficient but different votes as to give each of those parts differing majority support.) The plurality opinion contains notably polished prose – not least in its opening observation that: "Liberty finds no refuge in a jurisprudence of doubt."[85] Its critical element is also identified in well-crafted text:

> *Roe's essential holding, the holding we reaffirm, has three parts. First is a recognition of the right of the woman to choose to have an*

81	*Ibid*, 332–33.
82	Parkinson, 159.
83	Spann, 633.
84	505 US 833 (1992) (SC).
85	*Ibid*, 844.

abortion before viability and to obtain it without undue interference from the State ... Second is a confirmation of the State's power to restrict abortions after fetal viability, if the law contains exceptions for pregnancies which endanger the woman's life or health. And third is the principle that the State has legitimate interests from the outset of the pregnancy in protecting the health of the woman and the life of the fetus that may become a child. These principles do not contradict one another; and we adhere to each.[86]

The plurality opinion is not exclusively O'Connor's work and this is evident in its substance, which seems occasionally more lofty and less facts focused than her usual opinions. In essence, the opinion contains a lofty opening paragraph; a statement of the key issue presenting; a recital of the facts; a brief affirmation of the "essential holding"[87] of *Roe*; a consideration of applicable law, case law and legal theory; a detailed consideration of *Roe*; and the application of all that law to the impugned provisions; before concluding with yet more notably polished text:

Our Constitution is a covenant running from the first generation of Americans to us and then to future generations. It is a coherent succession. Each generation must learn anew that the Constitution's written terms embody ideas and aspirations that must survive more ages than one. We accept our responsibility not to retreat from interpreting the full meaning of the covenant in light of all of our precedents. We invoke it once again to define the freedom guaranteed by the Constitution's own promise, the promise of liberty.[88]

When it comes to "the promise of liberty", *Casey* has in fact been criticised for having constrained liberty and for having "taken the shell game to new heights"[89] – the street game in which one guesses under which of three shells a pea is concealed – suggesting to readers that *Roe* is "alive and well",[90] while reducing the fullest potency of the earlier decision.

In form (Principle–Issue–Facts–Law–Application of law–Conclusion), the plurality opinion is not very different from the

---

86	Ibid, 846.
87	Ibid.
88	Ibid.
89	Linton, 7.
90	Ibid.

form of analysis typically adopted by O'Connor in those others of her opinions considered here, conforming in essence to the approach espoused by the US Federal Judicial Center.[91]

In *Bush v Gore*,[92] the outcome of the 2000 presidential election was at stake. In that case, George W Bush, then the Republican Party candidate for president, challenged a recount that was being undertaken in Florida of so-called 'under-votes' (essentially votes that automatic counting machines had missed). Bush's concern was that the recount, if allowed to proceed, could see the rival Democratic Party candidate, Vice President Al Gore, win in Florida – and whoever won in Florida would win the presidency. The Supreme Court's eventual decision left standing a vote certification by the Florida secretary of state in favour of Bush, thus effectively handing Bush the presidency. It was likely impossible in such a politically charged case for the Supreme Court to avoid allegations that the conclusions of individual justices were politically motivated. However, there can be no doubt that the justices in the majority meant it when they observed as follows in their *per curiam* opinion (an opinion issued in the name of a court):

> *None are more conscious of the vital limits on judicial authority than are the Members of this Court, and none stand more in admiration of the Constitution's design to leave the selection of the President to the people, through their legislatures, and to the political sphere. When contending parties invoke the process of the courts, however, it becomes our unsought responsibility to resolve the federal and constitutional issues the judicial system has been forced to confront.*[93]

Equally, of course, there can be no doubt that Vice President Gore meant it when he stated in a televised address on 13 December 2000 that: "[W]hile I strongly disagree with the [Supreme] Court's decision, I accept it."[94] As an outsider, all one can say is that as the various opinions in *Bush v Gore* are written by great lawyers, one tends, as a reader, to find oneself nodding at what is said in each opinion before looking at the analysis of the same point in a rival opinion and nodding at that.

---

91 See Chapter 5.
92 531 US 98 (2003) (SC).
93 *Ibid*, 111.
94 *Ibid*, 239.

Because *Bush v Gore* was decided at high speed, what emerged from the nine Supreme Court justices was "an unlovely and hastily composed pile of opinions, dissents, half-agreements and bitter recriminations".[95] This is simply a downside of issuing opinions at high speed. As Justice Ginsburg later observed of the Supreme Court's deliberations in *Bush v Gore*:

> *[T]ime can make a difference:* Bush v Gore *yielded four dissenting opinions. If we had had time, it would have been one dissenting opinion. But the Court took it on a Saturday, briefs were filed on Sunday, argument on Monday, and opinions were out on Tuesday. There was simply no time to get together on a single dissent. We do try.*[96]

The end result was that, in its *per curiam* ruling, the court found (seven to two) that the Florida Supreme Court order of a manual recount violated the Equal Protection Clause. A smaller majority (five to four) found that no new recount could take place (because it could not be finished by the 'safe harbour' deadline by which federal law required states to have resolved disputes concerning choice of presidential electors). O'Connor's was the swing vote in the five-to-four majority.[97] However, one can only guess at her precise input into its substance, given that she did not issue a separate opinion in this regard. Notably, in 2013, O'Connor observed that the Supreme Court might have been better advised not to have taken the case at all, observing that in proceeding as it did, the court "probably ... added to the problem at the end of the day".[98] In making this observation, O'Connor was prepared honestly to acknowledge the capacity of the Supreme Court (and, by implication, its members) to err. There is, it is submitted, an appealing strength to a court/judge that can admit honestly to error.

3. Ruth Bader Ginsburg

Ruth Bader Ginsburg (1933–2020), a New Yorker, graduated joint first from her class in Columbia Law School in 1959. She worked as

---

95	Anon (2001), 226–27.
96	Metzger *et al* (2013), 23–24.
97	Blakemore.
98	Rosenthal.

an attorney (though, like O'Connor, she initially struggled to get employment) and a law teacher, and was a champion for equality and women's rights. In 1980, Ginsburg was appointed by President Carter to the US Court of Appeals.[99] She spent 13 years on that court before being nominated by President Clinton to the US Supreme Court in 1993. Her advancement from the Court of Appeals may have been delayed by the fact that she was nominated by a Democratic president and three terms of Republican presidents then followed, with Clinton being the next Democratic president after Carter. In any event, by the time she died in 2020, still a serving Supreme Court Justice, Ginsburg had been a judge for 40 years – a record almost matched on the European side of the Atlantic by Lord Denning's 38-year career as a British superior court judge. When nominated to the Supreme Court, "Ginsburg was advertised as a moderate ... but [proved] liberal on the bench".[100] (It may of course be that Ginsburg was actually moderate to liberal in her views, but that a rightward swing of the Supreme Court bench during her tenure made her appear considerably liberal.)

3.1 Observations

As with Sandra Day O'Connor, Ginsburg's personal writings offer a number of insights into the art and craft of judgment writing. So, for example, she has made the following observations.

(a)   General

- American jurisprudence is the loser if judges do not look to foreign precedents in their considerations of the law.[101]
- Humane concern in judgments is not "women's work";[102] it is the work of all.
- Academic writers are partners in the judicial search for wisdom.[103]
- "[W]omen speak in different voices, just as men do."[104] (In terms of writing style, Ginsburg saw her prose to be "not ...

---

99   Carter's role in diversifying America's federal judiciary goes generally unsung: see Brody *et al*, 368.
100   Choper and Sullivan, 60.
101   Ginsburg (2004), 329.
102   Ginsburg (1982), 275.
103   Ginsburg (1997), 832.
104   Ginsburg *et al* (2006), 1241.

immediately attention-grabbing ... but I hope ... what I write has staying power".)[105]
- "Being scholarly and being effective are not inconsistent."[106]
- When it comes to writing a brief for a court (these comments seem readily transferable to judgment writing), Ginsburg suggests that the best advice is to "keep it simple, never write a sentence that has to be read again to be understood".[107]
- "[A] lawyer who commits herself to public service ... should never lose sight of the people who desperately need representation".[108]
- "For the fact finder, fairness is the prime objective. 'Getting it right' looms larger when a court defines and applies the law."[109] (This seems a notable view.)
- In collegiate courts, there should be no written statements of position before the post-argument conference. "[A]n initial view committed to paper and circulated before collegial discussion might acquire a permanence it does not deserve."[110]
- When preparing a written reserved appellate court judgment:
  - "[t]he record defines and limits the facts and circumstances with which [the writing judge] ... may deal";[111]
  - "[t]he parties' contentions ordinarily determine the issues to be addressed";[112]
  - "[i]f the panel or ... writer spots a potentially dispositive question not raised by the parties ... invite supplemental briefs, thereby affording ... litigants a chance to have their say";[113]
  - "the author ... is ... guided, or restrained, by precedent";[114] and
  - "in most appellate cases the governing law is already made ... When a case ... invite[s] a decision moving forward or

---

105 Metzger *et al* (2013), 27.
106 Ginsburg (2002), 639.
107 Metzger *et al* (2013), 26.
108 Ginsburg (2013), 932.
109 Ginsburg (1985), 206.
110 *Ibid*, 212.
111 *Ibid*, 214.
112 *Ibid*.
113 *Ibid*.
114 *Ibid*, 215.

setting back the development of the law, 'the odds heavily favor the little against the much.'"[115]

- Some writers use "a thick mist of [legal] terms"[116] to keep the knowledge of the law "confined to its initiated votaries ... [T]his ought not to be the case."[117] Lawyers should "think and write for human consumption".[118]

(b) Dissenting and concurring judgments

- Dissenting and concurring judgments "are not consummations devoutly to be avoided".[119] To express an honestly and sincerely maintained conviction is not to violate some unwritten law. That said, Ginsburg cautions against "separate opinions that generate more heat than light",[120] quoting from Justice Brandeis' dissenting opinion in the income tax case of *Burnet v Coronado Oil & Gas Co*:[121] "[I]n most matters it is more important that the applicable ... law be settled than that it be settled right."[122]

- "[T]here is nothing better than an impressive dissent to lead the author of the majority opinion to refine and clarify her initial circulation."[123] (In an off-bench observation that points to a notable open-mindedness among Supreme Court members which sits uneasily with popular representations of them as ideologues, Ginsburg once indicated that up to four times a term a draft dissent ends up becoming the Supreme Court's majority opinion in a case.)[124]

- The most effective dissenting judgment stands on its own 'legal feet' and "spells out differences without jeopardizing collegiality or public respect for and confidence in the judiciary".[125]

---

115 *Ibid*, 216.
116 Ginsburg (1997), 831–32, quoting the Scottish-born James Wilson (one of America's 'Founding Fathers' and also one of the original associate justices of the US Supreme Court).
117 *Ibid*, 832.
118 *Ibid*.
119 Ginsburg (1992), 1194.
120 *Ibid*.
121 285 US 393 (1932) (SC).
122 *Ibid*, 406.
123 Ginsburg (2010), 3.
124 *Ibid*, 4.
125 Ginsburg (1992), 1196.

- There are two kinds of dissenting judgment: the great dissent written for a future age and a dissent that aims to prompt immediate legislative action.[126] As to the substance of a dissent, Ginsburg once lightly observed that "you can let out all the stops when you're a dissenter".[127]
- Hard cases do not make bad law; but on multi-judge panels, they too often produce multiple opinions.[128]
- More unsettling than a high incidence of dissent is a proliferation of separate opinions with no single opinion commanding a clear majority.[129]
- Ginsburg cautions against concurring judgments that register minor reservations, suggest additional reasons for the majority decision or criticise a dissenting view.[130]
- Ginsburg is critical of (confusing) concurring judgments that identify the writer's interpretation of what the majority means.[131]
- When writing for a collegiate court, one is never writing for oneself. "An opinion of the Court very often reflects views that are not a hundred percent what the opinion author would do, were she writing for herself."[132]

(c) **Politeness**

Ginsburg does not appear to have been a devotee of Justice Scalia's occasionally combative approach to judgment writing, observing:

> It is 'not good for public respect for courts and law and the administration of justice,' Roscoe Pound [an American legal scholar] decades ago observed, for an appellate judge to burden an opinion with 'intemperate denunciation of [the writer's] colleagues, violent invective, attributi[on]s of bad motives to the majority of the court, and insinuations of incompetence, negligence, prejudice, or obtuseness of [other judges].' Yet one has only to thumb through the pages of current volumes of [the law reports] ... to come upon condemnations by the

---

126	Metzger *et al* (2013), 16.
127	*Ibid.*
128	Ginsburg (1990), 148.
129	*Ibid.*
130	*Ibid*,149.
131	*Ibid*,149–50.
132	Metzger *et al* (2013), 15.

score of a court or colleague's opinion or assertion as, for example ... 'ludicrous', 'outrageous', one that 'cannot be taken seriously'" ... a 'blow against the People,' ... and 'Orwellian'.[133]

All of these observations are taken from opinions written by Justice Scalia.

3.2 Some key opinions

Ginsburg's Supreme Court career offers a wealth of interesting opinions worthy of dissection and analysis. Some of her opinions have been touched upon already. The constraints of space permit only that I consider her opinions in *United States v Virginia*[134] and *City of Sherrill v Oneida Indian Nation of New York*,[135] and her dissenting opinion in *Bush v Gore*.[136]

In *US v Virginia*,[137] the Supreme Court found, among other matters, that the single-sex (males-only) admissions policy of Virginia Military Institute (VMI) – "an extraordinarily challenging military school"[138] – denied the benefit of equal protection to women. (Virginia's primary concern, it seems, was that to operate a unisex school would destroy, at least for the initial period of boot camp-style training, "any sense of decency that still permeates the relationship between the sexes".)[139] The case was decided by an eight-person court. This was because Justice Thomas's son was a pupil at the VMI, so Thomas recused himself from participation in the case.

Ginsburg delivered the majority opinion of the court. It commences with a one-paragraph statement of the key issue and the court's decision. Next, she outlines the applicable facts, considers the applicable law (with O'Connor's opinion in *Hogan* being the closest guide to the applicable law) and treats with the various arguments made. Ginsburg ends with an eloquent conclusion to an opinion that is notably comprehensive in its reasoning:

A prime part of the history of our Constitution ... is the story of the

---

133 Ginsburg (1992), 1194–95.
134 518 US 515 (1996) (SC).
135 544 US 197 (2005) (SC).
136 531 US 98 (2003) (SC).
137 518 US 515 (1996) (SC).
138 *Ibid*, 523.
139 *Ibid*, 555.

> extension of constitutional rights and protections to people once ignored or excluded ... VMI's story continued as our comprehension of 'We the People' expanded ... There is no reason to believe that the admission of women capable of all the activities required of VMI cadets would destroy the Institute rather than enhance its capacity to serve the 'more perfect Union'.[140]

In form, her opinion roughly takes the following structure: Issue/Conclusion–Applicable Facts–Law and Arguments–Conclusion, which loosely corresponds with the form of opinion canvassed for by the Federal Judicial Center.[141]

In *City of Sherrill v Oneida Indian Nation of New York*,[142] the Oneida Indian Nation repurchased certain lands that had once been part of their traditional lands. When the city of Sherrill tried to impose property taxes on the land, the Oneida purported to exercise their aboriginal sovereignty over the lands and claimed that they were tax exempt. Given that Native Americans were given such an awful time by European 'settlers' of what is now the United States, instinctively one hopes on coming to the judgment that the Oneida will be proven right. Unfortunately for the Oneida, they lost. Ginsburg delivered the opinion of the court. Again, she commences with a brief summary of the issues and a recitation of the court's conclusion. She then considers the applicable facts, considers the applicable law and treats with the various arguments made, before reaching the conclusion that generations had passed as:

- the lands in issue were traditional Oneida lands;
- since the mid-19th century, most of the Oneida had resided elsewhere;
- the area in question had in consequence enjoyed a non-Native American character; and
- all of this, coupled with the long period in which the Oneida had not sought judicial relief against parties other than the United States, meant that they could not unilaterally revive their historical sovereignty over the relevant land.

---

140   *Ibid*, 558.
141   See Chapter 5.
142   544 US 197 (2005) (SC).

Again, in form, the opinion roughly takes the following structure: Issue/Conclusion–Applicable Facts–Law and Arguments–Conclusion. It can thus be seen as a variation of the Federal Judicial Center model or an example of the Mahoney model of judgment writing.

The facts of *Bush v Gore*[143] have already been considered above. In her dissenting opinion, Ginsburg gets straight to the points of dissent. Because the opinion was written at high speed, one also gets a sense of pathos that one does not see, for example, in the other Ginsburg opinions considered above; and her opinion, it is submitted, is the better for it. In her opening paragraph, Ginsburg makes the point that:

> *I might join THE CHIEF JUSTICE were it my commission to interpret Florida law. But disagreement with the Florida court's interpretation of its own State's law does not warrant the conclusion that the justices of that court have legislated. There is no cause here to believe that the members of Florida's high court have done less than 'their mortal best to discharge their oath of office'.*[144]

Ginsburg points repeatedly in her dissenting opinion to the difficulties that present as regards the US Supreme Court interfering with a state court's interpretation of state law:

> *THE CHIEF JUSTICE's willingness to reverse the Florida Supreme Court's interpretation of Florida law in this case is at least in tension with our reluctance in Fiore even to interpret Pennsylvania law before seeking instruction from the Pennsylvania Supreme Court. I would have thought the 'cautious approach' we counsel when federal courts address matters of state law ... demanded greater restraint. Rarely has this Court rejected outright an interpretation of state law by a state high court.*[145]

Ginsburg also rejects the proposition that there was a comprehensive line of Supreme Court case law which suggested that the Constitution impels the federal court "to train a skeptical eye on a state court's portrayal of state law",[146] positing that what Rehnquist

---

143   531 US 98 (2003) (SC).
144   *Ibid*, 136. The Florida Supreme Court, proceeding by reference to Florida state law, had ordered manual recounts of so-called 'under-votes'.
145   531 US 98, 139 (2003) (SC).
146   *Ibid*, 140.

contemplated in his opinion was a disruption of a state's republican regime by revising a state court construction of state law so as to protect one organ of government of that state from another.[147] And Ginsburg invokes the fundamental tenets of federalism "on which we all agree"[148] to show, in powerful prose, that what is being done by the majority involves, in her view, a fundamental departure from those tenets:

> *Federal courts defer to a state high court's interpretations of the State's own law. This principle reflects the core of federalism ... 'The Framers split the atom of sovereignty. It was the genius of their idea that our citizens would have two political capacities, one state and one federal, each protected from incursion by the other.' ... THE CHIEF JUSTICE'S solicitude for the Florida Legislature comes at the expense of the more fundamental solicitude we owe to the legislature's sovereign [ie, the People].*[149]

One cannot but wince at the seeming pointedness of Ginsburg's reference to the chief justice's "solicitude" for the Florida legislature.

Ginsburg was unconvinced by Bush's equal protection claim. Nor was she convinced by the 'safe harbour' argument (that it would not be possible to complete the recounts by the date by which federal law required states to have resolved disputes concerning choice of presidential electors, so why bother proceeding with the recount?), observing: "[T]he Court's reluctance to let the recount go forward ... turns on its own judgment about the practical realities of implementing a recount, not the judgment of those much closer to the process."[150] She noted too that the 'safe harbour' date did not enjoy the significance being accorded it by the majority: Florida's electoral votes could be delivered late and would still fall to be counted on 6 January 2001, unless both houses of Congress decided that the votes had not been regularly cast.[151] (In fact, had the Supreme Court decision gone the other way, this was a real possibility given that after the 2020 election, both houses of Congress were in Republican control.)

---

147   Ibid, 141.
148   Ibid, 142.
149   Ibid.
150   Ibid, 143.
151   Ibid, 144.

In summary, Ginsburg's dissenting opinion in *Bush v Gore* is a fiery, even exhilarating, opinion that avoids colourful rhetoric but manages nonetheless to be as passionate as it is persuasive. In structure, it focuses on Chief Justice Rehnquist's reasoning and makes some additional points. But while Ginsburg is pointedly critical of the chief justice's reasoning and, it seems, irritated by the majority conclusions, she never lets herself down by descending into pejorative prose. She vigorously disagrees but shows professional restraint in her language at all times.

4. Bertha Wilson

Bertha Wilson (1923–2007) was the first woman appointed to the Supreme Court of Canada. Following this appointment, Wilson faced "incidents of exclusion and hostility"[152] from some of her new workplace colleagues (though there were others who were well disposed and kindly). Wilson's biographer has described how one of Wilson's new colleagues struggled with having a female colleague, making clear that he did not enjoy sitting on panels with Wilson, describing her as "that woman" and once telling her that he had suggested she be replaced on a particular case because the subject matter was too difficult for her.[153] For Wilson, all of this must have been singularly unpleasant. It was also, it is submitted, anti-democratic: elected politicians placed Wilson on the Supreme Court in accordance with law; it was not for an unelected judge to decide in the face of that democratic imprimatur that Wilson was somehow undesirable as a colleague. It is testament to Wilson's personal character and professional calibre that she not only endured the unpleasantness directed towards her, but went on to craft multiple judgments of enduring value.

Wilson was born in Scotland, took her initial degrees in philosophy at the University of Aberdeen and then emigrated to Canada with her husband, a Presbyterian minister. In Canada, Wilson worked for a time as a dental receptionist before taking a law degree at Dalhousie University. After that, she commenced in private practice as a lawyer in Nova Scotia before moving to Ontario. In

---

152 Backhouse, 176.
153 Anderson, 94.

1975 she was appointed to the Court of Appeal of Ontario. In 1982 she was elevated to the Supreme Court of Canada by Prime Minister Trudeau (the father of Canada's present prime minister). Though ultimately it is a matter of personal opinion/taste, of the three judges considered in this chapter, Wilson's judgments, it is submitted, are the clearest to read. It is eminently possible to imagine a layperson reading one of Wilson's judgments and coming away with a perfect understanding of what she intended to convey. Though they do not perhaps have the 'fizz' of Lord Denning's writing, they consistently sparkle.

Sandra Day O'Connor considers that gender differences do not make a discernible difference in rendering judgment.[154] Wilson thought differently. In her extra-judicial writings, she pointed to "overwhelming evidence that gender-based myths, biases, and stereotypes are deeply embedded in the attitudes of many male judges, as well as in the law";[155] to "gender [as] ... a significant factor in judicial decision-making";[156] and to sexism as "the unarticulated underlying premise of many [historical] judgments".[157] She did not accept that existing understandings of law were invariably "the product of judicial neutrality";[158] and she saw a real role for women judges to "bring a new humanity to bear on the decision-making process"[159] – though one cannot but recall in this last regard Justice Ginsburg's observation that humane concern is not solely "women's work",[160] but the work of all.

There are broadly two schools of thought concerning Wilson's Supreme Court career. The first (and, it is submitted, the fairest) is that she:

> left large footprints in the sands of Canadian constitutional law ... [and] went further than her colleagues in using the [Canadian Charter of Rights and Freedoms] ... to change the way in which government operates and to raise the expectations of many Canadians, especially disadvantaged Canadians.[161]

---

154 Woodruff.
155 Wilson (1990), 512.
156 Ibid.
157 Ibid.
158 Ibid, 511.
159 Ibid, 522.
160 Ginsburg (1982), 275.
161 MacPherson, 239.

By contrast, there is a view that Wilson "breached the basic democratic principles of elected governance and accountability";[162] and that her decisions were "based ... on a subjective theory of interpretation ... [that] was ... an affront to liberal democracy".[163] As against these criticisms, Wilson would presumably respond with points such as those she made in her extra-judicial writings:

- The role of the judge is inherently anti-majoritarian;
- Constitutional interpretation is purposive; and
- In all cases a judge is tasked with resolving how a particular rendering of a right will work in a world of perpetual motion.[164]

(Wilson wrote an abundance of extra-judicial material that tends to be more interesting and profound than many judicial musings because it was informed by her studies in philosophy.)[165]

In a lecture on "Decision-Making in the Supreme Court" delivered at the University of Toronto in 1985, Wilson focused on what she perceived to be the four "tensions"[166] of judicial decision making – that is, the tensions:

- "between the desire to do justice in the individual case ... and ... to rationalize the development of ... jurisprudence";[167]
- "between attempting to achieve certainty in the law and ... ensuring its adaptability";[168]
- "between ... 'deciding only what is necessary for the case' ... and ... the [role of the] Court [as] ... overseer of the development of the jurisprudence";[169] and
- "between the judge as an individual member of the Court and the Court as ... institution".[170]

Even an awareness of these tensions offers a window onto what is at play when a judge sits down to write her judgment.

---

162 Hawkins and Martin, 1.
163 *Ibid.*
164 Wilson (1988), 338.
165 See, for example, Wilson (1986).
166 *Ibid*, 228.
167 *Ibid.*
168 *Ibid.*
169 *Ibid.*
170 *Ibid.*

Part II: The practice of the art and craft of judgment writing

4.1   Some key judgments

As with O'Connor and Ginsburg, Wilson's judicial career yielded a rich variety of judgments that offer valuable lessons on the art and craft of judgment writing. The constraints of space mean that only a limited number of them can be treated with here – specifically her judgments in *R v Morgentaler*[171] (on abortion), *Andrews v Law Society of British Columbia* (on equality)[172] and *R v Lavallée*[173] (on 'battered wife syndrome').

In *Morgentaler*,[174] a number of medical doctors, committed to securing freedom of choice and opposed to Canada's then restrictive abortion law, established a Toronto-based abortion clinic which operated in breach of the law. The doctors were prosecuted and acquitted, and their acquittals were appealed. The critical issue for the Supreme Court was whether Canada's law on abortion was in breach of Section 7 of the Canadian Charter of Rights and Freedoms (which is concerned with life, liberty and the security of the person). By a five-to-two majority, the court held that the impugned law violated Section 7. Wilson's concurring judgment is notable for its commitment to the *moral* freedom of choice enjoyed by women. Because the other majority judges took a more procedural[175] approach to determining the case, Wilson issued a separate concurring judgment.

In her judgment, Wilson identifies the key issue arising and indicates why her concurring judgment is necessary. Her opening rationale reads a bit like the justification for a dissent: "With all due respect, I think that the Court must tackle the primary issue first …"[176] Then she turns to the law, treating logically and methodically with the various issues presenting and peppering her analysis with profound observations concerning freedom, law and the individual before reaching her conclusion. Because it is a concurring judgment, Wilson can 'jump' straight into the law without much consideration of the facts. So her analysis is a near-classic Facts-Law-Application-Conclusion (FLAC) analysis of the type espoused by Atkinson,[177] just minus the facts.

171	[1988] 1 SCR 30 (SC).
172	[1989] 1 SCR 143 (SC).
173	[1990] 1 SCR 852 (SC).
174	[1988] 1 SCR 30 (SC).
175	*Ibid*, 161.
176	*Ibid*.
177	See Chapter 5.

In tone and thrust, Wilson's judgment in *Morgentaler* is a masterpiece in informed analysis and is doubly persuasive because of the understated professional tone it adopts. It is notable for its references to academic literature in addition to the expected treatment of case law (including relevant US case law). There is also a hint of Wilson's Scottish origins in her reliance on certain Scottish academic commentary.[178] The judgment is also interesting in showing the particular insight that a female judge can bring to the issue of abortion. So, for example, Wilson points with notable honesty to the reality that it is "probably impossible"[179] (one suspects fully impossible) for men ever to understand the full significance of what is at play for pregnant women when considering whether to have abortion:

This decision is one that will have profound psychological, economic and social consequences for the pregnant woman. The circumstances giving rise to it can be complex and varied and there may be, and usually are, powerful considerations militating in opposite directions. It is a decision that deeply reflects the way the woman thinks about herself and her relationship to others and to society at large. It is not just a medical decision; it is a profound social and ethical one as well. Her response to it will be the response of the whole person.

It is probably impossible for a man to respond, even imaginatively, to such a dilemma not just because it is outside the realm of his personal experience ... but because he can relate to it only by objectifying it, thereby eliminating the subjective elements of the female psyche which are at the heart of the dilemma.[180]

Returning to Cardozo's categorisation of judgment-writing styles,[181] there is a touch of the magisterial to the just-quoted prose, in the sense of its being eloquent, insightful and authoritative, even compelling.

In *Andrews*,[182] at issue was whether a requirement as to Canadian citizenship as a prerequisite for admission to the British Columbia bar was consistent with Section 15 of the Canadian Charter of

---

178   [1988] 1 SCR 30, 164 and 171–72 (SC).
179   *Ibid*, 171.
180   *Ibid*.
181   See Chapter 4.
182   [1989] 1 SCR 143 (SC).

Rights and Freedoms (which provides for equality before and under the law and for equal protection and non-discrimination). The types of issue presenting were akin to those that arose in the gender-related US Supreme Court cases of *Hogan* and *Virginia Military Institute* (considered above). The requirement as to citizenship was held by the Canadian Supreme Court to violate Section 15. Wilson delivered a co-authored majority judgment in which she briefly mentions the facts, gives a sense of her conclusion, makes some comment on the judgment of one of her colleagues (touching in particular on minority interests in the face of majoritarian rule) and then turns to the law more generally, establishing a (since modified) test for the assessment of Section 15 claims, before reaching her conclusion. In loose terms, save for a couple of diversions, Wilson's judgment essentially adopts a FLAC analysis, albeit that the facts are briefly treated with and there is some departure from this generic form.

Wilson's judgment in *Andrews* is notable for its concern for minority communities and interests, and its alertness to the threat posed to minority interests by majoritarian rule.[183] Wilson's original training in philosophy shows through in her invocation of John Stuart Mill in the following observation:[184]

> [N]on-citizens are a group lacking in political power and as such vulnerable ... Their vulnerability to becoming a disadvantaged group ... is captured by John Stuart Mill's observation ... that 'in the absence of its natural defenders, the interest of the excluded is always in danger of being overlooked' ... While legislatures must inevitably draw distinctions among the governed, such distinctions should not bring about or reinforce the disadvantage of certain groups and individuals by denying them the rights freely accorded to others.[185]

If one wanted a succinct summary of the nature and aim of government in a liberal democracy, this is it. Again, Wilson's understated but commanding style seems magisterial in nature.

In *Lavallée*,[186] the Supreme Court had to consider 'battered wife syndrome' as a basis for a plea of self-defence. There a much-abused

---

183   Ibid, 152.
184   Ibid.
185   Ibid.
186   [1990] 1 SCR 852 (SC).

woman had shot her partner in the back of the head one night. At her subsequent trial for murder, she claimed that she had acted in self-defence. This was a challenging line of defence to sustain when she had shot her partner from behind. In her support, a psychiatrist was called to give evidence on 'battered wife syndrome' ("a symptom complex of both physical (including sexual) and psychologic abuse of a woman by ... [someone] with whom a woman has an intimate relationship").[187] Ms Lavallée was acquitted by the trial jury. However, this verdict was overturned by the Manitoba Court of Appeal. On further appeal, the Supreme Court of Canada was asked to decide whether the evidence of the psychiatrist should have been called and whether the trial judge's instructions in relation to the evidence were adequate. In her judgment for the majority, Wilson identifies the key issues presenting and then treats with the facts at some length, including the procedural history of the case. She then re-identifies the issues before the court and proceeds with a comprehensive analysis of applicable law, applying that law to the facts and issues before the court, and proceeding eventually to her conclusion. Though the form of the judgment does not perfectly accord with any of those considered in Chapter 5, it perhaps comes closest to the forms identified by Bosielo (Introduction–Facts–Issues–Law–Application–Remedy–Costs) and the US Federal Judicial Center (Introduction–Issues–Facts–Legal Principles–Conclusion).

It has been suggested that: "Judges in discrimination cases must be able to put themselves in the 'shoes' of both the plaintiff and the defendant."[188] That is a proposition which, it is submitted, holds true in many types of case. In her judgment, Wilson brings a notable sympathy to bear when it comes to the problem of domestic violence, expressing in simple but powerful words why it is so objectionable, where the law had previously gone wrong and why expert evidence on the psychological effects on a woman of repeated battering was relevant and necessary:

Expert evidence on the psychological effect of battering on wives and common law partners must ... be both relevant and necessary in the

---

187   Swanson, 709.
188   Moyer and Haire, 669.

context of the present case. How can the mental state of the appellant be appreciated without it? The average member of the public ... can be forgiven for asking: Why would a woman put up with this kind of treatment? Why should she continue to live with such a man? How could she love a partner who beat her to the point of requiring hospitalization? We would expect the woman to pack her bags and go. Where is her self-respect? Why does she not cut loose and make a new life for herself? Such is the reaction of the average person confronted with the so-called 'battered wife syndrome'. We need help to understand it and help is available from trained professionals.

The gravity, indeed the tragedy of domestic violence can hardly be overstated ... Far from protecting women from it the law historically sanctioned the abuse of women within marriage as an aspect of the husband's ownership of his wife and his 'right' to chastise her. One need only recall the centuries old law that a man is entitled to beat his wife with a stick 'no thicker than his thumb'.

Laws do not spring out of a social vacuum. The notion that a man has a right to 'discipline' his wife is deeply rooted in the history of our society. The woman's duty was to serve her husband and to stay in the marriage at all costs 'till death do us part' and to accept as her due any 'punishment' that was meted out for failing to please her husband. One consequence of this attitude was that 'wife battering' was rarely spoken of, rarely reported, rarely prosecuted, and even more rarely punished. Long after society abandoned its formal approval of spousal abuse tolerance of it continued and continues in some circles to this day.

Fortunately, there has been a growing awareness in recent years that no man has a right to abuse any woman under any circumstances ... However, a woman who comes before a judge or jury with the claim that she has been battered and suggests that this may be a relevant factor in evaluating her subsequent actions still faces the prospect of being condemned by popular mythology about domestic violence. Either she was not as badly beaten as she claims or she would have left the man long ago. Or, if she was battered that severely, she must have stayed out of some masochistic enjoyment.[189]

These are notably powerful words that do not shrink from telling

---

189   [1990] 1 SCR 852, 871–3 (SC).

unpleasant home truths about the traditional treatment of women in Canadian society. As one reads them, one can almost imagine dead generations of Canadian women reaching up from their graves and applauding the fact that at last the truth was being told. And there is a place for honest, even revelatory, truth telling in judgments. Wilson, to use a colloquialism, clearly 'gets it' not only as to why domestic violence is wrong, but also as to where law and society continued to go wrong with regard to domestic violence, and what needed to be done. There is also an abiding sense in Wilson's judgment – and the same sense would likely *not* have arisen in the same judgment if delivered by a man – that the old days and ways were gone, and that there would be no tolerance for domestic violence in a modern, forward-looking Canada where a woman now served on the nation's highest court.

5. Conclusions

The following valuable lessons in judgment writing can, it is submitted, be derived from the above consideration of the opinions/judgments of Justices O'Connor, Ginsburg and Wilson:

- A judgment should avoid intemperate denunciation of others, violent invective and attributions of bad motives to (or insinuations of incompetence, negligence, prejudice or obtuseness on the part of) other judges.
- Brevity is preferable to wordiness.
- A judge is judged by the quality of what she does publicly. So she needs to be attentive to the art and craft of judgment writing.
- Judges have a persuasive role whereby, in their judgments, they have to convince the public that their 'take' on the law is right and correct.
- The judges we remember and admire are those whose originality makes a deep connection. (One cannot but recall Lord Denning in this regard and "the appeal his pronouncements made to popular common sense ... and the simple and comprehensible prose in which he made them".)[190]

---

190   Sedley (1999).

- Judges write for their time and all time. The best judgments may be ahead of their time.
- The best judgments are a fusion of reason/passion, learning/living and erudition/inspiration.
- There is a simple case against footnotes: "If you have something to say … say it. Don't weasel around down in the brush."[191]
- In treating with the ideal, one needs to acknowledge reality.
- Judicial sleight of action (whether perceived or real) is best avoided.
- In collegiate courts, time is required to prune an abundance of views into something more coherent. "[T]ime can make a difference."[192]
- Judges can admit previous error without damaging their reputation or the court system.
- A judgment should evince humane concern.
- Academic writers are partners in the judicial search for wisdom.
- Being scholarly and being effective are not inconsistent ends.
- A judgment should be simple in expression. Judges should "think and write for human consumption".[193]
- A judge committed to public service "should never lose sight of the people who desperately need representation".[194]
- "For the fact finder, fairness is the prime objective. 'Getting it right' looms larger when a court defines and applies the law."[195]
- In collegiate courts, there should be no written statements of position before the post-argument conference.
- When preparing a written reserved appellate court judgment:
  - "[t]he record defines and limits the facts and circumstances with which [the writing judge] … may deal";[196]
  - "[t]he parties' contentions ordinarily determine the issues to be addressed";[197]

---

191 Syverud, 1731.
192 Metzger *et al* (2013), 23–24.
193 Ginsburg (1997), 832.
194 Ginsburg (2013), 932.
195 Ginsburg (1985), 206.
196 *Ibid*, 214.
197 *Ibid*.

9. Three great and pioneering women judges: Justices O'Connor, Ginsburg and Wilson

- "[i]f the panel or ... writer spots a potentially dispositive question not raised by the parties ... invite supplemental briefs, thereby affording ... litigants a chance to have their say";[198]
  - "the author ... is ... guided, or restrained, by precedent";[199] and
  - "in most appellate cases the governing law is already made ... When a case ... invite[s] a decision moving forward or setting back the development of the law, 'the odds heavily favor the little against the much.'"[200]
- Dissenting/concurring judgments are not devoutly to be avoided. But one should avoid "separate opinions that generate more heat than light".[201]
- There are two kinds of dissenting judgment: the great dissent written for a future age and a dissent that aims to prompt immediate legislative action.[202]
- In appellate courts, what is more unsettling than the practice of issuing dissenting judgments is a proliferation of separate judgments with no single judgment commanding a clear majority.
- One should avoid concurring judgments that:
  - register minor reservations;
  - suggest additional reasons for the majority decision;
  - criticise a dissenting view; or
  - identify the dissenter's interpretation of what the majority means.
- When writing for a collegiate court, one is never writing for oneself. "An opinion of the Court very often reflects views that are not a hundred percent what the opinion author would do, were she writing for herself."[203]
- When approaching past judgments one should be heedful of the fact that:
  - "gender-based myths, biases, and stereotypes are deeply

---

198   Ibid.
199   Ibid, 215.
200   Ibid, 216.
201   Ginsburg (1992), 1194.
202   Metzger et al (2013), 16.
203   Ibid, 15.

185

embedded in the attitudes of many male judges, as well as in the law";[204]
- gender has long been "a significant factor in judicial decision-making";[205]
- sexism is "the unarticulated underlying premise of many [historical] judgments";[206] and
- traditional understandings of the law were not invariably "the product of judicial neutrality".[207]

- There are four "tensions"[208] at play when it comes to crafting a judgment:
  - "between the desire to do justice in the individual case ... and ... to rationalize the development of ... jurisprudence";[209]
  - "between attempting to achieve certainty in the law and ... ensuring its adaptability to [changing] social conditions";[210]
  - "between ... 'deciding only what is necessary for the case' ... and ... the [role of the] Court [as ... overseer of the development of the jurisprudence";[211] and
  - "between the judge as an individual member of the Court and the Court as ... institution".[212]

In this chapter, I have considered the many lessons in good judgment writing to be gleaned from the judgments of three great and pioneering women judges. In the next chapter, I expand this consideration by looking at the writing forms of three great US Supreme Court justices of the last century or so: Justices Holmes, Jackson and Scalia.

204	Wilson (1990), 512.
205	Ibid.
206	Ibid.
207	Ibid, 511.
208	Wilson (1986), 228.
209	Ibid.
210	Ibid.
211	Ibid.
212	Ibid.

10. Three great American judges: Justices Holmes, Jackson and Scalia

Justices Oliver Wendell Holmes, Jr, Robert Jackson and Antonin Scalia are perhaps the "three best writers" in the history of the US Supreme Court.[1] *In this chapter, I take a closer look at their opinions (judgments) and seek to identify some distinguishing features in their respective writing approaches that a judge wishing to improve her writing style might wish to bear in mind.*

1. **Justice Holmes**

    Justice Holmes (1841–1935) is a phenomenon: "as much a part of American legend as law",[2] the "Yankee from Olympus"[3] and a "patrician from Boston who made his mark on his own age and on ages still unborn".[4] (Holmes is also reputedly the man who, as a young captain in the Union Army, shouted at Abraham Lincoln, when the latter was touring the front lines during an ongoing battle, to "Get down you damn fool!")[5] Yet for all his prominence, were it not for the assassination of President McKinley, Holmes might have ended his days as a now-forgotten chief justice of the Supreme Judicial Court of Massachusetts, even if it was while on that court that "the literate and epigrammatic style for which Holmes often is now remembered began to emerge".[6] After McKinley's assassination, Theodore Roosevelt became president. Five months later, US Supreme Court Justice Gray resigned for health reasons. Under the then prevailing convention, Roosevelt needed to find a replacement justice from New England. Through

---

1   Roberts *et al*, 22.
2   Schwartz, B, 75.
3   Bowen.
4   Schwartz, B, 75.
5   *Ibid*, 76.
6   McHugh (2021), 140.

the good offices of Senator Henry Cabot Lodge, a friend of Holmes and Roosevelt, Holmes quickly became a serious candidate to replace Gray. Formal nomination came in July 1902 and Holmes' appointment was confirmed by the US Senate the following December.

Surprisingly, given what we now know as to what Holmes achieved on the Supreme Court, his nomination aroused a mixed response, one commentator suggesting that this was because "[t]he cutting edge of his mind was too fine ... for the coarser blades at the bar".[7] This mixed response is doubly surprising when one has regard to the fact that long years as a judge in Massachusetts meant that Holmes was a proven quantity when it came to opinion writing (and that what he had already proven was his singular competence):

> [He] liked to 'see a case to the bottom,' that is to see its larger legal and intellectual significance. He liked to write opinions that demonstrated that his thought process had gone beyond the question of which party in the case should prevail ... to include a consideration of the social policies, or the legal philosophy, behind those rules. He also liked to write opinions that included memorable and original language. He acted ... as much as a philosopher and literary craftsman as a judge in the writing of opinions. As a result, he sometimes wrote obscurely, which sometimes made the practical meaning of his opinions ... hard to determine.[8]

Unlike many modern US Supreme Court justices, but in common with Justices Jackson and Scalia – and there may be a lesson in this (it is submitted that there is) – Holmes wrote all of his own opinions. His productivity in writing opinions (and opinions of sometimes stunning impressiveness) was matched by a similar productivity when it came to writing addresses, articles, essays, speeches and his still-in-print masterpiece, *The Common Law*. That last-mentioned book contains the quote for which Holmes is perhaps best remembered today: "The life of the law has not been logic: it has been experience."[9] This notion of the common law as fundamentally wanting in systematic cohesion is now received logic; but in Holmes' time, it was a radical proposition, "pointing

---

7   Freund, 41.
8   White, G, 76.
9   Holmes (1882), 1.

the way to a new era of jurisprudence"[10] and, incidentally, offering a worked example of the truism that brevity is no impediment to profundity.

A good example of Holmes' opinion-writing style is offered by his dissenting opinion in *Northern Securities Co v United States*.[11] That was a case in which the Supreme Court was asked to decide whether the creation of holding companies by railroad competitors breached the antitrust provisions of the Sherman Act 1890. The government case was that such a breach arose. The court agreed. Holmes dissented. His dissenting opinion is famous for the line "Great cases, like hard cases, make bad law"[12] – a line which displays that "robust and epigrammatic style"[13] to which "his influence is due in part".[14] Holmes starts out in *Northern Securities* by acknowledging the general futility of dissenting opinions, writing: "I think it useless and undesirable, as a rule to express dissent."[15] Holmes seems, however, to think that the greatness of the case before the court merited a dissent in which he identified its particular significance in memorable terms:

> *Great cases, like hard cases, make bad law. For great cases are called great not by reason of their real importance in shaping the law of the future, but because of some accident of immediate overwhelming interest which appeals to the feelings and distorts the judgment. These immediate interests exercise a kind of hydraulic pressure which makes what previously was clear seem doubtful, and before which even well settled principles of law will bend. What we have to do in this case is to find the meaning of some not very difficult words.*[16]

The language is beautiful, though it does take more than one reading before the meaning becomes entirely clear – a common trait of Holmes' writing.

Following his introductory text, Holmes moves on to identify the issue presenting, considers some aspects of statutory interpretation, turns to the interpretative task at hand and then reaches

---

10   Schwartz, B, 78.
11   193 US 197 (1904) (SC).
12   *Ibid*, 400.
13   Balmer, 434.
14   *Ibid*.
15   193 US 197, 400 (1904).
16   *Ibid*, 400–01.

certain conclusions. In form, therefore, his dissent comes closest to that canvassed by Strong (as considered in Chapter 5) – that is, an opening paragraph or orientation, a summary of the issues to be discussed, a recitation of material adjudicative facts, an analysis of the legal issues and a conclusion. Holmes' closing paragraph is testament to the truth of the observation that when writing a dissent, "the ending should be a forceful last word".[17] Thus, Holmes writes:

> *In view of my interpretation of the statute, I do not go further into the question of the power of Congress ... I am happy to know that only a minority of my brethren adopt an interpretation of the law which in my opinion would make eternal the* bellum omnium contra omnes *[the 'war of all against all'; the language is Hobbesian] and disintegrate society so far as it could into individual atoms. If that were its intent, I should regard calling such a law a regulation of commerce as a mere pretense. It would be an attempt to reconstruct society. I am not concerned with the wisdom of such an attempt, but I believe that Congress was not entrusted by the Constitution with the power to make it, and I am deeply persuaded that it has not tried.*[18]

Again, the language is beautiful. Yet the comprehensibility of Holmes' intended meaning (and hence the accessibility of his opinion) seems somewhat encumbered by his taste for fine language. This is a man possessed of great power who clearly considers that the "augustness of the work"[19] before him requires augustness of language – though as a man who came of age in the era of Lincoln, he could not have been unaware that great issues can be treated with in the simplest of terms.

For all its occasional grandiosity, it is somehow hard not to fall in love with Holmes' overall writing style. In his opinions, he coined some great phrases, such as "The common law is not a brooding omnipresence in the sky, but the articulate voice of some sovereign or quasi-sovereign";[20] the phrase "clear and present danger";[21] and the very American notion of a "free trade in ideas".[22] But – an important lesson when it comes to judgment writing –

---

17   Lipez, 339.
18   193 US 197, 411 (1904).
19   Weinberg, 706.
20   *Southern Pacific Co v Jensen* 244 US 205, 222 (1917) (SC).
21   *Schenck v United States* 249 US 47, 52 (1919) (SC).

greatness in language does not necessarily equate to juridical greatness. Thus, it has been suggested that Holmes "was all presence, style – and is now legend", but achieved little of substance;[23] though as against that, one can set the view of Justice Frankfurter that: "In their impact and sweep and fertile freshness, [Holmes'] ... opinions have been a superbly harmonious vehicle for the views which they embody."[24]

One of the challenges facing progressive American legislators in the early 20th century was that their desire for social-minded legislation was repeatedly frustrated by a federal judiciary which perceived such legislation to be an unwarranted interference with freedom of contract. For example, in *Lochner v New York*,[25] in what is arguably one of the worst decisions in Supreme Court history, the court struck down legislation by which New York had sought to limit excessive work hours among New York bakers. Holmes was one of four dissenters. His notably brief (circa 600-word) dissent begins with a tacit acknowledgement that a dissenting judge need not always issue a dissent.[26] He then commences the mainstay of his opinion with an arresting sentence – "This case is decided upon an economic theory which a large part of the country does not entertain"[27] – and continues to the most famous line of the dissent: "The Fourteenth Amendment does not enact Mr Spencer's Social Statics."[28] (Herbert Spencer was a prominent apostle of *laissez faire* and social Darwinism. The thrust of Holmes' dissent is that the majority in *Lochner* showed insufficient deference to the determination of New York legislators that the maximum hours law was wise economic policy.)

Holmes' dissenting opinion in *Lochner* is of interest in the context of this book because of its clarity, accessibility and the way in which he manages to marry general principle with a specific conclusion. Its striking brevity does not diminish its potency and demonstrates the truth of Lord Macmillan's onetime observation

---

22 *Abrams v United States* 250 US 616, 630 (1919) (SC).
23 Weinberg, 722.
24 Frankfurter (1916), 698.
25 198 US 45 (1905) (SC).
26 *Ibid*, 75.
27 *Ibid*.
28 *Ibid*.

that: "The more we are swamped with precedents the more do we need the lifebelt of principles."[29] As one recent commentator has observed, it is nothing new to state that Holmes wrote powerfully and memorably:

> *But that ability is well worth reflection and emphasis at a time when lengthy citation – and jargon-filled judicial opinions on issues of significant social importance are all but indecipherable without the aid of a skilled interpreter. In his most well-known opinions, particularly his famous dissents, there is no doubt that Holmes was writing so that all could understand. Those opinions were succinct, focused and memorable, often containing passages broadly recognized today.*[30]

One such passage comes where Holmes observes as follows in *Lochner*:

> *Some ... laws embody convictions or prejudices which judges are likely to share. Some may not. But a constitution is not intended to embody a particular economic theory ... It is made for people of fundamentally differing views, and the accident of our finding certain opinions natural and familiar or novel and even shocking ought not to conclude our judgment upon the question whether statutes embodying them conflict with the Constitution of the United States.*
>
> *General propositions do not decide concrete cases. The decision will depend on a judgment or intuition more subtle than any articulate major premise. But I think that the proposition just stated, if it is accepted, will carry us far toward the end.*[31]

This is beautiful prose, clear in meaning and powerful in the sentiments it expresses.

Another leading case of the *Lochner* era is *Adair v United States*.[32] There, the Supreme Court struck down federal legislation aimed at ending so-called 'yellow dog' contracts (agreements not to join a trade union) in the interstate railroad industry. Holmes dissented. In form, Holmes' opinion makes brief reference to the facts ("As we all know, there are special labor unions of men engaged in the service of carriers ... "),[33] identifies the legal issue arising ("I turn to

---

29   Macmillan (1927), 48.
30   McHugh, J, 140.
31   *Supra*, at 75–76.
32   208 US 161 (1908) (SC).
33   *Ibid.*

the general question whether the employment can be regulated at all")[34] and treats with the issue at the level of principle:

> *I confess that I think that the right to make contracts at will that has been derived from the word liberty in the amendments has been stretched to its extreme by the decisions; but they agree that sometimes the right may be restrained. Where there is, or generally is believed to be, an important ground of public policy for restraint, the Constitution does not forbid it, whether this court agrees or disagrees with the policy pursued.*[35]

Holmes then brings this principled position to bear in the specific context of the case at hand, observing:

> *I quite agree that the question what and how much good labor unions do is one on which intelligent people may differ – I think that laboring men sometimes attribute to them advantages, as many attribute to combinations of capital disadvantages, that really are due to economic conditions of a far wider and deeper kind – but I could not pronounce it unwarranted if Congress should decide that to foster a strong union was for the best interest not only of the men, but of the railroads and the country at large.*[36]

What is notable in the above is Holmes' ability to marry general principle and a specific conclusion within a corpus of ascendant prose.

Sometimes Holmes' apparent desire for a 'snappy' line let him down. For example, in his opinion for the court in *Buck v Bell*,[37] a case concerned with forced sterilisation of so-called 'mental defectives', Holmes wrote: "Three generations of imbeciles are enough."[38] This observation has been described as "the most infamous sentence in the history of American jurisprudence",[39] "became the rallying cry for American eugenicists"[40] and would doubtless (and rightly) prompt calls for resignation if used by a judge today.

In structure, Holmes' opinion in *Buck* commences with a statement of the procedural/factual background, engages in some

---

34 *Ibid*, 191.
35 *Ibid*.
36 *Ibid*, 191–92.
37 274 US 200 (1927) (SC).
38 *Ibid*, 207.
39 Perlstein, 59.
40 Lombardo, 14.

(disturbing) social theorising about the legitimacy of forced sterilisation and then swiftly addresses the legal issue presenting. If nothing else, the opinion shows that when it comes to opinion writing, the aesthetically pleasing does not always equate to the morally correct. So, for example, Holmes observes as follows:

We have seen more than once that the public welfare may call upon the best citizens for their lives. It would be strange if it could not call upon those who already sap the strength of the State for these lesser sacrifices, often not felt to be such by those concerned, in order to prevent our being swamped with incompetence. It is better for all the world if, instead of waiting to execute degenerate offspring for crime or to let them starve for their imbecility, society can prevent those who are manifestly unfit from continuing their kind.

Not for nothing do "[w]riters today ... seem to have come to terms with a revised, rather mean Holmes".[41] Holmes never regretted what he said in *Buck*, contending that "brutal words"[42] in an opinion are justified "because of their power to cut through sentimentality and euphemistic evasion".[43] But brutality of language, it is respectfully submitted, has no place in a judgment.

Freedom of speech was at issue in *Schenck v United States*[44] and *Abrams v United States*.[45] In *Schenck*, Holmes delivered the majority opinion in a case concerned with the rights of persons who, in breach of America's Espionage Act of 1917, distributed fliers urging resistance to the wartime military draft. Holmes' opinion recites the procedural/factual background to the case, identifies the issues and applies the law to the issues. Speaking for the Supreme Court, Holmes concludes in essence that while in ordinary times, much that was said by the defendants would have been within their constitutional rights, "the character of every act depends upon the circumstances in which it is done".[46] He then skilfully manages to resolve matters in wording that speaks to the facts at hand, but also to a wider generality:

The question in every case is whether the words used are used in such

---

41 Weinberg, 691.
42 Quoted in McHugh, J, 141.
43 *Ibid*.
44 249 US 47 (1919) (SC).
45 250 US 616 (1919) (SC).
46 249 US 47, 52 (1919) (SC).

circumstances and are of such a nature as to create a clear and present danger that they will bring about the substantive evils that Congress has a right to prevent. It is a question of proximity and degree. When a nation is at war, many things that might be said in time of peace are such a hindrance to its effort that their utterance will not be endured so long as men fight, and that no Court could regard them as protected by any constitutional right.[47]

Again, Holmes' wording, though it involves powerful prose, can perhaps be flawed for its imprecision. In truth, one can read almost anything into his words. This became apparent in *Abrams*, where the freedom of speech rights of persons who supported the Russian Revolution and were opposed to the continuing war with Germany were in issue. The majority in that case, relying on *Schenck*, held that the defendants' freedom of speech rights were not violated. But Holmes dissented on the basis that the 'clear and present' danger which presented in *Schenck* did not present in *Abrams*, offering some memorable observations on free speech:

[T]he best test of truth is the power of the thought to get itself accepted in the competition of the market ... That at any rate is the theory of our Constitution. It is an experiment, as all life is an experiment ... While that experiment is part of our system I think that we should be eternally vigilant against attempts to check the expression of opinions ... unless they so imminently threaten immediate interference with the lawful and pressing purposes of the law that an immediate check is required to save the country.[48]

Despite Holmes' protestation of constancy in Abrams, he does seem to have been behaving inconstantly. Even today, it remains unclear "[w]hat happened to change the Holmes of *Schenck* into the Holmes of *Abrams*",[49] where his great dissent precipitated or acknowledged the modern American understanding of free speech. It may be that "almost without knowing",[50] the Holmes of *Schenck* was giving himself the materials that he needed to become the Holmes of *Abrams*. Or it could be that his thinking simply evolved. One cannot but recall in this regard Justice Jackson's observation in *Massachusetts*

47	*Ibid.*
48	250 US 616, 630 (1919) (SC).
49	Dewberry, 17.
50	Powell, 163.

v United States[51] that: "I see no reason why I should be consciously wrong today because I was unconsciously wrong yesterday."[52] It may be that some such sentiment was at play on Holmes' part.

Holmes has been described as a "poet *manqué*" – that is, as a man who could have been a poet but was not.[53] I am not sure that that is entirely true, for there is a poetic grandeur to Holmes' highest prose. And certainly, he is a shining example that a judgment can be a great judgment without being written in turgid language. Stylistically, it has been said that Holmes "can be compared only to Voltaire in his ability to compress profound thoughts into epigrams and aphorisms" – though, as will be seen, Justice Jackson is surely a close-run second (save that the distillation of intended meaning from Jackson's epigrammatic prose is generally an easier task than with some of Holmes' magical conjuring).

Of particular interest in the context of this book is Holmes' ability to combine the callings of writer and jurist and – as Justice Cardozo once observed – "to combine them to the glory of each".[54] Holmes, through his opinions, offers a continuing example of the truth that a great judge can be a great writer and lends credence to the proposition that to be a good judge, one should seek to be a good writer. In this regard, Cardozo has written of Holmes that:

> *Law in his hands has been philosophy, but it has been literature too. If anyone has ever been sceptical of the transfiguring power of style, let him look to these opinions. They will put scepticism to flight. How compact they are, a sentence where most of us would use a paragraph, a paragraph for a page! What a tang in their pointed phrases; what serenity in their placid depths; what a glow and a gleam when they become radiant with heat! One almost writhes in despair at the futility, too painfully apparent, of imitation or approach. These qualities of style are visible, of course, when he has spoken in great causes. What interests me as much is to find them as clearly visible in causes less pretentious, causes that to an art less consistent or fastidious might have seemed trivial and humble. He has known that greatness in such matters can be independent of the stakes.*[55]

---

51   333 US 611 (1948) (SC).
52   250 US 616, 639–40 (1919) (SC).
53   Schwartz, B, 92.
54   Hall, M, 84.
55   *Ibid.*

Perhaps four lessons might be drawn from these observations:
- Style is important in judgments.
- Brevity is no bar to profundity.
- While great judges offer lessons in style, imitation of style is best avoided as it will not ring true.
- So-called 'unimportant' cases (all cases are important to the parties involved) are as deserving of time and effort as 'important' ones.

If there is one criticism to be made of Holmes' writing, it is that "[h]is logic is not always easy to follow because it is not expressed in commonplace terms".[56] It is not simply, as Cardozo once suggested, that the person who finds Holmes occasionally hard to follow is a "sluggard unable to keep pace with the swiftness of [Holmes'] thought"[57] – though this may sometimes be so. It is more that in his choice of words or his condensing of logic, Holmes occasionally veers into the cryptical. For this reason, it is submitted that Lord Denning at his best is a better writer than Holmes, for (as will be seen) it can never be said of Denning that he is ever anything less than clear in what he writes.

2. Justice Jackson

Turning next to Justice Robert Jackson (1892–1954), although he spent 13 years on the US Supreme Court and became "one of the most influential Justices of the Supreme Court in the twentieth century",[58] he is perhaps most remembered today as the chief American prosecutor at the Nuremberg trials. As a judge, Jackson is one of the few US Supreme Court justices to have taken leave of absence from his judicial position to undertake other duties. Yet for all the strangeness of his temporary absence from the court, and despite his achievements as a Supreme Court justice, Jackson "considered his work in connection with Nuremberg [to be] the greatest accomplishment of his life".[59] (It was an

---

56 Jones, 143.
57 Cardozo (1939), 126.
58 Martin, C, 42.
59 Meltzer, 55. As will be seen in Chapter 12, there is an echo of Jackson's foreign interlude in the careers of Owen Dixon (who left the High Court of Australia to serve for a time as his nation's ambassador to the United States during World War II) and John Salmond (who spent time away from the New Zealand Supreme Court as his nation's delegate at the interwar Washington Conference on the Limitation of Armaments).

accomplishment that came at a price: Jackson's absence from Washington, coupled perhaps with strained personal relations with some other Supreme Court justices,[60] likely cost him the chief justiceship after Harlan Stone died in 1946.)[61]

As a Supreme Court Justice, Jackson has been described as a "compelling writer",[62] a "distinctively dazzling writer",[63] "brilliant and eloquent"[64] and "unusually eloquent",[65] with "[a] masterful command of the English language"[66] and "a gift for graceful and vivid expression",[67] writing prose of "extraordinary attractiveness".[68] "He is the peer of Holmes";[69] and like Holmes before him and Scalia after him, Jackson gave his all to his writing, one of his law clerks later observing that:

> *His credo was that a lawyer should give his best efforts to every professional assignment. First of all, every client is entitled to a first-class effort, and second, whatever you do, 'Somebody is watching, and you will attract clients, even from the other side, because you do a better job.' He completely believed it when he commented, 'There are no unimportant cases'.*[70]

Examples of Jackson's facility with English abound; only a few can be considered here. But first, it is worth recalling briefly a little of his career. Jackson was born in 1892 into a Pennsylvania farming family, to a father who was not willing to finance Jackson's desire to become a lawyer, forcing the future Supreme Court justice to

---

60 Martin, C, 52.
61 Barrett, 517. The position went to then Treasury Secretary Fred Vinson, a distinguished lawyer and a close friend of President Truman, the man who nominated him. "The Vinsons were practically members of the [Truman] family" (Cafardi *et al*, 703). During his time as chief justice, Vinson continued regularly to play poker with Truman (who loved the game):
> [O]ne day, right before lunch, they had been playing a poker hand. They interrupted it for lunch. After lunch, they came back, and they both discovered that there were five aces in the pack while they were playing. I will always remember Fred Vinson saying – you know, he is a very somber sort of an individual ...'What would the people of the United States of America think if they knew that the President of the United States and the Chief Justice were playing poker with five aces?' (ibid, 704).

One suspects that the American people might have been a little surprised to know that the heads of two branches of government remained so close personally.
62 Marsh, 306.
63 Barrett, 515.
64 Martin, C, 51.
65 Garner (2016), 24.
66 Koessler, 396.
67 Neal, 552.
68 *Ibid*.
69 Barry, G, 893.
70 Marsh, 309.

borrow from an uncle the funds necessary to realise his ambitions.[71] Jackson worked for a time in the law offices of a cousin in Jamestown, New York, attended Albany Law School for a year and then passed the New York Bar examinations. In a sense, however, his education never ended: Jackson was "a voracious reader"[72] and it shows in the elegance and potency of his writing.

Like President Lincoln before him, Jackson became a railroad trial lawyer, as well as general counsel of a number of companies. His chance at national prominence came when Franklin Roosevelt was elected president. Jackson, a Democrat, soon followed Roosevelt to Washington, starting out as a general counsel to the Internal Revenue Service in 1934 and rising to attorney general in 1940.[73] It was an ascent that was "extremely rapid";[74] however, it would be a mistake to see Jackson's successive job titles as offering a complete sense of his place in Washington: "He was, ahead of each of those titles, a figure in the inner, inner circles of Roosevelt's New Deal."[75]

At a meeting of the Supreme Court Bar held in late 1954 to mark Jackson's premature death, the spokesman for the assembled Bar observed of Jackson's writing style:

> *With little formal education, he developed a literary style wholly different from the styles of Holmes, Cardozo and other great stylists who have adorned the Court. He was as much given to aphorism as Holmes but was much less cryptic. One never had to labor over his pungent phrases to discover a hidden meaning ... He wrote with a trenchant, concrete, Saxon style of great beauty and vigor, nurtured chiefly on the King James version of the Bible and on Shakespeare. He contributed to the literature of the Court elements of freshness, clarity and originality.*[76]

There can be a touch of hagiography to such posthumous observations, but in Jackson's case they seem merited. Justice Frankfurter was later to add that Jackson wrote as he spoke and that he was, as

---

71 Jayasuriya, 9.
72 Adams, 2.
73 *Ibid*, 33.
74 Nielson, 383.
75 Barrett, 515.
76 Jayasuriya, 14.

a result, "one of those rare men whose spoken word survives in type".[77]

Some of Jackson's more prominent opinions include his opinion for the court in *West Virginia State Board of Education v Barnette*,[78] "one of his most eloquent decisions".[79] That was a case in which a group of Jehovah's Witnesses objected to a state law, enacted in a burst of wartime patriotism, which required children to salute the American flag and recite the Pledge of Allegiance at school. (The Jehovah's Witnesses considered that this was a breach of a biblical injunction contained in the Book of Exodus.) The Supreme Court agreed (six to three) that the Free Speech Clause protected students from such obligations. The whole of Jackson's opinion is an uplifting read for anyone committed to democracy – particularly today, when democracy seems so undervalued by so many in, of all places, the United States itself. So, for example, he observes:

> *As governmental pressure toward unity becomes greater, so strife becomes more bitter as to whose unity it shall be. Probably no deeper division of our people could proceed from any provocation than from finding it necessary to choose what doctrine and whose program public educational officials shall compel youth to unite in embracing ... It seems trite but necessary to say that the First Amendment to our Constitution was designed to avoid these ends by avoiding these beginnings.*[80]

This is a classic piece of Jacksonian prose, where he presents a particular state of affairs and then states his conclusion in epigrammatic form – here, that we avoid certain ends by avoiding certain beginnings, with a beautiful counterpoise between ends and beginnings.

Another notable opinion is Jackson's separate opinion – "concurring and dissenting, each in part"[81] – in *Communications Assn v Douds*,[82] where he showed a willingness to override First Amendment (free speech) rights in order that communist union leaders might be suppressed, yet dissented when it came to

---

77 Frankfurter (1955), 437.
78 319 US 624 (1943) (SC).
79 Barry, G, 896.
80 319 US 624, 641 (1943) (SC).
81 339 US 382, 442 (1950) (SC).
82 339 US 382 (1950) (SC).

requiring a union officer to swear an oath that he did not believe in the overthrow of the United States government, observing:

> It is not the function of our Government to keep the citizen from falling into error; it is the function of the citizen to keep the Government from falling into error. We could justify any censorship only when the censors are better shielded against error than the censored.[83]

Again, one sees Jackson's predilection for epigrams at play, this time in the form of a double epigram; while the first is clear, the second requires a little more consideration and perhaps offers a rare example in Jackson's writing of 'over-condensed' thought.

Jackson was prepared expressly to acknowledge his capacity for error. This can be seen in, for example, *McGrath v Kristensen*.[84] There, a Danish citizen had been prevented by the outbreak of World War II from returning home to Denmark from the United States. While in the United States, Kristensen applied for and was granted an exemption from military service. Seeking such relief was a basis for a later refusal of naturalisation if the person who obtained the exemption was 'residing' in the United States at the time it was obtained. The Supreme Court held that Kristensen could not be said to have been 'residing' in the United States within the meaning of the applicable statute. Jackson concurred. However, since he had given a contrary view when he was attorney general, he felt some explanation was owing. Thus, he suggested, in self-exculpatory terms, that his previous opinion "was as foggy as the statute the Attorney General [ie, he] was asked to interpret".[85] Then – ever a man for a snappy expression (not unlike Justice Holmes) – he offered a series of one-liners drawn from case law and literature, in which earlier judges had offered explanation for departing from a previous point of view:

> *Precedent ... is not lacking for ways by which a judge may recede from a prior opinion that has proven untenable ... Baron Bramwell extricated himself from a ... similar embarrassment by saying, 'The matter does not appear to me now as it appears to have appeared to me then.' ... Mr Justice Story, accounting for his contradiction of his own former*

---

83 *Ibid*, 442–43.
84 340 US 162 (1950) (SC).
85 *Ibid*, 176.

> opinion, quite properly put the matter: 'My own error ... can furnish no ground for its being adopted by this Court ...' [A]n escape less self-depreciating was taken by Lord Westbury, who ... rebuffed a barrister's reliance upon an earlier opinion of his Lordship: 'I can only say that I am amazed that a man of my intelligence should have been guilty of giving such an opinion.' If there are other ways of gracefully and good-naturedly surrendering former views to a better considered position, I invoke them all.[86]

Impressively, Jackson does not appear to have succumbed to the vanity that admission of error would diminish his standing as a judge.

Jackson dissented in part in *United States v South-Eastern Underwriters Association*,[87] a case in which the Supreme Court held that the Sherman Act (a federal antitrust statute) applied to the business of insurance. Jackson believed that such an extension (if extension it was) of the antitrust regime was properly the provenance of the other branches of government, again ultimately distilling his central thesis to the epigrammatic:

> A judgment as to when the evil of a decisional error exceeds the evil of an innovation must be based on very practical and in part upon policy considerations. When, as in this problem, such practical and political judgments can be made by the political branches of the Government, it is the part of wisdom and self-restraint and good government for courts to leave the initiative to Congress.[88]

In other words, Congress is better placed to gauge the advantages and drawbacks of extending federal law into a new area, so the initiative of such extension ought to be left by the courts to Congress.

More controversial was Jackson's willingness in *Kunz v New York*[89] to uphold constraints on free speech. *Kunz* was a case in which a Baptist minister was arrested for speaking without a permit in New York's Columbus Circle (and after he had used inflammatory words about other faiths). Jackson's pithy introduction to his opinion brilliantly anticipates the dangers in our Information Age of allowing untruths to reach the world unfiltered:

---

86   Ibid, 178.
87   322 US 533 (1944) (SC).
88   Ibid, 594.
89   340 US 290 (1951) (SC).

Essential freedoms are today threatened from without and within ... In such a setting, to blanket hateful and hate-stirring attacks on races and faiths under the protections for freedom of speech may be a noble innovation. On the other hand, it may be a quixotic tilt at windmills which belittles great principles of liberty. Only time can tell. But I incline to the latter view and cannot assent to the decision.[90]

Jackson brought similar insight to his dissent in *Terminiello v Chicago*.[91] There, another man of religion – this time a suspended Catholic priest – gave a hate-filled speech that amounted to a breach of the peace under a Chicago city ordinance. The Supreme Court held that the ordinance breached the First and Fourteenth Amendments. Jackson considered that the majority was engaging in piety and ignoring practicality:

The Court reverses this conviction by reiterating generalized approbations of freedom of speech with which, in the abstract, no one will disagree. Doubts as to their applicability are lulled by avoidance of more than passing reference to the circumstances of Terminiello's speech – and judging it as if he had spoken to persons as dispassionate as empty benches, or like a modern Demosthenes practicing his Philippics on a lonely seashore.[92]

Again, Jackson distils his central thesis into a familiar seesaw of thoughts; and if it be thought that his reasoning is less epigrammatic than usual, he proceeds a few lines later to deliver the following snappy one-liner: "An old proverb warns us to take heed lest we 'walk into a well from looking at the stars'."[93]

Jackson brought great executive branch experience to the Supreme Court. This can be seen in his opinion in the *Steel Seizure* case,[94] perhaps "the greatest single opinion ever written by a Supreme Court justice".[95] That was a case which followed on President Truman's seizure of control of steel production during the Korean War. The court held that Truman did not have the power to do as he did. Jackson delivered a concurring opinion in which he identified what has become the accepted schema for evaluating the

---

90   *Ibid*, 295.
91   337 US 1 (1949) (SC).
92   *Ibid*, 13.
93   *Ibid*, 14.
94   *Youngstown Sheet & Tube Co v Sawyer*, 343 US 579 (1952) (SC).
95   Levinson (2000), 242.

lawfulness of executive action. His observations as to the interconnectedness of government and the need for workable government are succinctly stated and perhaps even more true today, given the often logjammed state of Washington politics, than they were in Jackson's day:

> *The actual art of governing under our Constitution does not and cannot conform to judicial definitions of the power of any of its branches based on isolated clauses or even single Articles torn from context. While the Constitution diffuses power the better to secure liberty, it also contemplates that practice will integrate the dispersed powers into a workable government. It enjoins upon its branches separateness but interdependence, autonomy but reciprocity. Presidential powers are not fixed but fluctuate, depending upon their disjunction or conjunction with those of Congress.*[96]

Another case which shows Jackson's yielding of space to the other branches of government can be seen in *Shaughnessy v Mezei*.[97] There, Mr Mezei, an alien resident of the United States, travelled abroad and remained for 19 months in Hungary (behind the so-called 'Iron Curtain') at the height of the Cold War. On Mezei's return to the United States, the attorney general, without a hearing, ordered that he be excluded permanently from the United States, based on information of a confidential nature that the government declined to disclose to Mezei:

> *This man, who seems to have led a life of unrelieved insignificance [one might quibble with the notion that any human life could be insignificant], must have been astonished to find himself suddenly putting the Government of the United States in such fear that it was afraid to tell him why it was afraid of him.*[98]

The problem for the United States was that no other nation would accept Mezei. "Since we proclaimed him a Samson who might pull down the pillars of our temple, we should not be surprised if peoples less prosperous, less strongly established and less stable feared to take him off our timorous hands."[99] As a result, Mezei ended up being held at Ellis Island for 21 months. He brought

---

96   343 US 579, 635 (1952) (SC).
97   345 US 206 (1953) (SC).
98   Per Jackson J, *Ibid*, 219.
99   *Ibid*, 220.

an application challenging the lawfulness of this detention. The Supreme Court held that Mezei was not in unlawful detention and that courts could not temporarily admit him to the United States pending arrangements being made for him to leave. Jackson dissented. He commences with an introduction that has a Denning-esque flavour to it:

> *Fortunately it still is startling, in this country, to find a person held indefinitely in executive custody without accusation of crime or judicial trial. Executive imprisonment has been considered oppressive and lawless since John, at Runnymede, pledged that no free man should be imprisoned, dispossessed, outlawed, or exiled save by the judgment of his peers or by the law of the land. The judges of England developed the writ of habeas corpus largely to preserve these immunities from executive restraint. Under the best tradition of Anglo-American law, courts will not deny hearing to an un-convicted prisoner just because he is an alien whose keep, in legal theory, is just outside our gates. Lord Mansfield, in the celebrated case holding that slavery was unknown to the common law of England, ran his writ of habeas corpus in favor of an alien ... against the master of a ship at anchor in the Thames.*[100]

As he proceeds through his opinion, Jackson succinctly identifies the space owed by the judiciary to the other branches of government:

> *Substantively, due process of law renders what is due to a strong state as well as to a free individual. It tolerates all reasonable measures to insure the national safety, and it leaves a large, at times a potentially dangerous, latitude for executive judgment as to policies and means.*
>
> *After all, the pillars which support our liberties are the three branches of government, and the burden could not be carried by our own power alone. Substantive due process will always pay a high degree of deference to congressional and executive judgment, especially when they concur, as to what is reasonable policy under conditions of particular times and circumstances. Close to the maximum of respect is due from the judiciary to the political departments in policies affecting security and alien exclusion.*[101]

---

100 *Ibid*, 218–19. The judgment of Lord Mansfield is that given in *Somerset v Stewart* (1772) 98 ER 499 (KB), as considered in Chapter 4.
101 *Ibid*, 222.

Again, there is balance and counterbalance to this reasoning:
- an epigrammatic first line that posits a theory as to due process;
- an expansive second line which elaborates on the first line; and
- three further epigrammatic observations as to the nature of government, the deference owed to congressional and executive judgment and the extreme respect owed in policies affecting security and alien exclusion.

Jackson went on to conclude that detention of an alien would not be inconsistent with substantive due process, provided that the alien was accorded procedural due process. He did not see that procedural due process was done here.

Perhaps Jackson's most famous opinion is his dissenting opinion in *Korematsu v United States*.[102] There is a striking parallel between that case and *Liversidge v Anderson* (considered in more detail in Chapter 11). At issue in *Liversidge* was whether the English courts could enquire into whether the home secretary had reasonable grounds for his belief that a person was a person of hostile associations and hence subject to detention under wartime regulations. A majority of the House of Lords held, perhaps in an excess of patriotism, that there could be no enquiry into the reasonableness of the home secretary's views. Lord Atkin dissented and history has proven his view of the law to have been correct. Jackson took a not dissimilar stance in *Korematsu*. There, a majority of the Supreme Court held that the exclusion of American citizens of Japanese origin from certain areas of the American West Coast at the commencement of the war against Japan was valid. (In fact, President Roosevelt's actions in this regard were so controversial that Eleanor Roosevelt, his wife, privately remonstrated with her husband over the matter.)[103] In support of its conclusions, the Supreme Court observed that at the relevant time invasion by Japan was threatened, every possible precaution was necessary and there was not time enough to separate the loyal from the disloyal. Three

---

102   323 US 214 (1944) (SC).
103   Martin, C, 55.

justices dissented. Jackson's "passionate dissent"[104] is the most renowned.

Jackson's opening paragraph in *Korematsu* is Denning-esque in terms of its clarity and conviction. Its last two lines are especially powerful, deploying that epigrammatic brilliance which is commonplace throughout his opinions:

Korematsu ... has been convicted of an act not commonly a crime ... 'What is this act?' the reader is immediately driven to ask ... It consists merely of being present in the state whereof he is a citizen, near the place where he was born, and where all his life he has lived.[105]

Jackson then points to the racial dimension of what had occurred: that to be guilty of the crime, one had to be of Japanese descent. Then, in his classic style, he distils his sense and sentiments to their essence:

Now, if any fundamental assumption underlies our system, it is that guilt is personal and not inheritable. Even if all of one's antecedents had been convicted of treason, the Constitution forbids its penalties to be visited upon him, for it provides that 'no attainder of treason shall work corruption of blood, or forfeiture except during the life of the person attainted.' But here is an attempt to make an otherwise innocent act a crime merely because this prisoner is the son of parents as to whom he had no choice, and belongs to a race from which there is no way to resign. If Congress in peace-time legislation should enact such a criminal law, I should suppose this Court would refuse to enforce it.[106]

It was this last point which for Jackson was the 'killer point'. What would not stand if done by Congress had to fall when done, as here, by military order. With chop after chop, as if felling a tree, Jackson's opinion relentlessly demolishes the majority view with a beautiful shortness of sentence and remorselessness of logic, which arguably succeeds in a way that Lord Atkin's language in *Liversidge* does not, because what Lord Atkin delivered with something of an iron fist, Jackson takes care to wrap in a velvet glove:

Much is said of the danger to liberty from the Army program for deporting and detaining these citizens of Japanese extraction. But a

---

104　*Ibid*, 53.
105　323 US 214, 242–43 (1944) (SC).
106　*Ibid*, 243–44.

judicial construction of the due process clause that will sustain this order is a far more subtle blow to liberty ... A military order, however unconstitutional, is not apt to last longer than the military emergency ... But once a judicial opinion rationalizes such an order to show that it conforms to the Constitution, or rather rationalizes the Constitution to show that the Constitution sanctions such an order, the Court for all time has validated the principle of racial discrimination in criminal procedure ... The principle then lies about like a loaded weapon ready for the hand of any authority that can bring forward a plausible claim of an urgent need. Every repetition imbeds that principle more deeply in our law and thinking and expands it to new purposes ... A military commander may overstep the bounds of constitutionality, and it is an incident. But if we review and approve, that passing incident becomes the doctrine of the Constitution. There it has a generative power of its own, and all that it creates will be in its own image.[107]

To borrow from Cardozo's classifications of the language employed in judicial opinions, this is magisterial language, but delivered in bite-sized morsels that can be more readily digested.

3. Justice Scalia

Turning next to Antonin Scalia (1936–2016), he was one of the two most famous US Supreme Court justices of the late 20th/early 21st centuries – albeit latterly perhaps somewhat eclipsed in America's popular consciousness by Justice Ginsburg. Scalia's father was a professor of Romance languages at Brooklyn College. The young Scalia was educated at Catholic schools, then proceeded to Georgetown University before attending Harvard Law School. Following what one commentator has described as "a brief stop at a law firm in Cleveland",[108] he spent the 1970s and early 1980s "shuttling between academia and ... jobs in the Justice Department",[109] rising to the rank of assistant attorney general and also getting married and starting a family of nine children. Scalia was appointed by President Reagan to the US Court of Appeals in 1982. In 1986 he was nominated by Reagan to take the Supreme Court seat vacated upon Justice Rehnquist's elevation to the chief justiceship. Curiously, Scalia's ascent to the Olympian

---

107 *Ibid*, 245–46.
108 Toobin, 200.
109 *Ibid*.

heights of the US Supreme Court does not appear to have had quite the impact on his family that one might imagine. His son, Father Paul Scalia, a Catholic priest, has observed that:

> You have to understand, this was before the court took on the enormous role it has now in public life. I think my father would be the first to say that it should not have the enormous role it has now, that it's a distortion of its purpose. The court should have a more modest role. When he was appointed in '86, I was in high school with the children of senators and congressmen and governors, and they were the better-known names. Later, the name got to be better known, but it wasn't a big deal. He was dad, and the lawn better be mowed and you'd better not be late for dinner.[110]

In terms of writing style, Scalia's hallmark is "crisp writing",[111] to the point even of "using severe and forceful language".[112] Justice Kagan, one of the 17 justices who sat with Scalia during his time on the Supreme Court bench, has described Scalia's opinions as containing "distinctive splendid prose".[113] Another US Supreme Court Justice, Sonia Sotomayor, has described Scalia as "provocative"[114] and noted how his opinions, with their occasionally "searing words",[115] were "sometimes ... combative".[116] One of Scalia's former law clerks has suggested that Scalia's frankness was both a strength and a testament to Scalia's intellectual honesty, observing:

> Justice Scalia's outspokenness was part of what made him a great judge. Everyone has biases, and some are known to us. One of the best ways to neutralize conscious biases is simply to acknowledge their existence – openly, so that others are made aware of them.[117]

One current US Supreme Court Justice, Samuel Alito, has described being on the receiving end of what to an outsider seems combative language from Scalia in *Hein v Freedom from Religion Foundation*.[118] That was a case in which it was claimed that conferences held as part of President George W Bush's Faith-Based and

---

110 O'Donnell.
111 Greene, 144.
112 Kannar, 1323.
113 Roberts *et al*, 9.
114 Sotomayor, 1609.
115 *Ibid.*
116 *Ibid.*
117 Walsh R, 2190.
118 551 US 587 (2007) (SC).

Community Initiatives programme violated the Establishment Clause of the First Amendment to the US Constitution ("Congress shall make no law respecting an establishment of religion, or prohibiting the free exercise thereof"). This claim was made because, among other things, President Bush and his secretary of education gave speeches that used religious imagery and praised the efficacy of faith-based programmes in delivering social services. By a five-to-four majority, the Supreme Court held that the foundation did not have standing to sue. This is because, subject to narrow exceptions which did not present in *Hein*, American taxpayers cannot sue the government as to how it spends 'their' tax dollars. Scalia concurred in the majority decision but took aim at some of its reasoning, observing, for example, that the majority had engaged in "utterly meaningless distinctions",[119] and was offering logic that could not pertain "in any sane world".[120] In a tribute to Scalia, published after his death, Alito maintained that he "knew the comments were not personal. That was just Nino's way".[121] There is kindness in this observation. However, a question perhaps arises as to whether Scalia's combative tone always did him justice in terms of his courageous (even refreshing) willingness to take sometimes unpopular views which he perceived to be legally correct. After all, a too-combative style arguably risks diminishing a writing judge, her opinions and also the court in which she works.

One of contemporary America's best-known legal commentators, Professor Sunstein, ranks Scalia with Justices Holmes and Jackson as "not only one of the greatest justices in the [Supreme] Court's history ... [but] among its three best writers"[122] – a combination of achievements which, it is submitted, is not due solely to chance. Notably, Justice Kagan has directly linked Scalia's significance to the quality of his writing, observing:

> *A hundred years from now, no one will know what many of us on the Court today either wrote or accomplished. That is not true of Justice Scalia. He will go down in history as one of the most significant of Justices – and also one of the greatest.*[123]

119	*Ibid*, 618.
120	*Ibid*.
121	Alito (2017), 1606
122	Roberts *et al*, 22.
123	*Ibid*, 9.

During Scalia's career as a Supreme Court justice, he managed to move a particular American constitutional law theory (originalism) from the sidelines of legal philosophy to centre field. Originalism holds that the US Constitution must be interpreted by reference to its understood meaning at the time when that Constitution was adopted. This is a controversial school of interpretation, of which one learned commentator has observed:

> *It is ... naive. If the Board of Governors of the Federal Reserve relied on nineteenth century economics, or if the Surgeon General relied on nineteenth century medicine or if the Food and Drug Administration relied on nineteenth century chemistry, knowledgeable people in those fields would be properly dismayed.*[124]

Scalia was also a champion of the related but different theory of 'textualism', which holds that in legal interpretation, one looks primarily to the ordinary meaning of a legal text. In short, he considered that a statute means what it says and says what it means.

Scalia's championing of originalism and textualism led many to see him as "a powerful exemplar of neutrality and reason";[125] though some among his opponents considered that his decisions evinced "intolerance of social change ... limited imagination ... [and] jurispathic instincts".[126] Whatever stance one takes, few would deny that Scalia was a courageous judge and his courage falls perhaps to be respected, even if one disagrees with his reasoning/views in any one case.

One hindrance to Scalia's influence was that he was something of a great dissenter: "Scalia was often not on the winning side in many of the Court's most high-profile cases during his tenure."[127] As a result, it is probably correct to see him as a justice who had a great

---

124 Rubin, 1113. One also recalls in this regard the observation of Justice Brian Walsh, formerly of the Irish Supreme Court (his career is considered further in Chapter 12), during a onetime address in Ohio:
> *We in Ireland and the rest of Europe note that your Constitution is written in and construed in the present tense, as indeed is ours. One is often faced in and out of court with the type of argument which says that something is not what the founding fathers thought 200 years ago or some arguments to the like effect even in respect of our own 50 year old Constitution. We see your Constitution not as a document speaking from 1787, but as a law speaking from the present day. This is precisely the view which we have taken and followed in interpreting our own Constitution.* ((1987), 769–770).

125 Greene, 148.
126 *Ibid.*
127 Fitzpatrick and Varghese, 2232.

influence on legal and interpretative theory but a lesser influence on substantive constitutional law issues.[128]

Scalia gave a dissenting opinion in *United States v Virginia*.[129] In a tribute written for the *Harvard Law Review* following Scalia's death, Justice Ginsburg, who wrote the majority opinion (considered in Chapter 9), described Scalia's initial draft opinion in the case as "a zinger":[130]

> *Among the disdainful footnotes: 'The Court ... [refers] to 'the Charlottesville campus' of the University of Virginia ... Unlike university systems with which the Court is perhaps more familiar, such as those in New York ..., there is only one University of Virginia.' Thinking about fittingly restrained responses consumed my weekend, but I was glad to have the extra days to adjust the Court's opinion. My final draft was more persuasive thanks to Justice Scalia's searing criticism.*

Notably, Ginsburg does not state that "searing criticism" is an attribute in decision writing to which a judge should aspire. Nor did her amendments result in a particularly muted dissenting opinion from Scalia.

Consistent with the stance adopted in this book as to the very different role of majority and dissenting judgments (and the implications for the style of those judgments), Scalia appears to have taken a quite different approach to writing majority and dissenting opinions; and he was arguably clearer when he wrote a dissenting judgment – as can be seen, for example, if one looks at his majority opinion in *District of Columbia v Heller*[131] and his dissenting opinion in *Boumediene v Bush*.[132]

Heller[133] involved a challenge to a District of Columbia law that essentially prohibited possession of a handgun and possession of any gun in one's house, save in defined ways. The Supreme Court found the law to be unconstitutional. Rubin identifies a number of features to Scalia's majority opinion in *Heller* which he finds characteristic of Scalia's approach to majority opinion writing. From a

---

128   Ibid.
129   518 US 515 (1996) (SC).
130   Roberts *et al*, 3.
131   128 S Ct 2783 (2008) (SC).
132   553 US 723 (2008) (SC).

judgment-writing perspective, what is interesting is Rubin's contention that Scalia's opinion reads more "like an advocate's [advice]" than an "evaluation of conflicting evidence and points of view".[134] By contrast, there is Scalia's dissenting opinion in *Boumediene*.[135] That was a case concerned with the lawfulness of the suspension of the right of persons detained at Guantanamo Bay (as part of America's 'War on Terror') to bring a *habeas corpus* application challenging the lawfulness of their detention. The Supreme Court held that the suspension of this right had not been replaced with a suitable substitute. Scalia's dissent contains what seems to be quite heated language. So, for example, he decries the majority opinion as "nonsensical" and engaged in "manipulation"[136] of the law, offering reasoning that yielded "bizarre implication[s]",[137] and being driven by "an inflated notion of judicial supremacy".[138] Rubin contends that Scalia's rhetoric "might be appropriate for a commentator ... but is ... beyond the bounds of judicial discourse".[139]

One area where mainstream public opinion in the United States appears (happily) to have overtaken Scalia's views is in his treatment of LGBTQ+ rights – an area of litigation where Scalia's Supreme Court career is neatly 'bookended' by his opinions in *Lawrence v Texas*[140] (in which the court overruled its previous decision in *Bowers v Hardwick*)[141] a*nd Obergefell v Hodges*.[142] To understand the three cases, one must begin with *Bowers*, which was decided about three months before Scalia joined the Supreme Court bench. There, the Supreme Court upheld the constitutionality of a Georgia law that criminalised oral/anal sexual intercourse conducted privately and between consenting competent adults. The opinion was overruled by the Supreme Court less than two decades later in *Lawrence*, in which the majority reaffirmed the right to privacy and the traditional view that the state had no place in

---

133	128 S Ct 2783 (2008) (SC).
134	Rubin, 1113.
135	553 US 723 (2008) (SC).
136	*Ibid*, 833.
137	*Ibid*, 841.
138	*Ibid*, 842.
139	Rubin, 1129.
140	539 US 558 (2003) (SC).
141	478 US 186 (1986) (SC).
142	576 US 644 (2015) (SC).

regulating private sexual behaviour between consenting competent adults. Scalia dissented. He suggested that the majority were being "manipulative" of precedent[143] and engineering "a massive disruption of the current social order".[144] He evinced support for "the ancient proposition that a governing majority's belief that certain sexual behavior is 'immoral and unacceptable' constitutes a rational basis for regulation".[145] And he suggested that *"Bowers'* conclusion that homosexual sodomy is not a fundamental right ... is utterly unassailable".[146] In the closing segment of his opinion, Scalia made a series of observations that, one suspects, cannot but have hurt members of America's LGBTQ+ community, writing, for example:

> *Today's opinion is the product of a Court, which is the product of a law-profession culture, that has largely signed on to the so-called homosexual agenda ... [T]he Court has taken sides in the culture war ... Many Americans do not want persons who openly engage in homosexual conduct as partners in their business, as scoutmasters for their children, as teachers in their children's schools, or as boarders in their home. They view this as protecting themselves and their families from a lifestyle that they believe to be immoral and destructive ... So imbued is the Court with the law profession's anti-anti-homosexual culture, that it is seemingly unaware that the attitudes of that culture are not obviously 'mainstream'.*[147]

In his later dissenting opinion in *Obergefell*[148] (the five-to-four decision of the court that legalised same-sex marriage and thus marked a major step forwards for American society), Scalia commences with something of a paean to the civility of the ongoing gay marriage debate within the United States, observing that it "displayed American democracy at its best",[149] with "[i]ndividuals on both sides of the issue passionately but respectfully ... [attempting] to persuade their fellow citizens to accept their views".[150] Scalia's dissenting opinion also seems passionate. Thus, he criticises the majority opinion for "lacking even a thin veneer of

---

143 539 US 558, 587 (2003) (SC).
144 *Ibid*, 591.
145 *Ibid*, 589.
146 *Ibid*, 597.
147 *Ibid*, 602–03.
148 576 US 644 (2015) (SC).
149 *Ibid*, 714.
150 *Ibid*.

law";[151] for containing "mummeries and straining-to-be-memorable passages";[152] for involving "a naked judicial claim to legislative – indeed super-legislative – power";[153] for being guilty of "hubris"[154] and "o'erweening pride";[155] for engaging in a "judicial Putsch";[156] and for evincing a style that was "as pretentious as its content is egotistic",[157] containing "silly extravagances"[158] and "showy profundities [that] are often profoundly incoherent".[159] Though Scalia was perfectly entitled to hold and express his views, it is difficult when reading such observations not to recall Justice Frankfurter's onetime observation that: "The notion that the text [of the Constitution] should yield the same meaning to every conscientious member of the Supreme Court is the offspring either of ignorance or self-deception."[160] Scalia was not ignorant or self-deceived; he was a judge with a commanding intellect and a jurist of distinction. However, a question does perhaps arise whether he always did himself the fullest of justice in terms of the temper and tone of his opinions. Certainly, his sometimes combative style of opinion writing seems a less attractive model of opinion writing than, for example, the (often understated) finesse and sophistication that are the abiding judgment-writing traits of Justices Holmes and Jackson.

4. Conclusions

At least 10 lessons in judgment writing fall to be derived from the opinions of Justices Holmes, Jackson and Scalia:
- A good judgment sees the larger legal/intellectual significance of a case, taking the process of judgment beyond the issue of which party should win to a consideration of relevant social policy or legal philosophy.
- It seems to be a trait of the greatest judges that they write their own judgments.

151	*Ibid*, 716.
152	*Ibid*.
153	*Ibid*, 717.
154	*Ibid*, 718.
155	*Ibid*, 720.
156	*Ibid*, 718.
157	*Ibid*, 719.
158	*Ibid*.
159	*Ibid*.
160	Frankfurter (1955), 435.

- Greatness in language need not equate to juridical greatness in any one judgment.
- Brevity does not diminish potency or preclude profundity. The common law "need[s] the lifebelt of principles".[161]
- Substance should never yield to style. (In *Buck v Bell*,[162] Holmes' possible desire for a 'snappy' introductory line yielded "the most infamous sentence in the history of American jurisprudence".)[163]
- Holmes, through his opinions, offers a continuing example of the truth that a great judge can be a great writer and lends credence to the proposition that to be a good judge one should seek to be a good writer.
- A judge should give her best efforts to every professional assignment. Every litigant is entitled to a first-class effort. There are no unimportant cases.
- Admission of error need not diminish one's standing as a judge. Precedent is not lacking in examples of ways in which a judge may recede from a prior opinion that has proven untenable and perhaps misled others.
- In *Korematsu* (a case not unlike *Liversidge*), Justice Jackson's dissenting opinion proceeds with a beautiful shortness of sentence and remorselessness of logic, which succeeds in a way that Lord Atkin's language in *Liversidge* (considered in Chapter 11) does not, because what Lord Atkin delivers with something of an iron fist, Jackson takes care to wrap in a velvet glove.
- A good judgment should not involve the unmediated expression of self or be unduly combative. A too-combative style arguably risks diminishing the writing judge, her judgments and the court in which she works.

Having considered the many lessons in judgment writing to be gleaned from the judgments of three great and pioneering women judges and three great Supreme Court justices, I move on in the

---

161 Macmillan (1927), 48.
162 274 US 200 (1927) (SC).
163 Perlstein, 59.

10. Three great American judges: Justices Holmes, Jackson and Scalia

next chapter to consider the lessons to be gleaned from the speeches/judgments of three great British law lords: Lords Atkin, Denning and Bingham.

11. Three great British judges: Lords Atkin, Denning and Bingham

Judges operating in precedent-based systems 'stand on the shoulders of giants', bringing the wisdom of the past to bear in the present and adding to the cumulative evolution of the law into the future. In this chapter, I undertake an analysis of what lessons a judge minded to improve her judgment-writing style might glean from the judgments of three prominent law lords:[1] *Lord Atkin ("a great master of the common law");*[2] *Lord Denning ("possibly the most important English judge of the twentieth century");*[3] *and Lord Bingham ("a towering figure in the law").*[4]

1. **Lord Atkin**

    James Atkin (1867–1944), son of an Irish father and a Welsh mother, was born in Brisbane. However, he returned as an infant to Wales and was reared there by his mother after she was widowed. Atkin's career as a barrister had a slow start and though he eventually became a successful commercial lawyer, he was never hugely wealthy. In 1913 he was appointed to the High Court, where he appears to have enjoyed the solitary nature of the work. (There is, it must be said, a delightful freedom to sitting by oneself as a trial judge, deciding a case by oneself and then writing a judgment by oneself.) By contrast to the High Court, Atkin appears not to have been especially happy on the Court of Appeal, to which he was appointed in 1919 and where he had to contend with colleagues

---

1 As stated in the foreword, I have chosen not to comment on the work of judges whose working life continues. Because Lady Hale continues to be a working member of the House of Lords, I have not considered the many lessons that her speeches/judgments offer to the judge minded to improve her judgment-writing style. A consideration of Lady Hale's speeches/judgments will undoubtedly be a mainstay of this chapter in a future edition.
2 Gutteridge, 45.
3 Stevens, 237.
4 Layton, 893.

who held very different views from his own.[5] In 1928 he was elevated to the House of Lords and made a lord of appeal in ordinary ('law lord').

When it comes to the general style of Atkin's judgments, his biographer makes the following general observations:

> *Again and again ... his judgment ... reveals an uncommon perception of the commerce of daily life underlying a dispute. Such an understanding was essential for a humane law ... If the law were to detach itself from that everyday world it would lose its use, just as surely would commercial law if ... removed ... from the needs and intentions of businessmen ... Atkin's preoccupation was that neither should happen.*[6]

In terms of style, a onetime judge of the Irish Supreme Court has rightly suggested Atkin's judgments to have been enlivened "by clarity of style and language ... a flair for ... vivid example and ... a gift for aphorism and metaphor. Above all" – and this is a trait that seems always to separate a great judge from a good one – "he was able to rise above the ... immediate facts ... to see the problem in the perspective of a larger scheme of things".[7]

Atkin appears to have had a real sense of empathy/sympathy for those who were faring badly in life. The online *Oxford Dictionary of National Biography* describes him as a man whose "humane spirit ... ran through his work and ... was founded on his lifelong Christian beliefs". A good example of this occurs in *Everett v Griffiths*.[8] That was an action in negligence against the chairman of a board of guardians and a medical practitioner who had 'signed off' on Mr Everett's reception into an asylum as a pauper 'lunatic'. (The terminology employed when it came to mental health law in Atkin's era is to be deplored.) In the House of Lords, the majority held for the defendants. Atkin had dissented by way of a dissenting judgment that was described on appeal by Lord Haldane as "a powerful piece of reasoning",[9] albeit one that was noticeably long. Lord Justice Bankes' judgment occupies about 13 pages in the law reports. Lord

---

5 Lewis, G, 18.
6 *Ibid*, 28.
7 Henchy, 183.
8 [1920] 3 KB 163 (CA).
9 [1921] 1 AC 631, 652 (HL).

Justice Scrutton's takes about 11 pages. Yet Atkin's dissenting judgment comprises 23 pages and reads like the judgment he would have written if he had been tasked with writing the majority judgment. Atkin manages a notably strong opening and closing to his dissenting judgment:

[Introductory paragraph] *This case therefore raises the serious issue whether a sane man, who without reasonable care is imprisoned in an asylum, is by our law without redress against those whose negligence has caused him that terrible injury.*

...

[Closing paragraph] *[W]e are dealing with the liberty of persons ill able to protect themselves, paupers, and persons of weak mind who, though sane, may afford to the unthinking or careless mind evidences of insanity. In my opinion it is just as it is convenient that the law should impose a duty to take reasonable care that such persons, if sane, shall not suffer the unspeakable torment of having their sanity condemned and their liberty restricted; and I am glad to record my own opinion, ineffectual though it be, that for such an injury the English law provides a remedy.*[10]

In structure, Atkin's judgment roughly takes the form of Introduction–Issue–Facts–Law–Application of Law to Facts–Conclusion. Thus, it comes closest in form to that canvassed by the US Federal Judicial Center. Atkin's empathy for Mr Everett is clear and is comparable in eloquence to Justice Holmes at his best:

Grievous as is the wrong of unjust imprisonment of an alleged criminal, I apprehend that its colours pale beside the catastrophe of unjust imprisonment on an unfounded finding of insanity. Modern organization has no doubt done much to remove the horrors that were associated with Bedlam [a once-prominent London asylum] in the days when the victims were subject to public exhibition. Probably even now the insane ward or reception ward is not without its revolting incidents. But it is the effect on the mind sane, even if feeble, that knows itself wrongly adjudged unsound that produces the most poignant suffering.[11]

Atkin's judgment in *Everett* is also of interest in the hint it gives

---

10   [1920] 3 KB 163, 199 and 223 (CA).
11   *Ibid*, 211–12.

that his mind was already edging towards the idea of the general duty of care which he later iterated in *Donoghue v Stevenson*.[12] Thus, in his closing observation, Atkin observes that: "[I]t is just as it is convenient that the law should impose a duty to take reasonable care that ... persons, if sane, shall not suffer the unspeakable torment of having their sanity condemned and their liberty restricted."[13]

Workmen's compensation cases also offered Atkin an opportunity of showing his compassion for the so-called 'common man'. Two good examples of his approach to decision making in this area are offered by *Caswell v Powell Duffryn Associated Collieries*[14] and *Radcliffe v Ribble Motor Services*.[15] In *Caswell*, a mineworker was killed in circumstances where certain machinery that he was responsible for cleaning could be (and may have been) restarted without warning, posing a potentially fatal danger. The House of Lords, reversing the Court of Appeal, concluded that the mineworker's employer was liable. In terms of structure, Atkin gives the procedural and factual background to the case (in notable detail), considers the law in the context of the pertinent facts and arrives at a conclusion. In this, the form of his judgment comes closest to the Facts–Law–Application–Consideration (FLAC) judgment-writing style (as considered in Chapter 5). Atkin's description of the circumstances in which Caswell's body was found are eloquent and clear, with a staccato rhythm that was to be the hallmark of the best of Lord Denning's later judgments:

> *The men were engaged in loading the fifth journey; they had loaded three out of the fifteen trams, the fourth was under the chute when the machinery stopped. They went to the machine, and there they found the dead body of the unfortunate Caswell; his right hand was outstretched, caught between the belt and the roller and his head was drawn up against the roller; his neck was broken. The body was drawn up so that his feet were two feet from the ground, and beneath his feet and lying in water beneath his feet was one of the iron scrapers.*[16]

---

12 [1932] AC 562 (HL).
13 [1920] 3 KB 163, 223 (CA).
14 [1940] AC 152 (HL).
15 [1939] AC 215 (HL).
16 [1940] AC 152 (HL), 159–60.

Atkin's judgment in *Caswell* is also notable for the deft manner in which he marries principle with pragmatism. Lord Wright (who, as will be seen, had his occasional differences with Atkin in life) wrote posthumously of Atkin that it was "his insistence on the paramount importance of principles as opposed to casuistical subtleties which will give him a claim to be recognized by posterity".[17]

In *Radcliffe*, a bus driver engaged in his work had stopped in a street in Liverpool when he was knocked down by a bus being driven by another driver employed by the same employer. The employer pleaded the (later-abolished) defence of common employment whereby it could not be liable for injuries caused to an employee through the fault of another employee. The House of Lords held that the doctrine did not apply. In structure, Lord Atkin's judgment took the form of an introduction, a brief treatment of the relevant facts, identification of the legal issue presenting (the scope of the doctrine of common employment), a consideration of the law, an application of the law to the facts and a conclusion. In this it comes closest to the form of judgment canvassed by Bosielo and considered in Chapter 5 – that is, Introduction–Facts–Issues–Law–Application–Remedy–Order.

Atkin showed an occasional predilection for the caustic that has not aged well. Two cases in which this predilection shows are *Fender v Mildmay*[18] and *Liversidge v Anderson*.[19] The first of these cases was a breach of promise suit that has a decidedly yesteryear feel to it and yielded a judgment from Atkin which can be described as "a fine judgment of simple virtues"[20] – albeit a judgment that, it is respectfully submitted, is not without its deficiencies. The case arose from an extra-marital affair between Sir Anthony St-John Mildmay, MC and a certain Nurse Fender. Sir Anthony promised Nurse Fender that he would marry her when his wife divorced him. He reneged on that promise and Nurse Fender sued for breach of promise. Her action failed in the lower courts on the ground that as Sir Anthony had still been married when he made the promise, it was illegal and

---

17 Wright (1944), 338.
18 [1938] AC 1 (HL).
19 [1942] AC 206 (HL).
20 Harding, 439.

unenforceable as contrary to public policy. In a remarkable decision for the era in which it was given (in a nation which had only recently undergone a constitutional convulsion over the notion that the king might marry a divorcée), the House of Lords held that an action for breach of promise *could* be maintained where, as here, the promise had been made after the granting of a divorce decree *nisi* (a provisional divorce decree) and before the granting of the decree absolute (the decree which actually dissolved the marriage). It would be fair to say that Lord Russell waxes eloquent in his judgment about the solemnity of the institution of marriage (echoed to some extent by Lord Roche). But Atkin was unconvinced that what was at play in the case involved an attack on the institution of marriage, observing:

> *I can only say that if the lady yields to a promise with such an indefinite date she is probably of a yielding disposition, and it would appear difficult to predicate that immorality is either facilitated or accelerated by the promise. As to the suggestion that such a promise is bad because it tends to induce the husband to murder his wife, I reject this ground altogether. Alderson B. in* Egerton v Brownlow *incontinently classes such objections as ridiculous. They appear to afford another instance of the horrid suspicions to which high-minded men are sometimes prone.*[21]

With a word like "ridiculous" and mention of "horrid suspicions" being bandied about, Lords Russell and Roche could readily have taken offence. Atkin's observations also seem somewhat harsh when it comes to Nurse Fender. After all, her sole 'mistake' was to enter into a relationship with a man who appears to have acted as a cad towards her. Yet Atkin decries her as probably a woman of "yielding disposition".

In his dissenting judgment in *Liversidge v Anderson*[22] (considered further below), Atkin – in a judgment that Lord Bingham later described as "beautifully written"[23] – descended to a level of attack that grated with his colleagues and marred an otherwise great judgment. Indeed, one cannot but be reminded when one reads it of Justice Chauhan's more recent observations in the Supreme

---

21 *Supra*, at 15–16.
22 [1942] AC 206 (HL).
23 Bingham, T (2009b).

Court of India that while the formation and expression of honest opinion are key aspect of a judge's role, a judge should always show "poised restraint".[24]

Any common lawyer 'worth her salt' will know the two cases for which Lord Atkin is most famous. The first is his judgment in *Donoghue v Stevenson*,[25] the continuing importance of which has been attributed as being "due more than anything else to the moral spirit which animated Lord Atkin's speech".[26] The second is Atkin's already touched-upon dissenting judgment in *Liversidge v Anderson*.[27]

Donoghue v Stevenson's "inauspicious, somewhat ridiculous facts"[28] make for a slightly nauseating read. Ms Donoghue, a shop assistant, sought to recover damages from Mr Stevenson, a manufacturer of 'aerated waters' (fizzy drinks), for injuries she claimed to have suffered as a result of consuming part of the contents of a bottle of ginger beer which Stevenson had manufactured and which allegedly contained the decomposed remains of a snail. The House of Lords, by a three-to-two majority, held that the manufacturer of an article of food, medicine or the like which sold its product through a distributor in circumstances where neither the distributor nor the end user could discover any defect by inspection was under a legal duty to the end purchaser/user to take reasonable care that the said article was free from defect likely to cause injury to health. Atkin's judgment opens by identifying the issue arising. He points to the seriousness and significance of the issue presenting: "It is remarkable how difficult it is to find in the English authorities statements of general application defining the relations between parties that give rise to the duty [to take care]".[29] He discusses the legal issue, albeit with an invocation to Christian scripture (arguably a curious text on which to construct rational law), observing:

> *The rule that you are to love your neighbour becomes in law, you must not injure your neighbour; and the lawyer's question, Who is my*

---

24 *State of Gujarat v Justice RA Mehta (Retd)* [2013] 1 SCR 1, para 73.
25 [1932] AC 562 (HL).
26 Lewis, G, 67.
27 [1942] AC 206 (HL).
28 Van Rijswijk, 5.
29 [1932] AC 562, 579 (HL).

neighbour? receives a restricted reply. You must take reasonable care to avoid acts or omissions which you can reasonably foresee would be likely to injure your neighbour. Who, then, in law is my neighbour? The answer seems to be – persons who are so closely and directly affected by my act that I ought reasonably to have them in contemplation as being so affected when I am directing my mind to the acts or omissions which are called in question.[30]

The reference to "[t]he rule that you are to love your neighbour" is a reference to the Christian New Testament tale in which one of the Pharisees (a lawyer) tries to trick Jesus by asking which is the greatest of the divine Commandments, to which Jesus responds with two commandments, the second of which is that "Thou shalt love thy neighbour as thyself".[31]

Atkin next proceeds to apply the principle that he has identified to the facts at hand, though he does make a curious observation as to reliance on principle, noting that:

[I]t is of particular importance to guard against the danger of stating propositions of law in wider terms than is necessary, lest essential factors be omitted in the wider survey and the inherent adaptability of English law be unduly restricted.[32]

Atkin proceeds next to identify a basis for his neighbour principle in existing case law. In doing so, he refers, among other matters, to a judgment of Justice Cardozo (when in the New York Court of Appeals) in *MacPherson v Buick Motor Co*.[33] In *MacPherson*, Cardozo commences the story of the case at hand with a simplicity that is reminiscent of Lord Denning at his finest:

The defendant is a manufacturer of automobiles. It sold an automobile to a motor dealer. The retail dealer resold to the plaintiff. While the plaintiff was in the car, it suddenly collapsed. He was thrown out and injured. One of the wheels was made of defective wood, and its spokes crumbled into fragments.[34]

In the course of his judgment, Cardozo notes that when it came to the then law of England in this area, "a consistent principle is

---

30   *Ibid*, 580.
31   Matt: 37–40.
32   [1932] AC 562, 584 (HL).
33   217 NY 382 (1916) (CA).
34   *Ibid*, 384.

with difficulty extracted".[35] (Atkin was to do the necessary extraction, albeit in the context of a Scottish case, in *Donoghue*.) Cardozo then concludes, in a clear anticipation of the neighbour principle, that Buick as manufacturer owed a duty of care to MacPherson.

In his judgment in *Donoghue*, Atkin describes Cardozo's judgment in *MacPherson* as "illuminating"[36] and as stating the principles of law applicable to *Donoghue* "as I should desire to state them".[37] Of course, referring to American precedent also assisted in showing that Atkin and the majority in *Donoghue* were not introducing some radical innovation without the benefit of precedent, albeit that the best precedent available happened not to be British.

Liversidge v Anderson[38] was concerned with Regulation 18B of the wartime Defence (General) Regulations 1939, a provision which allowed for the detention of foreign nationals if the home secretary had "reasonable cause to believe any [such] person to be of hostile origin or associations". At issue before the House of Lords was whether the home secretary had to show reasonable cause to believe certain things alleged against a detainee. A majority of the Appellate Committee held that there could be no enquiry into the reasonableness of the home secretary's views. Lord Atkin dissented, and history has proven him to have been right in law. As early as 1951, there was, in *Nakkuda Ali v Jayartyne*,[39] the clearest distancing from the majority reasoning in *Liversidge*; and in *Inland Revenue Commissioners v Rossminster Ltd*,[40] Lord Diplock suggested, without contradiction, that "the majority of this House in *Liversidge v Anderson* were expediently and, at that time, perhaps, excusably, wrong and the dissenting speech of Lord Atkin was right".[41] It seems doubtful that Atkin thought the majority in *Liversidge* to be "excusably ... wrong" and doubtless Mr Liversidge would not have thought so either. "[I]n the midst of the practical anxieties of war-time, only Lord Atkin's sense of principle remained unimpaired."[42]

---

35 *Ibid*, 393.
36 [1932] AC 562, 598 (HL).
37 *Ibid*.
38 [1942] AC 206 (HL).
39 [1951] AC 66, 76 (HL).
40 [1980] 2 WLR 1 (HL).
41 *Ibid*, 49.
42 Harding, 436.

Atkin's judgment in *Liversidge* has at its core a concern that the words in the applicable regulations that "If the Secretary of State has reasonable cause" were being construed as if they read 'If the Secretary of State thinks that he has reasonable cause', yielding "an absolute power which, so far as I know, has never been given before to the executive, and I shall not apologize for taking some time to demonstrate that no such power is in fact given to the minister".[43] There is, arguably, a somewhat strident tone to the foregoing and an apology for what is a notably long dissent – which is suggestive that Atkin was conscious "that it is useful to keep dissents 'short and sweet'".[44] The stridency continues throughout the judgment. Thus, Atkin refers to the lower court judges (who were being upheld by the majority) as having been "infected with the 'subjective' virus"[45] (presumably the same being true of the judges upholding them). He dismisses his colleagues as "more executive minded than the executive".[46] He criticises counsel for the home secretary for making "arguments which might have been [made] ... in the time of Charles I"[47] (Charles I having been a 'high priest' of absolutism). And he states himself not merely to disagree with his colleagues but to "protest, even if I do it alone, against a strained construction put on words".[48] He then launches into perhaps the most astonishing attack ever made by a senior British judge on his colleagues:

> *I know of only one authority which might justify the suggested method of construction: '"When I use a word," Humpty Dumpty said in rather a scornful tone, "it means just what I choose it to mean, neither more nor less." "The question is," said Alice, "whether you can make words mean so many different things." "The question is," said Humpty Dumpty, "which is to be master – that's all."'* ('Through the Looking Glass,' c. vi.).[49]

The potency of Atkin's reference to Carroll's *Through the Looking-Glass* cannot be overstated. Lord Chancellor Simon even wrote to Atkin in advance of the judgment issuing, suggesting that the refer-

---

43 [1942] AC 206, 226 (HL).
44 Steel, 147.
45 [1942] AC 206, 242 (HL).
46 *Ibid*, 244.
47 *Ibid*.
48 *Ibid*.
49 *Ibid*, 245.

ence be dropped: "[M]y eye catches your very amusing citation from Lewis Carroll. Do you ... think this is necessary? I fear that it may be regarded as wounding to your colleagues who take the view you satirize."[50] Lord Wright (one of the majority judges) was so furious at Atkin's attack that Atkin's daughter, who went for dinner with her father in the House of Lords on the evening of the decision, was later to recall that Wright walked straight past them without stopping to speak, even though Wright had been a guest at their home.[51] Viscount Maugham even wrote to *The Times* to lend his public support to counsel for the home secretary, who was doubtless smarting at Atkin's reference to the absolutist dimension of his arguments. Eighty years later, it is hard to see that Atkin did not descend to discourtesy in his dissenting judgment, even if in his conclusions as to the law he was undoubtedly correct.

Atkin was first and foremost a commercial law judge. So no consideration of his judgment writing would be complete without mention of a couple of his more renowned commercial law judgments – namely *Banco de Portugal v Waterlow*[52] and *Bell v Lever Bros*.[53] The facts of *Banco de Portugal* read almost like the plot of an old Ealing Studios caper movie. A company that had been engaged by the Banco de Portugal to print *escudo* notes later did a further run of the notes for a criminal who introduced the notes into Portugal. Banco de Portugal had to withdraw the entire series of notes and sued for breach of contract. The appeals before the House of Lords concerned the question of whether the printers should be liable for the cost of printing the notes or the expressed value of the notes when issued (because once issued, they enjoyed a purchasing power in respect of commodities). Atkin reasons through why the latter approach is the correct approach; Lord Russell was among the dissenters and the case is notable for the apparent sniping between himself and Atkin. Thus, Atkin observes (forcefully) that:

> *It follows [from the cost of printing approach] that it makes no difference to the financial position of the Bank whether in exchange for a good note it receives a good note or a bad note. I should have thought*

---

50 For the exchange of correspondence between the two men, see Lewis, G, 139–42.
51 *Ibid*, 143.
52 [1932] AC 452 (HL).
53 [1932] AC 161 (HL).

Part II: The practice of the art and craft of judgment writing

> this result, in the language of one of your Lordships, 'manifestly impossible' [the phrase appears in Lord Russell's judgment]; but rules of law have to be tested in these days, and must survive the application of first principles.[54]

This is met by a forceful response from Russell, who states:

> One of your Lordships in his speech has, in effect, accused those of us who differ from him in this case, of upsetting a number of authorities governing our commercial law. Personally, I am unconscious of any such assault upon authority. I am only conscious of deciding that the Bank have not proved that they have suffered the enormous damages which they claim to recover ... I confess ... that I derive some consolation from the knowledge that, in this alleged act of violence I am abetted by one whose pre-eminence as a commercial lawyer is both well established and long established ... [that person being Scrutton L.J.].[55]

In *Bell v Lever Bros*,[56] the question at issue was whether a redundancy contract was void for common mistake in circumstances where a once-esteemed managing director was later found to have misconducted himself during his employment. The House of Lords by a three-to-two majority held that the contract was not void. The judgments as a whole did not bring the greatest of clarity to the law on mistake. Even the usually crystal-clear Atkin was reduced to occasional tongue-twisting logic, such as that a mistake concerning the quality of a thing contracted for "will not affect assent unless it is the mistake of both parties, and is as to the existence of some quality which makes the thing without the quality essentially different from the thing as it was believed to be".[57] In structure, Atkin's judgment takes the form of a one-sentence introduction, a consideration of the facts, an identification of the two points presenting for decision, a consideration in respect of each point of the applicable law followed by its application to the facts, and then a conclusion and indication of the form of the order to be made – that is, Introduction–Facts–Issues–Law–Application–Conclusion–Order, a form of approach which essentially mirrors that canvassed by Bosielo (as considered in Chapter 5).

---

54 [1932] AC 452, 486–87 (HL).
55 *Ibid*, 502.
56 [1932] AC 161 (HL).
57 *Ibid*, 218.

2. Lord Denning

Turning next to Lord Denning (1899–1999), his plain writing style is the abiding hallmark of his remarkable judicial career. As one commentator has succinctly put matters:

In giving judgment, Denning tried to make himself clear so that he could be easily understood by the parties. He called the parties by their names and did not speak of plaintiff and defendant. In telling the story, he set out the merits as the merits shew where justice lies. He used short sentences and tried to cultivate a style which commanded attention.[58]

In truth, Denning's prose – filled with "grace and felicity"[59] and "memorable as literature"[60] – is often so strikingly simple that it can be possible to underestimate the high intellectual, literary and legal skills that he brought to bear in attaining this level of simplicity. He shows – in a way that perhaps no other judge in the common law world has ever shown – "that problems are reducible to fairly clear and certain categories".[61] In terms of readability, his judgments remain head and shoulders above the judgments of most (perhaps all) other common law judges to this day, and place Denning in a very select group of judges (Justice Holmes is another) whose judgments can be taken down and read for pleasure.

Denning was renowned for his recitations of fact (and clearly enjoyed reciting them). Some of his opening lines read almost like the introduction to a novel – for example:

- "It appears that in the year 1965 M. Couvreur was interested in acquiring the products of a vineyard in France";[62] and
- "The centre-piece of this story is a pair of candelabra, made of well-cut glass, each supporting two candles with sparkling pear-drops all about."[63]

Sometimes Denning even conceived of his plots in novelistic terms, stating, for example, in *Midland Bank Trust Co Ltd v Green*[64]

---

58   Crowther, 734.
59   Martin, R, 7.
60   *Ibid.*
61   Klinck (1987), 388.
62   *Ionian Bank Ltd v Couvreur* [1969] 1 WLR 781, 783 (CA).
63   *Reid v Metropolitan Police Commissioner* [1973] QB 551, 557 (CA).
64   [1980] Ch 590 (CA).

that: "The Greens are a Lincolnshire farming family. This story might be called The Green Saga." There were even sequels to the saga. By the time of *Midland Bank Trust Co Ltd v Green (No 3)*,[65] Denning was writing: "This is another chapter in the long story of the Green family of Lincolnshire ... So many years have passed that several of the principal actors have died and are now represented by the executors of their estates."[66]

Harvey traces the evolution of Denning's writing style, pointing to the absence of his classic form in his earliest judgments, its sudden *entrée* in a nascent state in *James v Minister for Pensions*[67] ("Gunner James joined the army on July 24, 1941, at the age of thirty-two. In January 1943, he had a swelling on the right side of his neck which gradually spread"), and its evolution into the classic Denning 'openers', which Harvey divides into nine categories:

- the intriguing opener (eg, "It was a fine Chinese carpet worth £900, but it needed cleaning");[68]
- the historical opener (eg, "The village has an attractive name, Dibden Purlieu. It goes back to the times of the Norman French");[69]
- the fatal opener (eg, "A man's head got caught in a propeller. He was decapitated and killed");[70]
- the 'This is the case' opener[71] (eg, "This is the case of the Birmingham bombers");[72]
- the editorial opener (eg, "This case ought to have been simple, but the lawyers have made it complicated");[73]
- the *non sequitur* opener (eg, "Many years ago Sir Edward Coke had a case about six carpenters. Now we have a case about six car-hire drivers");[74]
- the 'This is an interesting case' opener (ie, "This is an

---

65 [1982] 2 WLR 1 (CA).
66 *Ibid*, 4.
67 [1947] KB 867 (CA).
68 *Levison v Patent Steam Carpet Cleaning Co Ltd* [1978] QB 69, 77 (CA).
69 *Jennings Motors Ltd v Secretary of State for the Environment* [1982] 2 WLR 131, 134 (CA).
70 *Allen v Jambo Holdings Ltd* [1980] 1 WLR 1252, 1254 (CA).
71 Harvey, 78.
72 *McIlkenny v Chief Constable of West Midlands Police Force* [1980] 2 All ER 227 (CA), As considered later in the main text above, Denning's description of the respondents as "the Birmingham bombers" was to prove controversial.
73 *Marsden v Regan* [1954] 1 All ER 423, 436 (CA). The lawyers in the case must have winced a little at this opening.
74 *Cinnamond v British Airports Authority* [1980] 1 WLR 582, 585 (CA).

interesting case ... ")[75] – the difficulty with this opening line is that it may suggest to other litigants that their particular case has failed to pique the deciding judge's interest;
- the whimsical opener (eg, "A gigantic ship was used for a gigantic fraud");[76] and
- the picturesque opener (eg, "In 1962 life was peaceful in Buckinghamshire").[77]

To these nine categories, it is submitted, a further category might be added: the occasionally disappointing opener. Two examples are *Rank Film Distributors Ltd v Video Information Centre*[78] ("'It is, it is a glorious thing, to be a Pirate King,' said W.S. Gilbert ... But he was speaking of ship pirates. Today we speak of film pirates. It is not a glorious thing to be, but it is a good thing to be in for making money");[79] and Denning's opening to his last judgment, in *George Mitchell Ltd v Finney Lock Seeds Ltd*,[80] which contains perhaps the worst opening to all of Denning's judgments:

> Many of you know Lewis Carroll's 'Through the Looking Glass.' In it there are these words (Ch. IV): 'The time has come,' the Walrus said, 'to talk of many things: Of shoes – and ships – and sealing-wax – Of cabbages – and kings – 'Today it is not 'of cabbages and kings' – but of cabbages and what-nots.

Even geniuses have their off days; and Denning was, without doubt, a genius when it came to crafting judgments. However, in reading the foregoing, one arguably catches a whisper of what Honoré means when he writes of the "gimmicks of style"[81] that Denning occasionally adopted in his late career.

In his judgments, Denning shows himself to be a proudly English judge – something that can be seen in the wonderful glimpses of England that he offers in his judgments. One of his most famous perspectives on England arises in *Hinz v Berry*,[82] a case in which he famously observes, in his opening text: "It was bluebell

---

75 *Southam v Smout* [1964] 1 QB 308, 319 (CA).
76 *Shell International Petroleum Ltd v Gibbs* [1982] 2 WLR 745, 771 (CA).
77 *Myers v Milton Keynes Development Corporation* [1974] 1 WLR 696, 699 (CA).
78 [1982] AC 380 (CA).
79 *Ibid*, 403.
80 [1982] 3 WLR 1036, 1040 (CA).
81 Friedman *et al*, 20.
82 [1970] 2 QB 40 (CA).

233

time in Kent."[83] As it happens, the fact that it was bluebell time in Kent had a relevance to the case: the reason Mrs Hinz was not injured in the car crash which formed the basis of the personal injuries lawsuit that came on appeal was because she had gone to the far side of the road to pick bluebells with one of her daughters. But as a line, its fame is perhaps due more to its reliance on the imagined sensation of the reader. To some, the line might conjure up a picture of a country road beneath old oak trees; a farm gate to one side opening onto a wide field and a view across the Kentish countryside; the sound of wind rustling through the overhead leaves; and the scent of bluebells, fresh grass and woodland all about. But for all the reader knows (at least until she reads further), the events could be taking place in an industrial estate just off the M20. Or the events may not take place in Kent at all; it may just happen to be bluebell time in Kent. The reader, at least initially, fills in the contours and colours of the scene depicted by Lord Denning, the reader's senses enhancing the vividness of her aesthetic experience and increasing her pleasure as she grasps the arrangement of and relation between the lines/colours/shapes/tones that constitute the experience afforded by Denning's words.

Continuing with his 'scenes of England', in *Gee v National Trust*,[84] Denning opens with the line: "In Cornwall there is a lovely inlet of the sea called the Helford River. In 1938 Mrs Hext owned a large house towards the head of the river, two or three farms and other buildings."[85] In *Burt v Claude Cousins & Co Ltd*,[86] he starts with the lines: "There is in Wiltshire a little village called Castle Combe, which is said to be the prettiest in England. The film 'Dr Doolittle' was made there."[87] And in *Ex parte Johnson Trust Ltd*,[88] one might almost be in the opening scene of a Sherlock Holmes mystery when, in his statement of the facts, Denning observes:

> *In Sussex, south of Petworth, there are two old villages nestling under the Downs. One is Graffham. The other is East Lavington. They are about a mile apart. In between them there is fine parkland attached to*

---

83 *Ibid*, 42.
84 [1966] 1 All ER 954 (CA).
85 *Ibid*, 956.
86 [1971] 2 QB 426 (CA).
87 *Ibid*, 433.
88 [1974] QB 24 (CA).

> *a mansion house called Lavington House. There is a carriage drive through the parkland from Graffham to East Lavington. It passes near to the mansion house. This drive was made over a hundred years ago by the owners of Lavington House so as to give access by carriage to and from their home. It was called the old coach road. It is no doubt a private carriage way for the owners of the big house.*[89]

'And it is there,' one almost expects Denning to say, 'that the body of the late baronet was found.' But in reality, the tale was a little more mundane: the villagers claimed simply that there was a public right of way for pedestrians along the carriageway.

Denning's introduction to *Johnson Trust* is beautifully written; albeit perhaps matched by the at points captivating statement of background facts in the judgment in *Walsh and Cassidy v County Council for the County Sligo*[90] – a recent decision of the Irish Supreme Court which, as with *Johnson Trust*, was concerned with whether there was a public right of way over private lands:

> *11 Lissadell was one of the major Anglo-Irish landed estates. Its history can be traced to Elizabethan times. It was, prior to its purchase by the plaintiffs, the home for centuries of the Gore-Booth family. At its greatest extent, the estate comprised some 32,000 acres of land comprising of the great house and demesne as well as tenanted lands. For large parts of its history, the title to the estate was entailed and held under strict settlements. Save for some short identifiable periods, during the entire period from 1800 until 1982, the owner in possession for the time being was a tenant in tail male.*
>
> *12 The present case is concerned with the claim by the respondent, the County Council of the County of Sligo, that the public enjoys rights of way to traverse all the roads through the demesne lands which remain after the disposal, in two stages, of the great bulk of the estate under the Land Acts.*[91]

Arguably, there can be a downside to Denning's understandable pride in his Englishness – namely, his occasionally controversial treatment of the non-English 'other'. For example, in *Kelly v London Transport Executive*,[92] Denning refers to Mr Kelly, an Irishman, as "a

---

89	*Ibid*, 31.
90	[2014] 2 ILRM 161 (SC).
91	*Ibid*, 167.
92	[1982] 2 All ER 842 (CA).

plausible Irishman and a chronic alcoholic".[93] And in *Secretary of State for Employment v Globe Elastic Thread Co Ltd*,[94] Denning, for no apparent reason, observes of Mr Wijaszko, an employee in a redundancy-related dispute, that "I expect he came from Poland originally." In *Kelly*, one gets the sense that Denning sacrificed clarity to eloquence, balancing the six syllables of "plausible Irishman" with the six syllables of "chronic alcoholic". But what exactly is a "plausible Irishman"; and to that end, what is an 'implausible Irishman'? In *Globe Elastic*, Denning's throwaway mention of Mr Wijaszko's supposed origins seems unnecessary. In *McIlkenny v Chief Constable of the West Midlands*,[95] in the face of evidence which suggested police misbehaviour in the prosecution of six alleged Irish terrorists, Denning – surprisingly for an undoubtedly savvy man – went out on a linguistic limb in a judgment that refused the men the opportunity to sue for assault following their murder convictions, observing as follows:

> If the six men win, it will mean that the police were guilty of perjury, that they were guilty of violence and threats, that the confessions were involuntary and were improperly admitted in evidence: and that the convictions were erroneous. That would mean that the Home Secretary would have either to recommend they be pardoned or he would have to remit the case to the Court of Appeal ... This is such an appalling vista that every sensible person in the land would say: It cannot be right that these actions should go any further ... [T]he actions should be stopped.[96]

Had Denning perhaps shown greater delicacy in his choice of words, he could have spared himself the embarrassment that befell him (even if he did not himself feel it) when the six men later had to be let free because their convictions were considered unsafe and unsatisfactory.[97] (The phrase "appalling vista" attracted such opprobrium in Ireland that when Denning died in 1999, one Irish national daily newspaper, the *Irish Independent*, reported his death under the headline "'Appalling vista' judge dies at 100".)[98]

---

93   *Ibid*, 845.
94   [1979] QB 183 (CA).
95   [1980] 2 WLR 689 (CA).
96   *Ibid*, 706.
97   See *R v McIlkenny* [1992] 2 All ER 417 (CA).
98   See Purcell.

11. Three great British judges: Lords Atkin, Denning and Bingham

An example of Denning hankering for a 'golden' England of yesteryear can be found in his judgment in *Dickson v Pharmaceutical Society of Great Britain*.[99] There he appears to trumpet the 'attractions' of a Victorian-Edwardian England that may have existed before the Great War and perhaps even endured in spirit into the interwar period, but which was surely dead or dying when *Dickson* was decided in the late 1960s. Thus, Denning writes:

We are all familiar with the traditional pattern of a chemist's shop. When you go in, there is on one side of the shop a qualified man dressed in a white coat. He is a registered pharmacist. He dispenses doctors' prescriptions: and from his counter he sells medicines and drugs; thermometers and bandages; and all needs for the sick. Those are called 'pharmaceutical goods.' On the other side there are shop girls dressed in their neat overalls. At their counters they sell toothpaste, lipstick, and all articles of toilet: also films, cameras and photographic equipment. Those are called 'traditional goods.'

This traditional pattern is being eroded ... [I]n some of the bigger shops ... 'non-traditional goods' assume a major role. You will there find that a large part of the space is devoted to the sale of books, gramophone records, even wines and spirits. So that the shop loses its individual character as a chemist's shop. It becomes part of a general emporium.

Even in the late 1960s, the just-quoted passage must have seemed antiquated in style. Denning presents the reader with an England populated exclusively by male pharmacists. (In reality, Frances Potter, the first woman to be registered under the Pharmacy Act of 1868, was registered as early as 1870.)[100] The picture Denning depicts of "a qualified man" on one side of the pharmacy and "shop girls" (not women) on the other seems anachronistic (though, in fairness, one of the great BBC sitcoms of the 1970s, *Are You Being Served?*, took place in an 'olde worlde' department store where the menswear and womenswear departments were run as separate fiefdoms on either side of a single shop floor, so there may have been a certain popular resonance to Denning's observations). As to the references to "articles of toilet", "gramophone records" and a

---

99   [1967] Ch 708 (CA).
100 Anon (2018). Curiously, Potter's achievement has not earned her a reference in the *Oxford Dictionary of National Biography*.

"general emporium", these are all usages of language that must have seemed somewhat dated in the 'swinging Sixties'.

In his essay on "Politics and the English Language", George Orwell points to what he considered to be two particular excrescences of English-language writing in his day. These were staleness of imagery and lack of precision. Imagery may seem something that a judge need not be concerned with. Yet what is a judge doing when writing the facts of a judgment other than creating an image in the reader's mind of the salient facts? Denning's often beautiful introductions to his judgments offer as good an introductory piece of prose as one will find within the covers of any novel of his day – for example, "Broadchalke is one of the most pleasing villages in England. Old Herbert Bundy was a farmer there";[101] and, perhaps most famously, his opening to *Miller v Jackson*,[102] which contains as good an example of image in judicial writing as exists:

> *In summertime village cricket is the delight of everyone. Nearly every village has its own cricket field where the young men play and the old men watch. In the village of Lintz in County Durham they have their own ground, where they have played these last 70 years. They tend it well. The wicket area is well rolled and mown. The outfield is kept short. It has a good club house for the players and seats for the onlookers. The village team play there on Saturdays and Sundays. They belong to a league, competing with the neighbouring villages. On other evenings after work they practise while the light lasts. Yet now after these 70 years a judge of the High Court has ordered that they must not play there anymore. He has issued an injunction to stop them. He has done it at the instance of a newcomer who is no lover of cricket ... with the consequence, I suppose, that the Lintz Cricket Club will disappear. The cricket ground will be turned to some other use. I expect for more houses or a factory. The young men will turn to other things instead of cricket. The whole village will be much the poorer. And all this because of a newcomer who has just bought a house there next to the cricket ground.*[103]

Any notion that imagery is not an important element of the fact-setting element of a judgment need merely be viewed in the context

---

101 *Lloyds Bank Ltd v Bundy* [1975] QB 326, 334 (CA).
102 [1977] QB 966 (CA).
103 *Ibid*, 976.

11. Three great British judges: Lords Atkin, Denning and Bingham

of the just-quoted passage to see that it is false. However, it may not be the only falseness that presents. There has been suggestion that Denning's ode to the Lintz Cricket Club is not factually correct, one commentator describing it as "pure fairy tale"[104] and another describing the club ground as "a scungy little ground surrounded by the worst artefacts of modern British industrialism".[105] (In fact, an internet search for the club brings up photographs which suggests it to be a pleasant venue, albeit not perhaps quite matching the mental image that Denning creates in his judgment.)

In his judgments, Denning engages repeatedly in (to borrow from Copland) a 'fanfare for the common man' – his sincere warmth for so-called 'ordinary' English people perhaps being born of his so-called 'ordinary' background as the son of a draper. So, for example, in *Beswick v Beswick*,[106] Denning pays homage to "Old Peter Beswick", a dead coal merchant whose widow brought a successful appeal seeking specific performance of a contract that her nephew had entered into with her late husband. Denning's maternal grandfather was a coal merchant and this memory may have informed the notable warmth in his description of Mr Beswick:

Old Peter Beswick was a coal merchant in Eccles, Lancashire. He had no business premises. All he had was a lorry, scales and weights. He used to take the lorry to the yard of the National Coal Board, where he bagged coal and took it round to his customers in the neighbourhood. His nephew, John Joseph Beswick, helped him in the business. In March, 1962, old Peter Beswick and his wife were both over 70. He had had his leg amputated and was not in good health. The nephew was anxious to get hold of the business before the old man died. So they went to a solicitor ... , who drew up an agreement for them.[107]

The text is magical. The main characters are all introduced. A sense of Beswick's background is conveyed. The mention of the amputated leg is suggestive of a hard life – and suggestive too of where Denning's fundamental sympathies lie; and that single sentence "The nephew was anxious to get hold of the business

---

104 Kiefel (2012), 5.
105 Priestley, 140.
106 [1966] Ch 538 (CA).
107 *Ibid*, 549.

before the old man died" is suggestive of a young man whose actions will play a part in the pages that follow.

In *Deeble v Robinson*,[108] a relatively early judgment that is devoid of the embroidery which can occasionally detract just a little from the greatness of some of Denning's later judgments, Denning paints yet another picture that honours a life lived by honest labour:

> Mr Deeble has a milk round. He sells milk to people at the doors of their houses. He runs his business from a dairy building where he keeps his equipment, refrigerator, spare milk bottles, and so forth, and a stable where he keeps his horse and float. His round is seven streets adjoining the premises. He does not actually have a shop as ordinarily understood. His lease of these premises is coming to an end, and he wants to stay on there. This depends on whether the premises come within the definition of a 'shop' in the Leasehold 1953 Property (Temporary Provisions) Act, 1951.[109]

Yet not all 'ordinary' people appear to be treated with the same affection by Denning. In *R v Slough Borough Council*,[110] Denning describes Ms Jack (an evicted council tenant) as:

> ... a coloured woman, aged 26. She is unmarried and has three children. The two older ones (a girl aged eight and a girl of four and a half) are in the care of the local authority. They have been put out with foster parents. The youngest (a boy aged two) is with his mother. In 1973 she was the tenant of a council house at Slough ... She often had men in the house.[111]

The fact that Ms Jack was a woman of colour is irrelevant to the judgment; one contemporary commentator described the reference to her ethnicity as "totally gratuitous".[112] As to the sentence "She often had men in the house", this is colloquial phraseology that seems wanting in exactness and – unusually for Denning – perhaps also wanting to a degree in kindness.

In *Lamb v Camden Borough Council*,[113] Denning seems to view squatters almost as a blemish on England. He commences with another beautiful vignette of England and English life:

---

108 [1954] 1 QB 77 (CA).
109 *Ibid*, 81.
110 [1981] QB 801 (CA).
111 *Ibid*, 808.
112 Anon. (1982), 18.
113 [1981] QB 625 (CA).

> *Off Hampstead Heath there is a terrace of houses of quality built in the early 19th century. They are called Villas on the Heath. One of them belonged to Mrs Lamb, the first plaintiff. In 1972 she went to New York and let the house to a tenant.*[114]

The tenant moved out of the house after it suffered flood damage and some squatters moved in. Mrs Lamb managed to have them evicted after "her father got some building labourers to put up a few boards at a cost of £10 ... [and] the neighbours helped too".[115] Then a second set of squatters came a-visiting:

> *[A] few months later, in the summer of 1975, there was a second invasion of squatters. A shifting population. As some went out, others came in. Mrs Lamb's agents did what they could to get them out ... Eventually the police arrested the squatters on a charge of larceny. Whilst they were at the police station, Mrs Lamb's agents got in and made the premises secure with elaborate reinforced defences. That was in May 1977. The end of the squatters.*[116]

Clearly, Mrs Lamb should not have had to suffer as she did. But Denning's language is, arguably, unfortunate. One would typically speak of a house being 'invaded' by rodents or some other pest. By using the verb 'to invade', Denning seems almost to diminish the squatters to the level of vermin, and they were not vermin.

Perhaps the two greatest judgments of Lord Denning's career are his establishment of the doctrine of promissory estoppel in *Central London Property Trust Ltd v High Trees House Ltd*[117] and his "path-breaking"[118] dissenting judgment in *Candler v Crane Christmas and Co*,[119] "one of the greatest judgments ever delivered in the common law world".[120] Both are considered here, not for their legal content but for what they can teach in terms of judgment writing.

High Trees, despite being a seminal judgment, briefly recounts the facts (which concerned a promised rent reduction), a succinct recitation of applicable case law (with cases being despatched with a one or two-sentence summary and never expressly quoted from),

---

114   *Ibid*, 632.
115   *Ibid*, 633.
116   *Ibid*.
117   [1956] 1 All ER 256 (KBD). (The judgment was delivered in 1946.)
118   Wilberforce, 441.
119   [1951] 2 KB 164 (CA).
120   Hogan (2007), 126.

followed by a conclusion as to the law and an indication of the practical effects of that conclusion. It is a judgment in the classic FLAC model and, if nothing else, points to the folly of the modern view that a judgment to be persuasive requires to be long – albeit not quite achieving the near-miracle that is Justice Holmes' circa 600-word dissent in *Lochner*.

In *Candler*, the plaintiff came to court looking for damages for negligent statements made by the defendant company. The Court of Appeal decided by a two-to-one majority that without a contractual/fiduciary relationship between the parties, the loss was not actionable. Denning dissented on the basis that an actionable duty of care should exist for negligent misstatements of the type that it was sought to sue upon. Over a decade later, his approach was endorsed by the House of Lords in *Hedley Byrne & Co Ltd v Heller & Partners Ltd*.[121] Because *Candler* is an appellate case and because his is a dissenting judgment, Denning does not deal with the substantive facts at length, but explores them on the basis that the detail is known. He then identifies the key issue in quite beautiful English:

> Now I come to the great question in the case: did the accountants owe a duty of care to the plaintiff? If the matter were free from authority, I should have said that they clearly did owe a duty of care to him.[122]

Denning then turns to applicable authority, commencing with an analysis of what he considers to have been "two cardinal errors"[123] that informed the case law which preceded more recent case law – most notably *Donoghue v Stevenson*,[124] which he considered justified a revisitation of standing precedent. Commencing with the words "Let me first be destructive", Denning assails the arguments of counsel for the defendant company, reasoning through applicable case law, but by reference only – that is, never quoting it at length. Proceeding next with the words "Let me now be constructive", he then suggests the circumstances in which he considers that a duty to use care in a statement does arise, to whom the duty is owed, the degree of proximity of relationship required and to what transactions it extends. And he ends with a warning

---

121 [1964] AC 465 (HL).
122 [1951] 2 KB 164, 176 (CA).
123 *Ibid*.
124 [1932] AC 562 (HL).

shot "that the law would fail to serve the best interests of the community if it should hold that accountants and auditors owe a duty to no one but their client".[125] Described in one journal article as a "powerful dissent",[126] Denning's judgment is also nothing short of a *tour de force* in terms of how to write persuasively. It is clear; it is brief; and though it treats comprehensively with precedent, it does not quote from it in excessive length.

3. Lord Bingham

As to Lord Bingham (1933–2010), "a towering figure in the law",[127] he is one of a select number of English judges who have managed in the 21st century to acquire a significant international reputation. The first person in English history to serve in the various positions of master of the rolls (responsible for the civil courts), lord chief justice (responsible for the criminal courts) and senior law lord, Bingham's reputation has, if anything, grown since his death. This is thanks in no small part to his book *The Rule of Law*, which was published in the last months before his death and treats at length with the role of the Rule – "an all but sacred flame which animates and enlightens ... society".[128] In an age when liberal democracy – never the strongest of plants – seems almost constantly confronted with near-withering attacks, it is a book that has acquired a fresh resonance.

Like Lords Atkin and Denning before him, Bingham did not initially study law at university, preferring instead to study history at Balliol College. (Atkin and Denning were also Oxford men: Atkin studied classics at Magdalen College and Denning studied mathematics, also at Magdalen.) Bingham's background in history arguably shines through in cases such as *A v Home Secretary (No 2)*,[129] where he trawls through hundreds of years of case law and other legal authorities before concluding, among other matters, that evidence obtained by torture cannot lawfully be admitted in a UK court.

As is the way with so many of Britain's leading judges, Bingham

---

125 [1951] 2 KB 164, 184 (CA).
126 Hogg and Amarnath, 138.
127 Layton, 893.
128 Bingham, T (2007), 85.
129 [2005] UKHL 71; [2006] 2 AC 221 (HL).

has a beguiling fluidity to his English, yielding a writing style that is understated but powerful. Bingham also gave some thought to the theory and practice of judgment writing. Some of his observations in this regard have been touched on elsewhere in this book. Before turning to consider a few of Bingham's judgments, it is worth recalling what might be styled as his 'Ten Commandments' when it comes to good appellate judgment writing (though many of these 'Commandments' are applicable to judgments written by courts at all levels):

- Accessibility is key: There is a problem with "the length, elaboration and prolixity" of common law judgments, with the result that such judgments have become to some extent inaccessible.[130]
- Multiple/dissenting judgments can be good: There is authoritative support for the proposition that multiple judgments and freedom to dissent "[foster] beneficial development in the law and [avoid] unsatisfactory compromises".[131]
- Composite judgments are sometimes desirable: Composite judgments from multi-judge panels are desirable in cases concerning:
  - professional conduct and responsibility;
  - criminal law and practice; or
  - an area which has become so complex that it would benefit from "a single lapidary and authoritative ... setting out [of] the law shorn of all superfluous excrescences".[132]
- Composite judgments are not unproblematic: Composite judgments can give rise to continuing issues of interpretation which could be avoided if the various judges on a panel summarise their reasoning.[133]
- The principle of law laid down should be clear: However many judgments are given (dissenting judgments included), the principle of law laid down should be clear.[134]

---

130 Bingham, T (2011), 42–43.
131 *Ibid*, 45.
132 Bingham, T (2009), 612.
133 Bingham, T (2007), 71.
134 Bingham, T (2011), 45.

- Judges should be cautious: It is one thing for a judge to move the law a little further along the line; quite another to recast it.[135]
- Trial judgments have limited audiences: The primary audience for a judgment is the parties and their advisers, "who must be told who has won and why, and what (if any) relief is to be given";[136] in unreserved first instance judgments, the sole audience will likely be the parties and their advisers.
- Appellate judgments have multiple audiences: Appellate court judgments have a wider audience, being:
  - the parties and their legal advisers (if any);
  - the legal profession;
  - law teachers;
  - non-legal professionals; and
  - the general public.[137]

  (These are such plentiful and varied audiences that it is more than arguable that one could not write a single judgment in the multiple formats such divergent audiences would require.)
- Dissenting judges write for future judges: In a dissenting judgment, the judge is addressing judges on successor courts.[138] (As Lord Dyson has separately observed: "[T]he product of today's buccaneer sometimes becomes tomorrow's orthodoxy.")[139]
- A good judgment will contain the following ingredients:[140]
  - (possibly) a succinct introductory identification of the central point in the case;
  - a summary of the salient facts;
  - some account of the history of the litigation;
  - a summary of the parties' respective contentions;
  - (for an appellate court) some attention to the trial judge's reasoning; and
  - clearly stated reasons for allowing/dismissing the appeal.

---

135 *Ibid.*
136 Bingham, T (2009), 607.
137 *Ibid.*
138 *Ibid.*
139 Dyson, 11.
140 Bingham, T (2009), 608-09.

In *A v Home Secretary*,[141] the House of Lords held that the rights of certain foreign terror suspects who had been detained without trial was a matter for the courts, and that there had been a breach of those rights. Bingham's judgment (technically it takes the form of a speech) deviates from his later-identified model as to the "ingredients which a good judgment should contain".[142] So, for example, he does not commence with a succinct introductory identification of the central point in the case; and he does not then follow his own suggested sequence of summarising the parties' respective contentions, attending to the reasoning of the Court of Appeal and then stating his reasons for allowing the appeal. Yet for all that (and testament to his skill as an author), Bingham's judgment is undeniably clear. It is not simple, though Bingham himself appears to see simplicity more as a desirable goal than as one that will invariably be attained. Thus, he has separately written:

> *To Einstein is attributed the aphorism: 'Everything should be made as simple as possible, but not simpler'. This seems to me to express a profound truth. There are some subject matters which cannot, without distortion or caricature, be made entirely simple. But simplicity should ... be a constant aim, well worth a struggle.*[143]

In an age when English judges have (unfairly) been decried by some among the UK press as "Enemies of the People"[144] (ironically, in relation to a case in which the judges in question were upholding the sovereignty of the people's Parliament), Bingham's judgment in *A v Home Secretary* gives something of a 'master-talk' as to due interaction between the judicial and legislative branches of government:

> *I do not accept the full breadth of the Attorney General's submissions. I do not ... accept the distinction which he drew between democratic institutions and the courts. It is of course true that the judges in this country are not elected and are not answerable to Parliament. It is also of course true ... that Parliament, the executive and the courts have different functions. But the function of independent judges charged to interpret and apply the law is universally recognised as a cardinal feature of the democratic state, a cornerstone of the rule of law itself.*

---

141 [2004] UKHL 56; [2005] 2 AC 68 (HL).
142 Bingham, T (2009), 608.
143 *Ibid.*
144 See the front-page headline to the Daily Mail of 4 November 2016.

The Attorney General is fully entitled to insist on the proper limits of judicial authority, but he is wrong to stigmatise judicial decision-making as in some way undemocratic.[145]

That is powerful prose – perhaps all the more powerful for being understated.

In *A v Home Secretary (No 2)*,[146] Bingham trawls through over half a millennium of case law and other legal authorities before concluding, among other matters, that evidence obtained by torture cannot lawfully be admitted in a UK court, regardless of where, by whom or on whose authority the torture was inflicted. He also, it is submitted, comes closer to incorporating into this judgment – in precisely the manner that he was later to write about – all the "ingredients which a good judgment should contain";[147] and his judgment does seem the better for it – which rather suggests that the ingredients he has separately identified as being necessary for a good judgment are rightly identified. Thus, Bingham commences with a one-sentence identification of "the central question which the House must answer".[148] He gives an account of the history of the litigation and then an account (it is too long to be described as a summary) of the salient facts. Then he embarks upon what can only be described as a *tour de force* of relevant case law and legal authorities from the late 15th century onwards, considering various dimensions of the appellants' arguments and also the case as put by the secretary of state.

There are a couple of memorable passages in Bingham's judgment in *A v Home Secretary (No 2)*, including a somewhat crushing dismissal of the test posited by Lord Hope as to when it can be said that a statement has been established as having been made under torture:

Lord Hope, proposes ... the following test: is it established, by means of such diligent inquiries into the sources that it is practicable to carry out and on a balance of probabilities, that the information relied on by the Secretary of State was obtained under torture? This is a test which, in the real world, can never be satisfied. The foreign torturer

---

145 Paragraph 42.
146 [2005] UKHL 71; [2006] 2 AC 221 (HL).
147 Bingham, T (2009), 608.
148 [2006] 2 AC 221, 243 (HL).

Part II: The practice of the art and craft of judgment writing

does not boast of his trade. The security services ... do not wish to imperil their relations with regimes where torture is practised. The special advocates have no means or resources to investigate. The detainee is in the dark. It is inconsistent with the most rudimentary notions of fairness to blindfold a man and then impose a standard which only the sighted could hope to meet.[149]

This is not the most exciting of English, but it is possessed of a sombre calmness that befits so troubling a subject matter and lends to the forcefulness of Bingham's observations.

At issue in *Regina (Jackson) v Attorney General*[150] was whether a law ostensibly passed in accordance with the Parliament Acts had in fact been duly enacted. The true target of this almost abstruse question was certain anti-hunting legislation – the Hunting Act 2004 – which had made it generally unlawful to hunt wild animals with dogs. The claimants' hope was that if the Parliament Act 1949 was invalid, then the Hunting Act (though enacted in accordance with the Parliament Acts) would also fall. The House of Lords held that the Parliament Act and hence the Hunting Act enjoyed full legal effect.

Bingham's judgment in *Jackson* is an eloquent and interesting piece of work that deals at length with British constitutional history. However, the abundance of quotations in the judgment makes it an occasionally testing read. (At one point, Bingham quotes almost the entirety of the text of the Parliament Act 1911.) Such an abundance of quotations is perhaps surprising from a man who has separately cautioned against "the reproduction of large chunks of quotation",[151] preferring instead "[the] giving [of] a summary which is both brief and completely accurate".[152] Nonetheless, in terms of the ideal judgment form for which Bingham separately canvassed, one can see elements of that ideal in his judgment in *Jackson*. Bingham's closing observations in *Jackson* also strike a particularly compelling note of concern as to the overweening powers of an omnipotent House of Commons. Thus, he states:

It has been a source of concern to some ... that the effect of the 1911

---

149   Ibid, 273.
150   [2005] UKHL 56; [2006] 1 AC 262 (HL).
151   Bingham, T (2009), 608.
152   Ibid.

11. Three great British judges: Lords Atkin, Denning and Bingham

... Act [as amended, this being an Act which ultimately allows the House of Commons extensive powers to override vetoes of proposed legislation by the unelected House of Lords] ... has been to erode the checks and balances inherent in the British constitution when Crown, Lords and Commons were independent and substantial bases of power, leaving the Commons, dominated by the executive, as the ultimately unconstrained power in the state. There is nothing novel in this perception. What, perhaps, is novel is the willingness of successive governments of different political colours to invoke the [said laws] ... not for ... major constitutional purposes ... but to achieve objects of more minor or no constitutional import ... There are issues here which merit serious and objective thought and study. But it would be quite inappropriate for the House in its judicial capacity to express or appear to express any opinion upon them, and I do not do so.[153]

In truth, he kind of does. No one reading this text could seriously be left in doubt as to what Lord Bingham thought of a situation in which legislation enacted to meet high constitutional needs would be used to meet lower political objectives.

In *Regina (Begum) v Governors of Denbigh High School*,[154] Bingham treated with the various rights issues that can present when it comes to wearing religious dress in secular schools. In that case, a Muslim girl complained that there had been a breach of her rights under the European Convention on Human Rights by virtue of a decision by her school to exclude her from attendance given her desire to attend school wearing a *jilbab* (a full-length outer garment that traditionally covers the head and hands) in preference to one of three alternative school uniforms that had been agreed upon following consultations between parents, pupils, staff and local mosques. The Court of Appeal (overruling the trial judge) upheld Ms Begum's claim but was itself overruled by the House of Lords. The political sensitivity of the case is captured by Lord Bingham in the second paragraph of his judgment when he observes that:

It is important to stress ... that this case concerns a particular pupil and a particular school in a particular place at a particular time ... The House is not, and could not be, invited to rule whether Islamic

---

153 [2006] 1 AC 262, 286–87 (HL).
154 [2007] 1 AC 100 (HL).

dress, or any feature of Islamic dress, should or should not be permitted in the schools of this country. That would be a most inappropriate question for the House in its judicial capacity, and is not one which I shall seek to address.[155]

There is perhaps a certain sleight of judicial hand in this observation. It is true in all it states. Yet clearly, what Britain's most senior judges had to say about the interactions between human rights law, religious belief, education and the wearing of religious dress/school uniforms was likely to impact on the design or redesign of relevant school policies in the wake of the case.

In form, Bingham's speech in *Begum* departs to some extent from the ideal that he separately identifies when he considers the "ingredients which a good judgment should contain".[156] Thus, he begins with a succinct introductory identification of the central issue in the case, including a brief mention of the litigation history (coupled with the just-quoted cautionary note). He then identifies, though not in summary form, the facts agreed between the parties and thereafter proceeds to identify the applicable law. He does not treat at any great length with the arguments of the parties. And there is more mention than is usual for him as to what had been decided in the court below. All this comes in the context where, it will be recalled, Bingham suggests a good appellate judgment will possibly contain a succinct introductory identification of the central point, as well as a summary of the salient facts, some account of the litigation history, a summary of the parties' respective contentions, some attention to the trial judge's reasoning and clearly stated reasons for allowing/dismissing the appeal. However, despite the departures from the ideal that he has separately posited, Bingham's judgment offers a most engaging read.

Begum and the various other Bingham judgments considered in the preceding pages raise one further issue. According to Bingham, the audience for appellate court judgments includes litigants and their lawyers (if any), the legal profession, law teachers, non-legal professionals and the general public.[157] If by this Bingham means that a judgment should be comprehensible to all of these audience

---

155   *Ibid*, 107.
156   Bingham, T (2009), 608.
157   *Ibid*, 607.

segments, a question arises as to whether it is actually possible to write such a judgment. If it is possible, then, arguably, none of the just-considered judgments meet this exacting standard – though my own sense is that such a standard is impossibly exacting.

4. Some lessons

Can one identify some key lessons on the art and craft of judgment writing from the foregoing? The following occur (I do not repeat Lord Bingham's insightful extra-judicial observations on judgment writing, as outlined above, but they repay careful reading):

- A good judgment possesses a clear style/language, vivid examples/imagery, aphorism and metaphor, and an ability to rise above immediate facts and to see a problem in the perspective of the larger scheme of things.
- Over the expanse of time, a sense of empathy/sympathy for those who are faring badly in life resonates well.
- There is nothing wrong with a distinctive style; snappy one-liners; even language that is occasionally flowery and ornate. However, the best judgments are crisp and persuasive.
- A good judgment may not be appreciated in its own time; a judge must take comfort in the fact that it may be appreciated at some time.
- Overt squabbling among members of an appellate panel ought to be avoided. There can be (sometimes unpleasant) squabbling behind closed doors but this does not need to be made public.
- Legal questions are often reducible to clear, certain categories.
- While the writing of common law judgments allows for individualism (to the point of genius), a judge needs to be careful not to reveal personal sentiment or to surrender substance to style.
- A good appellate judgment will possibly contain:
  - a succinct introductory identification of the central point, as well as a summary of the salient facts;
  - some account of the litigation history of the litigation;
  - a summary of the parties' respective contentions;
  - some attention to the trial judge's reasoning; and

- clearly stated reasons for allowing/dismissing the appeal.
- Brevity, clarity and simplicity are the gold standard of judgment writing. As to simplicity, everything should be made as simple as possible, but not simpler. This triple standard is likely impossible to attain if a judge writes (or perceives herself to be writing) for an abundance of divergent 'audiences'.

Having considered the lessons in judgment writing to be gleaned from the judgments of three great and pioneering North American women judges, three prominent US Supreme Court judges and three prominent British law lords, I proceed in the next chapter to consider some of the lessons in judgment writing to be gleaned from the judgments of some great (and often overlooked) judges from the wider common law world.

12. Some great judges from the wider common law world

This chapter considers some of the lessons in good judgment writing to be gleaned from the judgments of some of the most prominent judges from the wider common law world: Sir Owen Dixon (Australia); Bora Laskin (Canada); Hans Raj Khanna (India); Brian Walsh (Ireland); Shimon Agranat (Israel); and Sir John Salmond (New Zealand). All have participated in that "global conversation of judges"[1] which is such a remarkable feature of the common law world.

1. Introduction

One might sometimes imagine from reading existing literature on judgment writing that Lord Denning and Justice Holmes are the only judges ever to have crafted a masterful judgment. Their prominence is perhaps partly attributable to the 19th–20th century influence of the United Kingdom as an imperial power (and as the home country of the common law), as well as the centuries-long pre-eminence of American democracy as "the last best hope of earth".[2] Of course, both men also had a striking "capacity for … vivid writing".[3] However, there are several dozen pure or mixed common law jurisdictions worldwide, many of which have produced great judges with great writing styles, few of whom have received much consideration outside their home jurisdictions. In this chapter, I briefly consider some of the judgments written by prominent judges from several of these jurisdictions (regrettably, space means that it is not possible to consider more than a very few) and seek to identify what they have to teach the judge who seeks to be a better judgment writer. (The various judges are treated with in

---

1 Baudenbacher, 525.
2 Lincoln.
3 Hogan (2007), 120.

order of the jurisdiction from which they hail, each jurisdiction being treated with alphabetically.)

2. Sir Owen Dixon

Sir Owen Dixon (1886–1972) – a man "who occupies a magnificent place in the story of the Australian legal system"[4] and who was "[a]n internationally pre-eminent black-letter lawyer"[5] – was appointed in 1929 to the High Court of Australia. Save for brief periods as a wartime ambassador and international mediator (on the troubled issue of Kashmir), he served on the High Court (as chief justice from 1952) until his retirement in 1964. Under Dixon's leadership, the High Court is said to have "commanded a respect in other jurisdictions for its expositions of common law which exceeded that of any other superior court".[6] Dixon himself commanded remarkable prestige among his colleagues, to the point that he even 'ghost-wrote' judgments for some colleagues. (One recent survey suggests that 18% of one colleague's judgments may have been written by Dixon.[7] Additionally, two other colleagues "frequently free rode on the work ethic and intellect of Sir Owen ... by joining judgments written by Dixon ... or writing short concurring judgments".[8] Such 'freeloading' by fellow judges can only have enhanced Dixon's power within the High Court.)

Of Dixon's many judgments, space allows for the consideration of but a few. Yet even in the space available, it is also worth mentioning a paper he delivered in 1955 at Yale University. Entitled "Concerning Judicial Method", it is a paper "with which ... every lawyer in the common law tradition ... should be familiar", as one later judge of the High Court of Australia has suggested.[9] In it, in comments on "the classical period of English law"[10] (ie, from circa 1815 until the late 19th century), Dixon identifies what he perceived to be the limited role of the judgment writer:

---

4   Holloway, 688.
5   Bridge, 30.
6   Howard, 9. There is perhaps a touch of hyperbole in this observation. The US Supreme Court and the House of Lords have always enjoyed especial lustre in the common law world. However, it is true that the High Court of Australia does seem to have enjoyed an especial international lustre in Dixon's day.
7   Partovi, 682.
8   *Ibid*, 674.
9   Hayne, 223.
10 Dixon, 5.

12. Some great judges from the wider common law world

It is one thing for a court to seek to extend the application of accepted principles to new cases or to reason from the more fundamental of settled legal principles to new conclusions or to decide that a category is not closed against unforeseen instances which in reason might be subsumed thereunder. It is an entirely different thing for a judge, who is discontented with a result held to flow from a long accepted legal principle, deliberately to abandon the principle in the name of justice or of social necessity or of social convenience ... The objection [to this] is that in truth the judge wrests the law to his authority.[11]

In the just-quoted text, Dixon reveals his "unwavering faith"[12] in the classical common law perception of the judge as an actor limited in the scope of her freedoms and the form of her reasoning – what one commentator has described as "Dixonian 'legalism'".[13] Yet two immediate difficulties present with such an approach:

- It "perpetuates power structures and stymies the disruption required for ... reform";[14] and
- It requires a court "to decide issues of high moment to the community without, or with very little, consideration of the context".[15]

Dixon's limited conception of the judge's role is evident in his High Court judgments. An early judgment of note is *Birmingham v Renfrew*.[16] There, a husband and wife had agreed that the wife's property would be bequeathed to her husband in the event that she predeceased him (which she did), provided that he bequeathed his estate to certain of the wife's relatives. The husband defaulted on this arrangement in his will and the High Court held that a constructive trust had arisen in favour of those relatives which could be enforced against the husband's executors. Dixon's judgment from start to finish is marked by a striking clarity and crispness. His opening line neatly summarises the issue between the parties. After outlining the facts, his judgment then takes an interesting turn in that he states his conclusion and next proceeds to consider the applicable law

---

11 *Ibid*, 6.
12 Dawson, 543.
13 Aroney, 51.
14 Chaudhri, 163.
15 Howard, 7.
16 (1937) 57 CLR 666 (HCA).

before restating the conclusion that he has already trailed. In form, therefore, his judgment takes the following approach: Introduction–Facts–Conclusion–Law–Conclusion. So it takes an untypical approach that does not accord with the judgment forms considered in Chapter 5 and yet remains a model of clarity.

In *Yerkey v Jones*,[17] Dixon delivered a seminal judgment on what is now sometimes called 'sexually transmitted debt'[18] (the process whereby one person in a romantic relationship can become responsible for the financial debts of another). Though the judgment propounded an ostensibly sexist rule (in terms of favouring women over men),[19] it also involved a well-intentioned, if paternalist effort to ensure that a married woman was adequately protected from her husband's financial excess – in particular, where she was called upon to give a personal guarantee of his debts where there was no especial advantage to herself (a scenario which, unfortunately, continues occasionally to present). So while *Yerkey* yielded the position that "there is a species of guarantor to which the law accords special privilege – a married woman who guarantees her husband's debt"[20] – it may be that some such form of special privilege is justifiable if special needs present; though in a more enlightened age, any such privilege would, it is submitted, need to be moulded carefully so as to apply to any 'vulnerable' party in the context either of marriage (including same-sex marriages) or of non-marital romantic relationships.

Dixon's judgment in *Yerkey* commences with a captivating recitation of the relevant facts:

> About 10th August 1936 the respondent's husband, Estyn Jones, a clerk earning a slender salary, resolved to purchase at a price of £3,500 a bungalow standing on over three acres of land near Payneham, Adelaide. The place was fitted up as a poultry-farm, and from poultry keeping and from the breeding of dogs, a pursuit in which he took a great interest, he expected to make a certain profit. The respondent was less optimistic.[21]

---

17 (1939) 63 CLR 649 (HCA).
18 Fisher, 16.
19 See generally O'Donovan.
20 Walker, 6.
21 (1939) 63 CLR 649, 666–67 (HCA).

12. Some great judges from the wider common law world

Immediately, the reader senses that disaster beckons and that a lawsuit will ensue. After finishing the facts, Dixon turns to the law, expressly announcing that this is what he is doing ("Before dealing with the considerations of fact upon which the conclusion depends, some account should be given of the equitable principles upon which it is founded").[22] This takes some time. Dixon then applies the law to the facts at hand and reaches a conclusion – namely, that if a husband procures his wife to enter into a guarantee/security, it may be voided if the creditor trusted that procurement to the husband and had no independent ground for reasonably believing that the wife fully comprehended the transaction. (Leave to appeal the decision of the court to the Privy Council was refused.) In form, the judgment takes the classic Facts–Law–Application–Conclusion (FLAC) judgment form considered in Chapter 5.

Some of Dixon's prominent other judgments include those given in *Bank of New South Wales v The Commonwealth* (the 'Bank Nationalisation case')[23] and *Australian Communist Party v Commonwealth* (the 'Communist Party case').[24] The *Bank Nationalisation* case concerned the constitutionality of Australia's Banking Act of 1947, which would have given a monopoly in banking in Australia to the Commonwealth Bank of Australia. Thus, it was an overtly political case – albeit that Dixon somewhat unconvincingly suggested that this political dimension was an aspect of matters which the legalism of the common law was well placed to sidestep in its pursuit of truth:

> *Nor do I think that it is correct to say that courts cannot inquire into such matters. There are few, if any, questions of fact that courts cannot undertake to inquire into. In fact ... under the maxim* res iudicata pro veritate accipitur *['an adjudicated thing is regarded as truth'] courts have an advantage over other seekers after truth. For by their judgment they can reduce to legal certainty questions to which no other conclusive answer can be given.*[25]

A question perhaps arises as to whether Dixon was correct in his perception of the merits of strict legalism. "[F]or some ... Dixon's

---

22   *Ibid*, 670.
23   (1948) 76 CLR 1 (HCA).
24   (1951) 83 CLR 1 (HCA).
25   *Ibid*, 340.

legalism can be ... seen as ... reflecting an unsophisticated understanding of judging, or as a form of paternalism intended to hide from a credulous public the obvious freedom open to judges when they decide cases."[26] Certainly, the *Bank Nationalisation* case has more recently been touted as an example of "the unavoidability of the political role of the High Court [of Australia]".[27]

Dixon's judgment in the *Bank Nationalisation* case is a model of clarity. He identifies the purpose of the actions before the court, briefly describes the Banking Act, enters into a more comprehensive description, brings theory to bear and looks to the constitutionality of the act in a brilliant sequence of successive points which, though detailed, is easy to follow, with each point followed immediately by a crisp treatment of same; the judgment ends with an ultimate conclusion and an indication of the order to be made. In form (roughly Introduction–Law–Analysis–Conclusion–Order), Dixon's judgment takes an approach that bears a resemblance to the approach canvassed by Mahoney (Issues–Law–Facts–Conclusions–Order), as considered in Chapter 5.

At issue in the *Communist Party* case, "a celebrated victory for the rule of law",[28] was the constitutionality of Australia's Communist Party Dissolution Act 1950. The act was found by a six-to-one majority on the High Court to be unconstitutional – essentially because, as an act ostensibly targeting subversion, it empowered the government to proceed by declaration regardless of whether (apart from the declaration) there was any factual connection between affected persons and subversive activity.[29] For Australians, the case remains of significance from a human rights perspective "because if the majority had upheld the validity of the legislation, the defence power [a provision of the Australian Constitution allowing for defence-related laws] would have potentially been deemed limitless ... exercisable ... on the subjective opinion of the executive".[30] Dixon's judgment in the case proceeds with rigorous clarity. He identifies the purpose of the proceedings, briefly describes the act, brings theory to bear, enters into a compre-

---

26   See generally Gava (2011), 158.
27   McEvoy, 58.
28   Winterton, 630.
29   *Ibid*, 649 *et seq*.
30   Chetty, 22.

hensive consideration of the legislation, then treats with each of the various submissions made in detail before arriving at an ultimate conclusion. In form, he adopts an approach which might be summarised as Introduction–Law–Application–Conclusion, thus again taking an approach that bears a resemblance to that canvassed by Mahoney (as considered in Chapter 5). Yet for all that he is a 'black-letter' judge, some of Dixon's prose in the *Communist Party* case is quite beautiful – including his shrewd observation (which has a particular resonance in our own age, when liberal democracy seems endangered from within) that:

> *History and not only ancient history, shows that in countries where democratic institutions have been unconstitutionally superseded, it has been done not seldom by those holding executive power. Forms of government may need protection from dangers likely to arise from within the institutions to be protected.*[31]

There is real beauty in Dixon's black-letter expositions of the law. Arguably, however, he never quite reaches the literary heights scaled, for example, by Lord Denning or Justice Holmes, one commentator suggesting that Dixon echoes the attainments of those men but "to an admittedly lesser extent".[32] One cannot but wonder whether a greater spirit of adventure on Dixon's part might have won him a still-higher rank in the pantheon of common law judges than that which he has attained.

3. Bora Laskin

Bora Laskin (1912–84), the 14th chief justice of Canada – a "star of the Commonwealth judiciary",[33] "a wonderful writer ... [and] a sharp thinker who articulated a consistent vision"[34] – was a remarkable person and judge. Born of Jewish parents, in his early legal career Laskin (despite holding an LLM from Harvard University) was unable to find work at any of Canada's prominent law firms because of "the anti-Semitism of Anglophile Toronto's legal community".[35] Though he eventually managed to find a non-Jewish lawyer with

---

31 (1951) 83 CLR 1, 187 (HC).
32 Hogan (2007), 119.
33 Girard, 742.
34 Sossin, 263.
35 *Ibid*, 256.

whom to train, it is perhaps telling as to the lingering anti-Semitism of his day that Laskin pursued the mainstay of his pre-judicial career within academia.

As an academic and judge, Laskin has been described as having played an "activist role in the reform of labour law and human-rights law".[36] Appointed to the Ontario Court of Appeal in 1965, he became the first Jewish member of the Supreme Court of Canada, following his appointment to that court in 1970. In 1973, in a departure from convention, Laskin was appointed chief justice in preference to the then most senior ordinary member of that court.

As a judge, Laskin acquired a reputation for "commitment to modernity and the idea of law as a progressive force".[37] Though often in the minority – "perhaps more than any Canadian jurist, [he] is as celebrated for his dissents as his majority judgments"[38] – Laskin's dissent rate decreased over time.[39] Though he was prepared to take an "aggressive [activist] approach"[40] to the Canadian Charter of Rights and Freedoms following its adoption in 1982, he died before this proved possible. Among the more notable of his many judgments are his powerful dissents in *R v Burnshine*[41] ("a forceful dissenting opinion"),[42] *Nova Scotia Board of Censors v McNeil*[43] (a "strong dissent")[44] and *Attorney General for Canada & Dupont v Montreal*[45] (in which Laskin "dissented forcefully").[46]

Burnshine concerned the lawfulness of the sentencing powers of the courts of British Columbia by reference to the equality provisions of the Canadian Bill of Rights. *McNeil* concerned the lawfulness of censorship legislation which led to Bernardo Bertolucci's *Last Tango in Paris* being kept from the cinemas of Nova Scotia. *Dupond* concerned the lawfulness of what was in effect a prohibition on freedom of assembly within the precincts of the City of Montreal for a 30-day period.

---

36   Girard (2007), 730.
37   Sossin, 259.
38   *Ibid*, 260.
39   Belleau and Johnson, 65.
40   Girard, 4.
41   [1975] 1 SCR 693 (SC).
42   Sharpe (1985), 656.
43   [1978] 2 SCR 662 (SC).
44   Sharpe (1985), 652.
45   [1978] 2 SCR 770 (SC).
46   Sharpe (1985), 653.

12. Some great judges from the wider common law world

In *Burnshine*,[47] a onetime young offender maintained, among other matters, that he had been denied equality before the law because under the laws of British Columbia, he was exposed to a greater criminal sentence than applied elsewhere in Canada (apart from Ontario). The majority held in effect that the form of equality contended for did not present. Laskin's dissenting judgment contains a brief overview of the case before the court, a recitation of the facts, a consideration of applicable law and a conclusion, bringing it closest to the approaches to judgment writing canvassed by Atkinson and Wanderer (as considered in Chapter 5). As a judgment, it is notable for seeking to bring a more elastic concept to equality than the majority; and for Laskin's sharp observation that the majority view yielded a construction of the law which "appears ... alien to the very purpose which is said to animate it"[48] – that is, the majority was, Laskin intimated, prepared to sanction inequality under a measure that sought to promote equality.

In *McNeil*,[49] a closely divided (five-to-four) court upheld the validity of impugned censorship legislation pursuant to which Bernardo Bertolucci's erotic drama *Last Tango in Paris* was kept from Nova Scotian cinemas by the Nova Scotia Board of Censors. Laskin, by now chief justice, delivered a single dissenting judgment for the minority judges in which he maintained that the determination of decency/obscenity was a matter exclusively reserved to Canada's Parliament.[50] Laskin's dissenting judgment contains a brief overview of the case, identifies the issue presenting, looks at the facts and law, and then arrives at a conclusion. However, his dissenting judgment is perhaps most notable for what it does not do. Thus, it treats with the case before it as one concerning the issue of the validity of broadly drawn provincial legislation. In what may have been a necessary compromise in a collective dissent, Laskin does not treat with the broader issue raised by the Canadian Civil Liberties Association in the case as to the relationship of censorship to free speech – a line of approach which, had it been pursued, might have placed the case more to the fore internationally when it comes to judgments in this area.

---

47 [1975] 1 SCR 693 (SC).
48 *Ibid*, 718.
49 [1978] 2 SCR 662 (SC).
50 *Ibid*, 681.

Dupond[51] concerned the constitutionality of a blanket ban on public assembly in Montreal over a 30-day period. The Quebec Court of Appeal overturned an initial finding that the legislation was unconstitutional. On further appeal to the Supreme Court, a majority of the justices were prepared to uphold the city law as involving unobjectionable police/municipal regulations of a local character. Laskin and his two fellow dissenters were not. Laskin's judgment is notable for its clarity of reasoning and certainty of approach. So, for example, he observes:

> *There is a distasteful part of the challenged [laws] ... which, surprisingly, appears to be relied on to support their validity. The prohibition of assemblies or gatherings is not limited to those from which disorder or violence is anticipated but extends to all activities ... Here, persons who might seek to associate or gather for innocent purposes are to be barred ... because of a desire to forestall the violent or the likely violent. This is the invocation of a doctrine which should alarm free citizens even if it were invoked and applied under the authority of the Parliament of Canada ... [E]nforcement of the criminal law is often difficult ... Yet it has always been central to our criminal law that the police are expected to enforce it against violators and not against innocents.*[52]

It is hard not to blush at the bluntness of these stirring observations. The sense presents that, in Laskin, those who would seek to exercise their right to peaceful assembly have a champion. The straightforward simplicity with which Laskin expresses his views gives them a raw power. In form, the judgment takes the truncated form to be expected of a dissent, leveraging off the description of the law in the majority judgment and proceeding straight into a consideration of the (notable) points of difference with an at times almost breezy directness of style.

In each of *Burnshine*, *McNeil* and *Dupond*, Laskin cemented the perceived view of him as a civil libertarian and as someone prepared to depart from the Supreme Court's "tradition of legislative deference".[53] Notably, however – and surprisingly, perhaps, in a onetime

---

51 [1978] 2 SCR 770 (SC).
52 [1978] 2 SCR 770, 780 (SC).
53 Snell and Vaughan, 223.

academic – he is not prone to extensive consideration of "the philosophical or theoretical basis for civil liberties ... [or] the precise contours of any particular value or right".[54] So he clearly did not see his judgments as a place in which to engage in a PhD-style academic excursus. "He did, however, plainly hold strong views on the values he deemed important, and his commitment to those values was steady and constant."[55]

For all his achievements on the Supreme Court of Canada, perhaps the most interesting of Laskin's judgments is the "hammering eloquence"[56] of his dissent in the Ontario Court of Appeal in *R v Cameron*.[57] That involved a failed appeal by a Toronto art dealer, Dorothy Cameron, against a conviction for exhibiting 'obscene' pictures that nowadays likely would be – and (one suspects) 'then-a-days' likely were – viewed by most as unobjectionable. As Laskin himself observes in his dissenting judgment:

[C]onsidered in the light of the expert evidence, I have no difficulty in seeing emphasis in all the drawings on the human form ... Of course, there are sexual connotations; but it cannot ... be said that the drawings are merely vehicles for conveying such connotations ... I am quite satisfied that the Crown has failed to prove that the drawings are obscene.[58]

(They appear, in truth, to have been competent pictures by "reputable artists"[59] that were being displayed in "a first-rate gallery".)[60] In his judgment, Laskin was principally concerned by the fact that the conviction rested ultimately on the trial judge's reaction to the artworks in issue and thus was more in the nature of a personal reflex than representative of some breach of standards. Laskin's opinion was more in touch with changing social mores than the majority view and "continues to be one of the most widely cited judgments in obscenity cases around the world".[61] Certainly,

---

54 Sharpe, 633.
55 *Ibid*.
56 Horrall, 75.
57 [1966] 2 OR 777.
58 *Ibid*, para 91.
59 Braun, 63. There is, of course, a value to 'disreputable' artists also. With art as with judgments, "the [supposedly objectionable] dissent of today may become the [triumphant] orthodoxy of tomorrow" (Bingham (2009)).
60 Braun, *Ibid*.
61 Horrall, 77.

Part II: The practice of the art and craft of judgment writing

his enlightened liberal conclusions are a world away from the condemnatory stance of the majority judges, Justice Aylesworth observing as follows, for example:

> *I am quite unable to convince myself ... that it is either necessary or in service of the public good ... unduly to exploit the theme of sex as a dominant characteristic in the portrayal of the human figure ... Artistic merit in the portrayal of human forms singly or in relationship with one another – in the portrayal of appealing studies in contrast as to light and shade and in the treatment of the lines or other details of the human form do not require it.*[62]

In terms of style, Laskin has been described as "prolific in his judicial writing, [but] ... often highly formal in ... style, obscuring the policy aspect of his decisions behind a recitation of cases and consideration of precedent".[63] (This is a trait that is also discernible, for example, in the judgments of Justices Khanna of India and Walsh of Ireland.) In the context of this book, Laskin is additionally notable for having published on judicial writing styles, pointing to the need for judges on a panel "to show generous institutional faith in opinion ... prepared by others, unless strong conviction induces the preparation of a concurring opinion or ... a dissent",[64] though striking a somewhat sceptical approach as regards concurring judgments:

> *Each judge has or develops his own writing style; and collegiality dictates that one be generous enough in concurrence to tolerate literary compositions that are different from one's own, and hence to join in another's opinion where the only reason for writing separately would be a preference for a different literary style.*[65]

4. Hans Raj Khanna

Hans Raj Khanna (1912–2008) – "a great judge"[66] and an "ardent follower of [Justice] Holmes",[67] though "not an activist judge in terms of 'militant use of judicial power ...'"[68] – was born in

---

62 *Supra*, para 23.
63 Swinton, 354–55.
64 Laskin (1972), 339.
65 *Ibid*, 340.
66 Palshikar, 59.
67 Sudhir, 19.
68 Khosla, 65.

12. Some great judges from the wider common law world

Amritsar, in what was then British India. His family had historically been small traders, but his father was a successful lawyer. Khanna is one of three judges among those considered in this chapter who was born before the independent state he eventually served as judge came into existence. (The others are Justices Agranat and Walsh. Notably, all three were to pursue in their respective jurisdictions the path identified by Justice Walsh for an independent Ireland: "to develop our law after our own genius.")[69]

Appointed a judge in 1952, Khanna was elevated to the Punjab High Court in 1962, went from there to the Delhi High Court and proceeded to the Supreme Court in 1971. In *Kesavananda Bharati v State of Kerala*[70] ("the most important [Indian] case on the substantive limitation of Parliament's power to amend the constitution"),[71] Khanna was among the (seven-to-six) majority who held that the Indian Parliament's power to amend the Constitution was limited. The court appears initially to have split six to six, with Khanna not aligning himself with either group and only eventually, "as if by the quirk of history",[72] electing to join the majority view. In his judgment, Khanna iterated the 'basic structure' doctrine whereby certain elements of the Indian Constitution are not alterable/destroyable by the Indian Parliament, such as the democratic nature of India – though, ironically, "[t]he Basic Structure Doctrine proceeds upon a distrust of the democratic process"[73] (or, more accurately perhaps, a distrust of that self-destructive ochlocracy to which liberal democracy can tend).

Khanna's judgment in *Kesavananda Bharati* is strikingly long. It commences with a procedural history; outlines the legal background/issue; and then proceeds with an extensive interweaving of Indian law, constitutional law theory (as espoused by prominent theorists such as Bentham, Burke, Dicey, Laski, Mill, Paine and Pound), foreign law and case law (including case law from former British colonies such as Ireland which had initially been left by their onetime colonisers with a constitution akin to

---

69	O'Flaherty, 6.
70	(1973) 4 SC 225 (SC).
71	Singh, 9.
72	Kumar, 202.
73	Balasubramanian and Yadav, 56.

that of India). Finally, towards the end of his judgment, Khanna provides a helpful summary of his main conclusions, including the key finding that: "The power of amendment ... does not include power to abrogate the Constitution nor does it include the power to alter the basic structure or framework of the Constitution."[74] It is this 'basic structure' concept, described by former Chief Justice Babu of India as a "touchstone" of Indian democracy,[75] which continues to safeguard Indians – in particular, Indians who find themselves in a minority – from over-reach by the majority.[76]

There is no denying the intellectual sweep and power of Khanna's reasoning in *Kesavananda Bharati*. It may be that because the majority within the court was so narrow, he felt compelled to advance an essentially unanswerable case for the position staked out by the majority. Or he may have considered it desirable "to compensate for the absence of a developed constitutional history and tradition by assimilating" a wealth of common law theory and jurisprudence into his consideration of the law.[77] Whatever his motivation, his judgment is very long, comprising almost 200 lengthy and detailed paragraphs. And, like many literary classics, it is, at points, not the easiest of reads – though in reading it, one cannot but recall the observation in a onetime book review by Irish Supreme Court judge Brian Walsh (some of whose judgments are considered later below) that: "This is not an easy work to read but it is well worth the effort."[78] In form, Khanna's judgment is in a (distinguished) class of its own.

Kesavananda Bharati was one of a series of Indian Supreme Court cases which concerned limitations on the power to amend the Indian Constitution. Unsurprisingly, given the political implications of such case law, there followed an "increase in executive interference with judicial appointments to the higher courts".[79] This was a trend that was to impact directly on Khanna following his

---

74   *Supra*, para 1599.
75   Babu, 202.
76   See generally, Sood.
77   Lahav (1981), 36.
78   Walsh, B (1982), 387.
79   Rabboni and Kingsley, 465.
80   AIR 1976 SC 1207 (SC). Page references hereafter are to the pdf version of ADM Jabalpur available online at https://indiankanoon.org/doc/1735815/.

12. Some great judges from the wider common law world

dissenting judgment in *ADM Jabalpur v Shivkant Shukla*,[80] the case that earned him a lasting place in the world pantheon of judges.

ADM Jabalpur – the majority judgment in which has been described as "the Supreme Court of India's 'darkest chapter'"[81] – arose ultimately from the court-ordered suspension from the Indian Parliament of Prime Minister Indira Gandhi. Gandhi's government responded to this challenge by proclaiming a state of emergency, it seems a "Phoney Emergency"[82] designed to keep her in office. 'Phoney' or not, the state of emergency saw access to the courts for political detainees suspended. In *ADM Jabalpur*, the Supreme Court by a four-to-one majority (Khanna dissenting), in a "disastrous ruling",[83] held that such access could lawfully be suspended during a presidentially declared emergency (thereby refusing to support a number of courageous high court judges who had held *habeas corpus* hearings even after emergency laws prohibited access to the courts).[84] Khanna held to the view that access to the courts could not be suspended, even in an emergency.

More so perhaps than his judgment in *Kesavananda Bharati*, Khanna's "renowned dissent"[85] in *ADM Jabalpur* is riddled with phrases that would fire the soul of any common lawyer. He commences with a strong opening line – "Law of preventive detention, of detention without trial is anathema to all those who love personal liberty"[86] – and he never lets up:

- "Rule of law is the antithesis of arbitrariness";[87]
- "[T]he hard facts of human nature [have] demonstrated the essential egotism of men and the truth of the *dictum* that all power corrupts and absolute power corrupts absolutely";[88]
- "Sanctity of life and liberty was not something new when the Constitution was drafted. It represented a fact of higher values which mankind began to cherish in its evolution from a state of tooth and claw to a civilized existence";[89]

---

81 Ramnath (2016), 210.
82 Nariman, 16.
83 Noorani, 408.
84 Neuborne, 494.
85 Sarkar, 160.
86 *Supra*, 78.
87 *Ibid*, 96.
88 *Ibid*.
89 *Ibid*, 97.

267

- "Preventive detention, though not strictly punishment, is akin to punishment, because of the evil consequences of being deprived of one's liberty";[90]
- "One of the essential attributes of the rule of law is that executive action to the prejudice of or detrimental to the right of an individual must have the sanction of some law";[91] and
- "[T]here are certain aspects which constitute the very essence of the rule of law. Absence of arbitrariness and the need of the authority of law for official acts affecting prejudicially rights of individuals is one of those aspects".[92]

Axiom follows axiom as the law is carefully unveiled.

Like his judgment in *Kesavananda Bharati*, Khanna's dissenting judgment in *ADM Jabalpur* is notably long. There is also a similarity of form. He gives a relatively lengthy introduction, identifies the legal question presenting, considers the legal background and then proceeds again with an extensive consideration of a rich blend of Indian law, foreign law and case law, followed (eventually) by a helpful summary of conclusions, including the astute observation that:

There is no antithesis between the power of the State to detain a person without trial under a law of preventive detention and the power of the court to examine the validity of such detention. In exercising such power the courts only ensure that the detaining authority acts in accordance with the law providing for preventive detention.

But eloquence aside (and it is a most eloquent judgment), a striking feature of Khanna's judgment is the dispassionate professionalism of his text. His calmly reasoned and at points profound logic "belies the tumultuous political context in which it was decided".[93] And as with his judgment in *Kesavananda Bharati*, Khanna's judgment in *ADM Jabalpur* shows a talent that all of the judges considered in Part II of this book share – namely "an ability to probe beyond the formal realm of the law and to comprehend and to state the relevant principles from political philosophy".[94]

---

90 *Ibid*, 100.
91 *Ibid*, 105.
92 *Ibid*, 109–10.
93 Ramnath (2016), 210.
94 Lahav (1981), 36.

Khanna's 'reward' for his "celebrated dissent"⁹⁵ in *ADM Jabalpur* was that he was later snubbed by the Gandhi administration when, contrary to convention, it leapfrogged Justice Beg into the position of chief justice ahead of Khanna.⁹⁶ Khanna resigned over the snub and ended his days as "a symbolic figure of great importance ... [and] an example of ... moral courage".⁹⁷ And – testament to the truth of Lord Bingham's observation that "the dissent of today may become the orthodoxy of tomorrow"⁹⁸ – the Supreme Court of India in *KS Puttaswamy v Union of India*,⁹⁹ an important recent case on the right to privacy, latterly upheld Khanna's dissent in *ADM Jabalpur*. Justice Chandrachud overruled the majority judgment in the earlier case in the following memorable terms:

> *When histories of nations are written and critiqued, there are judicial decisions at the forefront of liberty. Yet others have to be consigned to the archives, reflective of what was, but should never have been. The decision of the US Supreme Court in* Buck v Bell *ranks amongst the latter. It was a decision in which Justice Oliver Wendell Holmes Jr. accepted the forcible sterilization ... of Carrie Buck as part of a programme of state sponsored eugenic sterilization. Justice Holmes, while upholding the programme opined that: 'three generations of imbeciles is enough'. In the same vein was the decision of the US Supreme Court in* Korematsu v United States, *upholding the imprisonment of a citizen in a concentration camp solely because of his Japanese ancestry.* ADM Jabalpur *must be and is accordingly overruled.*¹⁰⁰

5. Brian Walsh

Brian Walsh (1918–98) was a "great and creative judge"¹⁰¹ who "[let] in fresh air to legal and ethical debates in Ireland",¹⁰² and a man who "realised that judicial power is never surrendered by other

---

95 Ramnath (2016), 210.
96 Kachwaha, 29.
97 Neuborne, 482.
98 Bingham, T (2009), 607.
99 (2017) 10 SCC 1 (SC). In form, Justice Chandrachud's judgment is itself notable for its opening table of contents, with the judgment stated in the opening page to have "been divided into sections to facilitate analysis", so making his judgment, it is submitted, more accessible and comprehensible.
100 *Ibid*, para 121.
101 Kirby (2009), 78.
102 Manning, 208.

political forces and must always be asserted by the courts".[103] Walsh is the most consequential judge in the history of modern independent Ireland. One of his successors on the Supreme Court bench has written of Walsh "that his contribution [to Irish law] has been immense"[104] – though one must not imagine from this that the "Walsh years"[105] were especially radical from a social justice perspective. "[W]hat was evident was rather a paternalistic desire to protect the vulnerable than to assert the principle of equality as an engine for social change."[106]

Born at the close of World War I, when Ireland was still a part of the United Kingdom, Walsh went on to practise as a barrister and to teach law at St Patrick's College, a pontifical (Catholic) university outside Dublin. He was appointed to the High Court of Ireland in 1959 and elevated to the Supreme Court two years later. In 1980, Walsh was also elected a judge of the European Court of Human Rights (ECtHR). Notably, Walsh was not only an instigator of the new era of judicial dynamism that followed his appointment to the Supreme Court; in his time on the ECtHR, it "moved from the obscurity of a peripheral international tribunal ... to acceptance as a kind of constitutional court for human rights matters",[107] though the composite nature of its judgments makes it impossible to determine the scale of Walsh's involvement in this evolutionary process.

On appointment to the Supreme Court, Walsh apparently indicated that the then Irish prime minister (*taoiseach*) had indicated in private conversation that he would like the Supreme Court "to become more like the United States Supreme Court".[108] If so, the *taoiseach* got what he was looking for. One of Walsh's successors on the Supreme Court, former Chief Justice Ronan Keane, has observed how, throughout his judicial career, Walsh was "very concerned to make sure the Constitution was a living instrument".[109]

Justice Hogan, one of the current members of the Irish Supreme

---

103	Binchy, 152.
104	O'Flaherty, 2.
105	Binchy, 152.
106	*Ibid*.
107	See Hedigan, 31.
108	O'Flaherty, 1.
109	Keane, R (2004–06), 147.

Court, has described how Walsh "gathered up the driftwood of Irish constitutional law and left the waters pure".[110] Walsh achieved this 'gathering of driftwood' through a series of judgments that prodded a stagnating Irish legal system into rejuvenation. In truth, one can see in Walsh many of the attributes ascribed to Shimon Agranat, one of the "founding fathers"[111] of the Israeli Supreme Court;[112] and it seems likely that Agranat would have found much to agree with in Walsh's onetime analogy between a Constitution and railway building:

> *He said that in a new country, such as Australia or Canada, the railways were built in a straight line and the people followed the railways ... He thought our constitutional interpretation should be on the analogy of the straight line. The Constitution should not be bent to take into account some existing institution.*[113]

A striking feature of Walsh's judgments is that he consistently manages to achieve memorable advances without invariably deploying especially memorable language. Indeed, his judgments are testament to the power of understatement as a tool in the judicial armoury. The confines of space mean that only three of Walsh's more significant judgments can be considered here: *State (Quinn) v Ryan*,[114] *Byrne v Ireland*[115] and *McGee v Attorney General*.[116]

Quinn – still, to some extent, "the *fons et origo* of modern Irish extradition law"[117] – highlighted the unconstitutionality of a legacy arrangement from Ireland's time as part of the United Kingdom whereby a person could be arrested and removed from Ireland under an arrest warrant that issued in England (an entirely separate jurisdiction) without time for application to the Irish courts. Walsh begins with a general legal proposition ("Among the personal rights guaranteed by the Constitution is the right not to be deprived of personal liberty save in accordance with law"),[118] which he then reduces to the particular ("It is quite clear that a right to

---

110 Hogan (2017), 13.
111 Ramnath (2016), 210.
112 Lahav (1981), 27.
113 O'Flaherty, 5.
114 [1965] IR 70 (SC).
115 [1972] IR 241 (SC).
116 [1974] IR 287 (SC).
117 Hedigan, 24. The advent of the European arrest warrant has further transformed the extradition system in place between Ireland and its fellow member states of the European Union.
118 [1965] IR 70, 124 (SC).

apply to the High Court or any Judge thereof is conferred on every person who wishes to challenge the legality of his detention").[119] Next he briefly mentions the facts and then he embarks on a survey of applicable law and case law, reaching conclusions as he proceeds. In form (Propositions–Facts–Law–Conclusions), Walsh's judgment has a trace of the approach canvassed by Mahoney (Issues–Law–Facts–Conclusion–Order).[120] However, as with Khanna's style of reasoning, Walsh's reasoning in *Quinn* is perhaps best viewed as in a league of its own. The judgment led directly to the enactment of a revised extradition law. It was also "arguably the first building block in the Irish jurisprudence guaranteeing access to court".[121]

Byrne was "an absolutely momentous case"[122] which concerned whether royal immunity from suit had continued and vested in the post-independence Irish state. It arose out of a so-called 'trip and fall' accident in which Ms Byrne sought to sue Ireland and the attorney general as defendants. The Supreme Court held that the prerogative of immunity had not continued. Walsh delivered the lead judgment for the majority. In it, he briefly recites the facts and issue arising, then turns immediately to a consideration of constitutional theory and law (in Ireland, England, Australia and the United States), before bringing matters back to the facts at hand, again achieving a Khanna-like standard of clear but comprehensive reasoning. In form (Facts–Issue–Law–Conclusions), Walsh's judgment most closely resembles the form canvassed by Mahoney. There was, of course, an alternative conclusion that the Supreme Court might have reached (and which was advanced by the sole dissenting judge), which was that shaping governmental liability should have been left to Ireland's legislature. However, the legislature had had 50 years to act and essentially done nothing. Viewed from this perspective "[f]or the Supreme Court to have taken upon itself the task of reform and to have discharged it in so striking a fashion … was extremely propitious".[123] It has been

---

119 *Ibid.*
120 See Chapter 5.
121 Hedigan, 25.
122 Hogan (2017), 5.
123 Osborough (1976), 12.

suggested of Walsh's reasoning in *Byrne* that it "lacks depth of analysis".[124] However, as a judge one has to start somewhere: once a principle is acknowledged, any accretions and refinements (and even temporary setbacks) will follow.

Finally, *McGee v Attorney-General*.[125] This is a case from the Ireland of yesteryear in which the Catholic Church held great sway in national life. The case involved a challenge by Ms McGee to the constitutionality of legislation which prohibited the importation of contraceptives into Ireland. Ms McGee lost in the High Court but won in the Supreme Court, which held (by a four-to-one majority) that the relevant statutory provision was unconstitutional. Walsh begins his judgment in *McGee* with a passing reference to the facts, then turns to a consideration of applicable legislation, returns to the facts and then embarks on a survey of constitutional provisions, theory and applicable case law (including US case law). In his consideration of the natural (moral) law dimensions to *McGee*, Walsh (in notably eloquent language and as part of "an almost unique excursus by an Irish judge on the meaning of justice")[126] draws an explicit link between charity, justice and mercy, and the role of judges in the application of each:

> *Both Aristotle and the Christian philosophers have regarded justice as the highest human virtue. The virtue of prudence was also esteemed by Aristotle as by the philosophers of the Christian world. But the great additional virtue introduced by Christianity was that of charity – not the charity which consists of giving to the deserving, for that is attorney justice, but the charity which is also called mercy. According to the preamble, the people gave themselves the Constitution to promote the common good with due observance of prudence, justice and charity so that the dignity and freedom of the individual might be assured. The judges must, therefore, as best they can from their training and their experience interpret these rights in accordance with their ideas of prudence, justice and charity.*[127]

There is perhaps a danger in the last sentence of extending an open invitation to judges to become "latter-day philosopher kings

---

124 Lenihan, 3.
125 [1974] IR 287 (SC).
126 De Blacam, 324.
127 *Ibid*, 318–19.

[or queens] via the guise of constitutional adjudication".[128] But that does not detract from the quality of Walsh's analysis or prose. In form (Facts–Law–Facts–Law–Conclusion), Walsh's judgment is in a style of its own. And it is also possessed of a fundamental irony, of which Walsh cannot have been unaware: the Catholic Church is a champion of natural law. Yet in *McGee*, Walsh uses natural law to ground a right to privacy which rendered unconstitutional a statutory provision that criminalised the importation of contraceptives into (Catholic) Ireland. In the jousting yard of judgment writing, turnabout is fair play.

6. Shimon Agranat

Shimon Agranat (1906–1992), "the founding father of the right of free speech in Israel",[129] was born in Kentucky to Russian immigrant parents, grew up in Chicago, emigrated to British Palestine and ended up as the third chief justice of an independent Israel. As a jurisdiction, Israel is a "mixed system",[130] where common law, civil law, religious law and even traces of Ottoman law – "a degree of multiple influences rarely encountered in any other legal system"[131] – co-exist in a "living continuity".[132] However, a primary influence is the common law.[133] When it comes to the art and craft of judgment writing, the Israeli Supreme Court is notable among the courts considered in this book for consistently rendering judgments in language that is readily comprehensible.

Like Brian Walsh in Ireland, Agranat played a "major role in shaping ... the form and substance" of his nation's law in its formative post-independence period.[134] As one would expect of a judge whose Supreme Court career straddled almost three decades, his influence reaches into all areas of Israeli law. By way of example of the breadth of his contributions, he wrote the court's opinions in

---

128 Hogan (1990–92), 110.
129 Dalal, 47.
130 Hope (2001), 1.
131 Sassoon, 405.
132 Dainow, 435.
133 In one sense this is surprising, given the relatively recent arrival of the common law in what is now modern Israel. Sassoon (406–07) describes how common law was introduced by a Privy Council order as late as 1922, during a time when Palestine was a British protectorate:
> [T]hrough this gateway Palestine was suddenly given direct access to ... and ... able to share in the heritage and experience of close to a 1000 years of English law. The impact ... was immense ... [I]ts force on the Israel legal system of today is still very much in evidence.
134 Lahav (1992), 8.

the *Kol Ha'am* case (on free speech),[135] *Seedis v Seedis*[136] (on rabbinical courts) and *Mandelbrot v Attorney General*[137] (on insanity); and he delivered a concurring opinion in *Shmuel v Attorney General*[138] (on judicial recusals).

Kol Ha'am was a case that "radically transformed the landscape of political and civil liberties in Israel".[139] It arose from the suspension of two Communist newspapers by the Ben-Gurion administration after they published articles harshly critical of Israel's foreign policy. The Supreme Court (sitting as the High Court of Justice) lifted the suspension in a case that can now be seen to have been part of a process of establishment of "Israel's judicial bill of rights".[140] Agranat delivered the court's unanimous judgment. In it, he identifies the applicable law, describes the facts, considers the issues arising ("the relationship that exists between the right to freedom of the press ... and ... the power held by the authorities ... to place a limit on the use of that right"),[141] discusses the constitutional issues presenting (looking to authors from Mill to Milton and considering, for example, American and English case law), identifies the principles that require to be brought to bear and then reaches a conclusion. One of his more notable observations – though a question mark perhaps arises as to whether this holds good in the Information Age, when lies and false information fill the Internet and social media – was that: "As a general rule, there is a good chance that truth, in the end, will prevail; so ... it is better to act through discussion, education and counter-explanation, in order to cancel out the effect of ... false information."[142] In form (Law–Facts–Issue–Analysis–Conclusion), the judgment does not bear a close resemblance to any of the forms considered previously above.

Though the judgment in *Kol Ha'am* drinks deeply from the well of US case law – "The opinion incorporated a substantial portion of American First Amendment doctrine available in the early fifties"[143]

---

135   *Kol Ha'am Co Ltd v Minister of the Interior* (1953) HCJ 73/53 (SC/HCJ).
136   (1954) Special Tribunal 1/50 (SC/Special Tribunal).
137   (1956) CrimA 118/53 (SC/CCA).
138   (1964) CA 525/63 (SC).
139   Lahav (1990), 247.
140   Gross, 83.
141   (1953) HCJ 73/53 (SC/HCJ), 6.
142   *Ibid*, 28.
143   Lahav (1992) (1), 252–3.

– it is not perhaps quite in the league of *Marbury v Madison*. Thus, Agranat accepted that the Israeli judiciary did not have the power to invalidate statute. Even so, it is a significant decision in giving the Israeli courts a role in defining Israel's national way of life[144] and establishing the Israeli Supreme Court as "the guardian of civil rights in Israel".[145] It is also a model of clarity, utilising a free-flowing yet logical style that is worthy of imitation. In style, it has been described as "the Israeli version of a judicial opinion, Grand Style"[146] – that is (to borrow from Cardozo), a magisterial/imperative form of judgment in which "[w]e hear the voice of the law speaking by its consecrated ministers".[147]

Seedis v Seedis[148] is notable for staking out the respective jurisdictional 'territories' of Israel's secular and rabbinical courts.[149] The key question in *Seedis* was whether a rabbinical court had acted outside its jurisdiction in ruling on a property-related matter in a marital lawsuit. The Supreme Court, sitting as a special tribunal, held that it had not. Consistent with a general trend in Agranat's judgments, his judgment is notable for drawing on foreign case law and commentary. But even more striking is the extent to which he sets about constructing – and it really is constructing – the legal framework of a modern independent Israel by reference to established foreign/international practice. In form (Issue–Facts/Law–Law–Application of Law–Conclusion), the judgment comes closest to that espoused by Mahoney (Issues–Law–Facts–Conclusion–Order); but this does not do justice to the extent to which Agranat is taking various disparate threads of law and weaving them together into a newly coherent whole.

The creativity evident in *Seedis* can also be seen in *Mandelbrot v Attorney General*,[150] "[t]he most prominent example of independent creativity in ... [Israeli criminal] case law".[151] There, the medical evidence suggested that the accused (a paranoiac) could not bring

---

144 Burt, 2025.
145 Gross, 85.
146 Lahav (1981), 34.
147 Cardozo (1939), 10.
148 (1954) Special Tribunal 1/50 (SC/Special Tribunal).
149 For a roughly contemporary analysis of Israel's rabbinical court system and the interplay with the secular court system, see generally Chigier.
150 (1956) (Crim A, 118/53) (SC/CCA).
151 Gur-Aye, 562.

himself within the M'Naghten Rule, a test of insanity originally evolved by the English courts in the early 19th century. Agranat ("[who] considered *Kol Ha'am* and *Mandelbrot* his best and most significant opinions")[152] was among the majority who decided that this did not exhaust the accused's rights, and that he could also rely on the statutory defence of acting without the exercise of one's will. Agranat's judgment in the case has been described as "a daring affirmation of the judicial role in shaping the value system of ... society".[153] In terms of craftsmanship, the most striking feature of Agranat's judgment is its free-flowing, logical style and its crystal-clear clarity. Agranat describes the facts, considers the law (including a thorough analysis of relevant English and US law that features some of the same Anglo-American legal minds who populate Khanna's judgment in *Kesavananda Bharati*), brings a fresh analysis to bear on "whether the fundamental approach of the common law to the defence of insanity requires us to turn a favourable ear to the plea of irresistible impulse",[154] and then arrives at his conclusions. Agranat's judgment is so thorough, persuasive and comprehensible that it should almost be required reading for any common law judge seeking to improve her judgment-writing skills. In form, his FLAC style mirrors that canvassed by Atkinson (considered in Chapter 5).

Shmuel[155] was a case that derived from the rich mix of religions that co-exist in Israel. There, the attorney general sought an order removing children from a Christian missionary school and placing them in a Jewish school. The parents requested that the district judge (an orthodox Jew) recuse himself from acting in the case because, they claimed, his religion meant that he could not be seen to act impartially. The district judge declined to recuse himself and the applicants appealed to the Supreme Court. The Supreme Court considered that the law which the applicants sought to rely upon was concerned with a change of venue (not judge) which sufficed to deal with the appeal. However, it took the opportunity to offer various insights on recusal/disqualification of a judge. Agranat's concurring judgment, because it is a concurring judgment, does not

---

152 Kalman, 512.
153 Lahav (1990), 259.
154 (1956) (Crim A, 118/53), 41 (SC).
155 (1964) CA 525/63 (SC).

need to treat with the facts. Instead, it explains why a concurring judgment is needed (because there is a point of disagreement between other judges and Agranat therefore needs to indicate his view).[156] He then considers the question of jurisdiction by reference to English and US law (and some English commentary), bringing that foreign law and commentary to bear upon the case at hand (and pointing in particular to the availability of appeal to the applicants if they were dissatisfied with the decision of the district court).[157] As with all of the other just-considered judgments of Agranat, his judgment in *Shmuel* is striking in terms of how it seeks to construct a new post-independence legal order by reference to foreign law (and also for expressly pointing to the need for legislative reform[158] – thus showing a concurring judgment also to have that potential, which Justice Ginsburg ascribes to dissenting judgments,[159] of calling for necessary legislative reform). It is also a good example of how a short, focused concurring judgment can enhance a majority judgment. It meets the US Federal Judicial Center standard of including a statement as to why the concurrence has issued;[160] and, consistent with Lady Hale's observations on concurring judgments,[161] it adds a distinct perspective and is relatively short. In form, to borrow from McCormick (see Chapter 6), it is best viewed as an 'except for' concurring judgment, agreeing with the other judges except to the extent that it sides with Justice Witkon on a particular point in dispute.

As a judge, Agranat has been described as having "stood out for his uniqueness, drafting comprehensive judicial opinions with a decidedly didactic tone"[162] – observations that, to a greater or lesser extent, can be made of all of the judges considered in this chapter (particularly Laskin, Khanna and Walsh). One commentator, in an assessment of Agranat's judicial career, makes the following observations (which likewise find notable resonance in the careers of Laskin, Khanna and Walsh):

---

156   *Ibid*, 23–24.
157   *Ibid*, 26.
158   *Ibid*, 28.
159   Metzger *et al* (2013), 16.
160   Federal Judicial Center (2013), 30.
161   See Chapter 6.
162   Pardo and Zemer, 167.

When Agranat launched his Kol Ha'am *opinion in 1953, Israel's jurisprudence of rights was lean and arid, and the political climate was neither sympathetic to judicial review nor to civil liberties as understood in the liberal tradition. It took vision, confidence, a recognition of his role as a judge in rebuilding the homeland and, above all, enormous courage to reconstruct the legal system through judicial decision-making.*[163]

7. Sir John Salmond

Sir John Salmond (1862–1924) "was the leading legal intellect of his era in New Zealand",[164] as well as "a major international jurisprudential figure".[165] He is perhaps best known to generations of law students as the original author of one of the definitive texts on tort law in England and Wales. Born in England to a New Zealander father, he emigrated to New Zealand. This mixed upbringing carried through to his professional existence, which was marked by a strong connect "with the general current of Anglo-Imperial political and legal thought ... for this was an era when there was extensive fraternal dialogue amongst intellectuals of the British and American ... world in which Salmond moved without ... evident discomfort".[166]

Called to the New Zealand Bar in 1887, Salmond was a long-time university professor at the Universities of Otago, Adelaide (briefly) and latterly Victoria College (now Victoria University of Wellington), where he held the founding chair in law. Following a time as a legal draftsman, Salmond served as New Zealand's solicitor general, attracting some criticism in recent times for his apparent disinterest in Maori foreshore and lake claims, to which he "was both professionally (and probably personally) opposed".[167]

Salmond's time as a judge of the New Zealand Supreme Court lasted only four years, until his death (and was broken by a period as a New Zealand delegate at the interwar Washington Conference on the Limitation of Armaments). As a result, he is generally more

---

163   Lahav (1990), 269.
164   Morris, 813.
165   *Ibid*.
166   McHugh, P, 746.
167   Boast, 851.

Part II: The practice of the art and craft of judgment writing

remembered as "the author of books on jurisprudence and the law of torts which [were] ... standard works".[168] Even so, he managed a number of notable judgments, including but not limited to *Lodder v Lodder*,[169] *Park v Minister for Education*[170] and *Taylor v Combined Buyers Ltd*.[171] Salmond's dominance of the New Zealand legal arena of his time has led to the Supreme Court of his day being referred to as "Salmond's bench"[172] – though in truth it was a notably strong Supreme Court, containing a number of New Zealand's judicial 'greats', leading one commentator to describe it as "one of the strongest [New Zealand Supreme Court benches] ever".[173]

In *Lodder*, Salmond focused on conduct as a material element in divorce cases and also looked at the issue of whether a wife could insist on the continuation of a marriage which had long existed in name only, observing as follows in terms that are eloquent, if outdated:

It is true that the institution of lifelong marriage has been designed for the benefit of the woman rather than for that of the man. The nature of men and women is such that men commonly need no such legal protection against the evil chances of life. Nevertheless there seems no reason why a woman should be privileged to insist on the maintenance of her legal status as a wife, notwithstanding the fact that for years past she has lived apart from her husband and her marriage has been one in name only. Other considerations would doubtless apply if a wife's objection was not merely to the divorce but to the continuance of that separation by reason of which the divorce was claimed. Such an objection would be relevant in considering, as already indicated, whether the causes of the commencement or continuance of the separation are sufficiently grave and irremediable to justify a dissolution of the marriage.[174]

Throughout the judgment, Salmond is notably crisp: his sentences are short; he displays no emotion; and the abiding impression that arises is that one is in the hands of a competent

---

168 Anon (1925), 187.
169 [1921] NZLR 876 (SC).
170 [1922] NZLR 1208 (SC).
171 [1924] NZLR 627 (SC).
172 Morris, 813.
173 *Ibid*, 816.
174 [1921] NZLR 876, 880 (SC).

judge rendering dispassionate judgment and taking a "pragmatic approach to family law".[175] In form, the judgment has, arguably, a slightly unusual structure. It opens with a single paragraph in which the facts and law are summarised, the law is then stated and discussed, and only then are the facts detailed and the law (ever so briefly) applied. The sense presents, rightly or wrongly, that Salmond is more interested in the law and in speaking to the law than in the particular facts at hand.

In *Park*, the point at issue was whether the New Zealand minister of education could cancel a teacher's certificate in respect of (undetailed) disloyalty and gross misconduct which had been investigated by an education board, which decided to take no further action. The question was important as regards the security of tenure of teachers and also as regards the autonomous authority of education boards. The judgment follows a more traditional form than that of *Lodder*, commencing with the facts, identifying the law, applying the law to the facts and arriving at a conclusion – the conclusion being one that did not allow the effective usurpation of the role of an education board by the minister. Again, the language of the judgment is lucid and crisp, with a notable avoidance of especially long sentences. Insofar as it was necessary to criticise a previous decision of the House of Lords, Salmond's criticism is all the more effective for being understated; thus, he simply observes that: "It is not necessary for the purposes of the present case to consider the precise nature of this somewhat startling doctrine [as espoused by the House of Lords]".[176] As with *Lodder*, the judgment is notably short but no less (perhaps more) impressive for that.

In *Taylor*, a disappointed car buyer sought rescission of a contract of purchase on grounds of misrepresentation. Also in play was whether the car that was the subject of the dispute had been of merchantable quality and of reasonable fitness for the purpose for which it was bought. Salmond's judgment is slightly 'incomplete', in that he indicated at the end of the trial that the charge of fraud had not been sustained and reserved judgment solely on the issue of whether there had been breach of the implied statutory condi-

---

175 Morris, 823.
176 [1922] NZLR 1208, 1217 (SC).

tions of merchantable quality and of reasonable fitness for purpose. The judgment is longer and more discursive than those delivered in *Lodder* and *Park*, and it is difficult not to conclude that Salmond is dealing with issues with which he is instinctively more comfortable. Again, there are a couple of opening paragraphs that briefly identify the dispute at hand. The facts are treated with notable brevity and a lengthy and learned excursus on the law then follows – notable for the regard paid to English, Irish and Scottish case law. Only after settling on a definition of 'merchantable quality' for the purposes of New Zealand law does Salmond turn in detail to the facts of the case before him. So, as in *Lodder*, one gets a slightly unusual approach of a brief introduction, an excursus on the law, the application of the law to the facts (which are then recited in any detail), and then a consideration (by reference to previous New Zealand case law) as to the appropriate form of remedy, that law then being applied to the facts at hand. As with all of his judgments, Salmond's prose is crisp, his sentences are as short as they can be and the judgment is consequently an easy read.

8. **Conclusions**

To reach comprehensive conclusions on the careers of the major judicial figures considered in this chapter would be a huge task and better suited to a doctoral thesis (even several theses) than a short single book chapter. Nonetheless, even with the limited analysis possible in this chapter, it is possible to identify certain valuable lessons on judgment writing, such as the following:

- There is a wealth of case law in the wider common law world that has much to teach about the craft of judgment writing.
- There is no one methodology for writing a successful judgment.
- A 'black-letter' approach to law does not exclude the potential for eloquence, though it does seem to preclude that *éclat* which seems invariably to present in the very best judgments.
- There may be no especial eloquence to the views expressed in a judgment; however, stating the law with straightforward simplicity can exude a certain raw power.
- High-quality dissenting judgments can make a long-term difference and also enhance a judge's reputation.

- Formality in judicial style can obscure the policy aspect of decisions, especially when offered with detailed considerations of previous case law.
- Every judge has or develops her own writing style; and collegiality on an appellate court requires that one be generous enough to tolerate literary styles that are different from one's own.
- Judicial activism may sometimes need to be its own reward (as it can elicit a negative response from the executive branch in terms of personal advancement).
- The better judges/judgments show an ability to see beyond the particular of the moment to the greater issues at stake – that is, to probe beyond the formal realm of the law and to state applicable principle in a form that is clear, extensive and methodical.
- In the immediate post-colonial era, the greatest judgments of the greatest judges had a potent and significant role to play in forming the shape of democracy in newly independent nations.
- Great judgments, such as the best of those of Shimon Agranat, do not shy from revealing a struggle in the judge's soul.[177]

One further lesson arising, even from the limited consideration possible in a single chapter on the wider common law world, is that there is the clearest potential for a more expansive book examining the lessons in judgment writing to be gleaned from the judgments of more of the great judges from that wider world, including but not limited to the common law jurisdictions of Africa and the Caribbean.

With this chapter, I have concluded my consideration of the theory and practice of the art and craft of judgment writing. Given, however, the sheer number of *ex tempore* (ostensibly impromptu) judgments that continue to be delivered in common law jurisdictions, I proceed in the next chapter to consider the art, craft and delivery of *ex tempore* judgments – a process which can also involve some element of written preparation and result in a later written version of what was previously said.

---

177   Lahav (1990), 216.

Part III: Ex tempore *judgments*

13. The art and craft of *ex tempore* judgments

The Chief Justice [of Alberta] believes that the possibility of an erroneous decision given instanter *is more than off-set by the injustice, hardship, and weariness to the litigants, of a judgment long delayed, which might possibly be more correct. 'There is always the Court of Appeal,' he is apt to remark. A too prompt decision may be unjust to one of the litigants, but an unnecessarily delayed decision cannot help being unjust to both.* Canadian Law Times[1]

In this chapter, I address the art and craft of preparing and delivering ex tempore *judgments.*

1. Introduction

Though outside the scope of a book on judgment writing – especially one which canvasses for increased reliance on written reserved judgments – it is useful to touch briefly on the art, craft, preparation and delivery of *ex tempore* judgments, which Justice Cardozo once described as "ex tempore *decretals*".[2] This is not to retreat from the proposition that reserved written judgments represent the optimal form of judgment (albeit that *ex tempore* judgments are perfectly legitimate). It is to recognise the practical reality that in all common law jurisdictions, many judgments continue to be given orally on an '*ex tempore*' (ostensibly impromptu) basis when the hearing of a matter ends or very soon after.[3] Consequently, a chapter on this aspect of the judicial craft seems likely to be of interest and use to readers.

Ex tempore judgments tend nowadays to be more common in

---

1   Anon (1908), 225.
2   Cardozo (1935), 3.
3   It is also typically possible to give a reserved oral judgment.

Part III: *Ex tempore* judgments

lower, first instance courts which "are dominated by high case volume and limited time for each matter".[4] At a general level, it has been suggested that *ex tempore* judgments can be deployed in urgent cases, in easy/obvious cases[5] and when "[a] matter is ... not too complex"[6] – though my own experience is that there are few enough cases which are so easy, obvious, non-complex or even urgent that they cannot wait even a few days for a reserved written judgment.

The Latin term *'ex tempore'* means 'out of the time'. It is defined more broadly in the *Oxford English Dictionary* as meaning "without premeditation or preparation", with the phrase 'to speak *ex tempore'* meaning "to speak without notes or without reading from [a] manuscript". However, in the legal context, as will be seen, one of the key ingredients to giving a good *ex tempore* judgment is, to borrow from Baden-Powell, to 'be prepared': the better *ex tempore* judgments will have been subject to much prior thought and work. After all, with *ex tempore* judgments, as with all judgments, "[n]othing can be more contrary to equity and reason, than precipitate judgment".[7] Yet in the prior thought and work that goes into the substance of *ex tempore* judgments lies what is arguably their greatest deficiency. For if a judge is to give an *ex tempore* judgment at the end of a hearing or shortly thereafter, she will need to have a sense for some time before the hearing ends as to what her decision will be. But that involves largely making up one's mind on a dispute before all the arguments have been heard; and it surely "does nothing to engender confidence in the process for a judge ... to give the impression that the oral argument has been a waste of the parties' time and effort".[8]

The delivery of good *ex tempore* judgments is such a challenging task (and typically done alone by a trial court judge) that Lord Neuberger suggested, by way of "semi-serious point"[9] at a recent Denning lecture, that rather than starting alone in a district court

---

4   Hunter *et al*, 337.
5   Bell, A (2019), 16.
6   Bosielo, 5. By contrast, Fox (at 35) suggests that: "A trial judge should be able to deliver *ex tempore* judgment in a majority of cases."
7   Rippingham, 170.
8   Bell, A, 21.
9   Neuberger (2017), para 2.

and rising to the House of Lords, it would be better if novice judges started in the UK Supreme Court and moved in the opposite direction. This is because in the Supreme Court, the novice judge "would never have to deliver an *ex tempore* judgment".[10] After a time, she would proceed to the Court of Appeal, where she would find herself "not infrequently having to give *ex tempore* judgments".[11] Then – and only if she passed muster – she would be allowed out on her own as a trial judge "with ... the need to give immediate *ex tempore* judgments on tricky, procedural issues".[12]

In "The Judge Who Closed His Eyes",[13] Anglo-Irish barrister and humourist Theobald Matthew tells the tale of an experienced judge who falls asleep in a warm courtroom – this was before the threat of COVID-19 required all the doors and windows to be kept open at all times – and wakes up to find everyone waiting to hear what he has decided in the case before him. The judge pauses a moment and then speaks. He indicates that he sees no purpose in giving a reserved judgment and proceeds to give an *ex tempore* judgment. In that judgment, he mentions the one decision of the House of Lords that he recalls having been mentioned in argument and indicates that it inclines him to favour the plaintiff's case. He is subsequently pleased to see his decision upheld by the Court of Appeal and the House of Lords, "the Lord Chancellor Commenting, in the Latter Tribunal, on the Admirably Succinct Manner in which the Experienced Judge had Dealt with a Complicated and Difficult Problem".[14] The moral of the tale offered by Matthew is "Stick to the Point"[15] (presumably so as to keep the judge's attention). However, there is perhaps another lesson to be drawn from Matthew's Fables, which is that he saw *ex tempore* judgments occasionally to involve a degree of refined pretence. My own experience is that any such view is misplaced, and that the delivery of *ex tempore* judgments is

---

10 *Ibid.*
11 *Ibid.*
12 *Ibid.*
13 Matthew, 23.
14 *Ibid*, 24.
15 *Ibid.* In one review of a reissue of Matthew's funny fables, the reviewer – affecting the capitalisation and including the end-of-text moral that is the hallmark of Matthew's fables – humorously concludes by observing: "Within a Profession that Laughs at Itself Too Little, this book Ought to Be Read. You Might see in it Someone You Know. Moral. – It Might be You." (Smith, R, 332).

approached by devotees of this judgment form with the same seriousness of purpose and honest intent that they and others bring to written reserved judgments.

Though *ex tempore* judgments remain a continuing presence in common law systems, it is no longer the case that "the oral judgment is the rule", at least in UK courts.[16] Lord Neuberger, speaking in 2014 of the experience at superior court level in England and Wales, observed how "*Ex tempore* judgments, which were very common at first instance and in the Court of Appeal, when I started in the mid-1970s, are becoming rarer",[17] suggesting that this "in many ways is a shame".[18] (As mentioned, the position in lower courts is different.) It has been suggested that one factor contributing to the ascent of the reserved written judgment, at least within superior courts, is the decline of the jury trial in civil matters,[19] and with it the arrival of a more transparent system of decision making that is best achieved through writing (thus avoiding the singular deficiency of *ex tempore* judgments, being, as Lord Devlin once noted, that "they throw off things that are better left unsaid").[20] Lord Neuberger has suggested two further factors to explain the ascent of the written judgment. First, with the advent of written arguments, cases are argued more quickly than in the past, "so judges have much less time to prepare judgments during argument".[21] Second, the sheer abundance of material currently placed before judges means that giving a good *ex tempore* judgment is now much harder to do, because it is very hard for a judge to speak comprehensively to so much material.[22] (Lord Neuberger also suggests that if there is a greater move to televised court proceedings, there will be a still-greater decline in the number of *ex tempore* judgments that are delivered – a potential development that one suspects is not unrelated to his separate observation that, in his experience, "A good *ex tempore* was a work of art, but an ill-prepared one could be a rambling mess".[23] After all, no rational judge would

---

16	Lawson, 365.
17	Neuberger (2014), para 22.
18	*Ibid.*
19	Heydon (2012), 224.
20	Quoted in Barry, J, 28.
21	Neuberger (2014), para 22.
22	*Ibid.*
23	*Ibid.*

want to be recorded for posterity delivering a judgment that was embarrassingly bad.)

2. Advantages and drawbacks

Given that so much can be at stake for the parties to court proceedings (and that every case is important to those who are party to it), what conceivable advantage/s does the process of giving an *ex tempore* judgment offer over a more considered written judgment? Perhaps the principal perceived advantage of *ex tempore* judgments is that of speed:[24] parties get an instantaneous or near-instantaneous answer regarding the issue/s raised in court. This perceived advantage rests essentially on the proposition that: "The longer a judgment is reserved, the more difficult and time-consuming it is to write, and the scope for error may well increase."[25] However, in an age when a judge oftentimes (perhaps more often than not) enjoys post-hearing access to digital audio recordings of the proceedings to which her judgment relates, this supposed advantage seems less convincing than it was when a judge almost invariably had to rely upon "synoptic notes which he made during the trial ... inevitably scanty and frequently hard to decipher".[26] After all, what need has a judge of much memory when she can access the live recordings of what she has heard? Moreover, even if an *ex tempore* judgment entails the prospect of speed, "between an insufficiently considered, and possibly incorrect, outcome delivered on the spot and a considered outcome delivered a day or two later, the latter is much to be preferred".[27] Or as Sir Frank Kitto, a former member of the High Court of Australia, once observed:

In the great majority of cases it is more important that the purposes of an open statement of reasons should be well and fully achieved than that the parties and the Judge should have a quick end to their current preoccupation.[28]

A further perceived advantage of *ex tempore* judgments is that they offer a means whereby judges can give judgment while their

---

24 Côté (2003) (2), 436.
25 Bell, A (2019), 6–7.
26 De Navarre Kennedy, 38.
27 Bell, A (2019), 19.
28 Kitto (2003), 70–71.

memories remain "fresh";[29] and (on a not unrelated note) that it is preferable that parties hear the verdict "from the mouth of the person who heard the argument".[30] The concept of freshness is closely related to that of time and has already been considered. That of directness is informed by the traditional notion that *ex tempore* judgments are "more palatable to the loser ... [for] he can see the judges' decision-making process".[31] However, there is no reason why a written reserved judgment cannot be delivered (or, at least, its concluding paragraph read out) in open court to the parties. And while direct and immediate justice done when memory is at its freshest has much to recommend it, there is also a danger that judgment given in such circumstances will be given before the 'white heat' of courtroom battle between opposing counsel (and any emotion that they may have excited in the mind of the listening judge/s) has properly subsided, so allowing calm and collected judgment to prevail. The perceived advantages of freshness and directness, it might also (and again) be noted, rest on misplaced concern as to fading judicial memories in an age of wholesale digital audio recording of court proceedings. And while cognisance of a case may be at its height when a hearing ends – and this might be contended to ignore the fact that a more rounded understanding of matters may arise upon reflection – such freshness of mind does not necessarily yield clarity and eloquence of expression. It has been observed that: "The best ... oral judgment ever delivered does but read uncouthly when presented with verbal accuracy through the medium of a short-hand writer's notes."[32] And one commentator, writing of the realities of *ex tempore* judgment delivery, has observed how during same a judge:

> *will frequently have to pause to check something in his synoptic notes and his delivery will be disjointed. Sometimes his words may flow without interruption, at other times he will have to correct something he has said and say it over again with different words; and throughout he is unable to construct his sentences with appropriate punctuation.*[33]

---

29   Côté (2003), 437.
30   Bell, A (2019), 18.
31   Ehrenberg, 1195.
32   Anon (1871), 223.
33   De Navarre Kennedy, 38.

Such a scenario, it is submitted, is unlikely to persuade court users that a case has been heard and decided carefully. When one has regard to such practical realities, it is, with respect, difficult to accept the contention that (save perhaps in a few instances) "verbal communication may be a superior means of communication to written communication".[34] Comprehensive written reasons with an accompanying 'plain language' summary seem a more efficient means of ensuring clarity of communication and lasting comprehension by the affected parties.

A further reason offered for giving *ex tempore* judgments is that "the already overburdened judge does not have time to write reasons in every case".[35] There is a degree of truth in this. After all, every judgment in which nothing is written down is a case in which no further work has to be done by the judge on leaving the courtroom, thus in one sense heightening judicial efficiency. However, whether this 'efficiency' suffices to overcome the potential disadvantages that can present with *ex tempore* judgments is open to question. There can, after all, be a counter-efficiency in "using ... oral judgment as a vehicle for expanding the law"[36] (because the various implications of what a judge is doing may not have been completely thought through). As one commentator has observed in this regard: "It is harder to deal promptly and convincingly with a particular case if trying to fit the case to make a general statement about the law."[37]

In terms of the merits of *ex tempore* judgments, there is also perhaps a sense that this form of judgment may be "useful in an appeal that is clearly doomed or clearly irresistible".[38] But a question perhaps arises as to whether there are large numbers of such appeals. Moreover, given that many appeals involve some level of cross-appeal, the fact that one side has a doomed appeal does not mean that the other side's appeal is likewise doomed. (On a related note, it has been suggested that: "A brief oral judgment is fit for appeals with no new law, with no possibility of creating a

---

34 Bell, A (2019), 18.
35 Taggart, 18.
36 Ziegel, 400.
37 Emmett, 468.
38 Côté (2003), 439.

precedent, and with no one affected by the court's reasons except the parties."[39] However, it is open to question whether there are a great number of appeals cases that satisfy all three of the posited criteria.)

There may also be a sense abroad that a still-further attraction of *ex tempore* judgments is that they reduce the output of written case law in a world where such case law abounds. However, as one commentator has observed: "[T]he question of whether or not to publish reasons for judgment is ... distinct from whether reasons should be given in the first place."[40] In other words, a reserved written judgment may be desirable notwithstanding the existing abundance of such judgments. And in any event, as will be seen, when it comes to *ex tempore* judgments in superior courts, the best practice is that a permanent written record of such judgments should issue soon after.

It has been suggested that oral judgment is justified where "the appeal court should say little about the merits of the lawsuit or prosecution".[41] As against this, it might be suggested that there are many cases in which an appellate court is required to treat with the legal flaw presenting in one decision while being careful not to say anything that could trespass on a future decision on the same matter by a lower court.

Finally, there may be a sense among some lawyers that there can be instances where no reasons for judgment should issue – for example, where a judge seeks to achieve justice by departing from the law (and seeks through her silence to "ward off appellate review").[42] But, as Taggart observes, for a judge to behave so would be for her to abandon intellectual integrity and act contrary to the rule of law.[43] (And it is not clear that this 'trick' would work anyway, as a judgment so rendered could presumably be overturned for being unreasoned.)

3. Practical guidance

As can be seen from the foregoing, there are both potential advantages and drawbacks to the giving of an *ex tempore* judgment. But if

---

39 Ibid, 440.
40 Taggart, 20.
41 Côté (2003) (2), 440.
42 Taggart, 20.
43 Ibid.

a judge decides that she will give an *ex tempore* judgment, how might she best proceed to do so? Corbett and Elms have separately offered a number of helpful observations on preparing *ex tempore* judgments. These include the following.

First, it helps, by way of preparation, if each case is approached as though the intention is to give an *ex tempore* judgment in the end.[44]

Second, it is useful to consider all the documents involved in a case.[45] (Given the sheer abundance of documents that now seems to be a feature of so many modern cases, this may not always be fully possible, though advance review of the principal documents should typically be possible.)

Third, one should become absorbed in the trial throughout its duration.[46] (There is no doubt that the fuller the understanding of the nuances of a case, the easier and faster it is to construct an informed judgment following on the hearing.)

Fourth, it is useful to take copious, legible notes, noting key issues that arise and underlining points of significance.[47] (My own experience is that this process can be unsustainable over protracted periods and may ultimately yield a situation in which one focuses more on taking down a note of what is said than on the substance of what is said. A preferable approach, it is submitted, can be to write down headline notes of key points and, in a court where the proceedings are tape recorded, to jot down the date and time when the point was made. This list later functions as an *aide mémoire* to the key points presenting, and the note as to date and time enables one to listen back to the point if needs be.)

Fifth, it is useful to make a note of the key issues raised by counsel in their submissions and to ensure that these are answered in the ensuing judgment.[48] (At least in the Irish courts, it is now typical for counsel to provide written submissions in addition to their oral argument; and when this does not occur, there is nothing wrong in asking counsel for the various sides to identify and, if

---

44　Elms, 83.
45　Corbett, 119.
46　*Ibid.*
47　Elms, 83–84.
48　*Ibid*, 81–82.

Part III: *Ex tempore* judgments

possible, agree a list of the issues presenting for resolution. However, this can backfire if the different sides cannot agree on what issues arise to be resolved and end up providing separate and divergent lists of issues.)

Sixth, it is useful to keep brief notes on each side's case as it progresses, taking care, of course, to keep an open mind.[49] (Again, brevity is key here. There is always a risk that note taking will 'crowd out' the process of listening, and that the focus will become more on taking a note than on understanding the substance of what is being said.)

Seventh, reading up on the relevant law (if there is a point of law in dispute) is essential if one is to take an informed view on the law by case end.[50] (My own sense is that it is preferable to let counsel 'do the heavy lifting' in this regard: they know their case best; they know what they perceive the point/s of law presenting to be; and they know what submissions they wish to make.)

Eighth, if at all possible, one should write up the applicable legal principles and authorities.[51] This will form the basis of the ensuing judgment. (At least in the Irish courts, the competing written submissions provided by the respective parties seem more likely to form the bedrock of any future judgment, along with such notes as the presiding judge has made.)

Although the foregoing steps will not inevitably place a judge in a position of being able to give an *ex tempore* judgment at case end, they will shorten the delay between the end of the hearing and the delivery of whatever form of judgment a judge ultimately elects to give. "[T]he writing process will prove less burdensome and you will likely be in a better position to deliver judgment shortly thereafter."[52] Practical experience suggests that even if one is inclined to give judgment after counsel have finished speaking, it is sensible to rise for a time, both to be satisfied as to one's thoughts and to avoid the impression of a case having been decided even before the hearing was concluded.[53]

Côté, a onetime Canadian judge, has offered various insights

---

49 *Ibid*, 84.
50 Corbett, 119.
51 *Ibid*.
52 Bell, A (2019), 20.
53 Elms, 82–83.

regarding the practicalities of agreeing upon an *ex tempore* judgment between the members of a multi-judge appellate panel.[54] These include the following:

- A whispered on-bench ascertainment of views and agreement on what is to be said can quickly be agreed. (Presumably, some caution will be required in this regard if there is a digital audio recording system in the courtroom and judges do not wish a frank exchange of views to be recorded. In the online environment, it is possible for judges to adjourn briefly to a so-called 'breakout room'.)
- It is preferable that a common view be agreed between and communicated by the judges. (This is presumably because when matters are being communicated orally, greater potential arises for confusion among the parties – and unanticipated disagreement among the judges.)
- If a judgment is to be more than a couple of sentences long, it is preferable that the text be handwritten by one judge and reviewed by the others. (This suggestion presumably seeks to avoid confusion between the judges and among the parties.)
- If it becomes apparent that a dissenting judgment may issue, it may be appropriate to defer the delivery of any decision until a later date (presumably unless the dissenting judge can come up with a very quick oral dissent). Another possibility that presents is to render a brief oral judgment with written reasons to follow.
- It is a recipe for trouble for each judge to give a separate oral agreement that has not previously been discussed with the other judges (so allowing them to input on what each judge proposes to say).
- Appellate courts that give oral judgments should take care to record formally (whether by way of digital audio recorder, court reporter or their own handwritten or typed manuscript) the reasons for the decision. The Supreme Court of Canada offers an example of best practice in this regard: "[It] has all of its oral judgments transcribed and released to the parties and the public."[55]

---

54 Côté (2003), 442.
55 *Ibid*, 443.

There is a school of thought that if the issue of cost and delay presenting in many court systems is to be allayed, there will be need to be greater reliance in the future on *ex tempore* judgments.[56] Justice Kirby, a former member of the High Court of Australia, is prominent in his home country as among "those judges who urge the giving of *ex tempore* judgments as a general rule".[57] He has also identified some additional practical points that can usefully be brought to bear when it comes to the task that befalls every trial judge of preparing alone an oral judgment that is delivered on an *ex tempore* basis.[58] These include the following:

- (A generally accepted point), the more advance preparation done by a judge, the easier she will find the task of delivering oral judgment.
- Findings of fact (which determine most disputes) need not be lengthy; however, the judge should identify and resolve all factual issues and controversies presenting.
- Evidence not before the court should not be relied upon (a universal rule of judgment making).
- Unless the words of the applicable law are well known, it is a useful practice to state them verbatim.
- A judge should have the applicable law and/or case law to hand.
- When it comes to treating with the law in one's *ex tempore* judgment, identification of principle and a bare citation of authority are optimal. However, if there is no time for this, reading out the relevant passage of a textbook is satisfactory.
- If a point occurs to a judge's mind while delivering oral judgment that may tip the case in the opposite direction from that which she has resolved upon, such a judge has two 'options' (one of them, as Kirby makes clear, is not really an option). The dishonest one (the one that is not really an option) is to plough on regardless. The honest one (as recommended by Kirby) is to pause, invite submissions on the point and adjourn to reflect on matters. "The reasons must

---

56 See Kirby (1995), 231.
57 Bell, A (2019), 17.
58 Kirby (1995), 225–30.

then either start again or candidly explain the change of opinion and the ground which has occasioned it."⁵⁹
- A judge should be familiar with any rules which limit her power to alter the transcript or to deliver future written reasons that depart from what was orally stated. (It seems that in Australia, "Except for the case of the summing up or a direction to a jury, a wide latitude is given to judicial officers to refine their *ex tempore* reasons.")⁶⁰

Another practical tip (proffered separately by Bell) is the desirability of rising, however briefly, to consider matters, at the least when any issue of complexity presents. This is something of a 'halfway house' – and not a bad one – between the immediate *ex tempore* judgment and the more protracted (though not necessarily that much more protracted) process of preparing a written reserved judgment. Thus, Bell writes, a judge may:

> *adjourn for a short period, review notes or an outline that may have been prepared in advance ... consider whether ... any provisional views need alteration or qualification in light of the oral argument and ... integrate references to the oral argument into the notes or outline before returning to the bench to deliver reasons.*⁶¹

As to the amendment of later-provided transcripts of a previously delivered *ex tempore* judgment, there can be temptations and dangers for judges in this regard. Lord Neuberger has spoken of how "some judges just improve the punctuation and the syntax, [but] many judges use the opportunity to effect a fairly comprehensive rewriting".⁶² In *Bromley v Bromley*,⁶³ it was contended before the Court of Appeal that the amendments made by a trial judge to a stenographer's transcript yielded a judgment which departed so significantly from what the trial judge had actually said that the Court of Appeal should look at both the transcript and the corrected version to get a true sense of matters. This line of appeal was rejected by the Court of Appeal, given what it perceived to be a

---

59   *Ibid*, 228.
60   *Ibid*, 230.
61   Bell, A (2019), 21.
62   Neuberger (2014), para 23.
63   [1964] 3 All ER 226 (CA).

want of evidence showing that "the official transcript as approved by the judge [was] ... substantially different from what the judge actually said when he delivered his oral judgment at the trial".[64]

One would have expected *Bromley* to have sounded something of a warning bell for any judges who were minded to amend the written account of what they said *ex tempore* to such an extent that it no longer accurately or fully indicated what was said. Yet in *Langdon v Suremanor Ltd*,[65] the Court of Appeal was confronted with a situation where the transcript (assuming the revision was correct) was, per Lord Justice Lawton, "saying the opposite of what ... [the trial judge] had said orally when delivering judgment". Coming still closer in time, in *Yates v Yates*,[66] the trial judge, in a dispute concerning matrimonial property, appears to have sought to rewrite the basis for (though not the outcome of) his judgment. However, a tape recording of the oral judgment emerged and pointed to the divergence between what had been said and what the revised transcript indicated. On appeal, Stephen P for the Court of Appeal observed as follows:

> *[I]t is a very extensive revision. Almost two and a half pages have been deleted entirely, and a new page written to replace it. This ... on the face of it, show[s] that the judge revised his view from that stated in court ... [T]hat ... judgements should be revised by judges ... is quite proper. The spelling ... English ... precise expression ... may call for revision, so that a judge may make ... clear what he intended to say. However, it should never be the case that the basis of the judgment on any important issue should be entirely altered. Regrettably that appears to have happened in this case.*

Something of a more liberal disposition appears to present in the relatively recent judgment of Lord Phillips MR in the comparatively recent case of *Shirt v Shirt*,[67] in which "significant clarifications and amplifications"[68] were made by a trial judge to an oral reserved judgment – an approach which drew the following observations from Lord Phillips:

---

64 *Ibid*, 227.
65 [1984] Lexis Citation 1538 (CA).
66 [1988] Lexis Citation 1427 (CA).
67 [2012] EWCA Civ 1029 (CA).
68 See judgment of Lord Phillips, para [40].

13. The art and craft of *ex tempore* judgments

[33] ... [I]t is open to a Judge who gave judgment immediately after a hearing, to make amendments to the transcript after he receives it, not only to the punctuation and syntax, sentence construction and order of sentences, to improve the elegance and comprehensibility of his judgment; he can also add to it by way of amplifying and clarifying findings, and indeed amplifying and clarifying the reasoning, recorded in his oral judgment ...

[35] ... [I]f the law is too constraining on judges improving their ex tempore *judgments, then they will be loath to give* ex tempore *judgments. The delay caused by reserved judgments, and the extra time required from judges to prepare reserved judgments, are such that we should not discourage judges from giving* ex tempore *judgments.*

[36] *Once one accepts that it is open to a judge to amplify his judgment in this way, if he gives the judgment* ex tempore, *it seems ... very difficult to avoid the conclusion that, if a judge chooses to give oral judgment some time after the hearing, he should have the similar opportunity to amplify and improve the judgment when he receives it back in transcript form.*

[37] *However, I should make two points in relation to these observations. The first is that to amplify and improve is one thing; to make new or contradictory points ... is quite another. If a judge does have second thoughts after receiving a transcript, he should consider particularly carefully whether to include something wholly new, or something actually contradictory, to what he said in his* ex tempore *judgment. But if the judge does decide that he ought to include some such material, then he should make it clear on the face of the transcript what he has done.*

[38] *The second qualification which has particular reference to this case is that if significant amplifications and clarifications are made to a judgment not given* ex tempore, *ie, immediately after the hearing, but some time after the hearing, then it is almost inevitable that at least one of the parties ... will be concerned as to what has happened, and will wonder if the judge really ... concentrated on the issues when he gave his reserve judgment orally ...*

[39] *The course taken by the judge in this case was not one which I regard as generally desirable ...*

Part III: *Ex tempore* judgments

> [40] *Having made those points ... I do not consider that the significant clarifications and amplifications which the judge made have caused any injustice.*[69]

Despite all this, it seems notable that Lord Phillips nonetheless proceeded to limit his references to the judgment in its original form, not its amplified form.[70]

---

69   *Ibid*, paras [33]–[40].
70   The approach taken by the English courts is not the universal practice of all common law courts. In Texas, for example, a quite liberal regime presents in which:
      [b]ecause oral pronouncements ... are often tentative and incomplete, they can be reconsidered, supplemented, or modified by the written judgment ... When the writing adds to or differs from the oral judgment first announced, it is presumed to be what the judge intended (Peeples, 383).

Appendix: The judgment as the art of truth

Judgments are practical documents aimed at a practical end, being the resolution of real-life disputes. In the main body of this text, I have focused on the theory and practice of the art and craft of judgment writing. I have also touched on the art and craft of the continuing practice of ex tempore oral judgments. In this appendix (and I have deliberately consigned this text to the appendix because its focus is not the mainstay of this book), I consider some aspects of what the philosophy of aesthetics and art/literary theory may have to teach about judgments and judges.

In his *Lectures on Fine Art*, Hegel refers to three ideas of art, which can be brought to bear in the context of judgments:
- A work of art is not a natural product;
- It is made for human apprehension; and
- It has an end and aim in itself.

As to art not being a natural product, this rings true in the context of judgments also, with common law judgment writing to some extent involving non-formulaic artistry. As to art being made for human apprehension, in a judgment, a judge draws ultimately on an inner sense as to where the justice of a situation lies and then issues, for human apprehension, a judgment consistent with this sense. As to art having an end and aim in itself, judgments arguably have, among their goals, the goals of ethical instruction and improvement.

Margolis offers various shared properties of works of art and aesthetic judgment that can be seen also to point to the artistic character of judgments. These include the following. First, "[a] physical system functions as a work of art if its particular properties result from deliberate human work and can be construed as serving

303

some unified human goal".[1] A judgment satisfies these criteria: it is the product of deliberate human work and serves the pursuit of truth. Second, "[a] physical system functions as a work of fine art if ... the organization of its properties can be construed as inherently purposive without reference to an ulterior goal".[2] A judgment serves the primary goal of dispute resolution, albeit that this is not its sole goal. It also has the "ulterior" goal of facilitating legal discussion and affording, at least potentially, a fleeting glimpse of immanent truth. Third, "[a] physical system viewed as fine art may also be viewed as useful art, that is, as serving some human goal other than mere design".[3] Arguably a useful art such as judgment writing can also be viewed as a fine art. Fourth, "[u]se may be an element in the design of a work of art" and "[d]esign may be an element in the use of a work of art"; each proposition applies with equal vigour to a judgment.[4] Fifth, "the property of functioning as a work of art [involves] ... the power ... to appear to human perceivers as a purposively organized system".[5] This is arguably the case when one considers the ostensibly logical approach typically adopted in judgments. Sixth, "[t]o describe an object as a work of art is to describe its physical properties and to impute to it a unified human goal".[6] A judgment satisfies this criterion.

Art, in a post-religious age, is where an "encounter with transcendence continues to be sought".[7] This is as true of judgments as of any other form of artwork, with better judges seeking through rational eloquence to identify and speak to truth. Likely all judges will confirm that they sometimes experience a sense of inspiration when writing a judgment. But what is the object that yields such inspiration? Most likely truth. Moritz once observed of beauty that "[e]very instance of beauty ... is beautiful only insofar as ... the great whole is more or less revealed in it".[8] A judgment that is art, it is submitted, is one in which one finds "the great whole ... more or less revealed in it". In a judgment this "great whole" is truth.

---

1 Margolis (1959), 210.
2 Ibid.
3 Ibid.
4 Ibid.
5 Ibid.
6 Ibid.
7 Desmond, 1.
8 Bernstein, 143.

If one accepts the potential for a judgment to attain the level of art, what qualities might it be expected to possess? The following surely present. First, that it is susceptible to a "heightened power of perception".[9] Second, that it appears unified: "unity of some kind is necessary for our restful contemplation of the work of art as a whole."[10] A notable aspect of any well-written judgment is its unity of thought and capacity for restful contemplation. Third, that, to arouse emotion, it possesses rhythm, feeling, motion, proportion and colour; and draws the mind's eye to closer appreciation.[11]

When it comes to making value judgements of judgments, the traditional manner of assessing their potential effectiveness, the functions they are intended to serve, their relevant audience and the implicitly defined conditions under which an audience experiences that judgment have historically eschewed consideration of the artistic. That this has occurred is a challenge to lawyers, but also to students of art. Such students, Danto suggests, have long had a palette of qualities that are "too restricted ... [extending to] the beautiful, the ugly and the plain"[12] – though judgements about the ugly and the plain can and do often come within the realm of the beautiful.

What is the process whereby a judgment comes to be written? As an imaginative experience, it perhaps begins with a sensuous experience raised by the judge's consciousness to the imaginative level. The sensuous manifests in the "psycho-physical"[13] activity of judgment writing. Without the sensuous, there would be nothing from which consciousness could produce the aesthetic experience embodied in the judgment. But 'it takes two to tango': the consciousness works on the sensuous and the aesthetic unfolds. Danger presents for the writing process when judges perceive themselves as apart and different from the wider community. If a judge is to express through her judgments what all can feel, she "must share the emotions of all".[14] If judges form their own community, their emotions will be those of that community and their judgments fully intelligible only to that community. A judge who

---

9   Fry (1940), 33.
10 Ibid, 34–35.
11 Ibid, 36–37.
12 Danto (1998), 133.
13 Collingwood, 307.
14 Ibid, 119.

has lived a wide life but who joins herself to a narrow clique and then expresses only the emotions that pass muster within that clique is deliberately curtailing her freedom of expression.[15]

There is a close relation between the literary processes of poetry and law. Thus, it has been observed that: "The law has one way of seeing ... Poetry has another. But the journey is the same."[16] In the homage that he pays to poetry in his autobiography, 19th-century novelist Anthony Trollope makes a number of observations that might equally be applied to judgment writing, raising judgment writing, on Trollope's terms, to an art form beyond that of 'mere' prose. Thus, Trollope writes:

> By the common consent of all mankind who have read, poetry takes the highest place in literature. That nobility of expression, and all but divine grace of words, which she is bound to attain ... [w]hen that has been in truth achieved, the reader knows that the writer has soared above the earth and can teach his lessons somewhat as a god might teach.[17]

It can be said of judgment writing, as has been observed of poetry, that: "We should conceive of it as capable of higher uses ... than those which ... men have assigned to it hitherto."[18] And it is undoubtedly the case that in poetry, as in judgment writing, "there exist strong impulses ... that lead to truthfulness [and] ... to the apprehension of power behind all form".[19] The overlap between poetry and judgment writing can be seen in various of the general observations that Hegel makes as to the nature of poetry. First, poetry is "the original presentation of the truth, a knowing which does not yet separate the universal from its living existence in the individual".[20] A judgment proceeds likewise, identifying the universal and bringing it to bear in the individual. Second, poetry presents all subject matter "as a totality complete in itself and therefore independent".[21] Each judgment is likewise meant to form a whole and independent canvas. Third, apprehension and expres-

---

15   *Ibid*, 121.
16   Manderson and Caudill, 1325.
17   Trollope, 188.
18   Arnold, 161.
19   Dilthey, 32.
20   Hegel, II, 973.
21   *Ibid*.

Appendix: The judgment as the art of truth

sion remain contemplative in poetry.[22] Because law is not tangible, its apprehension and contemplation must likewise remain contemplative. There is clearly a practical import to judgments also; though that is not to suggest that poetry cannot serve a practical end – as evidenced, for example, by its occasional invocation in the service of reasoning within a judgment. Fourth, "even on its linguistic side, poetry has the vocation of being a sphere of its own".[23] There can be few who would deny that judgment writing likewise sits in a sphere of its own, devoted to truth, aimed at resolution of disputes and with its own conventions as to style and substance. Fifth, in poetic expression, "the words are only signs of ideas".[24] Judgment writing is similar. The words in a judgment conjure an image of the judge's creation and draw the reader into a world in which the judge seeks to reconcile rationality (law) and sentiment (justice). Sixth, while the objective form of poetry is words, the focus in a reading of poetry is linguistic. With judgments, though the immediate focus may seem to be on the parsing of words, the true focus is the ballooning legal concepts that soar from the pages of the law reports and ultimately from the mind of the judge whose judgment is being read. Seventh, poetry is "actual speaking".[25] When it comes to judgments, which are drafted as if to be spoken, one is equally dealing with 'actual speaking' – albeit speaking in a particular rhetorical style. Eighth, poetic writing, like judgment writing, is essentially figurative – that is:

it brings before our eyes not the abstract essence but its concrete reality ... and in this way we are confronted in the inner world of our ideas by the conception of the thing and its existence as one and the same whole.[26]

Stewart gives a sense of how the mind engages in play on the reading of poetry that is arguably akin to what occurs when one engages with a judgment:

[T]he poet avails himself of language, only to convey the ideas in his mind ... Imitation [of the ideas in his mind] ... is not the end ... he proposes ... but the means ... he employs ... When we peruse a descrip-

---

22 Hegel, II, 974.
23 *Ibid.*
24 *Ibid*, 1000.
25 *Ibid*, 1001.
26 *Ibid*, 1002.

> tion, we ... feel a disposition to form, in our own minds, a distinct picture of what is described; and in proportion to [our] ... attention and interest ... the picture becomes steady and determinate ... It is ... almost certain, that the imaginations of no two men coincide upon such occasions.[27]

Bringing these observations to bear in the context of judgment writing, a judge likewise avails of language to convey the ideas in her mind. Imitation of those ideas is the means she employs to communicate her ideas to the reader's mind. When the reader of a judgment reads a judgment, she forms in her mind a picture of what is described. That picture will almost certainly be different from the picture formed in the mind of another reader; but within (or more likely through) those readings, truth may be discerned. Stewart suggests that a distinguishing feature of poetry is that it seeks to please.[28] However, in this he is arguably mistaken: the truth discernible in and through judgments also pleases.

The judge, like the poet, has a new thought to describe.[29] Like the judge who authors a judgment, the function of the poet is that she "transforms the reader into one who is 'inspired'".[30] Emerson describes the intellectual journey involved in a poem in terms akin to the process which arises when one reads the finest judgments:

> With what joy I begin to read a poem ... [N]ow my chains are to be broken; I shall mount above these clouds and opaque airs in which I live – opaque, though they seem transparent – and from the heaven of truth I shall see and comprehend my relations ... [N]ow I am invited into the science of the real.[31]

There can be few lawyers who, in law school and/or in practice, have not encountered a judgment which has caused their spirit to soar at the truth – expected or unexpected – that is revealed therein, bringing them to a place or state where the immanent becomes, if not manifest, then at least less opaque. Such judgments are typically the work product of the highest and best practitioners of the art and craft of judgment writing.

---

27 Stewart, 416–17.
28 *Ibid*, 419–20.
29 Emerson, 11.
30 Valéry, 215.
31 Emerson, 13.

Table of cases

Australia
Australian Communist Party v Commonwealth (1951) 83 CLR 1 (HCA), 257–259
Bank of New South Wales v The Commonwealth [1948] HCA 7 (HCA), 257–258
Birmingham v Renfrew (1937) 57 CLR 666 (HCA), 255–256
Hadid v Redpath [2001] NSWCA 416 (NSW CA), 26–27
Yerkey v Jones (1939) 63 CLR 649 (HCA), 256–257

Canada
Andrews v Law Society of British Columbia [1989] 1 SCR 143 (SC), 178, 179–180
Cojocaru v British Columbia Women's Hospital & Health Center [2013] 2 SCR 357 (SC), 87
R v Cameron [1966] 2 OR777 (Ontario CA), 263–264
R v Burnshine [1975] 1 SCR 693 (SC), 260–261, 262
Nova Scotia Board of Censors v McNeil [1978] 2 SCR 662 (SC), 260, 261, 262
Attorney General for Canada & Dupond v Montreal [1978] 2 SCR 770 (SC), 260, 262
R v Morgentaler [1988] 1 SCR 30 (SC), 178–179
R v Lavallée [1990] 1 SCR 852 (SC), 178, 180–183
R v Sheppard [2002] 1 SCR 869 (SC), 19–20

England and Wales, Scotland
A v Home Secretary [2004] UKHL 56; [2005] 2 AC 68 (HL), 246–247
A v Home Secretary (No 2) [2005] UKHL 71; [2006] 2 AC 221 (HL), 243, 247–248
Allen v Jambo Holdings Ltd [1980] 1 WLR 1252 (CA), 232
Banco de Portugal v Waterlow [1932] AC 452 (HL), 229–230

Bell v Lever Bros [1932] AC 161 (HL), 229, 230
Beswick v Beswick [1966] Ch 538 (CA), 239-240
Bole v Horton (1673) 124 ER 1113 (CtCP), 19
Bromley v Bromley [1964] 3 All ER 226 (CA), 299–300
Burt v Claude Cousins & Co Ltd [1971] 2 QB 426 (CA), 234
Candler v Crane Christmas and Co [1951] 2 KB 164 (CA), 241, 242–243
Caswell v Powell Duffryn Associated Collieries [1940] AC 152 (HL), 222–223
Central London Property Trust Ltd v High Trees House Ltd [1956] 1 All ER 256 (KBD), 241–242
Cinnamond v British Airports Authority [1980] 1 WLR 582 (CA), 232
Deeble v Robinson [1954] 1 QB 77 (CA), 240
Dickson v Pharmaceutical Society of Great Britain [1967] Ch 708 (CA), 237–238
Distinctive Properties (Ascot) Ltd v Secretary of State for Communities and Local Government [2015] EWHC 729 (HC), 65–66
Donoghue v Stevenson [1932] AC 562 (HL), 222, 225–227, 242
DPP v Smith [1961] AC 290 (HL), 109
Everett v Griffiths [1920] 3 KB 163 (CA), [1921] 1 AC 631 (HL), 220–222
Ex parte Johnson Trust Ltd [1974] QB 24 (CA), 234–235
Fender v Mildmay [1938] AC 1 (HL), 223–224
Gee v National Trust [1966] 1 All ER 954 (CA), 234
George Mitchell (Chesterhall) Ltd v Finney Lock Seeds [1982] 3 WLR 1036 (CA), 69, 233
Gouriet v U.P.W. [1977] QB 729 (CA), 5
H v H [2020] EWFC 9 (Fam Ct), 65, 66
Hedley Byrne & Co Ltd v Heller & Partners Ltd [1964] AC 465 (HL), 242
Hinz v Berry [1970] 2 QB 40 (CA), 233–234
Inland Revenue Commissioners v Rossminster Ltd [1980] 2 WLR 1 (HL), 227
Ionian Bank Ltd v Couvreur [1969] 1 WLR 781 (CA), 231
James v Minister for Pensions [1947] KB 867 (CA), 232
Jennings Motors Ltd v Secretary of State for the Environment [1982] 2 WLR 131 (CA), 232
Kelly v London Transport Executive [1982] 2 All ER 842 (CA), 235–236
Lamb v Camden Borough Council [1981] QB 625 (CA), 240–241
Lancashire County Council v M [2016] EWFC 9 (HC), 120
Langdon v Suremanor Ltd [1984] Lexis Citation 1538 (CA), 300
Lau v Chu [2020] UKPC 24 (PC), 65
Levison v Patent Steam Carpet Cleaning Co Ltd [1978] QB 69 (CA), 232
Liversidge v Anderson [1942] AC 206 (HL), 206, 207, 216, 223, 224, 225, 227–229

Lloyds Bank Ltd v Bundy [1975] QB 326 (CA), 238
Marsden v Regan [1954] 1 All ER 423 (CA), 232
McIlkenny v Chief Constable of West Midlands Police Force [1980] 2 All ER 227 (CA), 232, 236
Midland Bank Trust Co Ltd v Green [1980] Ch 590 (CA), 231–232
Midland Bank Trust Co Ltd v Green (No 3) [1982] 2 WLR 1 (CA), 232
Miller v Jackson [1977] QB 966 (CA), 238–239
Mr Patrick v Mrs Patrick [2017] Lexis Citation 282 (Sh Ct), 120
Myers v Milton Keynes Development Corporation [1974] 1 WLR 696 (CA), 233
Nakkuda Ali v Jayartyne [1951] AC 66 (PC), 227
Pearse v Pearse (1846) 63 ER 950 (Ct Ch), 76
R (Forge Care Homes Ltd) v Cardiff and Vale University Health Board [2016] EWCA Civ 26 (CA), 65
R v McIlkenny [1992] 2 All ER 417 (CA), 236
R v Slough Borough Council [1981] QB 801 (CA), 240
Radcliffe v Ribble Motor Services [1939] AC 215 (HL), 222, 223
Rank Film Distributors Ltd v Video Information Centre [1982] AC 380 (CA), 233
Re A: A Letter to a Young Person [2017] EWFC 48 (HC), 120
Re C (Interim Care Order) [2011] EWCA Civ 918 (CA), 65
Read v J Lyons and Co Ltd [1947] AC 156 (HL), 32
Reid v Metropolitan Police Commissioner [1973] QB 551 (CA), 231
Rylands v Fletcher [1861–73] All ER Rep 1 (HL), 44
Secretary of State for Employment v Globe Elastic Thread Co Ltd [1979] QB 183 (CA), 236
Shell International Petroleum Ltd v Gibbs [1982] 2 WLR 745 (CA), 233
Shirt v Shirt [2012] EWCA Civ 1029 (CA), 300–302
Somerset's Case; Somerset v Stewart (1772) 98 ER 499 (KB), 50, 52–54, 205
Southam v Smout [1964] 1 QB 308 (CA), 232–233
SS v NS (Spousal Maintenance) [2014] EWHC 4183 (Fam) (HC), 65
Thomas v Roberts (1850) 64 ER 693 (VC Ct), 63–64
TuneIn Inc v Warner Music UK Ltd [2021] EWCA Civ 441 (CA), 70, 81
White v Jones [1995] 2 AC 207 (CA), 71
Yates v Yates [1988] Lexis Citation 1427 (CA), 300

European Court of Human Rights

Hutchinson v United Kingdom [2017] ECHR 57592/08, 65
Sunday Times v United Kingdom [1979] ECHR 6538/74, 24

India

ADM Jabalpur v Shivkant Shukla 1976 AIR 1207 (SCI), 267–269
Kesavananda Bharati v State of Kerala (1973) 4 SC 225 (SCI), 265–266, 267, 268, 277
KS Puttaswamy v Union of India (2017) 10 SCC 1 (SCI), 269
Shine v Union of India (2018) 46 BHRC 637 (SCI), 65
State of Gujarat v Justice RA Mehta (Retd) [2013] 1 SCR 1 (SCI), 72–73, 224–225

Ireland

Byrne v Ireland [1972] IR 241 (SC), 271, 272–273
McGee v Attorney General [1974] IR 287 (SC), 271, 273–274
State (Quinn) v Ryan [1965] IR 70 (SC), 271-272
Walsh and Cassidy v County Council for the County Sligo [2014] 2 I LRM 161 (SC), 235

Israel

Kol Ha'am Co Ltd v Minister of the Interior (1953) HCJ 73/53 (SC/HCJ), 275–276, 277, 279
Mandelbrot v Attorney General (1956) CrimA 118/53 (SC/CCA), 275, 276–277
Seedis v Seedis (1954) Special Tribunal 1/50 (SC/Sp Trib), 275, 276
Shmuel v Attorney General (1964) CA 525/63 (SC), 275, 277–278

New Zealand

Lodder v Lodder [1921] NZLR 876 (SC), 280, 280–281, 282
Park v Minister for Education [1922] NZLR 1208 (SC), 280, 281
Taylor v Combined Buyers Ltd [1924] NZLR 627 (SC), 280, 281–282

United States

Abrams v United States 250 US 616 (1919) (SC), 190, 194, 195
Adair v United States 208 US 161 (1908) (SC), 192–193
Boumediene v Bush 553 US 723 (2008) (SC), 212, 213
Bowers v Hardwick 478 US 186 (1986) (SC), 213, 214
Buck v Bell 274 US 200 (1927) (SC), 193–194, 216, 269
Burnet v Coronado Oil & Gas Co 285 US 393 (1932) (SC), 169
Bush v Gore 531 US 98 (2003) (SC), 159, 165–166, 171, 173–175
City of Sherrill v Oneida Indian Nation of New York 544 US 197 (2005) (SC), 171, 172–173
Commonwealth v Robin 421 Pa 70 (Pa 1966) (Penn SC), 105–106

Communications Assn v Douds 339 US 382 (1950) (SC), 200–201
District of Columbia v Heller 128 S Ct 2783 (2008) (SC), 212–213
Engle v Isaac 456 US 107 (1982) (SC), 156
Fisher v Lowe 333 NW 2d 67 (Mich Ct App 1983) (Michigan CA), 68
Grutter v Bollinger 539 US 306 (2003) (SC), 159, 162–163
Hein v Freedom from Religion Foundation 551 US 587 (2007) (SC), 209–210
Korematsu v United States 323 US 214 (1944) (SC), 206–208, 216, 269
Kunz v New York 340 US 290 (1951) (SC), 202–203
Lawrence v Texas 539 US 558 (2003) (SC), 213–214
Lee v Weisman 505 US 577 (1992) (SC), 156
Lochner v New York 198 US 45 (1905) (SC), 191–192, 242
Marbury v Madison 5 US 137 (1803) (SC), 39, 50–52, 276
Massachusetts v United States 333 US 611 (1948) (SC), 195–196
MacPherson v Buick Motor Co 217 NY 382 (1916) (New York CA), 226–227
McGrath v Kristensen 340 US 162 (1950) (SC), 201–202
Mississippi University for Women v Hogan 458 US 718 (1982) (SC), 159, 160–161
Northern Securities Co v United States 193 US 197 (1904) (SC), 104, 189–190
Obergefell v Hodges 576 US 644 (2015) (SC), 213, 214–215
Planned Parenthood of Southeastern Pennsylvania v Casey 505 US 833 (1992) (SC), 159, 163–164
Plaut v Spendthrift Farm Incorporated 514 US 211 (1995) (SC), 67–68
Reed v Allen 286 US 191 (1931) (SC), 55
Republican Party of Minnesota v White 536 US 765 (2002) (SC), 158–160
Roe v Wade 410 US 113 (1973) (SC), 159, 163, 164
Rosenberger v Rector 515 US 819 (1995) (SC), 156–157
Schenck v United States 249 US 47 (1919) (SC), 190, 194–195
Shaughnessy v Mezei 345 US 206 (1953) (SC), 204–206
Southern Pacific Co v Jensen 244 US 205 (1917) (SC), 190
Standard Fire Insurance Co v Reese (1979) 584 SW 2d 835 (Texas SC), 66–67
Terminiello v Chicago 337 US 1 (1949) (SC), 203
United States v South-Eastern Underwriters Association 322 US 533 (1944) (SC), 202
United States v Virginia 518 US 515 (1996) (SC), 161–162, 171–172, 180, 212
West Virginia State Board of Education v Barnette 319 US 624 (1943) (SC), 200
Youngstown Sheet & Tube Co v Sawyer 343 US 579 (1952) (SC), 203–204

Select bibliography

Abdullah, Aedit. "The 30th Singapore Law Review Annual Lecture: The Obsolescent Judge" (2018–19) 36 *Singapore Law Review* 1.

Abraham, David. "Liberty and Property: Lord Bramwell and the Political Economy of Liberal Jurisprudence Individualism, Freedom, and Utility" (1994) 38(3) *American Journal of Legal History* 288.

Adalberto, Jordan. "Imagery, Humor, and the Judicial Opinion" (1987) 41 *University of Miami Law Review* 693.

Adams, Harold. "A Tribute to Robert Jackson By His Nephew" (2004) 68(1) *Albany Law Review* 1.

Addison, Joseph. "Greatness, Novelty, or Beauty", *The Spectator*, 23 June 1712. https://web.english.upenn.edu/~cavitch/pdf-library/AddisonJ_Spectator411-21.pdf.

Alder, John. "Dissents in Courts of Last Resort: Tragic Choices?" (2000) 20 *Oxford Journal of Legal Studies* 221.

Alito, Samuel. "The Second Conversation with Justice Samuel A Alito, Jr: Lawyering and the Craft of Judicial Opinion Writing" (2009) 37 *Pepperdine Law Review* 33.

"A Tribute to Justice Scalia" (2017) 126(6) *Yale Law Journal* 1605.

Alschuler, Albert. *Law Without Values: The Life, Work, and Legacy of Justice Holmes*. Chicago: University of Chicago Press, 2000.

Amar, Akhil. "Marbury, Section 13, and the Original Jurisdiction of the Supreme Court" (1989) 56 *University of Chicago Law Review* 443.

Andenas, M and S Vogenauer (eds). *The Form of Judgment*. Hart: Oxford, 2012.

Anderson, Ellen. "Judging Bertha Wilson: Law as Large as Life". Toronto: University of Toronto Press, 2001.

Andrews, Neil. *Andrews on Civil Processes*, vol 1. Cambridge: Intersentia, 2017.

Anon. *Gorham v Bishop of Exeter: The Judgment of the Judicial Committee of*

the Privy Council. London: Seeleys, 1850.
"Reports and Reporters" (1871) 3 *Albany Law Journal* 222.
Editorial (1899–1900) 60 *Albany Law Journal* 76.
"Prompt Delivery of Judgments" (1908) 28(3) *Canadian Law Times* 225.
"Obituary: Sir John Salmond" (1925) 6 *British Yearbook of International Law* 187.
"Lord Denning and RACISM" (1982) 16 *Haldane Bulletin* 18.
"Garcia v National Australia Bank Ltd: Resurrecting the Corpus of Yerkey v Jones" (1998) 21(3) *University of New South Wales Law Journal* 845.
Deadlock: The Inside Story of America's Closest Election. New York: Public Affairs, 2001.
"Judgment Writing and Legal Scholarship: The Path Forward" (2014) 7(1) *National University of Juridical Sciences Law Review* i.
"Frances (Fanny) Elizabeth Potter", (2018) 300 (7911) *Pharmaceutical Journal*. https://pharmaceutical-journal.com/article/news/frances-fanny-elizabeth-potter.
"Stanford Stories". https://125.stanford.edu/the-law-school-class-of-1952/.

Appleton, Susan Frelich. "Telling the Story of Justice Sandra Day O'Connor" (2020) 62 *Washington University Journal of Law & Policy* 5.

Arden, Mary. "A Matter of Style? The Form of Judgments in Common Law Jurisdictions: A Comparison". Conference in Honour of Lord Bingham, June 2008, Oxford.
"Judgment Writing: Are Shorter Judgments Achievable?" (2012) 128 *Law Quarterly Review* 515.

Arkes, Hadley *et al*. "Antonin Scalia – A Justice in Full", *National Review*, 29 February 2016. https://perma.cc/KMY9-AFAP.

Arnold, Matthew. "The Study of Poetry" in Super, R (ed). *Matthew Arnold: English Literature and Irish Politics*. Ann Arbor: University of Michigan Press, 1973.

Aroney, Nicholas. "The High Court of Australia: Textual Unitarism vs Structural Federalism" in Aroney, Nicholas and John Kincaid. *Courts in Federal Countries*. Toronto: University of Toronto Press, 2017.

Asquith, Cyril. "Some Aspects of the Work of the Court of Appeal" (1950) 1(5) (ns) *Journal of the Society of Public Teachers of Law* 350.

Atkinson, Roslyn. "Judgment writing". https://archive.sclqld.org.au/judgepub/2010/atkinson060210.pdf.

Baar, Carl et al. "The Ontario Court of Appeal and Speedy Justice" (1992) 30 *Osgoode Hall Law Journal* 261.

Babu, S. Rajendra. "Contribution of the Supreme Court to the Growth of Democracy in India" (2013) 6(2) *National University of Juridical Sciences Law Review* 193.

Backhouse, Constance. "Chilly Climate for Women Judges. Reflections on the Backlash from the *Ewanchuck* Case" (2003) 15 *Canadian Journal of Women and the Law* 167.

Bacon, Francis. *Novum Organum*, Joseph Devey (ed). New York: Collier, 1902.

"Of Judicature" in *The Essays or Counsels, Civil and Moral*. Project Gutenberg.

"Of Studies" in *The Essays or Counsels, Civil and Moral*. Project Gutenberg.

Bagaric, Marko and James McConvill. "The High Court and the Utility of Multiple Judgments" (2005) 1(1) *High Court Quarterly Review* 13.

Balasubramanian, Archana and Namrata Yadav. "Amendmenace: The Constitution of India Unveiled (2004) 3 *Law Review, Government Law College* 29.

Bales, Scott. "Justice Sandra Day O'Connor: No Insurmountable Hurdles" (2006) 58(6) *Stanford Law Review* 1705.

Balmer, Thomas. "Present Appreciation and Future Advantage: A Note on the Influence of Hobbes on Holmes" (2005) 47(4) *American Journal of Legal History* 412.

Banks-Smith, Katrina. "More than Just Precedent: Perspectives on Judgment Writing" (2019) *University of Notre Dame Australia Law Review* 1.

Barak, Aharon. *The Judge in a Democracy*. Princeton: Princeton University Press, 2006.

Barak-Erez, Daphne. "Writing Law: Reflections on Judicial Decisions and Academic Scholarship" (2015) 41(1) *Queen's Law Journal* 255.

Barrett, John. "The Nuremberg Roles of Justice Robert H Jackson" (2007) 6(3) *George Washington University Global Studies Law Review* 511.

Barrow, Denys. "Judgment Delayed is Judgment Denied: Delays in Delivering Judgments in the Eastern Caribbean" (2009) 35(3) *Commonwealth. Law Bulletin* 429.

Barry, Graeme. "The Gifted Judge: An Analysis of the Judicial Career of Robert H Jackson" (2000) 38(3) *Alberta Law Review* 880.

Barry, John. "Morality and the Coercive Process" (1962) 4 *Sydney Law Review* 28.

Baudenbacher, Carl. "Judicial Globalization: New Development or Old Wine in New Bottles" (2003) 38(3) *Texas International Law Journal* 505.

Bazelon, David. "New Gods for Old: Efficient Courts in a Democratic Society" (1971) 46(4) *New York University Law Review* 653.

Beaumont, Brian. "Contemporary Judgment-Writing: The Problem Restated" (1999) 73 *Australian Law Journal* 743.

Beck, Luke. "The Constitutional Duty to Give Reasons for Judicial Decisions" (2017) 40(3) *University of New South Wales Law Journal* 923.

Behuniak-Long, Susan. "Justice Sandra Day O'Connor and the Power of Maternal Legal Thinking" (1992) 54(3) *Review of Politics* 417.

Bell, Andrew. "Delivering Reasons in the Tribunal Context", 21 October 2019. www.supremecourt.justice.nsw.gov.au/Documents/Publications/Speeches/2019%20Speeches/Bell_20191021.pdf.

Bell, Evan. "Letter to a New Judge" (2014) 40(1) *Commonwealth Law Bulletin* 95.

Belleau, Marie-Claire and Rebecca Johnson. "Judging Gender: Difference and Dissent at the Supreme Court of Canada" (2008) 15 *International Journal of the Legal Profession* 57.

Bennett, Robert. "A Dissent on Dissent" (1991) 74 *Judicature* 255.

Benson, Robert. "The End of Legalese: The Game is Over" (1984) 13 *New York University Review of Law and Social Change* 519.

Bentham, Jeremy. *The Works of Jeremy Bentham*. Edinburgh: William Tait, 1843.

Bernstein, J. *Classic and Romantic German Aesthetics*. Cambridge: Cambridge University Press, 2012.

Bianchi, Andrea. "International Adjudication, Rhetoric and Storytelling" (2018) 9 *Journal of International Dispute Settlement* 28.

Binchy, William. "The Irish Legal System: An Introduction" (2011) 11(3) *Legal Information Management* 151.

Binder, Guyora. "The Poetics of the Pragmatic: What Literary Criticisms of Law Offers Posner" (2001) 53 *Stanford Law Review* 1509.

Bingham, Joseph. "What is the Law?" (1912) 11(1) *Michigan Law Review* 1.
Bingham, Thomas. "The Common Law: Past, Present and Future" (1999) 25 *Commonwealth Law Bulletin* 18.
The Business of Judging. Oxford: Oxford University Press, 2000.
"The Rule of Law" (2007) 66(1) *Cambridge Law Journal* 67.
"What is the Law?" (2009) 40(3) *Victoria University of Wellington Law Review* 597.
"The Case of *Liversidge v Andersen*: The Rule of Law Amid the Clash of Arms" (2009b) 43 *International Law* 33.
The Rule of Law. London: Penguin Books, 2011.
Blakemore, Erin. "How Sandra Day O'Connor's Swing Vote Decided the 2000 Election". www.history.com/news/sandra-day-oconnor-swing-vote-bush-gore-election.
Boast, R. "Sir John Salmond and Maori Land Tenure" (2008) 38(4) *Victoria University of Wellington Law Review* 831.
Bobb-Semple, C. "English Common Law, Slavery, and Human Rights" (2007) 13 *Texas Wesleyan Law Review* 659.
Bodwin, Kelly, *et al.* "Opinion Writing and Authorship on the Supreme Court of Canada" (2013) 63(2) *University of Toronto Law Journal* 159.
Bose, Saikat Kumar. "4 Women Judges in Supreme Court After Historic Oath Today". www.ndtv.com/india-news/4-women-judges-in-supreme-court-after-historic-oath-today-2525198.
Bosielo, Ronnie. "Judgment Writing for Aspirant Judges", African Judicial Training Institute, 2013. www.joasa.org.za/newarticles/SA%20Judicial%20Training%20Institute%20Speech%20-%2021062013.docx.
Bosmajan, H. *Metaphor and Reason in Judicial Opinions*. Carbondale: Southern Illinois University Press, 1992.
Bowen, Catherine. *Yankee from Olympus*. Boston: Little, Brown & Co, 1944.
Bowman, Jeffery. "Review of the Court of Appeal (Civil Division) – Report to the Lord Chancellor". London: HMSO, 1997.
Braun, Stefan. "Freedom of Expression *v* Obscenity Censorship: The Developing Canadian Jurisprudence" (1985) 50 *Saskatchewan Law Review* 39.
Brennan, Francis. "Judging the Judges" (1979) 53 *Australian Law Journal* 767.
Brennan, G. "'In Review' Celebration of Scholarship" (2011) 37(3) *Monash University Law Review* 1.

Brennan, Jr, William. "In Defence of Dissents" (1986) 37 *Hastings Law Journal* 427.

Bridge, Carl. "Allies of a Kind: Three Wartime Australian Ministers to the United States, 1940–46" in Lowe, David *et al. Australia Goes to Washington*. Canberra: ANU Press, 2016.

Brierley, A. "Mutual Wills – Blackpool Illuminations" (1995) 58 *Modern Law Review* 95.

Brody, Anita *et al.* "Women on the Bench" (2003) 12(2) *Columbia Journal of Gender and Law* 361.

Brown, Judith *et al.* "The Rugged Feminism of Sandra Day O'Connor" (1999) 32(4) *Indiana Law Review* 1219.

Burns, Kylie. "In This Day and Age: Social Facts, Common Sense, and Cognition in Tort Law Judging in the United Kingdom" (2018) 45 *Journal of Law and Society* 226.

Burt, Robert. "Inventing Judicial Review: Israel and America" [1988–89] 10 *Cardozo Law Review* 2013.

Cafardi, Nicholas *et al.* "President Truman and the *Steel Seizure Case*: A 50-Year Retrospective" (2003) 41(4) *Duquesne Law Review* 685.

Campbell, Lord. *The Lives of the Chief Justices of England*, vol 2. London: John Murray, 1849.

The Lives of the Chief Justices, vol 3. New York: Cockroft & Co, 1873.

Cappalli, Richard. "Improving Appellate Opinions" (2000) 83 *Judicature* 286.

Cardozo, Benjamin. *The Nature of the Judicial Process*. New Haven: Yale University Press, 1921.

Paradoxes of Legal Science (1928). Westport: Greenwood Press, 1970.

Law and Literature and Other Essays and Addresses. New York: Harcourt, Brace, and Co, 1931.

"What Medicine Can Do for Law" (1935) 2(1) *Current Legal Thought* 1.

"Law and Literature" in Landis, J (ed). "Law and Literature" (1939) 39(1) *Columbia Law Review* 119.

The Growth of the Law (1924). New Haven: Yale University Press, 1963.

Carroll, Lewis. *Through the Looking-Glass and What Alice Found There*. New York: Rand McNally, c 1917.

Carroll, Noël. "Rough Heroes: A Response to A.W. Eaton" (2013) 71(4) *Journal of Aesthetics and Art Criticism* 371.

Carter, Jesse. "Dissenting Opinions" (1953) 4 *Hastings Law Journal* 118.

Casto, William. "Robert Jackson's Critique of *Trump v Hawaii*" (2020) 94(2) *St John's Law Review* 335.

Chaudhri, Rudhika. "Sir Owen Dixon and *Yerkey v Jones*: Considering the Feminist Implications of Strict and Complete Legalism" in Eldridge, John and Timothy Pilkington (eds). *Sir Owen Dixon's Legacy*. Canberra: Federation Press, 2019.

Chemerinsky, Erwin. "Justice O'Connor and Federalism" (2001) 32 *McGeorge Law Review* 877.

Chetty, Kate. "A History of the Defence Power: Its Uniqueness, Elasticity and Use in Limiting Rights" (2016) 16 *Macquarie Law Journal* 17.

Chigier, Moshe. "The Rabbinical Courts in the State of Israel" (1967) 2(2) *Israel Law Review* 147.

Choper, Jesse and Kathleen Sullivan. "The Current Justices of the US Supreme Court: Their Philosophies, Ideologies and Values" (1997) 51(1) *Bulletin of the American Academy of Arts and Sciences* 54.

Colbran, Stephen. "Temperament as a Criterion for Judicial Performance Evaluation" (2002) 21(1) *University of Tasmania Law Review* 62.

Collingwood, RG. *The Principles of Art*. Oxford: Clarendon Press, 1938.

Constable, Marianne. "Law as Claim to Justice: Legal History and Legal Speech Acts" (2011) 1(3) *UC Irvine Law Review* 631.

Coper, Michael. "The Seven Habits of a Highly Effective High Court" (2003) 28(2) *Alternative Law Journal* 59.

Corbett, M. "Writing a Judgment – Address at the First Orientation Course for New Judges" (1998) 115(1) *South African Law Journal* 118.

Côté, J. "The Oral Judgment Practice in the Canadian Appellate Courts" (2003) 5(2) *Journal of Appellate Practice and Process* 435.

The Appellate Craft. Ottawa: Canadian Judicial Council, 2009.

"A Practical Guide to Appellate Judging" (2015) *Journal of Appellate Practice and Process* 15.

Council of Europe. *Guidelines of the Committee of Ministers of the Council of Europe on Child-Friendly Justice* (2013). https://rm.coe.int/16804b2cf3.

Courts Service, The. *The Courts Service Annual Report 2000*. Dublin: Courts Service, 2000.

The Courts Service Annual Report 2019. Dublin: Courts Service, 2019.

Cover, Robert, *Justice Accused, Antislavery and the Judicial Process*. New Haven: Yale University Press, 1975.

"Violence and the Word" (1986) 95(8) *Yale Law Journal* 1601.

Cowen, Zelman. "1970 Turner Memorial Lecture – J.V. Barry: A Memoir" (1970) 3 *University of Tasmania Law Review* 237.

Crowther, Eric. "Book Review: *Lord Denning: A Biography*" 161(30) *Justice of the Peace & Local Government Law*, 26 July 1997, 734.

D'Amato, Anthony. "Can/Should Computers Replace Judges?" (1977) 11(5) *Georgia Law Review* 1277.

Dahlberg, Leif. "Pirates, Partisans and Politico-Juridical Space" (2011) 23(2) *Law and Literature* 262.

Dainow, Joseph. "The Civil Law and the Common Law: Some Points of Comparison" (1967) 15(3) *American Journal of Comparative Law* 419.

Dalal, Marwan. "Free Speakers and Their Repression: American Lessons to Israel" (2002) 38(1) *Stanford Journal of International Law* 43.

Daniels, Janet. "Patterns and Fashions in Reported Judgments" (1974) 6(1) *Review of Ghana Law* 19.

Danto, Arthur. "The End of Art: A Philosophical Defense" (1998)(2) 37(4) *History and Theory* 127.

Dawson, Daryl and Mark Nicholls. "Sir Owen Dixon and Judicial Method" (1986) 15 *Melbourne University Law Review* 543.

De Blacam, Mark. "Justice and Natural Law (1997) 32 (ns) *Irish Jurist* 323.

De Navarre Kennedy, John. "What Did the Judge Intend to Say?" (1968) 16 *Chitty's Law Journal* 38.

Dedek, Helge. "The Splendour of Form: Scholastic Jurisprudence and 'Irrational Formality'" (2011) 5(2) *Law and Humanities* 349.

Denneny, Michael. "The Privilege of Ourselves: Hannah Arendt on Judgment" in Hill, M (ed). *Hannah Arendt: The Recovery of the Public World*. New York: St Martin's Press, 1979.

Denning, Alfred. *Freedom Under the Law*. London: Stevens & Sons Ltd, 1949.

The Closing Chapter. London: Butterworths, 1983.

Desmond, William. *Art, Origins, Otherness*. Albany: SUNY Press, 2003.

Dessau, Linda and Tom Wodak. "Seven Steps to Clearer Judgment Writing". http://mja.gov.in/Site/Upload/GR/Title%20NO.182(As%20Per%20Workshop%20List%20title%20no182%20pdf).pdf.

Devlin, Lord. *The Judge*. Oxford: Oxford University Press, 1979.

Devlin, Richard. "From Archetypes to Architects: Re-Envisioning the Role Morality of Trial Level Judges" (2011) 43 *University of British Columbia Law Review* 277.

Dewberry, David. "In the Line of Fire: Reconsidering the Holmes of *Schenck* and the Holmes of *Abrams*" (2005) 42 *Free Speech Yearbook* 17.

Dicey, Albert. *Lectures on the Relation Between Law and Public Opinion in England during the Nineteenth Century*. London: Macmillan and Co, 1905.

Dilliard, Irving (ed). *The Spirit of Liberty*, 3rd ed. Chicago: University of Chicago Press, 1960.

Dilthey, Wilhelm. *Poetry and Experience*. Rudolf Makkreel and Frithjof Rodi (eds). Princeton: Princeton University Press.

Dinh, Viet. "Threats to Judicial Independence: Real & Imagined" (2008) 137(4) *Daedalus* 64.

Dixon, Owen. "Concerning Judicial Method". http://cloud.mrlegal.com.au/mrhomepage.nsf/565ff94daed36d5a48257b530051cc28/45793670f2c07e504825725e0014b1a5/$FILE/Jurisprudence%20Concerning%20Judicial%20Method.pdf.

Dolin, Kieran. "Law and Literature: Walking the Boundary with Robert Frost and the Supreme Court" (2003) 31 *University of Western Australia Law Review* 202.

Douglas, William. "The Dissent: A Safeguard of Democracy" (1948) 32 *Journal of the American Judicature Society* 104.

America Challenged. Princeton: Princeton University Press, 1960.

Dove Wilson, John. "A Scottish Judge Ordinar" (1908) 17(4) *Yale Law Journal* 232–56, 233.

Downes, G. "Writing Reasons for Judgment or Decision". Speech delivered to the Administrative Courts of Thailand, Thailand-Australia Mature Administrative Law Program, 3 May 2007.
www.aat.gov.au/AAT/media/AAT/Files/Speeches%20and%20Papers/WritingReasonsMay2007.pdf

Doyle, John. "Judgment Writing: Are There Needs for Change?" (1999) 73 *Australian Law Journal* 737.

Dyson, Lord. "Where the Common Law Fears to Tread. Annual Lecture for ALBA 2012" (2013) 34(1) *Statute Law Review* 1.

Earlsferry, Lord Roger of. "The Form and Language of Judicial Opinions" (2002) 118 *Law Quarterly Review* 226.

Ehrenberg, Suzanne. "Embracing the Writing-Centered Legal Process" (2004) 89 *Iowa Law Review* 1159.

Elias, Sian. "Transition, Stability and the New Zealand Legal System" (2004) 10(4) *Otago Law Review* 475.

Elms, Elwyn. "Ex Tempore Judgments" in Judicial Commission of New South Wales, *A Matter of Judgment: Judicial Decision-Making and Judgment Writing*, Sydney: Judicial Commission of New South Wales, 2003, 81.

"On the Use of Classical Allusions in Judgment Writing" (2008) 31(1) *University of New South Wales Law Journal* 56.

Emerson, Ralph Waldo. *Essays: Second Series*. Boston: James Munroe & Co, 1845.

Emmett, A. "Towards the Civil Law: The Loss of Orality in Civil Litigation in Australia" (2003) 26(2) *University of New South Wales Law Journal*, 447.

Epstein, Lee, William Landes and Richard Posner. "Why (and When) Judges Dissent: A Theoretical Analysis" (2011) 3 *Journal of Legal Analysis* 101.

Etlin, Richard. *In Defense of Humanism*. Cambridge: Cambridge University Press, 1996.

Fairfield, Charles. *Some Account of George William Wilshere, Baron Bramwell of Hever, and His Opinions*. London: Macmillan & Co, 1898.

Farganis, Dion and Justin Wedeking. "'No Hints, No Forecasts, No Previews': An Empirical Analysis of Supreme Court Nominee Candor from Harlan to Kagan" (2011) 45(3) *Law and Society Review* 525.

Fausten, Dietrich, Ingrid Nielsen and Russell Smyth. "A Century of Citation Practice on the Supreme Court of Victoria" (2007) 31 *Melbourne University Law Review* 733.

Federal Judicial Center. *Judicial Writing Manual*. United States General Publications Office, 1991.

Judicial Writing Manual: A Pocket Guide for Judges, 2nd edition. Washington, Federal Judicial Center, 2013. www.fjc.gov/sites/default/files/materials/16/Judicial%20Writing%20Manual_Second%20Edition_Fourth%20Printing_2020.pdf.

Feenan, Dermot. "Women Judges: Gendering Judging, Justifying Diversity" (2008) 35(4) *Journal of Law and Society* 490.

Ferguson, R. "The Judicial Opinion as Literary Genre" (1990) 2(1) *Yale Journal of Law and the Humanities* 201.

Fifoot, C. *Judge and Jurist in the Reign of Queen Victoria*. London Stevens and Sons, 1959, 15.

Finkelman, Paul. "Coming to Terms with Dred Scott: Response to Daniel Farber" (2011) 39 *Pepperdine Law Review* 49.

Fisher, Robert. "*De Facto* Relationships and *Yerkey v Jones*" (1996) 3 *James Cook University Law Review* 16.

Fitzpatrick, Brian and Paulson Varghese. "Scalia in the Casebooks" (2017) 84 *University of Chicago Law Review* 2231.

Flanders Jr, Robert. "The Utility of Separate Judicial Opinions in Appellate Courts of Last Resort: Why Dissents are Valuable" (1999) *Roger Williams University Law Review* 401.

Fletcher, William. "Dissent" (2009) 39 *Golden Gate University Law Review* 291.

Fordham, Margaret. "The Demise of the Rule in *Rylands v Fletcher*" (1995) *Singapore Journal of Legal Studies* 1.

Forrester, R. "Supreme Court Opinions – Style and Substance: An Appeal for Reform" (1995) 47 *Hastings Law Journal* 167.

Fox, Russell. *Justice in the Twenty-First Century*. Newport: Cavendish Publishing, 2000.

France, Steve. "Opinions With Style" (1999) 85(9) *ABA Journal* 38.

Francisco, Noel. "Justice Scalia: Constitutional Conservative" (2017) 84 *University of Chicago Law Review* 2169.

Frank, Jerome. "Words and Music: Some Remarks on Statutory Interpretation" (1947) 47 *Columbia Law Review* 1259.

Frankfurter, Felix. "The Constitutional Opinions of Justice Holmes" (1916) 29 *Harvard Law Review* 683.

Mr Justice Holmes and the Supreme Court. Cambridge: Belknap Press, 1938.

"Great Judge Retires: American Law Institute Honors Learned Hand" (1951) 37 *ABA Journal* 502.

"Foreword: Robert H Jackson" (1955) 55 *Columbia Law Review* 435.

French, Robert. "Swapping Ideas: The Academy, the Judiciary and the Profession". www.hcourt.gov.au/assets/publications/speeches/current-justices/frenchcj/frenchcj1Dec08.pdf.

Freund, Paul. "The New England Seat on the Supreme Court" (1975) 87 *Proceedings of the Massachusetts Historical Society*, 3rd Series, 32.

Friedman, Lawrence *et al.* "How I Write" (1993) 4 *Scribes Journal of Legal Writing* 3.

Friedman, Lawrence, Robert Kagan, Bliss Cartwright and Stanton Wheeler. "State Supreme Courts: A Century of Style and Citation" (1981) 33 *Stanford Law Review* 773.

Fry, Roger. *Vision and Design*. Harmondsworth: Penguin Books, 1940.

Fuld, Stanley. "The Voices of Dissent" (1962) 62(6) *Columbia Law Review* 923.

Gageler, Stephen. "Why Write Judgments?" (2014) 36(2) *Sydney Law Review* 189.

Garner, Bryan. *The Elements of Legal Style*, 2nd ed. New York: Oxford University Press, 2002.

"Powerful Eloquence" (2016) 102 *ABA Journal* 24.

"Clearing the Cobwebs from Judicial Opinions" (2001) 38(2) *Court Review* 4. http://aja.ncsc.dni.us/courtrv/cr38-2/CR38-2Garner.pdf.

Gault, Thomas. "Whose Day in Court Is It Anyway?" (2002) 33(3) *Victoria University of Wellington Law Review* 631.

Gautam, Khagesh. "Political Patronage and Judicial Appointments in India" (2017) 4(4) *Indonesian Journal of International and Comparative Law* 653.

Gava, John. "Law Reviews: Good for Judges, Bad for Law Schools?" (2002) 26 *Melbourne University Law Review* 560.

"When Dixon Nodded: Further Studies of Sir Owen Dixon's Contracts Jurisprudence" (2011) 33 *Sydney Law Review* 157.

Gerard, Gertrude. "A Reply to the A.A.P. Case" (1977) 2 *University of New South Wales Law Journal* 105.

Gibbs, Harry. "Judgment Writing" (1993) 67(7) *Australian Law Journal* 494.

Gibson, Judith. "Social Media and the Electronic New World of Judges" (2016) 7(2) *International Journal for Court Administration* 1.

Gibson, Walker. "Literary Minds and Judicial Style" (1996–97) 6 *Scribes Journal of Legal Writing* 115.

Giddens, Thomas. "Institution and Abyss" (2020) 2(2) *Law, Technology and Humans* 150.

Ginsburg, Ruth Bader. "From No Rights to Half Rights to Confusing Rights" (1978) 7(1) *Human Rights* 12.

"Women's Work: The Place of Women in Law Schools" (1982) 32(2) *Journal of Legal Education* 272.

"The Obligation to Reason Why" (1985) 37(2) *Florida Law Review* 205.

"Remarks on Writing Separately" (1990) 65(1) *Washington Law Review* 133.

"Speaking in a Judicial Voice" (1992) 67(6) *New York University Law Review* 1185.

"On the Interdependence of Law Schools and Law Courts" (1997) 83(5) *Virginia Law Review* 829.

"Memories of Gerald Gunther" (2002) 55(3) *Stanford Law Review* 639.

"Looking Beyond Our Borders: The Value of a Comparative Perspective in Constitutional Adjudication" (2004) 22(2) *Yale Law & Policy Review* 329.

Ginsburg, Ruth Bader *et al.* "A Tribute to Justice Sandra Day O'Connor" (2006) 119 *Harvard Law Review* 1239.

"Some Legal Scenery" (Keynote Address to the Judicial Conference of Australia, 5 October 2007). www.hcourt.gov.au/speeches/cj/cj_5oct07.pdf.

"The Role of Dissenting Opinions" (2010a) 95(1) *Minnesota Law Review* 1.

"The Supreme Court and Useful Knowledge" (2010b) 154(3) *Proceedings of the American Philosophical Society* 294.

"A Conversation with Justice Ginsburg" (2012–13) 122 *Yale Law Journal Forum* 283.

"A Conversation with Associate Justice Ruth Bader Ginsburg" (2013) 84(4) *University of Colorado Law Review* 909.

Girard, Philip. *Bora Laskin: Bringing Law to Life*. Toronto: University of Toronto Press, 2005.

"Who's Afraid of Canadian Legal History?" (2007) 57(4) *University of Toronto Law Journal* 727.

Gjesdal, Kristin. *Herder's Hermeneutics*. Cambridge: Cambridge University Press, 2017.

Glenza, Jessica. "How Dismantling Roe v Wade Could Imperil Other 'Core, Basic Human Rights'". *The Guardian*, 11 December 2021. www.theguardian.com/us-news/2021/dec/11/supreme-court-roe-v-wade-gay-rights-contraceptives-fertility-treatments.

Goelzhauser, Greg. "Diversifying State Supreme Courts" (2011) 45(3) *Law & Society Review* 761.

Goff, Lord. (a) "The Future of the Common Law" (1997a) 46 *International and Comparative Law Quarterly* 745.

(b) "Denning, Alfred Thompson [Tom], Baron Denning (1899–1999)", *Oxford Dictionary of National Biography*.

Gorman, Wayne. "Ours is to Reason Why: The Law of Rendering Judgment" (2015) 62(3) *Criminal Law Quarterly* 301.

Goutal, Jean. "Characteristics of Judicial Style in France, Britain and the USA" (1976) 24 *American Journal of Comparative Law* 43.

Graves, Robert. *Goodbye to All That*, London: Cassell and Company, 1958.

Greco, Michael and Stephen Wermiel. "Human Rights Hero: Sandra Day O'Connor" (2009) 36(1) *Human Rights* 25.

Greene, Jamal. "The Age of Scalia" (2016) 130(1) *Harvard Law Review* 144.

Greenwald, David and Frederick Schwartz. "The Censorial Judiciary" (2002) 35 *UC Davis Law Review* 1133.

Gregory, Herbert. "Shorter Judicial Opinions" (1948) 34(3) *Virginia Law Review* 362.

Grey, Thomas. "Holmes and Legal Pragmatism" (1989) 41(4) *Stanford Law Review* 787.

Gross, Aeyal. "The Politics of Rights in Israeli Constitutional Law" (1998) 3(2) *Law and the Transformation of Israeli Society* 80.

Groves, Matthew and Russell Smyth. "A Century of Judicial Style: Changing Patterns in Judgment Writing on the High Court 1903–2001" (2004) 32(2) *Federal Law Review* 255.

Gur-Aye, Miriam. "Forty Years of Criminal Law: Developments in Case law Re. the Requirement of Fault" (1990) 24 *Israel Law Review* 560.

Gutteridge, H. "Lord Atkin of Aberdovey" (1945) 9 *Cambridge Law Journal* 44.

Hale, Lady. "Judgment Writing in the Supreme Court" (2010). http://ukscblog.com/judgment-writing-in-the-supreme-court-brenda-hale/.

Hall, Kermit (ed). *The Oxford Companion to the Supreme Court of the United States*, 2nd ed. Oxford: Oxford University Press, 2005.

Hall, Margaret (ed). *Selected Writings of Benjamin Nathan Cardozo*. New York: Fallon Law Book Company, 1947.

Hamilton, Alexander. "Other Defects of the Present Confederation" 21 *The Federalist* (see the *Federalist Papers Online* at https://guides.loc.gov/federalist-papers/text-21-30#s-lg-box-wrapper-25493335).

Handsley, E. "Public Confidence in the Judiciary: A Red Herring for the Separation of Judicial Power" (1998) 20 *Sydney Law Review* 183.

Hanly, Conor. "The Decline of Civil Jury Trial in Nineteenth-Century England" (2005) 26(3) *Journal of Legal History* 253.

Harding, R. "Lord Atkin's Judicial Attitudes and Their Illustration in Commercial Law and Contract" (1964) 27(4) *Modern Law Review* 434.

Harrington, John and Ambreena Manji. "'Mind with Mind and Spirit with Spirit': Lord Denning and African Legal Education" (2003) 30(3) *Journal of Law and Society* 376.

Harvey, Cameron. "It All Started with Gunner James" (1986) 1 *Denning Law Journal* 67.

Hasson, R. "The Doctrine of *Uberrima Fides* in Insurance Law. A Critical Evaluation" (1969) 32(6) *Modern Law Review* 615.

Hawkins, Robert and Robert Martin. "Democracy, Judging and Bertha Wilson" (1995) 41 *McGill Law Journal* 1.

Hayne, Kenneth. "Concerning Judicial Method – Fifty Years on" (2006) 32 *Monash University Law Review* 223.

Hearne, Brian. "Beauty is Truth, Truth Beauty" (1990) 41(1) *The Furrow* 9.

Hedigan, John. "Brian Walsh and the European Convention on Human Rights – The Strasbourg Years" (2001) 10 *Irish Journal of European Law* 22.

Heerey, Peter. "The Judicial Herd: Seduced by Suave Glittering Phrases" (2013) 87 *Australian Law Journal* 460.

Hegel, Georg. *Aesthetics: Lectures on Fine Art*, vols I and II. T Knox (trans). Oxford: Oxford University Press, 1975.

Henchy, Seamus. "Lord Atkin by Geoffrey Lewis" (1983) 18(1) (ns) *Irish Jurist* 182.

Henderson, Andrew. "Symbolic Logic and the Logic of Symbolism" (2014) 41(1) *Critical Inquiry* 78.

Henderson, Lynne. "Legality and Empathy" (1987) 85(7) *Michigan Law Review* 1574.

Herz, Michael. "'Do Justice!': Variations of a Thrice-Told Tale" (1996) 82(1) *Virginia Law Review* 111.

Herz, Ruth. "Review Essay: Anatomy of a Judge" (2015) 9(1) *Law & Humanities* 123.

Heydon, J. "Varieties of Judicial Method in the Late 20th Century" (2012) 34 *Sydney Law Review* 219.

"Threats to Judicial Independence: The Enemy Within" (2013) 129 *Law Quarterly Review* 205.

Ho, HL. "The Judicial Duty to Give Reasons" (2000) *Legal Studies* 42.

Hobbes, Thomas. *Leviathan*. Oxford: Clarendon Press, 1965.

Hoffman, D, A Izerman and J Lidicker. "Docketology, District Courts and Doctrine" (2007) 85 *Washington University Law Review* 681.

Hogan, Gerard. "Unenumerated Personal Rights: Ryan's Case Re-Evaluated" (1990–92) 25–27 (ns) *Irish Jurist* 95.

"Holmes and Denning: Two 20th Century Legal Icons Compared" (2007) 42 (ns) *Irish Jurist* 119.

"Mr Justice Brian Walsh: The Legacy of Experiment and the Triumph of Judicial Imagination" (2017) 57 *Irish Jurist* 1.

Hogg, Peter and Ravi Amarnath. "Why Judges Should Dissent" (2017) 67(2) *University of Toronto Law Journal* 126.

Holloway, Ian. "'A Bona Fide Attempt': Chief Justice Sir Owen Dixon and the Policy of Deference to Administrative Expertise in the High Court of Australia" (2002) 54(2) *Administrative Law Review* 687.

Holmes, Oliver Wendell, Jr. *The Common Law*. London: Macmillan & Co, 1882.

"The Path of the Law" (1897) 10 *Harvard Law Review* 457.

Holmes, Oliver Wendell and Frederick Pollock. *Holmes-Pollock Letters*, 2nd ed. Mark deWolfe Howe (ed). Cambridge: Belknap Press, 1961.

Holmes, Oliver Wendell and Harold Laski. *Holmes-Laski Letters: The Correspondence of Mr Justice Holmes and Harold J Laski 1916–1935*, Mark deWolfe Howe (ed). Cambridge: Harvard University Press, 1953.

Hope of Craighead, Lord. "The Place of a Mixed System in the Common Law World" (2001) 35(1) *Israel Law Review* 1.

"Writing Judgments", 9th Annual Lecture to the Judicial Studies Board, London, 16 March 2005.

Horrall, Andrew. "'Adult Viewing Only': Dorothy Cameron's 1965 Trial for Exhibiting Obscene Pictures" (2013) 34(1) *Journal of Canadian Art History* 56.

Horwitz, P. "Law's Expression: The Promise and Perils of Judicial Opinion Writing in Canadian Constitutional Law" (2000) 38(1) *Osgoode Hall Law Journal* 101.

Howard, Colin. "Sir Owen Dixon and the Constitution" (1973) 9(1) *Melbourne University Law Review* 5.

Hughes, Charles. *The Supreme Court of the United States*. New York: Columbia University Press, 1928.

Hunter, Rosemary, Sharyn Roach Anleu and Kathy Mack. "Judging in lower courts: Conventional, procedural, therapeutic and feminist approaches" (2016) 12(3) *International Journal of Law in Context* 337.

Hussain, Aishah. "'Legal Font Wars': Supreme Court's Switch to Calibri Sparks Debate Among Lawyers". www.legalcheek.com/2021/12/legal-font-wars-supreme-courts-switch-to-calibri-sparks-debate-among-lawyers/.

Hutchinson, Thomas. *The Diary and Letters of His Excellency Thomas Hutchinson, Esq*, vol II. Boston: Houghton, Mifflin & Co, 1886.

International Association of Youth and Family Judges and Magistrates. *Guidelines on Children in Contact with the Justice System*. London: International Association of Youth and Family Judges and Magistrates, 2017.

Irons, Peter. *A People's History of the Supreme Court*. London: Penguin Books, 2006.

Jacob, Robin. "How to write a judgment". *Prospect*, 7 December 2000. www.prospectmagazine.co.uk/philosophy/how-to-write-a-legal-judgment-robin-jacob-court-of-appeal-law.

Jayasuriya, Kumar (ed). *Memorials of the Justices of the Supreme Court of the United States*. Buffalo: WS Hein, 1981–2009.

Jefferson, Thomas. Letter of 12 June 1823 to William Johnson. https://founders.archives.gov/documents/Jefferson/98-01-02-3562.

Jeffries, Stuart. "Dido Belle: the artworld enigma who inspired a movie". *The Guardian*, 27 May 2014. www.theguardian.com/artanddesign/2014/may/27/dido-belle-enigmatic-painting-that-inspired-a-movie.

Jerome, Frank. "Words and Music: Some Remarks on Statutory Interpretation" (1947) 47 *Columbia Law Review* 1259.

Jones, Leonard. "Oliver Wendell Holmes, the Jurist" (1935) 69(3) *United States Law Review* 136.

Judicial Commission of New South Wales. "A Matter of Judgment – Judicial Decision-Making and Judgment-Writing". Sydney: Judicial Commission of New South Wales, 2003.

Juliano, Ann and Stewart Schwab. "The Sweep of Sexual Harassment Cases" (2001) 86(3) *Cornell Law Review* 548.

Kachwaha, Mamta. *Judiciary in India: Determinants of Its Independence and Impartiality*. Geneva: Centre for the Independence of Judges and Lawyers, 1988.

Kalman, Laura. Book Review: *"Judgment in Jerusalem: Chief Justice Simon Agranat and the Zionist Century* by Pnina Lahav" (1998) 23(2) *Law and Social Inquiry* 479.

Kane, Matthew. "Accessible Judgments as a Practical Means to Reengage African Interest and Salvage the International Criminal Court" (2015) 1 *African Journal of International Criminal Justice* 6.

Kannar, George. "The Constitutional Catechism of Antonin Scalia" (1990) 99(6) *Yale Law Journal* 1297.

Kaplan, Benjamin. "An American Lawyer in the Queen's Courts: Impressions of English Civil Procedure" (1971) 69(5) *Michigan Law Review* 821.

Kaufman, Andrew. "Cardozo" (2018) 34(1) *Touro Law Review* 7.

Kaushik, Shivam and Anushri Singh. "All India Judicial Services: Problems and Prospects" (2018) 11(4) *National University of Juridical Sciences Law Review* 519.

Keane, P. "The Idea of the Professional Judge: The Challenges of Communication". www.ajoa.asn.au/wp-content/uploads/2021/01/P01_14_02_28_1-Justice-P-A-Keane.pdf.

Keane, Ronan. "Murder: The Mental Element" (2002) 53(1) *Northern Ireland Legal Quarterly* 1.

"Reflections on the Irish Constitution" (2004–06) 5/7 *Radharc* 135.

Keith, Ben. "Seeing the World Whole: Understanding the Citation of External Sources in Judicial Reasoning" (2008) 6(1) *New Zealand Journal of Public and International Law* 95.

Kennedy, Anthony *et al.* "William Rehnquist and Sandra Day O'Connor: An Expression of Appreciation [with Response]" (2006) 58(6) *Stanford Law Review* 1663.

Keyes, Evelyn. "The Literary Judge: The Judge as Novelist and Critic" (2007) 44(3) *Houston Law Review* 679.

Khanna, Hans. *Law, Men of Law, and Education*. Bombay: NM Tribathi (P) Limited, 1981.

Khosla, Madhav. "Addressing Judicial Activism in the Indian Supreme Court: Towards an Evolved Debate" (2009) 32(1) *Hastings International and Comparative Law Review* 55.

Kiefel, Susan. "Reasons for Judgment: Objects and Observations". Speech delivered at the Sir Harry Gibbs Law Dinner, Emmanuel College, University of Queensland, 18 May 2012.

"The Individual Judge" (2014) 88(8) *Australian Law Journal* 554.

Kierstead, Shelly. "Therapeutic Jurisprudence and Child Protection" (2011) 17(1) *Barry Law Review* 31.

Kilkelly, Ursula. *Listening to Children About Justice: Report of the Council of Europe Consultation with Children on Child-Friendly Justice.* Strasbourg, 5 October 2010. CJ-S-CH (2010) 14 Rev.

King, Henry. "Robert Jackson's Transcendent Influence Over Today's World" (2004) 68 *Albany Law Review* 23.

Kirby, Michael. "On the Writing of Judgments" (1990) 64(11) *Australian Law Journal* 691.

"*Ex Tempore* Reasons" (1992) *Australian Bar Review* 93.

"Reasons for Judgment" (1994) 12 *Australian Bar Review* 121.

"Ex Tempore Judgments – Reasons on the Run" (1995) 25 *University of Western Australia Law Review* 213.

"What Is It Really Like to Be a Justice of the High Court of Australia" (1997) 19 *Sydney Law Review* 514.

"Law at Century's End – A Millennial View from the High Court of Australia" (2001) 1 *Macquarie Law Journal* 1.

"Judging: Reflections on the Moment of Decision" in Judicial Commission of New South Wales. *A Matter of Judgment: Judicial Decision-Making and Judgment Writing.* Sydney: Judicial Commission of New South Wales, 2003, 43.

"Appellate Courts and Dissent: Diversity in the Protection of Freedom" (2004) 16 *Judicial Officers Bulletin* 25.

"Judicial Dissent" (2005) 12 *James Cook University Law Journal* 4.

"Judicial Dissent – Common Law and Civil Law Traditions" (2007) 123 *Law Quarterly Review* 379.

"A Solitary Judicial Voice in India's Crisis". *Sydney Morning Herald*, 26 April 2008, 50.

"The Rise and Rise of the Australian Magistracy". Association of Australian Magistrates XVI Biennial Conference, 7 June 2008.

Kirby, Michael. "Ten Requirements for Successful Law Reform" (2009) 11 *Flinders Journal of Law Reform* 77.

Kitto, Frank. "Some Recollections of Sir Owen Dixon" (1986) 15 *Melbourne University Law Review* 577.

"Why Write Judgments?" in Judicial Commission of New South Wales. *A Matter of Judgment: Judicial Decision-Making and Judgment Writing.* Sydney: Judicial Commission of New South Wales, 2003, 69.

Klarman, Michael. "Has the Supreme Court Been More a Friend or Foe to African Americans?" (2011) 140(2) *Daedalus* 101.

Klinck, Dennis. "Style, Meaning, and Knowing: Megarry J. and Denning M.R. in *In Re Vandervell's Trusts (No. 2)*" (1987) 37(4) *University of Toronto Law Journal* 358.

"'This Other Eden: Lord Denning's Pastoral Vision" (1994) 14(1) *Oxford Journal of Legal Studies* 25.

Koessler, Maximilian. "*Robert H Jackson: Lawyer's Judge. By Eugene Gerhart*" (1962) 62 *Columbia Law Review* 395.

Komar, Roman. *Reasons for Judgment: A Handbook for Judges and Other Judicial Officers*. Toronto: Butterworths, 1980.

Koniak, Susan. "When Law Risks Madness" (1996) 8(1) *Cardozo Studies in Law and Literature* 65.

Krikler, Jeremy. "The *Zong* and the Lord Chief Justice" (2007) 64 *History Workshop Journal* 29.

Kumar, Virendra. "Statement of Indian Law – Supreme Court of India Through Its Constitution Bench Decisions Since 1950. A Juristic Review of Its Intrinsic Value and Juxtaposition" (2016) 58(2) *Journal of the Indian Law Institute* 189.

Lahav, Pnina. "American Influence on Israel's Jurisprudence of Free Speech" (1981) 9 *Hastings Constitutional Law Quarterly* 21.

"Foundations of Rights Jurisprudence in Israel" (1990) 24 *Israel Law Review* 211.

"Jurisprudence and Biography: The Case of Shimon Agranat" (1992) 8(1) *Israel Studies Bulletin* 8.

Lamond, Grant. "Do Precedents Create Rules?" (2005) 11(1) *Legal Theory* 1, 23–24.

Laskin, Bora. "The Institutional Character of the Judge" (1972) 7(3) *Israel Law Review* 329, 333.

"The Function of the Law" (1973) 11 *Alberta Law Review* 118.

"A Judge and His Constituencies" (1976) 7 *Manitoba Law Journal* 1.

Lasok, D et al (eds). *Fundamental Duties*. Oxford: Pergamon Press, 1980.

Law, Jonathan (ed). *Oxford Dictionary of Law*, 9th ed. Oxford: Oxford University Press, 2018.

Lawson, F. "Comparative Judicial Style" (1977) 25(2) *American Journal of Comparative Law* 364.

Layton, Alexander. "Rt Hon Lord Bingham of Cornhill KG" (2010) 59 *International and Comparative Law Quarterly* 893.

Lebovits, Gerald. "Short Judicial Opinions: The Weight of Authority" (2004) 76 *New York State Bar Journal* 64.

"Thoughts on Legal Writing from the Greatest of Them All: Benjamin N Cardozo". https://nysba.org/thoughts-on-legal-writing-from-the-greatest-of-them-all-benjamin-n-cardozo/.

Leflar, Robert. "Some Observations Concerning Judicial Opinions" (1961) 61 *Columbia Law Review* 810.

Lenihan, Niall. "Royal Prerogatives and the Constitution" (1989) 24(1) (ns) *Irish Jurist* 1.

Levin, A. "Mr Justice William Johnson, Creative Dissenter" (1944) 43(3) *Michigan Law Review* 497.

Levinson, Sanford. "Law as Literature" (1982) 60 *Texas Law Review* 373.

"Why the Canon Should Be Expanded to Include the Insular Cases and the Saga of American Expansionism" (2000) 17 *Constitutional Commentary* 241.

Levitt, Stephen. "The Life and Times of a Local Court Judge in Berlin" (2009) 10 *German Law Journal* 169.

Lewis, CS. "On Three Ways of Writing for Children". https://myweb.scu.edu.tw/~jmklassen/scu99b/chlitgrad/3ways.pdf.

Lewis, G. *Lord Atkin*. Hart: Oxford, 1999.

Lincoln, Abraham. "Annual Message to Congress". 1 December 1862. www.abrahamlincolnonline.org/lincoln/speeches/congress.html.

Linton, M DeSales. "The 'Right' to Choose: Now You See It Now You Don't" (1992) 22(8) *Off Our Backs* 7.

Lipez, Kermit. "Some Reflections on Dissenting" (2005) 57 *Maine Law Review* 313.

Llewellyn, Karl. "On the Good, the True, the Beautiful, in Law" (1942) 9 *University of Chicago Law Review* 224.

The Bramble Bush. New York: Oceana Publications, 1951.

Lombardo, Paul. "Facing Carrie Buck" (2003) 33(2) *The Hastings Center Report* 14.

Longford, Elizabeth. *Wellington*. London: Abacus Books, 2001.

Lorand, Ruth. "The Purity of Aesthetic Value" (1992) 50(1) *Journal of Aesthetics and Art Criticism* 13.

Lynch, Andrew. "Dissent: The Rewards and Risks of Judicial Disagreement in the High Court of Australia" (2003) *Melbourne University Law Review* 724.

"Collective Decision-Making: The Current Australian Debate (2015)

21 *European Journal of Current Legal Issues.* http://webjcli.org/index.php/webjcli/article/view/407/518.

Macdonald, Roderick. "Legal Bilingualism" (1997) 42(1) *McGill Law Journal* 119.

"Epistles to Apostles" (2001a) 39(3) *Alberta Law Review* 668.

"The Fridge-Door Statute" (2001b) 47 *McGill Law Journal* 11.

MacLeish, Archibald and E Prichard. *Law and Politics: Occasional Papers of Felix Frankfurter, 1913–1938, xvii.* New York: Harcourt, Brace and Co, 1939.

Macmillan, Lord. "Canadian and British Law" (1927) 5 *Canadian Bar Review* 44.

"Law and Language". Birmingham: The Holdsworth Club, 1931.

"The Writing of Judgments" (1948) 26 *Canadian Bar Review* 491.

MacPherson, James. "Canadian Constitutional Law and Madame Justice Bertha Wilson" (1992) 15(1) *Dalhousie Law Journal* 217.

Macrossan, John. "Queensland Judicial Perspective – A Century On" (1994) 3 *Griffith Law Review* 194.

Mahapatra, Dhananjay. "Supreme Court Judges Bat for Succinct Judgments". *The Times of India*, 3 November 2014. https://timesofindia.indiatimes.com/india/Supreme-Court-judges-bat-for-succinct-judgments/articleshow/45017501.cms.

Mahoney, Dennis. "Judgment Writing: Form and Function" in Judicial Commission of New South Wales. *A Matter of Judgment: Judicial Decision-Making and Judgment Writing.* Sydney: Judicial Commission of New South Wales, 2003, 103.

Mailhot, Louise and James Carnwath. *Decisions, Decisions... A Handbook for Judicial Writing.* Montreal: Les Editions Yvon Blais, 1998.

Malik, Lokendra and Arora Manish. *Two Outstanding Indian Judges.* Delhi: Universal Law Publishing, 2015.

Manderson, Desmond and David Caudill. "Modes of Law: Music and Legal Theory – An Interdisciplinary Workshop Introduction" (1999) 20 *Cardozo Law Review* 1325.

Manning, Maurice. "Utopianism and Hard Pounding – The Quest for Human Rights and the Role of National Human Right Commissions" (2006) 13 *Irish Journal of European Law* 207.

Manson, Edward, *Builders of Our Law During the Reign of Queen Victoria,* 2nd ed. London: Horace Cox, 1904.

Margolis, Joseph. "The Mode of Existence of a Work of Art" (1958) 12(1) *Review of Metaphysics* 26.

"Proposals on the Logic of Aesthetic Judgments" (1959) 9(36) *Philosophical Quarterly* 208.

Marsh, James. "The Genial Justice: Robert H. Jackson" (1974) 60 *ABA Journal* 306.

Marshall, Jeremy, Helen Stalford and Liam Cairns. "Achieving child friendly justice through child friendly methods: let's start with the right to information" (2017) 5 *Social Inclusion* 207.

Marshall, Rudolph. "Judicial Humor: A Laughing Matter?" (1989) 41 *Hastings Law Journal* 175.

Martin, Constance. "The Life and Career of Justice Robert H. Jackson" (2008) 33(1) *Journal of Supreme Court History* 42.

Martin, Robert. "Criticising the Judges" (1982) 28(1) *McGill Law Journal* 1.

Martineau, Robert. "Restrictions on Publication and Citation of Judicial Opinions: A Reassessment" (1994) 28 *University of Michigan Journal of Law Reform* 119.

Mason, Anthony. "Opening Address New South Wales Supreme Court Judges Conference" (1993) 1 *The Judicial Review* 185.

"The Nature of the Judicial Process and Judicial Decision-Making" (2003a) in Judicial Commission of New South Wales. *A Matter of Judgment: Judicial Decision-Making and Judgment Writing*. Sydney: Judicial Commission of New South Wales, 1.

"The High Court of Australia: A Personal Impression of Its First 100 Years" (2003b) 27 *Melbourne University Law Review* 864.

"The Role of the Judge" (2004) 16(10) *Judicial Officers Bulletin* 77.

"The Art of Judging" (2008) 12 *Southern Cross University Law Review* 33.

"Reflections on the High Court: Its Judges and Judgments" (2013) 37(2) *Australian Bar Review* 102.

"The High Court of Australia – Reflections on Judges and Judgments" (2013) 16 *Southern Cross University Law Review* 3.

"Sir Anthony Mason Reflects on Judging in Australia and Hong Kong, Precedent and Judgment Writing". University of Melbourne Law School High Court Blog, 28 July 2014. https://blogs.unimelb.edu.au/opinionsonhigh/2014/07/28/barnett-mason/.

Matthew, Theobald. *Forensic Fables*. London: Butterworths, 1926.

Maugham, Somerset. *The Summing Up*. London: William Heinemann, 1951.

McColl, Ruth. "The Art of Judging" (2008) 12 *Southern Cross University Law Review* 43.

McCormick, Peter. "Supreme Court Cites the Supreme Court: Follow-Up Citation on the Supreme Court of Canada 1989–1993" (1995) 33(3) *Osgoode Hall Law Journal* 453.

"Standing Apart: Separate Concurrence and the Modern Supreme Court of Canada" (2008) 53(1) *McGill Law Journal* 137.

"Structures of a Judgment: How the Modern Supreme Court of Canada Organizes Its Reasons" (2009) 32(1) *Dalhousie Law Journal* 35.

McCullough, David. *John Adams*. New York: Simon and Schuster, 2001.

McEvoy, Kathleen. "Elements of the Australian Constitution" in Corkery, J (ed), *Study of Law*. Adelaide: The Adelaide Law Review Association, 1988.

McGlynn Gaffney, Jr, Edward. "The Importance of Dissent and the Imperative of Judicial Civility" (1994) 28 *Valparaiso University Law Review* 583.

McGregor, Ruth. "Justice Sandra Day O'Connor" (2006) 119 *Harvard Law Review* 1245.

McGinness, John. "Judicial Education in Australia" (2009) 17(3) *Australian Law Librarian* 150.

McHugh, James. "Book Review: Oliver Wendell Holmes: A Life in War, Law, and Ideas" (2021) 102(4) *Massachusetts Law Review* 138.

McHugh, M. "The Judicial Method". Speech delivered at the Australian Bar Association Conference, 5 July 1998. www.hcourt.gov.au/assets/publications/speeches/former-justices/mchughj/mchughj_london1.htm.

McHugh, P. "Sir John Salmond and the Moral Agency of the State" (2007) 38 *Victoria University of Wellington Law Review* 743.

McIntyre, Joe. "In Defence of Judicial Dissent" (2016) 37 *Adelaide Law Review* 431.

McLachlin, Beverley. "Legal Writing: Some Tools" (2001) 39(3) *Alberta Law Review* 695.

"Preserving Public Confidence in the Courts and the Legal Profession" (2002) 29 *Manitoba Law Journal* 277.

McLuhan, Marshall. *The Gutenberg Galaxy: The Making of Typographic Man*. Toronto: University of Toronto Press, 1969.

Meehan, Michael. "The Good, the Bad and the Ugly: Judicial Literacy and Australian Cultural Cringe" (1990) 12 *Adelaide Law Review* 431.

Megarry, Robert. "The Judge" (1983) 13 *Manitoba Law Journal* 189.

Meltzer, Bernard. "Robert H. Jackson: Nuremberg's Architect and Advocate" (2004) 68(1) *Albany Law Review* 55.

Metzger, Gillian *et al*. "A Conversation with Justice Ruth Bader Ginsburg" (2013) 25(1) *Columbia Journal of Gender and Law* 6.

Meyer, Philip, "Visual Literacy and the Legal Culture: Reading Film as Text in the Law School Setting" (1993) 17 *Legal Studies Forum* 91.

Mian, Ajmal. *A Judge Speaks Out*. New York: Oxford University Press, 2004.

Mikva, A. "For Whom Judges Write" (1988) 61 *Southern California Law Review* 1357.

Montrose, JL. "Reasoned Judgment" (1958) 21 *Modern Law Review* 80.

"The Treatment of Statutes by Lord Denning" (1959) 1(1) *University of Malaya Law Review* 87.

Moore, Richter. "Justice Sandra Day O'Connor: Law and Order Justice?" (1988) 63(4) *International Social Science Review* 147.

Morgan, Ted. *FDR*. New York: Touchstone, 1985.

Morris, Grant. "Salmond's Bench: The New Zealand Supreme Court Judiciary 1920–24" (2007) 38 *Victoria University of Wellington Law Review* 813.

Mortimer, Debbie. "Some Thoughts on Writing Judgments in, and for, Contemporary Australia" (2018) 42(1) *Melbourne University Law Review* 274.

Mous, Anon Y. "The Speech of Judges: A Dissenting Opinion" (1943) 29 *Virginia Law Review* 625.

Moyer, Laura and Susan Haire. "Trailblazers and Those that Followed: Personal Experiences, Gender, and Juridical Empathy" (2015) 49(3) *Law & Society Review* 665.

Mulcahy, Sean. "Can a Literary Approach to Matters of Legal Concern Offer a Fairer Hearing than that Typically Offred by the Law?" (2014) 8(1) *Law & Humanities* 111.

Munby, James. "Unheard voices: the involvement of children and vulnerable people in the family justice system". The Annual Lecture of the Wales Observatory on Human Rights of Children and Young People delivered by Sir James Munby, President of the Family Division at the College of Law, Swansea University on 25 June 2015. www.swansea.ac.uk/media/Sir-James-Munby-Annual-lecture-2015.pdf.

Munday, Roderick. (a) "Judicial Configurations. Permutations of the Court and Properties of Judgment" (2002) 61(3) *Cambridge Law Journal* 612.

(b) "All for One and One for All: The Rise to Prominence of the Composite Judgment within the Civil Division of the Court of Appeal" (2002) 61(2) *Cambridge Law Journal* 321.

"Judicial Footnotes: A Footnote With Footnotes" (2006) 170 *Justice of the Peace* 864.

Murchison, Melanie. "Making Numbers Count: An Empirical Analysis of Judicial Activism in Canada" (2017) 40(3) *Manitoba Law Journal* 425.

Murphy, John. "The Merits of *Rylands v Fletcher*" (2004) 24(4) *Oxford Journal of Legal Studies* 643.

Murphy, Tim. "The Irish Constitution in Context" (2019) 108(431) *Studies* 332.

Murphy, W and R Rawlings. "After the *Ancien Régime*: The Writing of Judgments in the House of Lords, 1979–80" (1982) 45(1) *Modern Law Review* 34.

Murray, Sarah. "'A Letter to the Loser'? Public Law and the Empowering Role of the Judgment" (2014) 23(4) *Griffith Law Review* 545.

Murynka, Daniella. "Give Me One Good Reason: The Principled Approach in the Canadian Judicial Opinion" (2015) 40(2) *Queen's Law Journal* 609.

Nariman, Fali. "Fifty Years of Human Rights Protection in India – The Record of 50 Years of Constitutional Practice" (2013) *National Law School of India Review* 13.

Neal, Phil. "Justice Jackson: A Law Clerk's Recollections" (2005) 68 *Albany Law Review* 549.

Nelson, Goodman and Catherine Elgin. *Reconceptions in Philosophy*. Indianapolis: Hackett, 49.

Neuberger, Lord. "Insolvency, Internationalism and Supreme Court Judgments", 11 November 2009. www.ilauk.com/docs/lord_neuberger_ila_pre-dinner_lecture_11_nov_09.pdf.

"Developing Equity – A View from the Court of Appeal", 20 January 2012.

www.judiciary.uk/wp-content/uploads/JCO/Documents/Speeches/mr-speech-chancery-bar-assoc-lecture-jan12.pdf.

"No Judgment – No Justice". First Annual BAILII Lecture, 20 November 2012. www.bailii.org/bailii/lecture/01.html.

"Sausages and the Judicial Process: The Limits of Transparency", 1 August 2014. www.supremecourt.uk/docs/speech-140801.pdf.

"Judgment and Judgments – The Art of Forming and Writing Judicial Decisions", Denning Society Lecture 2017. www.lincolnsinn.org.uk/wp-content/uploads/2018/11/denningsocietylecture2017.pdf.

Neuborne, Burt. "The Supreme Court of India" (2003) 1 *International Journal of Constitutional Law* 476.

Newark, F. "Non-Natural User and *Rylands v Fletcher*" (1961) 24(5) *Modern Law Review* 557.

Nielson, James. "Robert H Jackson: The Middle Ground" (1944) 6 *Louisiana Law Review* 381.

Niv, M. "The Undesirability of Detailed Judicial Reasoning" (1999) 7 *European Journal of Law and Economics* 161.

Noorani, A. "The Judiciary and the Bar in India During the Emergency" (1978) 11(4) *Law and Politics in Africa, Asia, and Latin America* 403.

Oberman, Michelle. "Thirteen Ways of Looking at *Buck v Bell*: Thoughts Occasioned by Paul Lombardo's 'Three Generations, No Imbeciles'" (2010) 59(3) *Journal of Legal Education* 357.

O'Connell, Mary Ellen. *The Art of Law in the International Community*. Cambridge: Cambridge University Press, 2019.

O'Connor, Sandra Day. "Portia's Progress" (1991) 66(6) *NYU Law Review* 1546.

"Full Text of Justice Sandra Day O'Connor's Commencement Address (2004)". https://news.stanford.edu/news/2004/june16/oconnortext-616.html.

"Music and the Law" (2005) 18 *Western Legal History* 41.

"Remembering Rehnquist" (2006) 31(1) *Journal of Supreme Court History* 5.

"Remarks at the Inaugural Sandra Day O'Connor Distinguished Lecture Series" (2009) 41(4) *Texas Tech Law Review* 1169.

O'Connor, Sandra Day and Kim Azzarelli. "Sustainable Development, Rule of Law, and the Impact of Women Judges" (2011) 44(1) *Cornell International Law Journal* 3.

O'Donnell, Paul. "Antonin Scalia's Catholic Priest Son Doesn't Like Being Called a Conservative". *The Washingtonian*, 2 May 2017. www.washingtonian.com/2017/05/02/antonin-scalias-catholic-priest-son-doesnt-like-being-called-a-conservative/.

O'Donovan, James. "The Retreat from *Yerkey v Jones*: From Status Back to Contract" (1996) 26 *University of Western Australia Law Review* 305.

O'Flaherty, Hugh. "Brian Walsh, 1918–98" (1998) 7(1) *Irish Journal of European Law* 1.

O'Loghlen, M. "Whether Courts Must Give Reasons for Decision" (1999) 73 *Australian Law Journal* 630.

O'Regan, Catherine. "From Form to Substance: The Constitutional Jurisprudence of Laurie Ackerman" (2008) *Acta Juridica* 1.

O'Reilly, James (ed). *Human Rights and Constitutional Law: Essays in Honour of Brian Walsh*. Dublin: Round Hall Press, 1992.

Olsson, Leslie. *Guide to Uniform Production of Judgments*. Melbourne: Australian Institute of Judicial Administration, 2nd ed, 1999.

Oosterhoff, Albert. "Mutual Wills" (2008) 27 *Estates, Trusts and Pensions Journal* 135.

Orth, John. "Sir William Blackstone: Hero of the Common Law" (1980) 66(2) *ABA Journal* 155.

Orwell, George. "Politics and the English Language". www.public-library.uk/ebooks/72/30.pdf.

Osborough, Nial. "The State's Tortious Liability: Further Reflections on *Byrne v Ireland*" (1976) 11(1) *Irish Jurist* 11.

Literature, Judges and the Law. Dublin: Four Courts Press, 2008.

Oxner, Sandra. "The Quality of Judges" (2003) 1 *World Bank Legal Review* 307.

Pahl, Dennis. "Sounding the Sublime" (2009) 42(1) *Poe Studies* 41.

Paley, Ruth. "Imperial Politics and English Law: The Many Contexts of 'Somerset'" (2006) 24(3) *Law and History Review* 659.

Palshikar, V. "Judicial Activism" (2007) 7 *The Law Review* 55.

Pannick, David. *Judges*. Oxford: Oxford University Press, 1987.

Parkinson, Jerry. "Admissions After *Grutter*" (2003) 35(1) *University of Toledo Law Review* 159.

Pardo, Sharon and Lior Zemer. "The Image of European Union Law in Bilateral Relations" (2021) 54 *Vanderbilt Journal of Transnational Law* 147.

Partovi, Andisheh *et al.* "Addressing Loss of Identity in the Joint Judgment: Searching for the Individual Judge in the Joint Judgments of the Mason Court" (2017) 40(2) *University of New South Wales Law Journal* 670.

Peeples, David. "Trial Court Jurisdiction and Control Over Judgments" (1986) 17 *St Mary's Law Journal* 367.

Pérez-Gómez, Alberto. *Built Upon Love: Architectural Longing After Ethics and Aesthetics*. Cambridge: MIT Press, 2006.

Perju, Vlad. "Reason and Authority in the European Court of Justice" (2009) 49 *Virginia Journal of International Law* 307.

Perlstein, Rick. "Outsmarted: on the Liberal Cult of the Cognitive Elite" (2017) 34 *The Baffler* 52.

Perrin, Benajmin. "The Court Had Been Oft Divided Lately. And That's a Good Thing" *National Post*, 19 January 2016.

Petersson, Sandra. "Poetic Justices and the Legalities of Love" (2000) 31(1) *Victoria University of Wellington Law Review* 103.

Pether, Penelope. "Pursuing the Unspeakable: Toward Critical Theory of Power, Ethics and the Interpreting Subject in Australian Constitutional Law" (1998) 20(1) *Adelaide Law Review* 17.

Pickering, Harold. "On Learning to Write: Suggestions for Study and Practice" (1955) 41(12) *ABA Journal* 1121.

Pillai, KN Chandrasekharan and Sood, Jyoti Dogra. "Supreme Court – In Retrospect and Prospect" (2006) 48(1) *Journal of the Indian Law Institute* 3.

Poe, Edgar Allen. "Poetry, Tales, and Selected Essays". New York: The Library of America, 1996.

Popkin, William. *Evolution of the Judicial Opinion*. New York: NYU Press, 2007.

Posner, Richard. *Law and Literature: A Misunderstood Relation*. Cambridge: Harvard University Press, 1988.

"Judges' Writing Styles (And Do They Matter)?" (1995) 62 *University of Chicago Law Review* 1421.

Frontiers of Legal Theory. Cambridge: Harvard University Press, 2001.

Divergent Paths: The Academy and the Judiciary. Harvard: Harvard University Press, 2016.

Pound, Roscoe. "The Theory of Judicial Decision" (1924) 2(4) *Canadian Bar Review* 263.

Powell, H. "Law as a Language, Law as an Art: Reflections on James Boyd's White's *Keep Law Alive*" (2021) 10(1) *British Journal of American Legal Studies* 155.

Presser, Stephen. "The Development and Application of Common Law" (2004) 8 *Texas Review of Law and Politics* 291.

Priestley, L. "The Writing of Judgments; A Forum" (1992) 9 *Australian Bar Review* 130.

Purcell, Bernard. "'Appalling vista' judge dies at 100", *Irish Independent*, 6 March 1999. www.independent.ie/irish-news/appalling-vista-judge-dies-at-100-26155585.html.

Rabboni, Ansuman and P Kingsley. "*Actio Popularis*: A Perspective Analysis on Public Interest Litigation" (2011) 72(2) *Indian Journal of Political Science* 463.

Rackley, Erika. "Judicial Diversity, the Woman Judge and Fairy Tale Endings" (2007) 27(1) *Legal Studies* 74.

Radcliffe, Lord. "Law and Order" (1964) 61 *Law Society Gazette* 820.

Ramnath, Kalyani. "The Runaway Judgment: Law as Literature, Courtcraft and Constitutional Visions" (2011) 3(1) *Journal of Indian Law and Society* 1.

"*ADM Jabalpur*'s Antecedents: Political Emergencies, Civil Liberties, and Arguments from Colonial Continuities in India" (2016) 31(6) *American University International Law Review* 209.

Ransom, William. "Associate Justice Robert H Jackson" (1941) 27 *ABA Journal* 478.

Rappaport, Michael. "It's the O'Connor Court: A Brief Discussion of Some Critiques of the Rehnquist Court and Their Implications for Administrative Law" (2004) 99 *Northwestern University Law Review* 369.

Raveendran, R. "Rendering Judgment – Some Basics" (2009) 10 *Supreme Court Cases* (J) 1.

Re, Edward. *Appellate Opinion Writing*. Washington, DC: Federal Judicial Center, 1975.

Reagan, Ronald. *An American Life*. London: Random Century, 1990.

Réaume, Denise. "The Judicial Philosophy of Bora Laskin" (1985) 35(4) *University of Toronto Law Journal* 438.

Reid, Lord. "The Judge as Law Maker" (1972) *Journal of the Society of Public Teachers of Law* (1972) 12(1) (ns) 22.

Reynolds, Joshua. *Seven Discourses Delivered in the Royal Academy by the President*. Cambridge: Cambridge University Press, 2014.

Reynolds, Maura. "Judge Roberts' View from the Bench", *Los Angeles Times*, 10 August 2005. www.latimes.com/archives/la-xpm-2005-aug-10-na-roberts10-story.html.

Richardson, Ivor. "The Role of an Appellate Judge" (1981) 5(1) *Otago Law Review* 1.

"Closing Remarks" (2004) 2 *New Zealand Journal of Public and International Law* 115.

Rippingham, John. *The Art of Public Speaking Ex-Tempore*. London: Longman, Hurst et al, 1814.

Ritter, David. "The Myth of Sir Owen Dixon" (2005) 9(2) *Australian Journal of Legal History* 249.

Roberts, Heather and Laura Sweeney. "Why (Re)Write Judgments?" (2015) 37 *Sydney Law Review* 457–66, 464.

Roberts, Dorothy. "Sandra Day O'Connor, Conservative Discourse, and Reproductive Freedom" (1991) 13(2) *Women's Rights Law Reporter* 95.

Roberts, John, *et al*. "In Memoriam: Justice Antonin Scalia" (2016) 130(1) *Harvard Law Review* 1.

Rodell, Fred. "Goodbye to Law Reviews" (1936–37) 23(1) *Virginia Law Review* 38.

"Goodbye to Law Reviews – Revisited" (1962) 48 *Virginia Law Review* 279.

Rodger, Lord. "The Form and Language of Judicial Opinions" (2002) 118 *Law Quarterly Review* 226.

Rosenthal, Andrew. "O'Connor Regrets Bush *v* Gore", *The New York Times*, 29 April 2013. https://takingnote.blogs.nytimes.com/2013/04/29/oconnor-regrets-bush-v-gore/.

Rothenburg, Kevin. "Book Review: *First: Sandra Day O'Connor*" (2020) 112(1) *Law Library Journal* 152.

Roussy, Alain. "Cut-and-Paste Justice: A Case Comment on *Cojocaru v British Columbia Women's Hospital and Health Centre*" (2015) 52(3) *Alberta Law Review* 761.

Rubenstein, Kim. "Returning to 'Representation/s of Women': Feminist Analysis and Job-Sharing as Core Constitutional Concerns" in Rubenstein, Kim (ed). *Traversing the Divide: Honouring Deborah Cass's Contributions to Public and International Law*. Canberra: ANU Press, 2021.

Rubin, Edward. "Question Regarding *DC v Heller*: As a Justice, Antonin Scalia Is (A) Great, (B) Acceptable, (C) Injudicious" (2008) 54 *Wayne Law Review* 1105.

Sands, Philippe. "Lord Bingham of Cornhill obituary". *The Guardian*, 11 September 2010. www.theguardian.com/law/2010/sep/11/lord-bingham-of-cornhill-obituary.

Santayana, George. *The Sense of Beauty*. New York: Dover Publications, 1955.

Sarkar, Arpita. "A Journey with the Due Process of Law: Recording Some Revelations and Disappointments with the Work of Abhinav Chandrachund" (2011) 3(1) *Journal of Indian Law and Society* 158.

Sassoon, David. "The Israel Legal System" (1968) 16 *American Journal of Comparative Law* 405.

Scalia, Antonin. "The Dissenting Opinion" (1994) *Journal of Supreme Court History* 33.

Schaefer, Walter. "Precedent and Policy" (1966) 34 *University of Chicago Law Review* 3.

Schauer, F. "Precedent" (1987) 39 *Stanford Law Review* 571.

Schnoor, Randal. "The Contours of Canadian Jewish Life" (2011) 31(3) *Contemporary Jewry* 179.

Schlag, Pierre. "The Aesthetics of American Law" (2002) 115 *Harvard Law Review* 1047.

Schotland, Roy. "Republican Party of Minnesota v White: Should Judges Be More Like Politicians?" (2002) 41 *Judges' Journal* 7.

Schuck, P. "Legal Complexity: Some Causes, Consequences and Cures" (1992) 42 *Duke Law Journal* 1.

Schwartz, Bernard. *Some Makers of American Law*. Calcutta: Ajoy Law House, 1985.

Schwartz, Louis. "Justice, Expediency, and Beauty" (1987–1988) 136(1) *University of Pennsylvania Law Review* 141.

Sedley, Stephen. "Denning's Law" (1979) 11(2) (ns) *Bulletin (Haldane Society of Socialist Lawyers)* 15.

"Lord Denning obituary". *The Guardian*, 6 March 1999. www.theguardian.com/news/1999/mar/06/guardianobituaries.

Sharlow, Karen. "Why Judges Need Academics" (2012) 32 *Windsor Review of Legal and Social Issues* 13.

Sharpe, Robert. "Bora Laskin and Civil Liberties" (1985) 35(4) *University of Toronto Law Journal* 603.

"Brian Dickson, the Supreme Court of Canada, and the Charter of Rights: A Biographical Sketch" (2002) 21 *Windsor Yearbook of Access to Justice* 21.

Sharpe, Robert and Vincent-Joul Proulx. "The Use of Academic Writing in Appellate Judicial Decision-Making (2011) 50 *Canadian Business Law Journal* 550.

Shiels, Trevor. "Multiple Judgments and the New Zealand Supreme Court" (2015) 14 *Otago Law Review* 11.

Shientag, Bernard. "A Modern Judicial Mind – The Writings of the Rt Hon. Lord Macmillan" (1936) 36 *Columbia Law Review* 615.

Simmons, Robert. "Better Opinions – How?" (1941) 27 *ABA Journal* 109.

Singh, Ravindra. "Substantive Limitation on the Power of Parliament to Amend the Constitution: The Indian Standpoint" (2020) 10 *GNLU Journal of Law Development and Politics* 1.

Sivakumar, S. "Judgment or Judicial Opinion: How to Read and Analyse" (2016) 58(3) *Journal of Indian Law Institute* 273.

Smith, George. "A Primer of Opinion Writing, For Four New Judges" (1967) 21 *Arkansas Law Review* 197.

"A Primer of Opinion Writing for Law Clerks" (1973) 26 *Vanderbilt Law Review* 1203.

Smith, Robert. "Book Review: *Forensic Fables*. London: Butterworth, 1961" (1962) 15(2) *Florida Law Review* 326.

Smyth, Russell. "Judicial Robes or Academic Gowns? Citation of Secondary Authority and Legal Method in the New Zealand Court of Appeal" in Bigwood, Rick (ed). *Legal Method in New Zealand Court of Appeal*. Wellington: Butterworths, 2001.

"Trends in the Citation Practice of the Supreme Court of Queensland over the Course of the Twentieth Century" (2009) 28(1) *University of Queensland Law Journal* 39.

Snell, James and Frederick Vaughan. *The Supreme Court of Canada: History of the Institution*. Toronto: University of Toronto Press, 1985.

Solan, Lawrence. "Communicative Content and Legal Content" (2013) 89 *Notre Dame Law Review* 479.

Sonnenfeldt, Richard. "For Me, Robert H Jackson Is Alive" (2004) 68 *Albany Law Review* 71.

Sood, Ankur. "The Basic Structure Unbound" (2008) 2 *NUALS Law Journal* 145.

Sossin, Lorne. "In Search of Bora's Head" (2009) 59 *University of Toronto Law Journal* 251.

Sotomayor, Sonia. "A Tribute to Justice Scalia" (2017) 126(6) *Yale Law Journal* 1609.

Spann, Girardeau. "Neutralizing *Grutter*" (2005) 7(3) *University of Pennsylvania Journal of Constitutional Law* 633.

Spiegelman, J. "Reasons for Judgment and the Rule of Law", Paper presented at the National Judicial College, Beijing and the Judges' Training Institute, Shanghai, 10 November 2003.

St George Stubbs, Roy. "Sir George Jessel: Master of the Rolls" (1951) 29(2) *Canadian Bar Review* 147.

Stack, Kevin. "The Practice of Dissent in the Supreme Court" (1996) 105 *Yale Law Journal* 2235.

Stalford, Helen and Kathryn Hollingsworth. "'This case is about you and your future': Towards Judgments for Children" (2020) 83(5) *Modern Law Review* 1030.

Steel, Freda. "The Role of Dissents in Appellate Judging" (2017) 67(2) *University of Toronto Law Journal* 142.

Steigelfest, Jack. "The End of an Era for Single-Sex Schools: Mississippi University for Women v Hogan" (1983) 15(2) *Connecticut Law Review* 353.

Stein, Joshua. "Tentative Oral Opinions: Improving Oral Argument Without Spending a Dime" (2013) 14 *Journal of Appellate Practice and Process* 159.

Stevens, Robert. "Judicial Legislation and the Law Lords – II" (1975) 10(2) (ns) *Irish Jurist* 216.

Stewart, Dugald. *Elements of the Philosophy of the Human Mind*. Brattleborough: William Fessenden, 1808.

Stone, Geoffrey. "The Supreme Court in the 21st Century" (2013) 142(2) *Daedalus* 36.

Stone, Harlan. "Dissenting Opinions Are Not Without Value" (1942) 26 *Journal of the American Judicature Society* 78.

Strong, S. "Writing Reasoned Decisions and Opinions: A Guide for Novice, Experienced and Foreign Judges" (2015) *Journal of Dispute Resolution* 93.

Sudhir, Abhishek. "Discovering Dworkin in the Supreme Court of India – A Comparative Excursus" (2014) 7(1) *National University of Juridical Sciences Law Review* 13.

Sunstein, Cass. "One Case at a Time: Judicial Minimalism on the Supreme Court". Harvard: Harvard University Press, 1999.
 Why Societies Need Dissent. Cambridge: Harvard University Press, 2005.
Swanson, Richard. "Battered Wife Syndrome" (1984) 130 *Canadian Medical Association Journal* 709.
Sweeney Byrne, Lucy. "Tropic of Cancer by Henry Miller: Vibrant, sexy, terrible and free". www.irishtimes.com/culture/books/tropic-of-cancer-by-henry-miller-vibrant-sexy-terrible-and-free-1.4414735.
Swinton, Katherine. "Bora Laskin and Federalism" (1985) 35(4) *University of Toronto Law Journal* 353.
Syverud, Kent. "Lessons from Working for Sandra Day O'Connor" (2006) 58(6) *Stanford Law Review* 1731.
Taggart, Michael. "Should Canadian Judges Be Legally Required to Give Reasoned Decisions in Civil Cases?" (1983) 33(1) *University of Toronto Law Journal* 1.
Temple Lang, John. "Book Review: Human Rights and Constitutional Law Essays in Honour of Brian Walsh" (1992) 14 *Dublin University Law Journal* 201.
Tolstoy, Leo. *What is Art?* New York: Funk & Wagnalls, 1904.
Toobin, Jeffrey. *The Nine: Inside the Secret World of the Supreme Court.* New York: Doubleday, 2007.
Traister, Rebecca. "The Body Politic". *New York Magazine*, 2 December 2021. https://nymag.com/intelligencer/2021/12/the-betrayal-of-roe.html.
Traynor, Roger. "Some Open Questions on the Work of State Appellate Courts" (1957) 24 *University of Chicago Law Review* 211.
Trochev, Alexei and Rachel Ellett. "Judges and Their Allies" (2014) 2(1) *Journal of Law and Courts* 67.
Trollope, Anthony. *Autobiography of Anthony Trollope.* London: Dodd, Mead and Company, 1905.
Turnbull, George. *A Treatise of Ancient Painting.* London: 1740. www.archive.org.
Turner, J. "Middleton's Case and the Larceny Act 1916" (1941) 7 *Cambridge Law Journal* 337.
Twain, Mark. "Fenimore Cooper's Literary Offences". Project Gutenberg.
Uelmen, Gerald. "The Tragedy of Rose Bird" (2016) 38 *Thomas Jefferson Law Review* 143.

United States Judiciary Committee. *Confirmation Hearing on the Nomination of John G Roberts, Jr to be Chief Justice of the United States* (S Hrg 109-158; Serial J-109-37), 12–15 September 2005.

Valentine, G. "Sir John Salmond's Jurisprudence and Some Reflections" (1938) 50 *Juridical Review* 1.

Valéry, Paul and Charles Guenther. "Poetry and Abstract Thought" (1954) 16(2) *Kenyon Review* 208.

Van Detta, Jeffrey. "The Decline and Fall of the American Judicial Opinion, Part I" (2009) 12(1) *Barry Law Review* 53.

Van Rijswijk, Honni. "Mabel Hannah's Justice: A Contextual Re-Reading of *Donoghue v Stevenson*" (2010) 5 *Public Space* 1.

Wald, Patricia. "The Rhetoric of Results and the Results of Rhetoric" (1995) 62 *University of Chicago Law Review* 1371.

"A Reply to Judge Posner" (1995) 62 *University of Chicago Law Review* 1451.

Walker, Greg. "Inter-Spouse Guarantees – Limits on the Liability of a Wife for Her Husband's Debts" (1992) 6(4) *Commercial Law Quarterly* 6.

Walsh, Brian. Book Review: "George Gavan Duffy 1882–1951. A Legal Biography by G.M. Golding" (1982) 17(2) (ns) *Irish Jurist* 384.

"200 Years of American Constitutionalism – A Foreign Perspective" (1987) 48 *Ohio State Law Journal* 757.

Walsh, David. "On the Meaning and Pattern of Legal Citations Evidence from State Wrongful Discharge Precedent Cases" (1997) 31 *Law & Society Review* 337.

Walsh, Ryan. "The Forthrightness of Justice Scalia" (2017) 84 *University of Chicago Law Review* 2189.

Wanderer, N. "Writing Better Opinions: Communicating with Candor, Clarity and Style" (2002) 54 *Maine Law Review* 47.

Warren, Earl. "Chief Justice John Marshall: A Heritage of Freedom and Stability" (1955) 41(11) *ABA Journal* 1008.

Watt, Gary. "Law-Suits: Clothing as the Image of the Law" in Dahlberg, Leif (ed). *Visualizing Law and Authority, Essays on Legal Aesthetics*. Boston: De Gruyter, 2012, 23.

Waye, Vicki. "Who Are Judges Writing For?" (2009) 34(2) *University of Western Australia Law Review* 274.

Weidenfeld, Matthew. "Visions of Judgment: Arendt, Kant, and the Misreading of Judgment" (2013) 66(2) *Political Research Quarterly* 254.

Weinberg, Louise. "Holmes' Failure" (1998) 96(3) *Michigan Law Review* 691.
Wells, Michael. "French and American Judicial Opinions" (1994) 19 *Yale Journal of International Law* 81.
West, Robin. "Jurisprudence as Narrative: An Aesthetic Analysis of Modern Legal Theory" (1985) 60 *New York University Law Review* 145.
Weyrauch, Walter. "The Art of Drafting Judgments: A Modified German Case Method", (1956) 9 *Journal of Legal Education* 311.
Wharton, Edith. *The Writing of Fiction*. New York: Charles Scribner's Sons, 1925.
https://archive.org/details/writingoffiction0000whar/page/n7/mode/2up.
White, George. *Oliver Wendell Holmes, Sage of the Supreme Court*. New York: Oxford University Press, 2000.
White, James Boyd. "Law as Language: Reading Law and Reading Literature" (1981–82) 60 *Texas Law Review* 415.
Heracles' Bow: Essays on the Rhetoric and Poetics of the Law, Madison: University of Wisconsin Press, 1985.
"What's an Opinion For?" (1995) 62 *University of Chicago Law Review* 1363.
Wigmore, J. *Evidence in Trials at Common Law*. Boston: Little, Brown, 1983. P Tillers (ed).
Wilberforce, Lord. "The Academics and Lord Denning" (1985) 5(3) *Oxford Journal of Legal Studies* 439.
Williams, Joseph and Joseph Bizup. *Style: Lessons in Clarity and Grace*. New York: Pearson, 2021.
Wilson, Bertha. "Decision-Making in the Supreme Court" (1986) 36(3) *University of Toronto Law Journal* 227.
"The Scottish Enlightenment: The Third Shumiatcher Lecture in The Law as Literature" (1986–87) 51 *Saskatchewan Law Review* 251.
"The Making of a Constitution" (1988) 71(6) *Judicature* 334.
"Will Women Judges Really Make a Difference?" (1990) 28(3) *Osgoode Hall Law Journal* 507.
Winterton, George. "The Significance of the Communist Party Case" (1992) 18 *Melbourne University Law Review* 630.
Wisdom, John. "Wisdom's Idiosyncrasies" (2000) 109 *Yale Law Journal* 1273.

Wolff, Michael. "Making Judge-Speak Clear Amidst the Babel of Lawspeakers" (2014) 79(4) *Missouri Law Review* 1039.

Woodruff, Judy. "Sandra Day O'Connor: *The Majesty of the Law*". http://edition.cnn.com/2003/ALLPOLITICS/05/20/judy.page.oconnor/index.html.

Wright, Lord. *Legal Essays and Addresses*. Cambridge: Cambridge University Press, 1939.

"In Memoriam: Lord Atkin of Aberdovey 1867–1944" (1944) 60 *Law Quarterly Review* 332.

Young, P. "Judgment Writing" (1996) 70 *Australian Law Journal* 513.

Young, Stephen. "Reconceptualizing Accountability in the Early Nineteenth Century: How the Tort of Negligence Appeared" (1989) 21 *Connecticut Law Review* 197.

Younger, Irving. "On Judicial Opinions Considered as One of the Fine Arts" (1980) 51 *University of Colorado Law Review* 341.

Ziegel, Jacob. "Bora Laskin's Contributions to Commercial, Contract, and Corporate Law" (1985) 35(4) *University of Toronto Law Journal* 392.

Index

Note: Because this book is international in scope, the nationality of each person named in this index is, for purposes of clarity, mentioned in brackets after her/his name. The abbreviation (fn) followed by a number denotes that the index reference is in a footnote.

Academics and academic references
    academics as audience, 35
    academics as partners, 167
    academic references, 69–72
    anti-intellectualism, 70
    attractions of academic commentary, 71
    Chief Justice Brennan (Australia) on Academy, 70
    drawbacks of academic commentary, 71–72
    embrace of Academy a recent development, 70–71
    judgment not a PhD thesis, 31–32, 69–70
    judgments and rationalisation of law, 32
    Justice Sharlow (Canada) and role of Academy, 70
    respective roles of academics and judges, 70

Accessibility
    and composite judgments, 24–25
    judgments to be accessible, 22–23
    to people with disabilities, 22(fn39), 127

Adams, John, (US)
    role in *Marbury v Madison*, 51

Agranat, Shimon, (Israel), 274–279
    and concurring judgments, 277–278
    background, 274
    breadth of judgments, 274–275
    compared to Justice Khanna (India), 265, 278
    compared to Justice Laskin (Canada), 278
    compared to Justice Walsh (Ireland), 265, 271, 274, 278
    construction of modern Israel, 278
    creativity as judge, 276–77
    didacticism, 278
    early post-independence judge, 274
    'founding father' of Israeli Supreme Court, 271
    freedom of speech, 275
    influence as judge, 274–276
    judicial role in shaping value system, 277
    Kol Ha'am and *Marbury v Madison*, 275–276
    lessons from judgments of wider common law world, 282–283
    magisterial style, 276
    on role of truth, 275
    reliance on foreign/US case-law, 275, 276, 277, 278
    some cases considered, 275–279
    Supreme Court as civil rights guardian, 276
    visionary judge, 279

Alito, Justice, (US)
    on judgment audiences, 33–34
    on Justice Scalia (US), 209–210

Alternative judgment forms, 17–18; see also **Children; Simplified judgments**

Anti-intellectualism, 70

Anwar, Sheriff, (UK)
    simplified judgment, 120

Aphorisms, 76–77
    as substitute for analysis, 76
    cause of reluctance to amend judgment, 77
    Justice Holmes (US) as aphorist, 196
    Justice Jackson (US) as aphorist, 196

Appellate court judgments
    accessibility is key, 244

Index

agreeing *ex tempore* judgment, 297
composite judgments and interpretation, 244
composite judgments sometimes desirable, 244
dissenting judges write for future judges, 245
ingredients of, 87–88, 245, 251–252
judge on appellate court not writing for self, 170
judges should be cautious, 245
multiple audiences, 245
multiple/dissenting judgments beneficial, 244
no written statement before post-argument conference, 168
overt squabbling best avoided, 251
politeness, 117
preparing written reserved judgments, 168–169
principle of law laid down to be clear, 244
types of, 103

Arnold, Lord Justice, (UK)
and synopsising of law, 81–82

Art
artistic value judgment of judgments, 305
judgment as, 304–305

Artificial intelligence
AI-aided judgments, 17

Asylum and immigration; see Simplified judgments

Atkin, Lord, (UK), 219–230
and Lord Russell (UK), 229–230
background, 219, 243
compared to Justice Jackson (US), 207
danger of wide propositions, 226
dissent in *Liversidge*, 227–229
empathy/sympathy for unfortunate, 220, 222
evolution of thinking in *Donoghue*, 221–222
invocation of *Through the Looking Glass* in *Liversidge*, 228–229
landmark judgment in *Donoghue*, 39
length of speech in *Donoghue*, 39
lessons from Lords Atkin, Bingham and Denning (all UK), 251–252
letter of Viscount Maugham (UK) to *The Times* after *Liversidge*, 229
Liversidge and *Korematsu* compared, 207, 216

Lord Simon's (UK) bid to modify *Liversidge* speech, 228–229
Lord Wright (UK) and, 223, 229
occasional predilection for caustic, 223, 228–229
occasional tongue-twisting logic, 230
on Justice Cardozo (US), 227
primacy of principle over casuistry, 223
reliance on Christian scripture, 226
vindication of judgment in *Liversidge*, 227
writing style, 220

Atkinson, Justice, (Australia), 85, 161, 178, 277
on judgment structure, 85–87

Audience
academics as, 35
and style, 58–59
appellate court audiences, 33–34
configuration and institutional role, 35
confusion of audiences and prolixity, 34
for apex courts, 33
for law-revealing court, 35
growth of administrative state and, 34
impact on judgment, 35, 82–83
legal profession as, 35
Lord Bingham (UK) on, 34
possible audiences, 34–35, 82–83
posterity as, 35–36, 157–158
primary audience, 36
secondary audience, 36
terrible irony, 37
US Federal Judicial Center on, 82–83
who US judges write for, 33
writing to entire audience, 37

Australia
stylistic innovations, 57
to fore in judgment reforms, 56

Aylesworth, Justice, (Canada), 264

Babu, Chief Justice, (India)
on 'basic structure' doctrine, 266

Bacon, Francis, (UK)
on over-speaking judges, 39

Bacon, Vice-Chancellor, (UK)
and overconfidence, 22

Bankes, Lord Justice (UK)
and Lord Atkin (UK), 220

Index

Beg, Chief Justice, (India), 269

Bentham, Jeremy, (UK), 29

Bertolucci, Bernardo, (Italy), 261

Bingham, Lord, (UK)
  background, 243
  gold standard, 18, 42–43, 126
  intelligible, clear, predictable judgments, 22
  international reputation, 243
  lessons from Lords Atkin, Bingham and Denning (all UK), 251–252
  on audience, 34
  on dissenting judgments, 106, 109, 263(fn59)
  on judicial and legislative branches, 246–247
  on judgment structure, 85, 87–88
  on omnipotent House of Commons, 248–249
  simplicity as desirable goal, 246
  synopsising of law, 81–82
  'Ten Commandments' of judgment writing, 244–245
  The Rule of Law, 243
  towering figure, 243
  use of quotations, 248
  writing style, 243–244
  versus Lord Reid (UK), 109–110

Bird, Chief Justice Rose, (US), 153, 153(fn4)

Blackburn, Lord, (UK)
  and perils of humour, 62–63
  impoliteness, 73
  Rylands v Fletcher, 44

Bohr, Niels, (Denmark), 65

Bosielo, Judge, (South Africa), 181, 223, 230
  on judgment structure, 85, 88–89

Bramwell, Lord, (UK), 201

Brandeis, Justice, (US)
  more important that law be settled than right, 169

Brennan, Chief Justice, (Australia)
  on scope for theory in judgments, 70

Brennan, Justice, (US)
  criticism of Justice O'Connor (US) 156

Brevity, 34, 157
  crystallisation of laws and, 43–44
  disincentivising of, 45
  no bar to potency/profundity, 197, 216
  Poe (US) on undue brevity, 142
  principles as solution to prolixity, 191–192
  Rylands v Fletcher and, 44

Breyer, Justice, (US)
  literary allusion (in Plaut), 67–68

Briggs, Lord, (UK)
  referred to Shakespeare in judgment, 65, 66

Burger, Chief Justice, (US)
  on brevity, 20

Burke, Edmund, (UK), 265

Burns, Robert, (UK), 65

Bush, George W, (US), 165, 209

Byron, Lord, (UK), 65

Cardozo, Justice, (US)
  on overemphasis of facts, 90(fn37)
  on re-reading own judgment, 4
  on styles of judgment, 50, 51(fn25), 54, 55, 56
  own style, 55–56
  preciosity, 56

Carroll, Lewis, (UK)
  reference to his writing in *Liversidge*, 228–229
  reference to his writing by Lord Denning (UK), 69, 233

Carter, Jimmy, (US), 167
  role in diversification of judiciary, 167(fn99)

Chandrachud, Justice, (India)
  criticism of judgment of Justice Holmes (US) in *Buck* 269
  criticism of US Supreme Court judgment in *Korematsu*, 269
  structuring judgment to facilitate reading/analysis, 269(fn99)
  upholding Justice Khanna's (India) dissent in *ADB Jabalpur*, 269

355

Index

Charles I (UK), 228
  controversial reference to in *Liversidge*, 228
  'high priest' of absolutism, 228

Chauhan, Justice, (India)
  on harsh language, 72–73, 224–225

Children
  and child-friendly judgments, 122–123, 127–131
  and child-friendly justice, 122–123
  as a special public, 128
  Chief Justice McLachlin (Canada) on evolution of judicial role, 121
  Child Friendly Justice Guidelines, 124
  complexity as barrier to simplicity, 125
  CS Lewis (UK) on writing for, 123, 127–131
  efficiency as barrier to plain language, 125
  emoting as judge, 126
  ex tempore judgments for children, 121
  exposing children to sensitive information, 125
  Guidelines on Children in Contact with Justice System, 124
  idealising/patronising children, 131
  judgments for, 119–133
  judicial independence as barrier to 'plain language', 125–126
  Justice Jackson (UK) and simplified judgment forms, 120
  Justice Munby (UK) on writing to/for children, 121
  length of judgment, 129–130
  moralising to children, 130–131
  not frightening children, 130
  'plain language' notes, 119–122
  possible objections to writing to/for children, 125–127
  seeking emotional contact, 123–124
  Sheriff Anwar (UK) and simplified judgment form, 120
  therapeutic justice, 122
  UN Convention on Rights of Child, 124, 127
  writing child-friendly judgments, 127–131
  writing for child of today/tomorrow, 121, 129

Christianity
  used as basis for law, 225–226

Citations, 95

Clarity, 4, 21–22, 22–23, see also 'Gold standard'
  and footnotes, 74–76
  does not demand length, 22
  good judgment possesses clear style/language, 251
  Lord Neuberger (UK) on, 22–24
  wastepaper basket the judge's friend, 22

Clinton, Bill, (US), 167

Cockburn, Lord, (UK)
  choosing judgments to promote himself, 36

Coleridge, Lord, (UK)
  law courts or courts of justice? 75

Common law
  law as dynamic medley, 15
  'Open Sesame' myth, 7, 31

Composite judgments
  aid to accessibility, 24–25
  clarity and certainty, 24
  deficiencies of, 24–25
  Lord Bingham (UK) on, 109, 244
  Lord Neuberger (UK) on, 109–110
  Lord Reid (UK) on, 109
  undesirability of, 24

Concurring judgments, 114–118
  advantages of, 115–116
  and dissenting judgments, 114
  appropriate when judicial dialogue needed, 23–24
  confusing concurring judgments to be avoided, 170
  drawbacks of, 117
  explain why given, 115
  'fantastic beasts', 114
  free speech, 24
  instructive, not pedantic, 115
  Justice Ginsburg (US) on, 169–170
  Justice Laskin (Canada) on, 264
  Justice O'Connor (US) and types of, 160
  Lady Hale (UK) on, 116, 160
  need for politeness, 117
  not devoutly to be avoided, 169
  self-indulgence and, 114
  types of, 115

Copland, Aaron, (US), 239

Index

Corbett, Chief Justice (South Africa)
  on judgment structure, 85, 89–91

Côté, Justice (Canada)
  on appellate court judgments, 117–118
  on politeness, 117

Danto, Arthur, (US), 305

Denham, Chief Justice (Ireland), 154

Denning, Lord, (UK)
  aesthetic experience, 234
  anachronisms of language, 237–238
  and non-British people, 235–236
  and 'ordinary' people, 239–241
  and people of colour, 240
  'appalling vista' remarks, 236
  as 'pop icon', 154, 157
  background, 239, 243
  brevity of *High Trees* and *Lochner* dissent, 241–242
  colloquial phraseology, 240
  compared to Justice Ginsburg (US), 154
  compared to Justice Holmes (US), 197, 231
  compared to Justice Jackson (US), 205
  compared to Justice Wilson (Canada), 176
  conversational/homely style, 55
  evolution of writing style, 232–233
  gimmicks of style, 233
  hankering for 'golden' England, 237
  imagery, 139, 238–239
  immortality, 36
  inaccuracy in imagery, 239
  intellectual ostentation, 69
  length of career, 167
  lessons from Lords Atkin, Bingham and Denning (all UK), 251–252
  Lintz Cricket Club, 238–239
  literary brilliance, 231
  notable prominence in common law world, 253
  novelistic plotlines of judgments, 231
  on making meaning clear, 4
  opening lines, 231–233
  originality, 157
  persuasiveness, 243
  pride in Englishness, 233, 235
  reference to writing of Lewis Carroll (UK), 233
  renowned recitations of fact, 231
  scenes of England, 233–235
  style compared to Irish Supreme Court style, 235
  vivid writing style, 145, 253

Dicey, Albert Venn, (UK), 265

Disabilities
  Judgment accessibility to people with disabilities, 22(fn39), 127

Dissenting judgments
  ABA historical opposition to, 111
  and concurring judgments, 114
  and illusion of certainty/infallibility, 112
  as act of egotism, 105
  as product of individualistic judging, 111
  brevity of Justice Holmes' (US) dissent in *Lochner*, 191
  Chief Justice Taft (US) on, 111
  closing of dissent to be forceful, 190
  disrupt smooth running of court, 113
  dissent aversion, 111
  dissent without dissenting judgment, 110
  dissenting judges write for future judges, 245
  drawbacks, 111–113
  effectiveness, 169
  evolutionary change and, 106
  freedom of speech and, 105
  functions of, 105
  good on date of issuance only, 107
  how to write, 113–114
  imprecision of, 112
  ingredients of good judgment, 245
  Justice Douglas (US) on, 105
  Justice Ginsburg (US) on, 169–170
  Justice Holmes (US) and, 104
  Justice Laskin (Canada) on, 263
  Justice Scalia (US) on, 107
  Justice Stewart (US) on, 104
  Justice Stone (US) on, 108
  Lord Bingham (UK) on, 106, 244
  merits of, 104, 107–109
  minor reservations best avoided, 170
  motivations for, 110–111
  need for politeness, 117
  not devoutly to be avoided, 169
  politically charged, 112–113
  possibility for fewer, 23
  separate opinions with no majority, 170
  stifling clarification of law, 112
  stimulant to clarity, 105, 169
  tomorrow's orthodoxy, 245, 263(fn59)
  too many multiple opinions, 170
  two kinds of, 170
  views of dissenting judge, 104–105

Dixon, Sir Owen (Australia)
  ambassador and mediator, 254

357

Index

background, 254
'black-letter lawyer', 254, 255, 257–258
extra-judicial commentary on judgment writing, 254–255
greater adventure might have yielded greater reputation, 259
lessons from judgments of wider common law world, 282–283
parallel with Justice Jackson (US) and Justice Salmond (New Zealand), 197(fn59)
paternalism, 256
reputation of High Court in his day, 254
quality of prose, 259
rigorous clarity, 258
rule of law, 258
some prominent cases, 256–259

Douglas, Justice, (US)
on dissenting judgments, 105

Dyson, Lord, (UK)
on dissenting judgments, 245

Editing
correction after issuing judgment, 83–84
cutting judgment lengths, 23
editing checklist, 97–99

Elias, Chief Justice, (New Zealand), 154

Epigrams, 76–77
as cause of reluctance to amend judgment, 77
as substitute for analysis, 76
Justice Holmes (US) as epigrammatist, 196
Justice Robert Jackson (US) as epigrammatist, 76, 196, 200
Lord Justice Knight Bruce (UK) and, 76
may not yield clarity, 76–77
Oliver Wendell Holmes, Jr, (US), and, 76

Esgrove, Lord Justice Clerk, (Scotland), 19

European arrest warrant, 271(fn117)

European Convention/Court of Human Rights, 24, 126

Ex tempore judgments, 287–302
amendment of later-provided transcripts, 299–302
agreeing *ex tempore* judgment in appellate court, 296–297
as refined pretence, 289
attractions of, 27, 291–294
commonly delivered, 287
defined, 288
drawbacks of, 26–27, 291–294
greater need for in future, 298
greatest deficiency, 288
in child law cases, 121
Jessel, Sir George (UK) and, 26
Justice Kirby (Australia) on, 298–299
less likely if proceedings televised, 290
Lord Neuberger (UK) on, 288–289, 299
nature of, 25
no longer the rule, 290
practical guidance on preparation/delivery of, 294–299
reasons for choosing to give, 293–294
unwritten judgments as 'legal untouchables', 27
when to be given, 288

Fenimore Cooper, James, (US) 143

Font style, 18(fn15)

Footnotes, 74–76
as wasteland of needless *dicta*, 75
causes and consequences, 75
Justice O'Connor (US) and, 158
need to quit them 'cold turkey', 75
Oliver Wendell Holmes, Jr, (US) and, 75
precedential standing, 75

Frankfurter, Felix, (US)
evanescent fate of judgments, 36
on differences in interpretation, 215
on Justice Holmes' (US) opinions, 190–191

Freedom of choice
considerations of *Roe v Wade*, 163–164
risks to *Roe v Wade*, 159

Frost, Robert, (US), 67–68, 100

Gandhi, Indira, (India), 267

Ginsburg, Ruth Bader, (US)
as 'pop icon', 154
background, 154, 166–167
commentary on judgment writing, 167–171, 176
compared with Lord Denning (UK), 154, 167
films about, 154(fn7)
length of career, 167
lessons from Justices O'Connor (US),

Ginsburg (US) and Wilson (Canada), 183–186
on a 'nine woman' US Supreme Court, 153
on Justice O'Connor (US), 161
on Justice Scalia (US), 156
pointedness in *Bush v Gore*, 174
reforming potential of dissenting judgments, 278
restraint in *Bush v Gore*, 175
some opinions considered, 171–175

'Gold standard', see also Bingham, Lord, (UK)
and divergent audiences, 252
brevity, clarity, simplicity, 18, 22, 42–43, 146, 252

Gore, Al, (US), 165

Graves, Robert, (UK), 22

Gray, Justice, (US), 187

Haldane, Lord, (UK)
on Lord Atkin (UK), 220

Hale, Lady, (UK), 154, 219(fn1)
on concurring judgments, 116, 278

Harsh language, 72–74, see also Politeness
Justice Chauhan (India) on, 73
Lord Blackburn (UK) and, 73

Hegel, Georg, (Germany)
relating Hegel's ideas on art to law, 303
relating Hegel's ideas on poetry to law, 306–307
three ideas of art, 303

Heydon, Justice, (Australia)
on *ex tempore* judgments, 26–27

Hogan, Justice (Ireland)
on Justice Walsh (Ireland), 270–271

Holmes, Oliver Wendell, Jr, (US)
aphorist, 196
as *poet manqué*, 196
august language for august task, 190
background, 187–188
brevity of dissent in *Lochner*, 191
brutality of language, 194
coining of phrases, 190
combining callings of writer and jurist, 196
common law wanting systematic cohesion, 188
compared to Justice Jackson (US), 198, 201
compared to Justice Scalia (UK), 210, 215
compared to Lord Denning (UK), 197, 231
compared to Voltaire (France), 196
complex writing style, 189
desire for snappy line, 193
epigrammatist, 196
footnotes, 75
forceful last word at end of dissent, 190
'Great Dissenter', 104
immortality, 36
imprecision of language, 195
inconstancy, 195
Justice Cardozo (US) on, 196–197
Justice Frankfurter (US) on, 191
laconic/sententious style, 54
lessons from Justices Holmes, Jackson and Scalia (all US), 215–216
marrying principle and law, 191, 193, 194
meanness, 194
nomination, 187–188
notable prominence in common law world, 253
objectionable opinion in *Buck v Bell*, 193–194
on freedom of speech, 194–195
on futility of dissenting opinions, 189
opinions as fusion of reason and passion, 158
Professor Sunstein on, 210
some opinions considered, 189–196
The Common Law, 188
writing style, 187, 253
wrote own opinions, 188

Hughes, Chief Justice, (US)
on dissenting judgments, 106
on politeness, 74
on undue pursuit of unanimity, 107

Humour, 62–63

Imagery and metaphor, 76, 139
Lord Denning (UK) and imagery, 139, 238–239
words in judgment yielding image, 307

India
to fore in judgment writing development, 56

Information age, 16, 83, 202

Index

'Information overload', 17

Ireland
increase in written judgments, 43–44

Irish Supreme Court
making it like US Supreme Court, 270
style compared to Lord Denning's (UK), 235

Israel Supreme Court
as civil rights guardian, 276
notable quality of judgments, 274

Israeli legal system, 274
arrival of common law, 274
mixed nature, 274
see also Agranat, Shimon

Jackson, Justice (UK)
simplified judgments, 120

Jackson, Justice (US)
aphorist, 199
background, 197–198
capacity to admit error, 201
compared to Justice Cardozo, (US), 199
compared to Justice Holmes, (US), 198, 199, 201
compared to Justice Scalia (US), 198, 210
compared to Lord Atkin (UK), 207
compared to Lord Denning (UK), 205
desire for snappy line, 201
dissenting judgment in *Korematsu*, 206–207
epigrammatist, 200, 201, 202, 203, 206, 207
failure to become US Chief Justice, 198
future Chief Justice Rehnquist (US) as clerk, 155
Justice Frankfurter (US) on, 199–200
Korematsu and *Liversidge* compared, 206–207, 216
lessons from Justices Holmes, Jackson and Scalia (all US), 215–216
magisterial language in 'bite sizes', 208
masterful opinion in *Steel Seizure* case, 203–204
'New Deal' lawyer, 199
Nuremberg trials, 197
on dangers of untruths in free society, 202–203
on free speech, 200–201, 202–203
on role of citizenry/Government, 201
on tripartite government, 204–205
over-condensation of thought, 201
parallel with Dixon, Chief Justice, (Australia) and Justice Salmond (New Zealand), 197(fn59)
praise of writing style, 198, 199
Professor Sunstein (US) on, 210
some opinions considered, 200–208
support for democracy, 200
wrote as he spoke, 199–200
wrote own opinions, 188

Jacob, Sir Robin, (UK)
contemporary expectation of long judgments, 40
life too short to read modern judgments, 39
no need to lay down law for all time, 142
on academic references, 69
respective roles of academics and judges, 35

Jefferson, Thomas, (US)
comments on *Marbury v Madison*, 51

Jessel, Sir George, (UK)
accent, 26
ex tempore judgments, 26
judgment in *St Leonards Will Case*, 26

Johnson, Justice, (US), 51
laconic style, 51
support for slavery, 51

Johnson, Samuel (UK), 65

Judge
admission of error does not diminish, 166, 202, 216
as architect, 99–100
as 'human link' in justice system, 131
better judges see beyond the immediate, 283
self-curtailment of freedom of expression, 306
judicial activism may need to be own reward, 283
judicial courage, 157–158
Justice O'Connor (US) on judicial elections, 158–160
need to speak with dignity, 47
never losing sight of the desperate, 168
theoretical weakness in not electing judges, 160
types of, 79

Index

Judgment
  academic references, 69–72, 167
  as art, 303–305
  aim is dispute resolution, 79–80
  anti-intellectualism, 70
  anti-Roma sentiment, 64(fn73)
  anxious parade of knowledge, 22
  aphorisms, 76–77
  appellate court judgment, ingredients of, 87–88
  appellate court judgment, types of, 103
  as encounter with truth, 304
  as intellectual creation, 48
  as letter to loser, 31
  as part of continuum, 32
  as performative act, 16, 157
  as persuasive act, 16, 17, 157
  as self-aggrandisement, 36
  as temporary crystallisation of law, 106
  as tool for re-legitimising court system, 120, 132
  as violent act, 16
  brisk adjudication, 50
  by way of poem, 68
  children, see Children
  citations, 95–96
  classical rhetorical form, 93–94
  closing out potential for appeal, 45
  commentary on gender and judgment, 176
  conceals underlying thoughts, 84
  conclusion of, 61–62, 93
  concurring judgments, see Concurring judgments
  definition, 15
  dissenting judgments, see Dissenting judgments
  drawback of high-speed judgments, 166
  editing, see Editing
  emoting as judge, 132
  empathic reasoning, 31
  enabling scrutiny of judges, 28
  epigrams, 76–77
  evanescent fate of, 36, 40
  evolution of judgment writing, 120–121
  facts, identifying, 92–93
  facts, obsession with, 90
  fairness as prime objective, 168
  family law judgments, see Children
  footnotes, 74–76
  foreign precedent in US cases, 167
  form, 84
  good judgment sees larger significance, 215
  grammar, 62, 136
  guidance on structure/contents, 23
  harsh language, 72–74
  humane concern as work of all, 167
  humour, 62–63
  identification of issues, 91
  imagery, 139
  impact of audience on, 35
  impact of technology, 41
  'important' and 'unimportant' cases, 197, 216
  information overload, 81
  institutional role of judges, 21
  intelligible, clear, predictable, 22
  judge as mouthpiece of God, 54
  judgment openings, 59
  literary allusion, 64–69
  metaphors, 76
  more important that law be settled than right, 169
  nineteenth-century judgments, 39–40
  no right answer, 30–31, 112
  non-mechanistic application of law, 94
  not a PhD thesis, 31–32
  not intended to rationalise law, 32
  objective facts an illusion, 90
  people with disabilities, 22(fn39), 127
  plain language, see Plain language
  precedent, reliance on, 72
  producing desired product, 132
  prolixity, 34, 40–42, 146
  public accountability, 39
  publishing, 83
  pure and impure form, 49
  purposes of, 29–33
  quotations, 95–96
  racism, 53
  reasoning style, 59–60
  re-stating principle, 44–45
  right answer not enough, 121
  role in communicating reasons, 32
  sarcasm, 63–64
  short-form judgments, 45–46
  simplicity, 43
  soft power, 30
  statement of issues, 95
  structure, 79–101
  summary at start, 23
  synopsising law, 70, 81–82
  types of, 80
  typographical errors, 83–84

Judgment publication
  on whether to publish, 83

Index

Judgment structure
    alternative formats, 85
    appellate court judgment, ingredients of, 87–88
    as cause of information overload, 81
    citations, 95
    complexity of facts and, 80–82
    conceals underlying thoughts, 84
    conclusion of, 61–62, 93
    conventions of form, 84
    Corbett, Chief Justice, (South Africa) on, 89–91
    eliciting issues from counsel, 92
    factors affecting form, 80
    facts, identification of, 92–93
    facts, obsession with, 90
    four tensions of judicial decisions, 177
    identification of issues, 91
    Judge Bosielo (South Africa) on, 88–89
    Justice Atkinson (Australia) on, 86–87
    Justice Mahoney (Australia) on, 91–93
    Lord Bingham (UK) on, 87–88
    nature of issues and, 80–82
    objective facts an illusion, 90
    quotations, 95–96
    statement of issues, 95
    Strong on, 93–94
    synopsising law, 81–82
    US Federal Judicial Center on, 80–81, 94–96
    Wanderer, 96–99

Judgment writing
    accessibility is key, 244
    and writing a brief, 168
    barriers to better writing, 44–45
    'black letter' approach no bar to eloquence, 282
    brevity no bar to potency/profundity, 197, 216
    composite judgments sometimes desirable, 244
    danger of stating wide propositions, 226
    dissenting judges and future judges, 245
    drawback of high-speed writing, 166
    empathy/sympathy for those faring badly, 251
    evolution of, 120–121
    four tensions of judicial decisions, 177
    good judgment may not be appreciated, 251
    good judgment possesses clear style/language, 251
    grammar, 62, 136
    great judges and great writing, 215, 216
    interpersonal nature of task of judgment, 128
    judges should be cautious, 245
    legal questions often reducible to the simple, 252
    lessons from judgments of wider common law world, 282–283
    lessons from Justices Holmes, Jackson and Scalia (all US), 215–216
    lessons from Justices O'Connor (US), Ginsburg (US) and Wilson (Canada), 183–186
    lessons from Lords Atkin, Bingham and Denning (all UK), 251–252
    moralising, 130–131, 142
    multiple audiences of appellate judgments, 245
    multiple/dissenting judgments beneficial, 244
    need for greater consideration of wider common law world, 283
    no one methodology for successful judgment, 282
    originality, 157
    patronising, 131
    personal sentiment not to be revealed, 251
    preparing written reserved appellate judgments, 168–169
    principle of law to be clear, 244
    process of writing, 197
    producing desired product, 132
    revealing of struggle in judge's soul, 283
    sentimentality and, 129
    trial judgments have limited audiences, 245
    substance should not yield to style, 216, 251
    writing clearly for asylum seekers and immigrants, see Simplified judgments
    writing clearly for children, see Children
    writing for human consumption, 169
    writing own judgments, 215
    'writing out', 44

Juries
    obviating need for written judgment, 19

Kagan, Justice, (US)
    on Justice Scalia (US), 209, 210

Keane, Chief Justice, (Ireland),
    on Justice Walsh (Ireland), 176

Keene, Justice, (UK)
    referred to Tennyson (UK) in judgment, 65

Index

Kennedy, Justice, (US), 163

Khanna, Hans Raj, (India) 264–269
  ability to see 'larger picture', 268
  and Indira Gandhi (India), 267
  background, 264–265
  'basic structure' doctrine, 265
  compared with Justice Agranat (Israel), 265, 278
  compared with Justice Laskin (Canada), 264, 278
  compared with Justice Walsh (Ireland), 264, 265, 272, 278
  didacticism, 278
  dispassionate writing-style, 268
  dissenting judgment in *ADM Jabalpur*, 266–269
  early generation of post-Independence judges, 265
  language to fire the soul, 267–268
  lessons from judgments of wider common law world, 282–283
  overlooked for promotion, 269
  prolific in writing; formal in style, 264
  renowned judgment in *Kesavananda Bharati*, 265–266
  some judgments considered, 265–269
  vindicated in *KS Puttaswamy*, 269

Kiefel, Chief Justice, (Australia), 154

Kirby, Justice, (Australia)
  on alternative judgment forms, 17–18
  on *ex tempore* judgments, 298–299

Kitto, Sir Frank, (Australia), 25, 74, 115, 291

Knight Bruce, Lord Justice, (UK)
  anti-Roma sentiment, 64(fn73)
  as epigrammatist, 76
  use of sarcasm, 63–64

Laski, Harold, (UK), 265

Laskin, Bora (Canada), 259–264
  background, 259–260
  celebrated dissenter, 260
  commitment to modernity/progressivism, 260
  compared with Justice Agranat (Israel), 278
  compared with Justice Khanna (India), 264, 278
  compared with Justice Walsh (Ireland), 278
  didacticism, 278
  extra-judicial commentary on judgment writing, 264
  first Jewish member of Supreme Court of Canada, 260
  freedom of assembly, 262
  freedom of expression, 263–264
  freedom of speech, 261
  hammering eloquence, 263
  lessons from judgments of wider common law world, 282–283
  occasional bluntness, 262
  on concurring/dissenting judgments, 264
  practical bent of judgments, 262–263
  some judgments considered, 260–264
  victim of anti-Semitism, 259–260
  writing style, 259

Law and economics
  why judges dissent, 111

Laws, Lord Justice, (UK)
  refers to Milton in judgment, 65

Lawton, Lord Justice, (UK), 300

Length; see also Clarity
  causes of prolixity, 39–42, 146
  conduct of trial and, 45
  cutting judgment lengths, 23
  'in judgment' quotations, 44
  judgments for children and, 129–130
  length to be determined by subject, 147
  not necessary for clarity, 22
  Poe (US) on length, 141–142
  public accountability, 39

Lewis, CS, (UK)
  and writing for children, 123, 127–131

Lincoln, Abraham, (US), 40, 187, 199
  US as last best hope of earth, 253

Literary allusion, 64–69
  cause of, 66
  drawbacks of, 68–69
  merits of, 64
  Lord Denning (UK) and, 69
  poetry, 67, 68
  reasons for, 67
  serves real purpose, 66
  striving for effect, 69

Literature
  judgments as literary compositions, 16

363

Index

Lodge, Henry Cabot, (US), 188

Lord Hope of Craighead (UK), 247

Macmillan, Lord, (UK)
    judgment as literary composition, 16
    judgment not intended to rationalise law, 32
    on identification of facts, 92
    on itch to legislate, 41
    on literary allusion, 64
    on metaphors, 76
    on precedent versus principle, 191–192
    on style, 47
    on synopsising law, 70
    undesirability of composite judgments, 32

Mahoney, Justice, (Australia), 161, 173, 258, 272, 276
    on judgment structure, 85, 91–93

Mansfield, Lord, (UK)
    and Dido Belle (UK), 53
    judge as mouthpiece of God, 54
    magisterial style, 50
    on never volunteering reasons, 20
    racist language, 53
    Somerset case, 50, 52–54, 205

Margolis, Joseph, (US)
    commentary points to artistic character of judgments, 303

Marshall, Chief Justice, (US)
    magisterial style, 52
    Marbury v Madison, 39, 50, 51–52

Matthew, Theobald, (UK) 289

Maugham, Somerset, (UK), 135–138
    acquaintance with great writing beneficial, 137
    digression, 137
    good prose is rococo, 136
    good writing takes time, 137, 138
    grammar not critical, 136
    no need for literary genius, 135
    no need for perfect prose, 135
    on euphony, 136
    on lucidity/simplicity, 135
    on obscurity in writing, 136
    simplicity needs discipline, 136
    sticking to the point, 138
    write in manner of one's period, 137

Maugham, Viscount (UK)
    letter to *The Times* after *Liversidge* decision, 229

McKinley, William, (US), 187

McLachlin Chief Justice, (Canada), 154
    on evolution of judicial role, 121

Media, 28(fn70), 36
    criticism and unfair criticism, 28(fn70), 246

Mill, John Stuart, (UK), 180, 265, 275

Miller, Henry, (US), 106

Milton, John, (UK), 65, 275
    recent burst of references internationally, 65(fn83)
    referred to in English judgment, 65

Mostyn, Justice, (UK)
    reference to Byron (UK), Bohr (Denmark), Pope (UK) and Twain (US), 65, 66

Munby, Lord Justice, (UK)
    on writing to/for children, 121

Music and law, 157–158

Mussumano, Justice, (US)
    strong dissent re Miller's *Tropic of Cancer*, 105–106

Neuberger, Lord, (UK)
    and composite judgments, 109–110
    on clarity in judgment writing, 22
    on *ex tempore* judgments, 288–289, 299
    on televised proceedings, 290

New Zealand
    successive women Chief Justices, 154

O'Connor, Justice Sandra Day, (US), 154–166
    attractions of judgment style, 155–156
    background, 154–155
    capacity to admit error, 166
    criticism of style by Justice Brennan (US), 156
    extra-judicial commentary on judgment writing, 157–158
    first woman appointed to US Supreme Court, 155

freedom of choice, 159, 163–164
instance of possibly harsh criticism, 161
lessons from Justices O'Connor (US), Ginsburg (US) and Wilson (Canada), 183–186
music and the law, 157–158
on diversity, 161–163
on election of judges, 158–160
on equality, 160–162
on footnotes, 158
on gender and judgment, 176
on gender discrimination, 160–162
on judicial courage, 157–158
on law as fusion of reason and passion, 158
on rule of law, 158
on teamwork, 158
pragmatism, 156
praise of style by Justice Ginsburg (US), 156
preference for narrow opinions, 160–161
reputation, 155
some opinions considered, 156–157, 158–166

Originalism, 211

Orwell, George, (UK) 138–141, 238
bad writing curable, 138
four questions to ask of each sentence, 140
hackneyed phraseology, 140
language and clear expression, 138
meaningless words, 140
'padding', 140, 140–141
poor deployment of language, 138
precision, 139
pretentiousness, 140
rules for better writing, 141
staleness of imagery, 139
stringing text together, 140

Paine, Thomas, (UK/US), 265

Persuasion
judgment as persuasive act, 16–18
Lord Denning (UK) and, 243

Phillips, Lord, (UK), 300–302

Plain language, 37, 119–133
efficiency as barrier to plain language, 125, 132
imprecision in, 126
interference with judicial independence, 125–126
online response to use of, 122–123
international law justification for, 126–127

Poe, Edgar Allen, (US), 141–143
'heresy of the Didactic', 142
length of text, 141–142
moralising, 142
tone, 142–143
undue brevity, 142

Poetry
engagement with poetry/judgment, 307–308
judgment by way of, 68
Penn Warren (US) on pure/impure poetry, 48–49
poetic references, 67, 68
relating Hegel's (Germany) ideas on poetry to law, 306–307
relation between poetry and law, 306–308
US Supreme Court and, 67–68

Politeness, 73–74, 144 see also Harsh language
Chief Justice Hughes (US) on, 74
impoliteness of Lord Blackburn (UK), 73
in appellate courts, 117–118
in concurring/dissenting judgments, 117
Justice Ginsburg (US) on, 170–171
no need to be impossible, 74
refrain from condemning witnesses, 74

Pope, Alexander, (UK), 65

Posner, Justice, (US)
on style, 48–49
pure and impure judgments, 48–49
why judges dissent, 110–111

Potter, Frances, (UK)
first woman registered as pharmacist, 237

Pound, Roscoe, (US), 265

Precedent
and footnotes, 75
reliance on, 72
versus principle, 192

Ptah-Hotep (Ancient Egypt), 36

Quotations, 95–96
as sign of intellectual confidence/indolence, 44

Index

Rationalisation of law
  judgments not to rationalise law, 32

Reagan, Ronald (US)
  nomination of Justice O'Connor (US), 155
  nomination of Justice Scalia (US), 208

Reasons, see also Written reasons
  American reasoning types, 21
  English reasoning types, 20
  purposes of reasoned judgments, 29–33
  reasons do not yield reasoned judgment, 20
  reasons for reasons, 18, 19–20
  role of judgment in communicating reasons, 32

Rehnquist, Chief Justice, (US), 173, 174
  and Justice O'Connor, (US), 155
  as clerk to Justice Jackson, (US), 155

Reid, Lord, (UK)
  on dissenting judgments, 109
  'Open Sesame' myth, 7, 31
  simplicity as a goal, 43
  undesirability of composite judgments, 24–25
  versus Lord Bingham, (UK), 109
  written reasons in Scotland, 19

Religion
  used as basis of judgment, 225–226

Reserved judgment, see Judgment, Judgment structure, Judgment writing, Written reasons

Roberts, Chief Justice, (US),
  on getting to the 'right' answer, 30–31

Roosevelt, Eleanor (US), 206

Roosevelt, Franklin, (US), 199, 206

Roosevelt, Theodore, (US), 187–188

Rowling, JK, (UK), 114

Rule of law, 15, 112, 243
  Justice O'Connor (US) on, 158

Russell, Lord, (UK),
  and Lord Atkin (UK), 229–230

Salmond, Sir John, (New Zealand), 279–282
  and Maori rights, 279
  author, 279, 280
  background, 279–280
  crisp writing style, 280
  diplomat while judge, 279
  fraternal judicial dialogue in imperial era, 279
  lessons from judgments of wider common law world, 282–283
  member of strong New Zealand Supreme Court, 280
  ostensible comfort with commercial issues, 282
  parallel with Dixon, Chief Justice, (Australia) and Justice Jackson (US), 197
  pragmatic approach to family law, 281
  shortness of judgments, 282
  some judgments considered, 280–282

Sarcasm, 63–64

Scalia, Justice, (US), 208–215
  and Justice Ginsburg, 208
  and originalism, 211
  and poetry, 67–68
  and textualism, 211
  approach as majority/minority author, 212
  as great dissenter, 211–212
  as pop icon, 208
  background, 208–209
  compared with Justice Holmes (US), 210, 215
  compared with Justice Jackson (US), 210, 215
  Father Paul Scalia (US) (son), 209
  great judge and writer, 210
  Justice Alito (US) on, 209–210
  Justice Ginsburg (US) on, 156, 170–171, 212
  Justice Kagan (US) on, 209, 210
  Justice Sotomayor (US) on, 209
  lessons from Justices Holmes, Jackson, and Scalia (all US), 215–216
  literary allusion (in *Plaut*), 67–68
  on dissenting judgments, 107
  on LGBTQ+ rights, 213–214
  on separation of powers, 67
  opinion like advocate's advice, 213
  Professor Sunstein (US) on, 210
  writing style, 117, 156, 170–171, 209, 212, 213, 215
  wrote own opinions, 188

Index

Scrutton, Lord Justice, (UK)
and Lord Atkin, 221

Shakespeare, William, (UK), 27, 65

Sharlow, Justice, (Canada)
on role of Academy, 70

short-form judgments, 45–46

Simon, Lord Chancellor (UK)
bid to modify Lord Atkin's (UK) speech in *Liversidge*, 228–229

Simplified judgments
Chief Justice McLachlin (Canada) on evolution of judicial role, 121
child-friendly judgments, 119–131
complexity as barrier to simplicity, 125
efficiency as barrier to plain language, 125
judicial independence as barrier to 'plain language', 125–126
Justice Jackson (UK) and simplified judgment forms, 120
length of judgment, 129–130
'plain language' notes, 119–123
Sheriff Anwar (UK) and simplified judgment form, 120
therapeutic justice, 122
writing child-friendly judgments, 127–131

Soft power
judgments yield national influence, 30

Sotomayor, Justice, (US)
on Justice Scalia (US), 209

Souter, Justice, (US), 163

Steakley, Judge, (US)
on inappropriateness of literary allusion, 66–67

Stewart, Justice, (US)
on dissenting judgments, 104

Stone, Justice, (US)
on dissenting judgment, 108

Story, Justice, (US), 201

Style
and grammar, 62
and judgment conclusion, 61–62
and judgment openings, 59
and purpose, 49
and treatment of law, 60–61
aspects of, 47–49
audience and, 58–59
conversational/homely style, 54–55
definition, 48
demonstrative judgments, 56
good judgment possesses clear style/language, 251
imitation of style best avoided, 197
importance of style, 197
judge as mouthpiece of God, 54
Justice Cardozo (US) on, 50–56
laconic/sententious style, 54
Lord Macmillan (UK) on, 47, 49
Lord Mansfield's (UK) style, 50
magisterial imperative style, 50
majestic prose and moral substance, 54
nothing wrong with distinctive style, 251
of reasoning, 59–60
on improving writing-style, 57–58
persuasiveness and, 47
preciosity, 56
refined/artificial style, 55, 56
scholarliness and effectiveness not inconsistent, 168
substance should not yield to style, 216, 251
stylistic types, 49–56
tonsorial/agglutinative style, 56
versus ornamentation, 47

Taft, Chief Justice, (US),
on dissenting judgments, 111

Tennyson, Lord, (UK), 65

Textualism, 211

Therapeutic jurisprudence, 31
ancient Egypt, 36
for children, 132
judgment as letter to loser, 31

Trollope, Anthony (UK)
relating his observations on poetry to law, 306

Trudeau, Pierre, (Canada), 176

Truman, Harry (US)
and *Steel Seizure* case, 203–204
friendship with Vinson, Chief Justice, (US), 198
nomination of Vinson, Chief Justice, (US), 198

367

Index

Twain, Mark, (US), 143–145
    arrive at particular end, 144
    confine self to facts pleaded, 144
    distilled judgment-writing rules, 144–145
    every element should be necessary, 144, 145
    language/tone should be consistent, 144
    observe good grammar, 145
    on Fenimore Cooper (US), 143–144
    ordinary language to be preferred, 144
    person/event should be included for reason, 144
    politeness, 144
    reason through the law, 144
    referred to in judgment, 65
    relevance a key criterion, 144
    slovenliness/surplusage undesirable, 145
    state what mean to state, 144
    stop writing when no more to be said, 144

UK Supreme Court
    font change, 18(fn15)
    Justice Ginsburg (US) on 'nine woman' court, 153
    lustre in common law world, 164
    possible decline in influence of judgments, 30

United Kingdom
    possible decline in influence of judgments, 30

US Federal Judicial Center, 160, 162, 172, 181, 221
    on audiences, 82–83
    on concurring judgments, 115, 117, 278
    on dissenting judgments, 113–114, 117
    on judgment structure, 80–81, 85, 94–96

US Supreme Court
    as post-war standard-bearer of rights and freedoms, 30
    diminished influence, 30
    first Jewish woman appointed to, 154
    first woman appointed to, 154
    lustre in common law world, 254
    making Irish Supreme Court like US Supreme Court, 270

Vaughan, Chief Justice, (UK)
    early supporter of written reasons, 19

Voltaire, 196

Vos, Sir Geoffrey, (UK)
    on synopsising law, 81

Walsh, Justice Brian, (Ireland), 269–274
    background, 269–270
    Chief Justice Ronan Keane (Ireland) on, 270
    compared to Justice Agranat (Israel), 265, 271, 278
    compared to Justice Khanna (India), 264, 265, 272, 278
    compared to Justice Laskin (Canada), 264, 278
    deploying natural law contra Catholic teaching, 274
    didacticism, 278
    encouragement of judges as philosopher kings/queens, 273–274
    establishment of principle, 273
    Justice Gerard Hogan (Ireland) on, 270–271
    lessons from judgments of wider common law world, 282–283
    making Irish Supreme Court like US Supreme Court, 270
    memorable advances without memorable language, 271
    most consequential post-independence Irish judge, 270
    on Constitution as living document, 211
    on justice, charity, and mercy, 273
    paternalist, 270
    role in European Court of Human Rights, 270
    role of post-independence judges, 265
    prolific in writing; formal in style, 264
    shaping governmental liability, 272–273
    some judgments considered, 271–274
    writing style, 271, 273, 274

Ward, Lord Justice, (UK)
    reference to Robert Burns (UK), 65, 66

Warren, Robert Penn, (US), 48

Wellington, Duke of, (UK), 110

Westbury, Lord, (UK), 202

Wharton, Edith, (US), 145–148
    avoid the misleading, 145
    brevity, clarity and simplicity, 146
    choose and explain angle, 145–146
    convention the first necessity of art, 147
    deep familiarity with subject desirable, 146
    genius and writing, 146

inattention/irrelevance undesirable, 145
length to be determined by subject, 147
mediocre text too long; great text too short, 147
narrative should furnish substance, 147
on novel-writing, 147–148
on short story writing, 145–147
opening page to contain germ of whole, 145, 148
presentation determined by subject, 147
proportionality, 148
refinement of text/thought, 146
'Three Bears' approach to writing, 147
tenuous and tight versus dense and prolix, 146
vitality arises from dramatic rendering, 145
weakest text of great writers offer completeness, 148

Wilson, Justice Bertha, (Canada), 175–183
background, 154, 175–176, 179
compared with Lord Denning (UK), 176
extra-judicial writing, 176, 177
first woman on Canadian Supreme Court, 154
hostility from some colleagues, 175
lessons from Justices O'Connor (US), Ginsburg (US) and Wilson (Canada), 183–186
magisterial style, 179
nature/aim of liberal democratic government, 180
on four tensions of judicial decisions, 177
on gender and law/judgments, 176
on women and the law, 153–154, 181–183
perspectives on Supreme Court career, 176–177
some judgments considered, 178–183
strength brought to judgment on domestic violence as woman, 182–183

Wilson, Justice James, (US), 169(fn116)

Winkelmann, Chief Justice, (New Zealand), 154

Witkon, Justice, (Israel), 278

Witnesses
refrain from condemning, 74

Wright, Lord (UK)
ignoring Lord Atkin (UK) after *Liversidge*, 229
on Lord Atkin (UK), 223

Written reasons
attractions of, 25–28
Chief Justice Vaughan (UK) on, 19
evolution in Scotland, 19
evolution of need for, 19–20
half-writing judgment, 25
increase public scrutiny, 28
juries obviating need for, 19
personal motivations for, 18–19
purposes, 29–30

About the author

Max Barrett
Justice of the High Court of Ireland

Mr Justice Max Barrett is a judge of the High Court of Ireland. Having worked as a solicitor in private practice and also as an in-house lawyer in the financial services sector, he was appointed to the High Court in January 2014. As a judge, he worked initially on the Commercial Court. Over time he has worked in all major areas of the High Court's activity, including the Asylum, Chancery, Family, Immigration, Insolvency, Judicial Review, Jury and Non-Jury Lists. Justice Barrett has also headed the Competition List since his appointment to the bench. During his time as a judge, Justice Barrett has delivered close to 600 reserved judgments. On the Asylum and Family Law Lists, he has taken a pioneering role in evolving a novel form of judgment – a traditional-form judgment to which a litigant-friendly letter in 'plain English' is appended – in a bid to maximise the comprehensibility of judgments for court users. Some of Justice Barrett's many judgments are now prominent/leading judgments in their respective areas. In addition to his judicial experience, Justice Barrett holds a PhD in law, a first-class master's in English literature and first-class postgraduate diplomas in arbitration and financial services law. He is among the most widely published of the current Irish judiciary (books and articles). Justice Barrett is a member of the Law Society of Ireland and a bencher of King's Inns.

About Globe Law and Business

Globe Law and Business was established in 2005. From the very beginning, we set out to create law books which are sufficiently high level to be of real use to the experienced professional, yet still accessible and easy to navigate. Most of our authors are drawn from Magic Circle and other top commercial firms, both in the UK and internationally.

Our titles are carefully produced, with the utmost attention paid to editorial, design and production processes. We hope this results in high-quality publications that are easy to read, and a pleasure to own. Our titles are also available as ebooks, which are compatible with most desktop, laptop and tablet devices. In 2018 we expanded our portfolio to include journals and Special Reports, available both digitally and in hard copy format, and produced to the same high standards as our books.

In the spring of 2021, we were very pleased to announce the start of a new chapter for Globe Law and Business following the acquisition of law books under the imprint Ark Publishing. We are very much looking forward to working with our Ark authors, many of whom are well known to us, to further developing the law firm management list, and to welcoming our new Ark customers.

We'd very much like to hear from you with your thoughts and ideas for improving what we offer. Please do feel free to email me at sian@globelawandbusiness.com with your views.

Sian O'Neill
Managing director
Globe Law and Business
www.globelawandbusiness.com

Related new title

The Rule of Law in the 21st Century

A Worldwide Perspective
Second Edition

Consulting Editors **Professor Robert A Stein**, **Justice Richard J Goldstone** and **Homer E Moyer, Jr**

Go to **www.globelawandbusiness.com/ROL2** for full details including free sample chapters

Related title

Globe Law and Business

The Independent Bar

Featuring a foreword by Chantal-Aimée Doerries QC

Insights into a Unique Business Model
Consulting Editor **David Barnes**

> " "
> Does this book succeed? It is without doubt an excellent primer about the business of chambers and does so well within its one-volume constraints.
>
> **Robin Jackson**
> 3 Verulam Buildings

Go to **www.globelawandbusiness.com/TIB**
for full details including free sample chapters